The Egyptian Labor Market in an Era of Reform

The Economic Research Forum for the Arab Countries, Iran and Turkey (ERF) is an independent, nonprofit, regional networking organization for the Middle East and North Africa region. Established in 1993, with headquarters in Cairo, the Forum's mission is to initiate and fund policy-relevant economic research, to organize conferences and meetings, to publish and disseminate the results of research activity to scholars, policymakers, and the business community of the region, and to function as a resource base for researchers through its databank and documentation library. A major concern is to build regional research capacity through the application of quality standards, as well as through specialized workshops. ERF also initiates joint research programs with other regional and international institutions, coordinating comparative cross-country research and assisting its constituency in accessing data and information. Website:<www.erf.org.eg>

The Egyptian Labor Market in an Era of Reform

Editor

Ragui Assaad

An Economic Research Forum Edition

The American University in Cairo Press
Cairo • New York

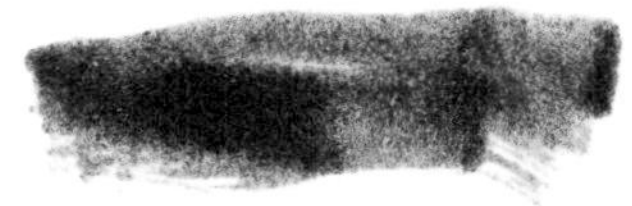

First published in 2002 by
The American University in Cairo Press
113 Sharia Kasr el Aini, Cairo, Egypt
420 Fifth Avenue, New York 10018
www.aucpress.com

in association with
The Economic Research Forum for the Arab Countries, Iran, and Turkey
7 Boulos Hanna Street, Dokki, 11123 Cairo, Egypt
www.erf.org.eg

Dar el Kutub No. 16736/01
ISBN 977 424 712 4

Printed in Egypt

Contents

Acknowledgments

The Economic Research Forum for the Arab Countries, Iran and Turkey (ERF) wishes to thank the Central Agency for Public Mobilization and Statistics (CAPMAS) for its assistance in conducting the Egypt Labor Market Survey 1998 and its permission to use the data from the October 1988 round of the Labor Force Sample Survey to carry out the studies included in this volume.

ERF wishes to thank in particular Mr. Ahab Elwi, president of CAPMAS, and Mr. Mostapha Gaafar for their guidance and support. Special thanks is also due to Mr. Amin Fouad for his tireless efforts to make this project a success. Our warmest thanks are due to all the other CAPMAS staff who participated in all stages of the survey, including sampling, questionnaire design, pretesting, training of field workers, managing and supervising field operations, office checking, coding, data entry, validation, and tabulation.

ERF also wishes to thank Ghada Barsoum for her masterful coordination of every aspect of the project, Adel Shaban for his skill in organizing the training of field workers and overseeing the fieldwork, and Ali Rashed for his competent computer support. Special thanks are also due to Andrea Matthews for copy editing the manuscripts in consultation with the editor and the authors and for her efforts in preparing the text for publication.

At the ERF office, the editor and authors received invaluable assistance on all administrative aspects of the project from Hana' Al-Sagban, Naima Loutfy, Anais Hagopian, Ingi Magdy, and Hind Rasheed. They are particularly grateful to Gillian Potter for her efforts in bringing this project to fruition.

ERF gratefully acknowledges the financial and technical support of the International Center for Economic Growth (ICEG) through its Economic Policy Initiative Consortium project in Egypt, which is funded by USAID. ERF also wishes to thank the Ford Foundation, the World Bank, the Population Council and ICEG for providing the funds to undertake the Egypt Labor Market Survey of 1998.

Contributors

Mona Amer has a masters degree in Applied Microeconomics from the University of Paris I-Sorbonne, France, and is a Ph.D. candidate in economics at the Institut d'Etudes Politiques de Paris, where her specialization is labor and youth. She is a lecturer in labor economics at the Faculty of Economics and Political Science, Cairo University.

Ragui Assaad obtained his Ph.D. from Cornell University in the USA. He is currently Associate Professor at the Humphrey Institute of Public Affair, University of Minnesota, where he teaches and conducts research in the areas of labor markets and labor policy in MENA, poverty and poverty alleviation strategies, the informal economy, and the role of institutions in development. He is a Research Fellow of the Economic Research Forum and has served as a consultant to the World Bank, the International Labor Office, the Ford Foundation, UNDP, and UNICEF.

Safaa El Kogali is currently an Economist in the World Bank in Washington, DC working in the Africa region's Human Development Department. She holds an M.Phil in Development Studies from the Institute of Development Studies at the University of Sussex, UK. She is a Research Associates with the Economic Research Forum and a consultant economist with the Population Council in Cairo. Her principal research interest is in human development, with special focus in education, labor market and gender.

Alia El Mahdi obtained her Ph.D. from Cairo University. She is currently Professor of Economics at the Faculty of Economics and Political Science, Cairo University and also Vice Dean for Post-graduate Studies and Research. Her main area of research interest is labor markets, with a special emphasis on informal economic activity, and micro and small enterprises. She is a Research Fellow of the Economic Research Forum.

May Mokhtar has an M.S. in statistics from Cairo University, where her main research focus was on child labor in Egypt. Currently, she is a Ph.D. candidate in biostatistics at the University of California at Los Angeles, with research focused on socioeconomic issues.

Mona Said is currently an economist in the Policy Development and Review Department of the International Monetary Fund. She holds a Ph.D. in economics from Cambridge University, England, and her current research interests and publications are in the areas of labor market segmentation, gender discrimination, wage inequality, transaction costs in trade, and fiscal decentralization.

Jackline Wahba holds a Ph.D. in economics from the University of Southampton in the United Kingdom, where she is currently a lecturer. Her research has focused on the Egyptian labor market, and in particular on migration, remittances, mobility, the public sector, and child labor. She is a Research Fellow of the Economic Research Forum.

Nadia Zibani is a Ph.D. candidate in demography at the Ecole des Hautes Etudes en Sciences Sociales, in Paris, France. Her research interests include child labor and education. She works as a consultant to the Population Council.

Introduction

In 1991 Egypt embarked on a major Economic Reform and Structural Adjustment Program (ERSAP) with support from the IMF and the World Bank. The program was adopted after many years of attempted economic stabilization and reform, beginning with the open door policies of the 1970s to stabilization attempts in the late 1980s in response to sharply falling oil prices. ERSAP included, *inter alia*, a stabilization component that aimed to eliminate large and unsustainable fiscal and external imbalances, trade, exchange rate and financial sector reforms, and an ambitious privatization program. An explicit objective of ERSAP was a reorientation of the economy toward the market and a reduction the role of the state, including its role as a dominant employer.

Although there was a great deal of speculation about the effects of ERSAP on the Egyptian labor market throughout the 1990s, the data available at the time on labor market conditions simply did not permit an accurate assessment of how the effects of ERSAP were transmitted to workers and households through the labor market. Because of the scarcity of official data on employment issues, little was known about the evolution of labor force participation, employment, unemployment, and wages in Egypt since the implementation of reforms. The official data sources suffer from comparability problems across time and are not available in a form that allows for serious, in-depth analysis.

Cognizant of this severe lack of recent data, the Economic Research Forum for the Arab Countries, Iran and Turkey (ERF)—in cooperation with the Egyptian Central Agency for Public Mobilization and Statistics (CAPMAS)—conducted the Egypt Labor Market Survey 1998 (ELMS 98), a nationally representative in-depth labor market survey of 5000 households. The survey was designed to be as comparable as possible to a special round of the LFSS carried out in October 1988 (LFSS 88) on a sample of 10,000 households. The ELMS 98 was conducted 10 years to the day after the LFSS 88 using a similar sample and questionnaire design. Utmost care was used to ensure that the bulk of the data would be strictly comparable, while allowing for some issues to be added and others to be dropped.

This collection of articles assembles the first set of studies based on these two surveys. Because the thorny comparability issues that normally plague Egyptian data sources could be set aside, the various studies are able to accurately assess how various aspects of the Egyptian labor market have been transformed over this significant period of economic reform. The authors analyze changes in the supply and demand for labor during the ten-year period, including the growth in the working age population, changes in participation behavior, the extent to which the private sector has contributed to employment creation, and the continued role of the government in the labor market. They also analyze the trends and structure of wages and earnings, the changing trajectories of youth employment, trends in child labor and schooling, and the evolution of female employment over the period. Finally, the role of the informal sector in employment creation is explored, as well as the extent to which the labor market itself has become more informal over the period.

The papers use a common set of definitions that correspond as closely as possible to international recommendations for labor force statistics. Both surveys use the definition of the economically active population adopted by the Thirteenth International Conference of Labor Statisticians in October 1982. The definition, which is sometimes referred to as the extended labor force definition, counts as economic activity any activity involving the production and processing of primary products, whether for the market, for barter, or for own consumption, and the production of all other goods and services for the market. Thus, those engaged in subsistence activities in agriculture, animal husbandry, or the processing of agricultural goods are counted as active, but not those who engage in other domestic activities such as food preparation, house cleaning, or child rearing. A previous definition referred to as the market labor force definition, limited the economically active population to those engaged in production of goods and services for the purpose of market exchange or barter.

As a result of using this extended definition of economic activity, the rate of female participation in the labor force, as measured in the two surveys, is considerably higher than that regularly reported by the Egyptian Labor Force Sample Survey, especially in rural areas where subsistence activities are more common. It also results in significantly lower unemployment rates that had been previously reported, which, in practice, use a definition of economic activity that approaches the market labor force. In ELMS 1998, the questions used to detect economic activity were asked in such a way to allow a distinction to be made between individuals engaged in market work and those who are economically active according to the extended definition. Unfortunately, however, no similar provisions were made in the LFSS 1988. Accordingly, all our comparisons with 1988 are done on the basis of the extended labor force definition.

In what follows, I briefly summarize the most important findings of each of the studies included in the collection. In the overview papers, Assaad and Said discuss the major trends in employment and wages. Assaad shows that although female labor force participation has increased and that of males has fallen, women's employment prospects have worsened significantly over the economic reform period. Outside the public sector, which has continued to grow relatively fast for both males and females, the only sector where female employment grew at a higher than average rate is nonwage agriculture, which includes the difficult-to-measure subsistence agriculture sector. Paid employment in the private sector grew fairly rapidly for males, but stagnated for females. Employment in state-owned enterprises declined in absolute terms for both males and females, but the decline was more severe for females. Unemployment rates increased for both males and females, but the increase was more pronounced in rural areas, where the most rapid increase in the working age population occurred over the period. Evidently, rural-to-urban migration flows over the period were insufficient to make up for the historically higher fertility rates in rural areas, resulting in severe demographic pressures on rural labor markets.

Said shows that the 1990s decade has been one of real wage erosion and overall wage compression. Wage differentials due to experience, education, and while-collar/blue-collar occupational differences all declined. Government workers continued to see their wages being eroded relative to those in the private sector. In contrast, state-owned enterprise workers saw their wage premia increase despite significant contraction in the size of that sector. On the whole, wage inequalities decreased among males and increased among females. Although there is practically no unexplained gender difference in wages among government workers, there is a large and persistent difference in the private sector and a growing gender gap in the state-owned sector, which increasingly resembles the private sector in its wage structure.

The papers in Part II address the role of the informal sector in labor absorption and the degree to which the labor market itself has been informalized. El-Mahdy focuses first on "informal workers," i.e., employees who are hired without the benefit of a contract or socially insurance coverage. This group represented about a third of the nonagricultural labor force and four fifths of the private nonagricultural workforce in 1998. She then turns to informal entrepreneurs, the employers and self-employed workers who operate informal enterprises. With regards to informal workers, she finds that their share in the total and private nonagricultural workforces has declined slightly from 1988 to 1998, indicating that there is no trend toward greater informality in the wage labor market. In comparing the wages of formal and informal workers, El-Mahdi finds that in terms of money wages, informal workers are often paid more than their formal counterparts, but they lack all the nonwage benefits that formal workers receive. With regards to informal entrepreneurs, El-Mahdi finds that their share in total employment has increased from 1988 to 1998, especially in rural areas. Wahba and Moktar investigate the informalization question by examining the job history data for workers in the ELMS 98 sample, focusing on those who were at least 18 in

1990 and at most 64 in 1998. According to this analysis, the proportion of workers in a variety of employment arrangements than can be described as informal increased slightly in the 1990s. This includes workers with no contracts and/or no social insurance, and workers with no contracts and irregular employment, or no social insurance and no regular employment. They find that the groups experiencing the greatest informalization of their employment are female workers and youth under the age of 30. Among workers already employed in 1990, more moved from informal to public employment than the other way around. However, new entrants to the labor market in the 1990s have been disproportionately drawn into informal employment. Because job security regulations protect the status of workers who are already employed, the brunt of informalization in Egypt has fallen on new entrants to the labor market.

The two papers in Part III examine the labor market experience of women and children over the reform period. El-Kogali shows that women in private sector wage employment in Egypt, and particularly the young new entrants among them, are working longer hours. Their jobs have also become casualized in the sense that they are less likely to be protected by an employment contract, or by social or medical insurance coverage, and are more likely to be temporary. Zibani investigates changes in child labor and schooling over the study period. She finds that rates of children's participation in the labor force have dropped significantly in the ten-year period, a trend that can be partially explained by significant increases in school enrollment rates. She also finds major differences along gender lines in children's activity patterns. Working boys are predominantly engaged in market work, whereas working girls are mostly engaged in subsistence work. A significant proportion of girls are engaged in domestic work, which, although it does not count as employment under conventional definitions, can be a significant impediment to schooling.

The two papers in the final part of the volume examine the dynamics of the labor market by assessing changes in the labor mobility patterns of the population as a whole, and the youth population in particular, a critical group that is the focus of much policy debate. Wahba uses detailed data on job mobility in the 1988 and 1998 surveys to examine how labor mobility patterns have changed and whether these changes can be attributed to economic reform and structural adjustment. Wahba shows that mobility rates for employed workers across occupations or sectors actually dropped in the 1990s compared to the 1980s, although mobility across industries (economic activity) increased slightly. Labor market adjustment was taking place at the margin through changed patterns of labor market entry and exit. Young workers were less likely to enter into the public sector and more likely to be channeled toward private and informal employment. By the same token, older workers were more likely to retire early from public sector employment in the 1990s compared to 1980s, but this trend was much stronger for public enterprise than for the government. In fact, female civil servants tended to stay on longer to their government jobs in the 1990s compared to the 1980s.

Given the growing concern with youth unemployment in a period of rapid increases in youth labor supply, Amer investigates changes in youth labor market trajectories from the 1980s to the 1990s. She begins by reviewing the general trends in labor force participation and unemployment for youth and then examines in some detail changes in the school-to-work trajectories of youth from the 1980s to the 1990s. She finds that the public sector continues to be the largest destination for youth seven to eight years after entry, and that the proportion of youth ending up in the public sector after eight years in the 1990s is fairly similar to what it was in the 1980s. On the other hand, the proportion entering to private sector jobs, especially unprotected jobs, has increased. One positive indicator is that a smaller proportion of youth remained in the unemployed state after eight years in the 1990s compared to the 1980s, but there were sharp differences along gender lines in this respect. Young women tend to remain in the unemployed state much longer than young men. Amer also finds that two-thirds of women in private sector jobs will have left these jobs after four years, mostly because of marriage. In contrast, those in the public sector tend to hold on to their jobs there.

In conclusion, the papers in the volume indicate that although economic reforms have slowed down employment in the public sector, government employment continues to be one of the largest labor absorption sectors in Egypt. Young workers are increasingly being pushed toward private jobs that lack contract or social insurance protection, but young females are finding it much harder to access even these private sector jobs. Due to slowing rural-to-urban migration, rural areas are experiencing severe demographic pressures and thus poor labor market prospects for their youth. Young men are able to adjust by commuting to work elsewhere, an option that is not always open to young women in this culture. The 1990s have been a decade of real wage erosion and one of growing gender gaps in wages in the private sector. Informality has also increased in the labor market, especially when it comes to new entrants. Although no major legal reforms of labor market rules were adopted since 1991, Egyptian labor markets are becoming de facto less regulated through a more lax enforcement of existing rules.

Ragui Assaad

Part I. Overview

1 The Transformation of the Egyptian Labor Market: 1988–98

Ragui Assaad

Introduction

Because of the scarcity of official data on the Egyptian labor market, little is known about the evolution of labor force participation, employment, and unemployment in Egypt in recent years. Although the most recently published Labor Force Sample Survey (LFSS) dates from 1998, it suffers from serious comparability problems with previous rounds of the survey. Data from the recently released 1996 Population Census (PC) cannot be compared with any source other than previous censuses. Moreover, with concepts that are difficult to define and operationalize—such as "economically active population," "employment," and "unemployment"—a large-scale operation like the census does not provide accurate results. Finally, neither the census data nor the LFSS data are available to researchers in the form of microdata, which would allow them to conduct the kind of multivariate analysis that is now typically expected in labor market studies.

Driven by this severe lack of recent data, the Economic Research Forum for the Arab Countries, Iran, and Turkey (ERF)—with the cooperation of the Egyptian Central Agency for Public Mobilization and Statistics (CAPMAS)—conducted the Egypt Labor Market Survey 1998 (ELMS 98), a nationally representative in-depth labor market survey of 5,000 households in Egypt. The survey was designed to be comparable to a special round of the LFSS carried out in October 1988 (LFSS 88).[1] The ELMS 98 was conducted 10 years to the day after the LFSS 88 using a similar sample and questionnaire design. Utmost care was used to ensure that the bulk of the data would be strictly comparable, even if some questions were added or dropped from the ELMS 98 survey.

This chapter provides an overview of the changes in the main labor market aggregates and rates in Egypt from 1988 to 1998. It examines changes that occurred in recent years in unemployment, underemployment, and employment, and in the working-age population and labor force. It also explores the changing structure of employment and the sectors that contributed most to employment creation in the 1990s. Special care was taken to ensure that the variables used were strictly comparable across the two time periods covered by the LFSS 88 and the ELMS 98. This necessitated the use of the extended definition of "labor force" and "employment," which include employment in subsistence agriculture (see definitions at the end of this section). The extended definition yields a larger labor force and a lower unemployment rate than the more conventional market labor force definition, which unfortunately cannot be obtained for 1988 due to the way the relevant questions were asked in LFSS 88.

The Egyptian civilian labor force has grown at an average rate of 2.7 percent per year from 1988 to 1998, which is equal to the rate of growth of the working-age population (ages 15–64). This means that overall participation rates remained stable over this 10-year period. This overall stability masked significant changes along gender lines, with the male labor force participation rate falling by 4 percentage points and the female labor force participation rising by the same amount. Moreover, the size of the rural labor force has been growing faster than that of the urban labor force, reflecting the more rapid rise of the rural population. The labor force will continue to grow faster than the overall population for the next 10 years, as the large cohort of 10- to 19-year-olds makes its transition to the labor market. Egypt is now at a stage in its demographic transition where it is beginning to see a declining proportion of dependents, but where labor supply pressures are at their peak.[2] However, the rate of growth of the labor force will drop significantly as the smaller cohort of those currently under the age of 10 reaches working age.

The drop in male labor force participation is due in part to increasing school enrollments among young males, but the bulk of the effect comes from earlier withdrawals from the labor force by uneducated males above the age of 50. The rise in female labor force participation is also due to the combination of an increasing share of females with a secondary or higher-than-secondary education—who tend to participate at higher rates than their less-educated counterparts—as well as greater persistence of married women above the age of 30 in the labor force.

The increase in educational attainment of both males and females over this relatively brief period is remarkable. The government seems to have succeeded in making the necessary educational investments to significantly increase enrollments, despite great budgetary pressures in a period of economic stabilization and structural adjustment. This can also be seen in the very rapid growth of the number of teachers in the decade under study. The increasing educational attainment of the female population is likely to drive rising female participation rates for the foreseeable future.

Overall unemployment increased during the study period from 5.4 percent to 7.9 percent, with the number of unemployed increasing by 6.6 percent per annum, from 0.89 million in 1988 to 1.72 million in 1998, a rate of increase that is considerably higher than the rate of growth of either the working-age population or the labor force. However, it is worth noting that the growth in unemployment is lower than what it was in the 1980s, when it grew at nearly 9 percent per annum (Assaad, 1997b).

Underlying the overall increase in the unemployment rate is a relative stability in the urban unemployment rate and a sharp increase in the rural rate. This basically means that employment growth for rural residents, although slightly more rapid than for urban residents, did not keep pace with the much more rapidly expanding rural working-age population. The concentration of unemployment among young, educated, new entrants is largely the result of a rapidly growing labor supply that is outstripping the ability of the economy—in particular, the rural economy—to generate new employment. The absence of migration flows to the cities has also prevented rural surplus labor from moving to the cities at the same rates as it did in the past. There is some evidence, however, that commuting rates among rural males to jobs in urban areas have increased significantly.

The growth in labor supply is driven primarily by past demographic growth, but the resulting labor surplus is being increasingly manifested as open unemployment, rather than underemployment, because of education-induced behavioral and preference changes. Educated youth are much more likely than their uneducated counterparts to want to hold out for a regular job—one regulated by the formal institutions and regulations of society, with relatively steady paychecks and social service benefits—rather than engage in casual, irregular employment, which generally offers more unstable employment, and provides no social service benefits.

A broader measure of employment inadequacy—which includes visible underemployment, discouraged unemployment, as well as open unemployment—reveals a similar pattern by education, except for lesser-educated males, whose visible underemployment rates are high. In fact, the rates of underemployment among illiterate males rival the rates of open unemployment among graduates. Because of their heavy household responsibilities, females who work part-time do not generally declare themselves as available for more work, and therefore do not show up as underemployed.

The most dramatic finding with respect to employment is the continued rapid increase in government employment. While employment in state-owned enterprises contracted significantly over the study's 10-year period, the public sector as a whole increased its share of total employment because of the continued rapid growth of government employment. This somewhat puzzling result can be explained in two ways. First, it appears that female civil servants are not quitting public service after marriage and childbearing in the 1990s at the same rate as they used to. Thus, even with a reduction in the rate of hiring of new entrants, the government workforce can continue to expand due to this lower female exit rate. Second, despite the fact that hiring rates have declined among the groups eligible for guaranteed public employment—namely secondary school and university graduates—the size of this group has expanded dramatically in the 1990s, further fueling the growth of public payrolls. Much of the government hiring in the 1990s was for new teachers, but the number of clerical workers also increased significantly.

The private sector outside agriculture also contributed significantly to job creation, primarily for men. Employment growth for women in the private nonagricultural sector was significantly slower than the growth of the female labor force in general. There appears to be a large exodus of male labor from agriculture in contrast to a substantial increase in female participation in the sector. The increase in female agricultural employment is mostly attributable to those engaged in subsistence agriculture. Agricultural wage labor has declined in both relative and absolute terms, for both males and females.

1. Basic Definitions Used in This Study

1.1 Economically Active Population

The most recent internationally accepted definition of the "economically active population" was adopted by the Thirteenth International Conference of Labor Statisticians (ILO) in October 1982. It states that the "economically active" comprises all persons of either sex who furnish the supply of labor for the production of economic goods and services as defined by the United Nations (UN) system of national accounts. These include: "The production and processing of primary products, whether for the market, for barter, or for their own consumption; the production of all other goods and services for the market; and, in the case of households that produce such goods and services for the market, the corresponding production for their own consumption" (ILO, 1982). Thus, those engaged in subsistence activities in agriculture, animal husbandry, or the processing of agricultural goods are counted as active, while those who engage in other domestic activities, such as food preparation, housecleaning, or child-rearing, are not.

In the definition of employment that follows, the international recommendations state that persons engaged in the production of goods and services for their own consumption and that of the household should be considered employed "if such production comprises an important contribution to the total consumption of the household." (ibid.) Throughout the rest of this paper, I refer to this definition as the "extended labor force" definition, in contrast to the "market labor force" definition, which excludes production for own consumption. Individuals whose production does not constitute "an important contribution to household consumption" are not classified anywhere else in the economically active population. Thus, besides the obvious problem with operationalizing the term "important," there are two seemingly contradictory recommendations for the treatment of those engaged in production for their own consumption.[3]

The recommendations further suggest distinguishing between the "currently active population," or the labor force, as comprising those who are economically active during a short reference period of one week, and the "usually active population" comprising those who are economically active during a long reference period (anywhere from three months to a year). The labor force and the usually active population are further subdivided into the "employed" and the "unemployed." Although the LFSS 88 and the ELMS 98 allow for estimates of both the current and usual versions of these variables, the analysis presented here is based exclusively on the short reference period of one week.

In the LFSS 88, the extended definition of the economically active population was strictly applied with no attempt to determine what constituted an "important contribution to household consumption." Therefore, any person engaged in primary activities for purposes of their own or their household's consumption was considered economically active, including women who had a few chickens in the backyard, or girls who assisted their mothers in such subsistence activities. As a result, the rate of female participation in the labor force measured in that survey was considerably higher than that reported by official labor force surveys, especially in rural areas, where subsistence activities are more common. It also resulted in significantly lower unemployment rates than had been previously reported, or that have been reported since in official labor force surveys, which effectively use a definition of labor force that approaches the market labor force definition.

In ELMS 98, the employment questions were asked so as to allow for the separate identification of the market labor force and the extended labor force. As a result, we can produce estimates based on either definition. Unfortunately, no similar provisions were made in the LFSS 88 to separately identify those engaged only in production for their own or household consumption. Accordingly, all comparisons with 1988 are done on the basis of the extended labor force definition.

1.2 Employment

For a person to be classified as employed, according to the international recommendations, they would either have had to be: (1) "at work" for at least one hour during the reference period; (2) formally attached to a job (if a paid employee) or to an enterprise (if self-employed); (3) an employer; or (4) an unpaid family worker. As mentioned above, persons engaged in the production of goods and services for their own or household consumption should be considered employed only if such production comprises an important contribution to the total consumption of the household. Since there is no effective way of operationalizing this rather vague criterion, I use an extended definition of employment that includes all those engaged in any subsistence production. With ELMS 98 data, as in the case of the labor force, it is possible to limit the definition of employment to those whose activity is at least in part for the purposes of exchange.

1.3 Unemployment

The unemployed comprise all persons "above a certain age"—which for our purposes is 14—who were: (1) without work; (2) currently available for work, either in paid employment or self-employment; or (3) seeking work (i.e., had taken specific steps in a recent reference period to seek employment). For operational purposes, the ELMS 98 interpreted "available for work" as wishing to work and willing to start working within 15 days of work becoming available. The reference period for "seeking work" was set at 3 months, with the exception of those who registered with the Ministry of Manpower's employment offices, who were considered to be seeking work even if such registration was prior to the 3-month reference period.

The international recommendation states that in situations where the labor market is organized or limited in scope, or where labor absorption is at the time inadequate, the "seeking work" criterion can be relaxed. This, in fact, was done for the estimates of unemployment reported from the LFSS 88. However, the practice in Egypt since then is to impose the "seeking work" criterion. I am therefore reporting estimates of unemployment that impose all three criteria on the data from the 1988 and 1998 surveys on the basis of a series of questions asked about actions taken to seek employment. Those who declared themselves as not working and available for work but who did not take actions to seek employment are considered "discouraged unemployed," and are classified as out of the labor force (see Section 4).

2. Labor Force Growth, Demographic Composition, and Labor Force Participation

Labor force growth, or the growth in aggregate labor supply, is determined by the overall population growth rate, the changing age composition of the population, and the change in age-specific participation rates. Changes in participation rates are usually attributable to behavioral changes in areas such as school enrollment, retirement, and female withdrawal from the labor force upon marriage. In the following discussion, I will try to disentangle these various influences on the growth and the changes in the demographic composition of the labor force from 1988 to 1998. Most of the discussion centers on the labor force participation of those between the ages of 15–64. However, when discussing the pattern of participation by age, I open the age range to those ages 6-75 in an attempt to see how child labor and the economic participation of older adults has changed over the 10-year period.

2.1 Labor Force Growth and Trends in Participation

The labor force, using the extended definition, has grown at an annual rate of 2.7 percent from 1988 to 1998, which was exactly the rate of growth of the working-age population. The overall rate of participation of those between the ages of 15–64 has, therefore, remained constant at about 59.1 percent. Although the rate of growth of the working-age population has slowed somewhat from 2.8 percent per annum in the previous decade, the stability in overall participation rates continues a trend that extends at least to the mid-1970s (Assaad, 1997b).

Table 1.1: Population and Labor Force Growth Rates (percent/year) Ages 15–64, 1988–98

	Male	Female	Total
Population			
Urban	2.3	2.1	2.2
Rural	3.2	3.0	3.1
Total	**2.8**	**2.6**	**2.7**
Labor Force			
Urban	1.8	3.6	2.4
Rural	2.5	3.5	2.9
Total	**2.2**	**3.6**	**2.7**

Source: Author's calculations based on data from LFSS 1988 and ELMS 1998.

The stability in the overall participation rate masks significant differences in how participation has changed over time along gender lines and by urban/rural location. These changes resulted in important shifts in the gender and geographic composition of the labor force. While male participation rates declined by approximately 4 percentage points from 1988 to 1998, female participation increased by the same percentage. As a result, the female labor force grew at a rate of 3.6 percent per annum, whereas the male labor force grew at only 2.2 percent per annum.

Higher accumulated fertility in rural areas and relatively insignificant rural-to-urban migration in the 1990s have resulted in a rate of population growth that is nearly 50 percent higher in rural areas than in urban areas. However, this was not fully reflected in the differential rate of growth of the urban and rural labor forces. The difference in the rate of growth of the labor force relative to that of the population is the result of falling overall participation in rural areas and rising participation rates in urban areas, as shown in Table 1.2. This is due primarily to the fact that female participation rates have been growing more rapidly in urban than in rural areas. In fact, the growth rate in the female labor force is about equal in urban and rural areas, despite widely different rates of growth in the underlying populations.

Table 1.2: Labor Force Participation Rate (percent) by Gender, Market, and Extended Labor Force Definitions, Ages 15–64, 1988, 1998

	Urban		Rural		Total	
Sex	**1988**	**1998**	**1988**	**1998**	**1988**	**1998**
Males						
Market labor force	N.A.	70.8	N.A.	73.5	N.A.	72.3
Extended labor force	74.4	70.8	78.8	73.6	76.7	72.3
Females						
Market labor force	N.A.	25.5	N.A.	17.7	N.A.	21.2
Extended labor force	28.5	33.0	53.5	56.6	41.8	46.0
All						
Market labor force	N.A.	48.1	N.A.	45.7	N.A.	46.0
Extended labor force	51.2	51.9	66.0	65.1	59.1	59.2

Note: N.A. = not available.
Source: Author's calculations based on data from LFSS 88 and ELMS 98.

Table 1.3: Comparative Labor Force Participation Rates (percent) by Gender and Urban/Rural Locations from Various Sources, Ages 15–64

		Source				
		LFSS 1995	**PC 1996**	**EIHS 1997**	**LFSS 1997**	**LFSS 1998**
Male	Urban	69.9	77.1	72.8	70.0	70.3
	Rural	76.3	83.4	75.4	75.9	74.6
	All	73.3	80.5	74.1	73.2	72.6
Female	Urban	19.5	20.4	26.2	20.3	20.2
	Rural	23.0	10.9	17.3	20.9	19.6
	All	21.4	15.2	21.5	20.6	19.8
All	Urban	44.8	49.3	50.1	46.1	46.2
	Rural	49.7	47.6	46.5	47.9	46.5
	All	47.4	48.4	48.2	47.1	46.4

Sources: LFSS= Labor Force Sample Survey (CAPMAS); PC = Population Census (CAPMAS); EIHS = Egypt Integrated Household Survey (IFPRI).

A comparison of the market labor force and the extended labor force definitions in 1998 shows that female participation rates are strongly determined by the definition that is used (comparable figures on market labor force are not available for 1988). If the market labor force definition is used instead of the extended definition, female participation rates in 1998 are reduced by 25 percentage points, a relative change of more than 50 percent. Since the difference involves women engaged in subsistence agriculture and animal husbandry, the biggest change occurs in rural areas. But the change in urban areas is significant, as well. These differences emphasize how important it is to specify which definition of participation is being used and how it is operationalized. Because of problems relating to definitions and field implementation, measurement of female labor force participation rates in Egypt have been notoriously unstable. Table 1.3 provides a sample of recent estimates of labor force participation rates (ages 15–64) from various sources.

The first thing to note from this comparison is that the 1996 Population Census (PC) provides much higher estimates of male labor force participation rates than the other survey-based sources. Among the survey-based sources, the estimates of male labor force participation rates are similar across the various sources and also fairly similar to the estimates provided by ELMS 98 (Table 1.2) under either definition of the labor force. It is in the measurement of female labor force participation that the various estimates differ the most. The 1996 PC has the lowest estimates, with the difference being essentially concentrated in rural areas, where the census does a particularly poor job capturing women outside paid employment. The EIHS 1997, which uses a market labor force definition, provides estimates that are very close to those of ELMS 1998 when the market definition is used there as well. In theory, the regular rounds of LFSS use the extended definition, but the estimates they provide are lower in urban areas and slightly higher in rural areas than those provided by EIHS and ELMS using the market definition. They fall well short of the estimates provided by ELMS using the extended definition.

These large variations in the measurement of female labor force participation, especially in rural areas, underscores the need for caution in comparing across different sources any labor force statistics that depend in some way on the size of the female labor force.

2.2 Determinants of the Decline in Male Labor Force Participation

In this section, I examine the demographic and behavioral changes that underlie the falling labor force participation rates among males. Male labor force participation declined from 76.7 percent in 1988 to 72.3 percent in 1998, with urban and rural areas experiencing roughly similar rates of decline.

Figure 1.1a: Male Labor Force Participation Rates by Age, Urban/Rural Location, Males Ages 6–75

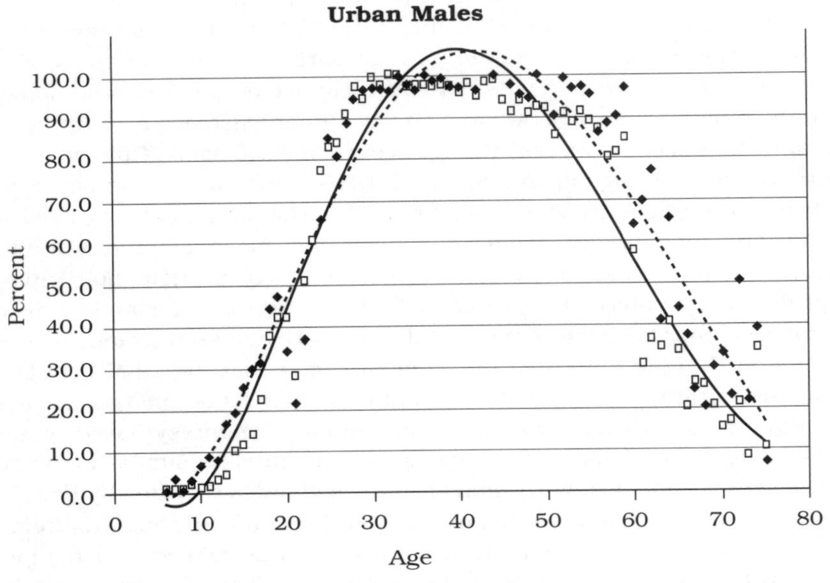

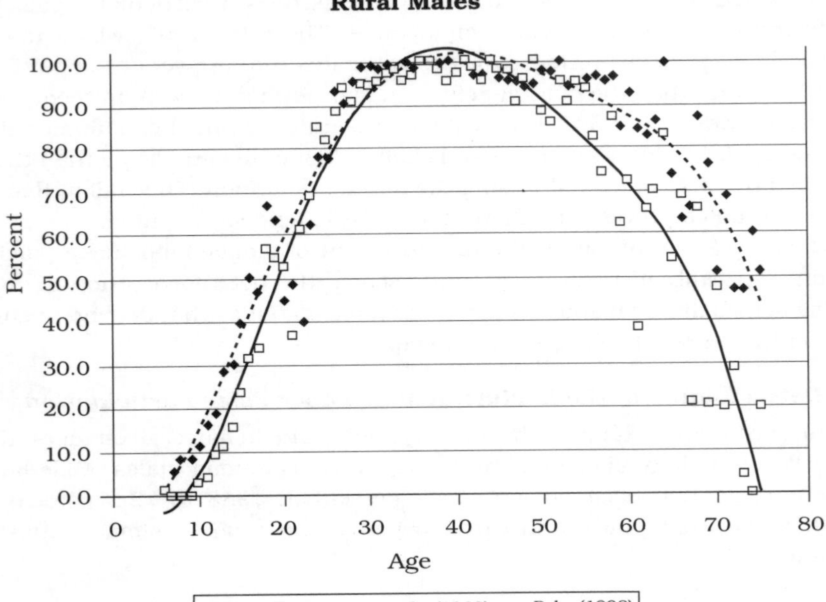

Figure 1.1b: Age Distribution of the Male Population by Urban/Rural Location, 1988–98

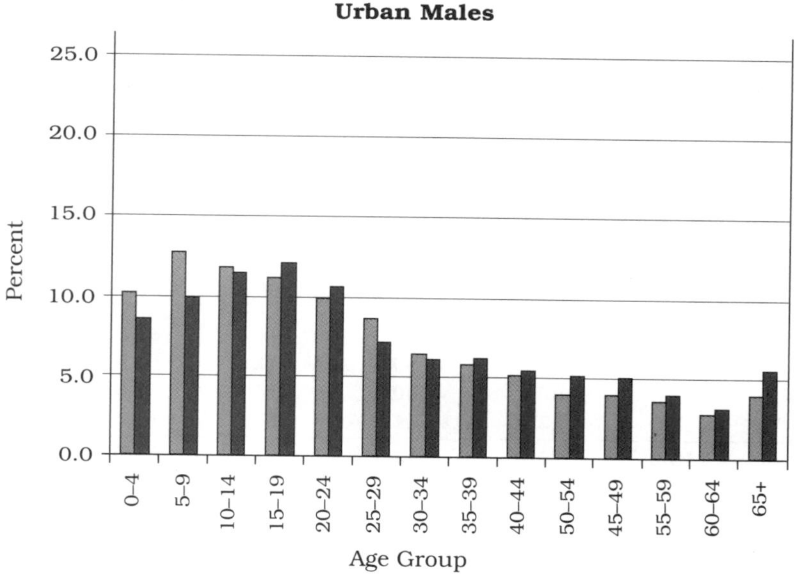

Rural Males

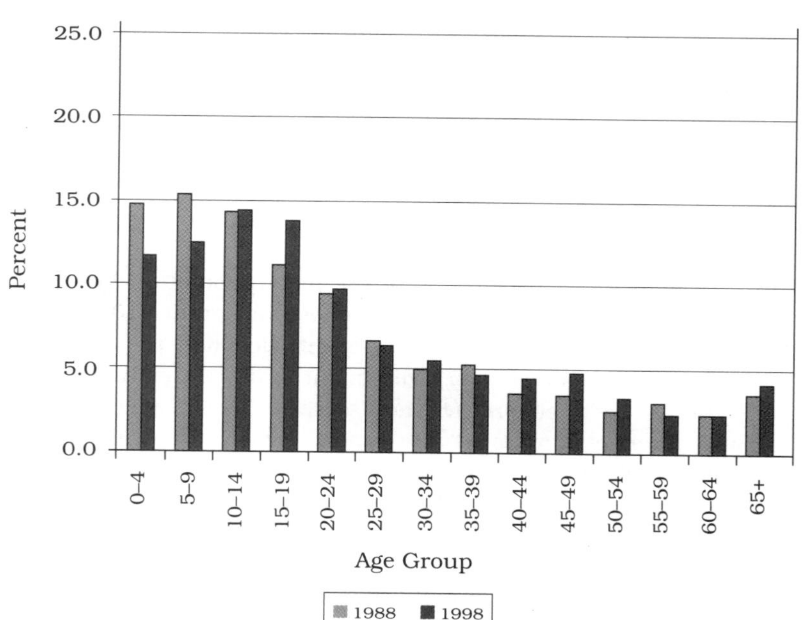

As shown in Figure 1.1a and Appendix Table A1.3, the decline in male participation occurred at the two ends of the age distribution, with a somewhat larger drop at older ages. The black-and-white symbols on the figures indicate mean participation rates by age in 1988 and 1998, respectively. The dashed-and-solid lines are a 5th order polynomial fit through these points. Participation rates for males ages 6–19 fell noticeably from 1988 to 1998, a trend that is reflected in the rising school enrollment rates shown in Table 1.4.

Table 1.4: Net School Enrollment Rates Males (percent), Ages 6–24, 1988, 1998

Age	Urban		Rural		Total	
	1988	1998	1988	1998	1988	1998
06–11	94.5	96.4	90.0	93.6	91.8	94.6
12–14	86.2	92.6	80.5	84.9	82.6	87.7
15–19	64.5	69.6	50.1	56.8	56.3	61.7
20–24	21.9	28.0	11.7	17.1	16.2	21.9
Total	**68.3**	**70.4**	**62.7**	**65.5**	**65.0**	**67.4**

Source: Author's calculations based on data from LFSS 88 and ELMS 98.

In both time periods, male participation falls sharply between the ages of 20–22, the ages at which most males undertake their military service in Egypt.[4] From age 23 onwards, the participation rate rises sharply in both 1988 and 1998, until it becomes virtually universal by age 30, and remains so until age 44 or 45. After that, participation begins to drop, though by much more in 1998 than in 1988. In 1988, males in rural areas continued to work at rates close to 100 percent until age 60, dropping to 70 percent by age 70. By 1998, male participation rates in rural areas had dropped to close to 70 percent by age 60 and 20 percent by age 70. In urban areas, the decline is less pronounced, but only because the trend toward earlier retirement had already set in by 1988.

Figure 1.1b shows the distribution of the male population by age group (see also Table A1.1). Although the proportion of males under 10 years of age is declining significantly, reflecting recent fertility declines, the proportion of those 15–19 is still increasing, especially in rural areas. Combined with the 10–14 age group, they constitute the largest 10-year cohort in 1998. Currently, rising school enrollment rates and the concomitant fall in participation are dampening the pressure this age group is exerting on labor supply. However, once they complete their educations and reach the 20–24 age group, their participation rates will rise sharply, putting significant pressure on the labor market. The growing proportion of young new entrants to the labor market means that demographically-induced labor supply pressures are still growing in Egypt, and will continue to do so for at least another decade.

As shown in Figure 1.2a, education-specific participation rates are declining only for uneducated males. Urban males with some formal schooling are participating at about the same rates as in 1988, and the participation rates of their rural counterparts are increasing. Thus, the decline in the overall participation rates of males can be attributed to the combined effect of lower participation for older males with low levels of education, and increasing educational enrollments. This is putting a larger fraction of younger males in intermediate educational levels, which have lower participation rates.

Figure 1.2b shows that the proportion of males in the ages of 15–64 who have not completed the primary level of education has declined markedly from 1988 to 1998. Conversely, the proportion that has completed each educational level has increased, with the most marked increases occurring at the intermediate and less-than-intermediate levels (secondary and preparatory and primary levels, respectively). Since these levels allow for further schooling, they have lower participation rates.

We can therefore conclude that the decline in male participation rates is due, in large part, to a significant drop in participation among older, uneducated males, who are withdrawing from the labor force at an earlier age. Although this phenomenon had been occurring for some time in urban areas, it has accelerated markedly in rural areas during the study period. To a lesser extent, the drop in male participation can also be attributed to increasing enrollments at the secondary and tertiary education levels.

2.3 Determinants of the Increase in Female Labor Force Participation

According to the extended definition of the labor force, female participation rates increased from 42 percent to 46 percent, with the increase about one-and-a-half times faster in urban areas than in rural areas. As shown in Figure 1.3a and Appendix Table A1.3, as in the case of males, there is a decline in participation up to age 19 in both urban and rural areas, which reflects the increasing female enrollment rates shown in Table 1.5. In fact, female school enrollment rates increased considerably more than what is implied by the reduction in the labor force participation rates of girls. Girls in rural areas appear to have made important strides in school enrollment, with enrollment rates increasing by nearly 25 percent for girls ages 6–11 and by nearly 60 percent for those 12–14. Although rural enrollment rates are still significantly lower than urban rates—and female rates lower than male rates—both gaps are closing fast.

At the other end of the age distribution, the change in the pattern of female participation is notably different from that of males. For every age group beyond the early twenties, up to age 75, the general pattern is that participation has increased between 1988 and 1998 in both urban and rural areas (Figure 1.3a). There is no question that although females are now more likely to delay their entry to the labor force until their late teens and early twenties, they are also more likely to remain economically active for a longer time.

Figure 1.2a: Male Labor Force Participation Rates by Educational Attainment and Urban/Rural Location, Ages 15–64

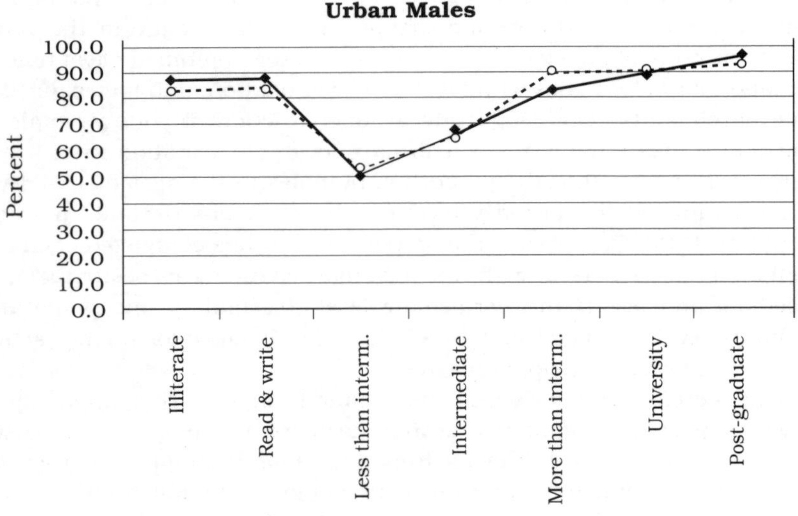

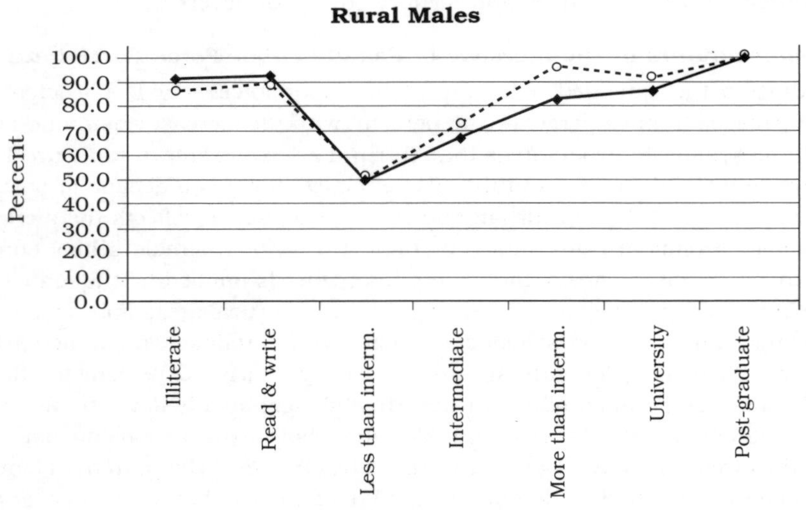

Figure 1.2b: Distribution of the Male Population by Educational Attainment and Urban/Rural Location, Ages 15–64, 1988–98

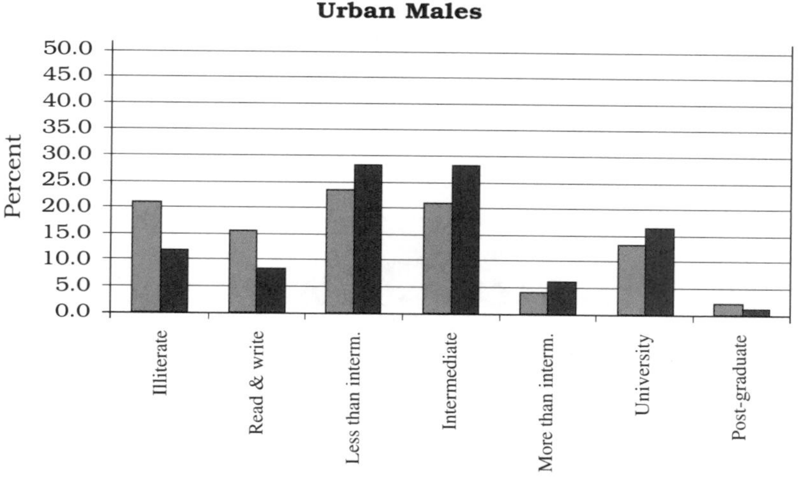

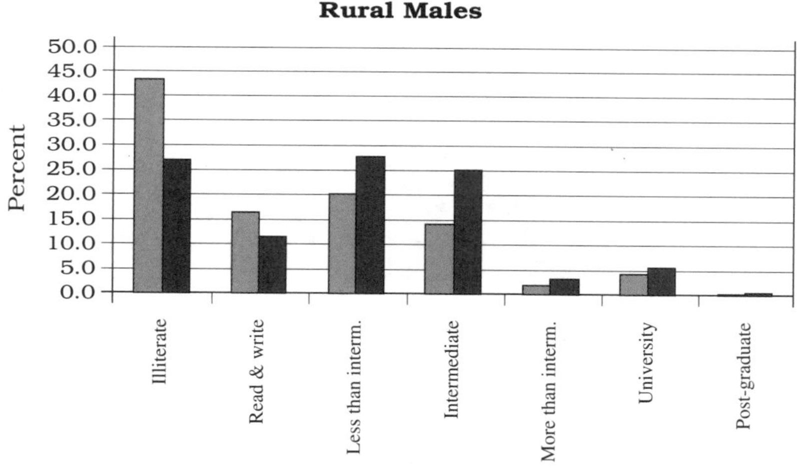

Figure 1.3a: Female Labor Force Participation Rates by Age, Urban/Rural Location, Ages 6–75, Extended Labor Force Definition, 1988, 1998

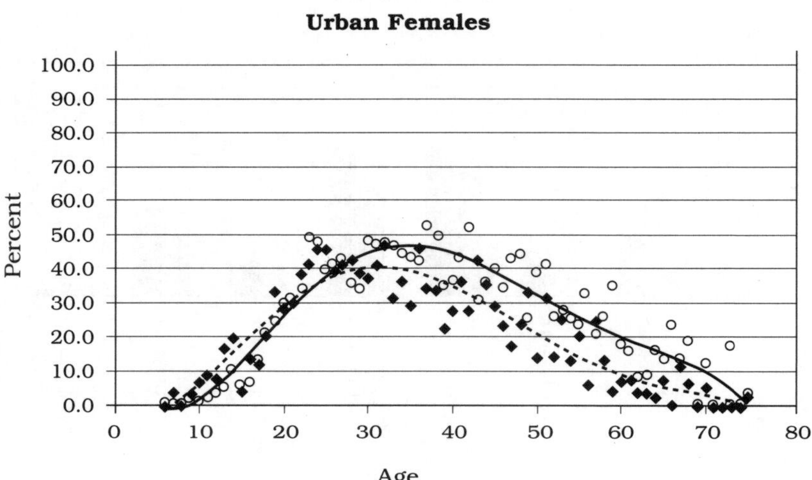

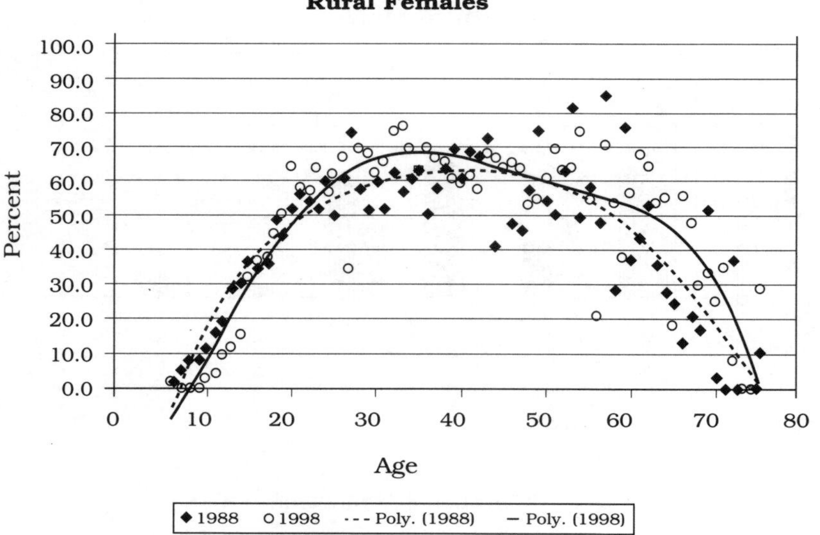

Figure 1.3b: Age Distribution of the Female Population by Urban/Rural Location, 1988–98

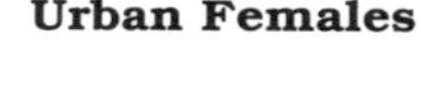

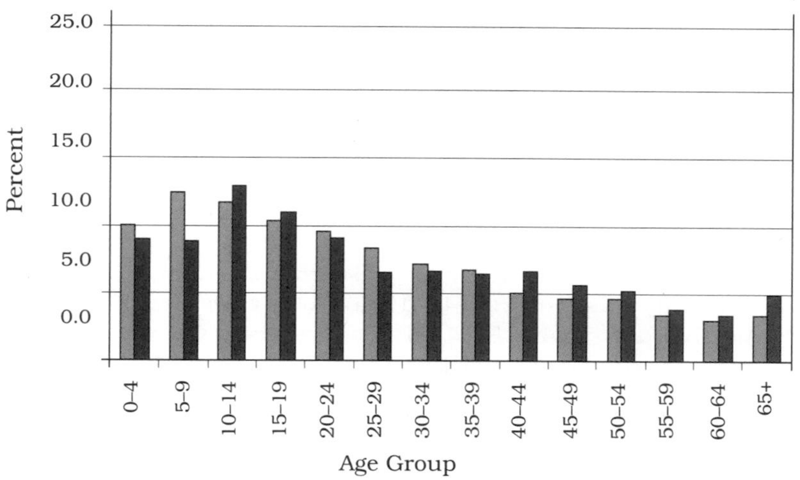

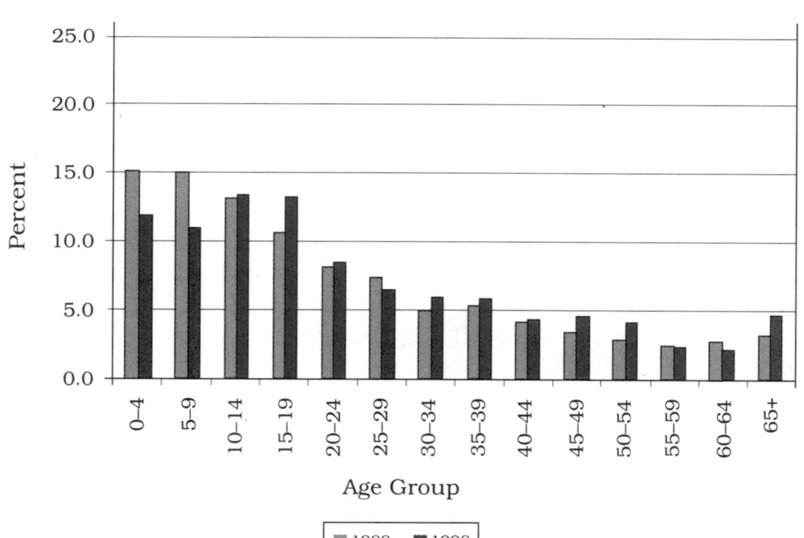

In urban areas, at every age from 30 to 65, female participation rates are nearly 10 percentage points higher in 1998 than in 1988. In 1988, the highest female participation rate in urban areas, nearly 46 percent, occurred at age 25. By 1998, the maximum of nearly 52 percent occurred close to age 40.

A similar rising trend in female participation is apparent in rural areas, but because of the predominance of subsistence agriculture activities in rural female employment, participation is not only higher, but the age pattern is also more complex. It appears that rural females have a bimodal activity pattern. Participation first peaks at age 30, declines in the prime childbearing ages, and increases again between ages 50 and 60. The participation of those females ages 25–35 has clearly increased in the 10-year period, but there is no clear trend among those 45–65.

As in the case of males, demographic pressures will continue to drive female labor supply as the large cohort of 10–19 year-olds moves into the labor force over the next decade (Figure 1.3b). In this case, however, the demographic effect is compounded by rising participation of those above the age of 20.

Table 1.5: Net School Enrollment Rates (percent), Females Ages 6–24, 1988, 1998

Age	Urban		Rural		Total	
	1988	1998	1988	1998	1988	1998
06–11	92.6	95.4	69.2	84.8	78.4	88.9
12–14	79.8	88.8	46.8	74.4	59.5	80.6
15–19	60.3	68.7	25.2	45.2	40.0	54.1
20–24	17.9	26.0	4.2	7.3	10.6	15.5
Total	**64.8**	**71.0**	**41.9**	**55.6**	**51.3**	**61.8**

Source: Author's calculations based on data from LFSS 88 and ELMS 98.

The trend in the pattern of female participation by educational attainment is virtually the reverse of the one found for males. There is rising participation for uneducated females and declining participation among females at the intermediate levels of education, the most rapidly growing segment of the female population. However, the biggest effect on overall participation comes from the change in the distribution of the female population by educational level. As shown in Figure 1.4b the proportion of illiterate females in the working-age population has fallen sharply, from 42 percent to 28 percent in urban areas and from 80 percent to 56 percent in rural areas. This decline is counteracted by increases in the proportion of females at every level of formal education, but the most notable increases are at the intermediate and less-than-intermediate levels. It is by now a well-established fact in Egypt that female participation increases sharply once an intermediate (or secondary) educational level is reached.

This is confirmed by this study (see Figure 1.4a and Appendix A1.4). Thus, despite somewhat falling participation at that level over time, overall participation has increased because of the increase in the proportion of secondary-school graduates, who participate at higher rates than their lesser-educated counterparts. Though holders of less-than-intermediate certificates participate at relatively low rates because they are still likely to be in school, they participate at high rates once they have completed their schooling. Therefore, their increasing numbers will fuel increased female participation in the near future.

Table 1.6: Proportion Ever-Married Among Females Ages 15–39, 1988, 1998

	Urban		Rural		Total	
	1988	**1998**	**1988**	**1998**	**1988**	**1998**
15–19	8.6	2.9	32.9	15.9	22.7	11.0
20–24	38.5	30.7	77.2	57.6	59.2	45.7
25–29	71.7	70.2	93.9	86.4	83.8	79.5
30–34	90.2	88.7	97.4	90.2	93.7	89.5
35–39	98.2	93.0	98.4	97.2	98.3	95.3

Source: Author's calculations based on data from LFSS 88 and ELMS 98.

Previous studies on female participation in Egypt have shown that the biggest drop in participation occurs at marriage, rather than at childbearing (Assaad and El-Hamidi, 2001). Rising participation could thus be the result of delayed marriage as well as higher persistence in the labor force after marriage. Table 1.6 shows the proportion of those females who have ever been married according to age group, in both surveys. There is clearly a strong trend toward delayed marriage. The proportion of ever-married females has dropped significantly for every age cohort until age 34 in both urban and rural areas, and has even dropped noticeably for those 35–39 in urban areas. Although marriage is virtually universal among females in Egypt by age 40, early marriage is no longer the norm. The largest decline in marriage is among young women ages 15–19, whose marriage rate fell by more than 50 percent. Marriage rates have also fallen precipitously for females in their early twenties.

Besides delaying marriage, a growing number of Egyptian women at all educational levels, and in both urban and rural areas, are continuing to work after marriage. Table 1.7 shows that the participation rate among married women has increased more significantly over the study's 10-year period than it has among unmarried women, especially in urban areas. Because it is easier to combine work and household chores in rural areas, married rural women participate at higher rates than both their urban and unmarried counterparts. However, even urban married women are now participating at rates similar to unmarried urban women, which was not the case in 1988.

Figure 1.4a: Female Labor Force Participation Rates by Educational Attainment and Urban/Rural Location, Ages 15–64 1988, 1988, Extended Labor Force Definition

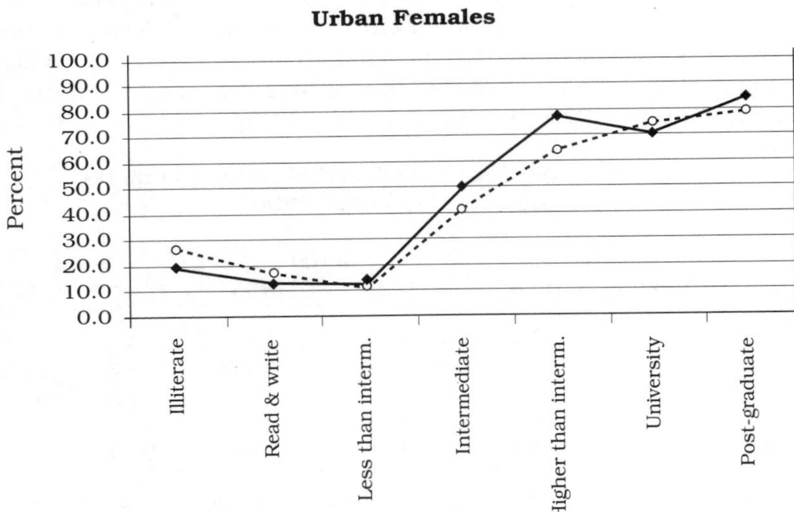

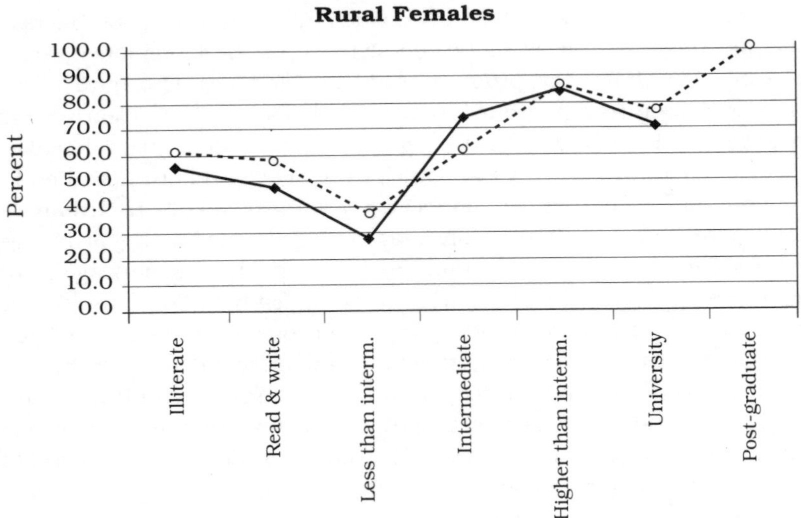

Figure 1.4b: Distribution of the Female Population by Educational Attainment and Urban/Rural Location, Ages 15–64 1988, 1988, Extended Labor Force Definition

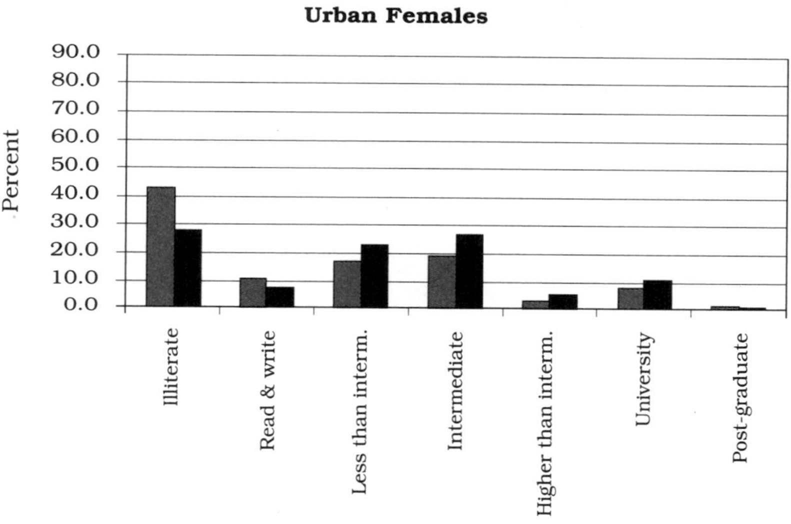

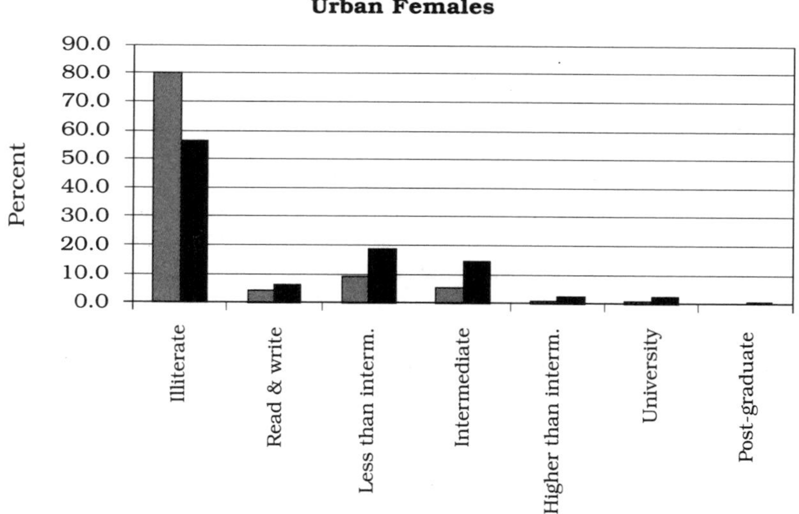

What is even more remarkable is that the largest increases in participation have occurred among lesser-educated married women. As noted above, women with intermediate levels of education, whether married or unmarried, have decreased their participation.

Table 1.7: Female Labor Force Participation Rates by Marital Status, Ages 16–64, 1988, 1998

	Urban		Rural		Total	
	1988	**1998**	**1988**	**1998**	**1988**	**1998**
Married Women:						
Illiterate	17.5	26.7	55.8	61.1	43.9	51.5
Read & write	8.5	13.7	49.0	60.2	21.0	36.8
Less than intermediate	14.7	14.4	52.1	57.0	27.4	34.0
Intermediate	50.5	45.0	74.3	68.5	57.7	54.9
Higher than intermediate	68.0	59.0	92.9	83.4	76.7	67.9
University	66.3	66.2	70.7	76.6	67.0	68.6
All married women	26.8	34.6	56.8	62.6	43.9	50.5
Unmarried Women:						
Illiterate	21.0	26.7	52.8	59.2	41.4	49.8
Read & write	23.8	26.3	41.9	49.0	28.5	38.6
Less than intermediate	13.3	9.3	16.9	30.1	14.7	20.0
Intermediate	47.7	37.3	70.8	51.1	51.8	42.5
Higher than intermediate	83.7	71.6	58.7	88.4	79.7	76.8
University	76.3	88.0	70.8	73.4	76.0	85.7
All unmarried women	33.4	34.4	47.6	50.7	39.7	42.8

Source: Author's calculations based on data from LFSS 88 and ELMS 98.

We can conclude from the analysis of female participation patterns that a combination of demographic, educational, and behavioral factors will continue to push female participation rates higher in the foreseeable future. Not only is the proportion of females at the age of entry to the labor market increasing, these new entrants are increasingly educated and are therefore more likely to participate in economic activity. In addition, older women are persisting in the labor force longer. I will show, in Section 5 below, that most of the older women who remain economically active after marriage are in fact civil servants who are holding on to their government jobs.

3. Unemployment

I now move to an assessment of unemployment trends in the Egyptian economy from 1988 to 1998. Unless otherwise stated, I will be using the extended definition of the labor force, rather than the market definition. As a result, the unemployment rates reported here will seem low compared to the figures normally reported for Egypt. The extended definition, which counts the large number of females who engage in subsistence agriculture, is much more likely to increase measured employment relative to unemployment, and thus results in a lower unemployment rate estimate. However, the trend in the unemployment rate should not be affected by the use of the extended labor force definition. To provide estimates that are comparable to the official unemployment rate reported by the regular LFSS, I also provide estimates based on the market definition of unemployment for 1998. Finally, to abstract from problems of measuring the employed component of the economically active population altogether, I report changes in the unemployment ratio, the ratio of the unemployed to the working-age population (ages 15–64). This measure provides a reliable estimate of the trend in the share of the unemployed among all potential workers.

I adopt the standard international definition of unemployment: no work of any kind for more than an hour in the reference week, readiness to work, availability for work, and an active search for it. In the published results from LFSS 88, the search requirement was dropped, which tended to increase the measured rate of unemployment. In the results I present below, however, the search requirement is imposed in both 1988 and 1998. In a subsequent section, I consider those who have not searched for work as "discouraged unemployed," and examine how their proportion has changed over time.

3.1 The Overall Trend in Unemployment

The aggregate unemployment rate, based on the extended labor force and search definitions, increased from 5.4 percent to 7.9 percent from 1988 to 1998, or by nearly 48 percent. The number of unemployed increased from 0.89 million in 1988 to 1.72 million in 1998, which translates into an annual growth rate of 6.6 percent, nearly two-and-a-half times the rate of growth of the labor force or the working-age population. However, even this relatively high rate of growth of unemployment in the 1990s is lower than the equivalent rate in the 1980s, which was about 8.9 percent per annum, as measured by the regular LFSS (see Assaad, 1997).

If the definition of the labor force is limited to market work, the rate of unemployment rises to 11.7 percent in 1998. The difference is due entirely to a change in the female unemployment rate, which increases from 9.4 percent, according to the extended definition, to 27.6 percent, according to the market definition. The unemployment ratio, which is the proportion of unemployed to the working-age population (15–64), increased from 3.2 percent in 1988 to 4.7 percent in 1998.

As in the case of participation, these overall trends mask considerable variations by gender, urban/rural location, region, age, and educational attainment. As shown in Figure 1.5, rural unemployment rates have increased significantly more than urban rates, and male unemployment rates have increased more than female rates. The latter is somewhat surprising, since previous studies that relied on the regular LFSS data, up to 1995, have shown that not only were female unemployment rates higher than male rates (which is confirmed here), but they were also rising faster (Assaad et al, 2000). The increase in the female unemployment rate in the LFSS data appears to be the result of declining effort over time to detect female employment in agriculture and informal activities, which tends to gradually shrink the denominator of the unemployment rate.

3.2 Urban and Rural Unemployment

Urban unemployment rates have remained fairly stable over the 10-year period, increasing only from 9.0 to 9.7 percent. There is, in fact, a slight decline in unemployment for urban females, but I would discount this decline since it seems to result from an exaggeration of the unemployment rate among uneducated females in 1988 (an issue to which I return below). An examination of the unemployment ratio (Figure 1.6) shows also that the proportion of the unemployed to the working-age population has remained fairly stable in urban areas.

The situation in rural areas is significantly worse. As shown in Figure 1.5, unemployment rates in rural areas have tripled for males and increased by 80 percent for females. Although male unemployment rates in rural areas were less than half of what they were in urban areas in 1988, the difference had virtually disappeared by 1998.

Unemployment rates for urban females are still considerably higher than rural rates, but the difference is narrowing there as well. The higher female unemployment rate in urban areas is due to the easier threshold for being considered in the labor force in agriculture, which tends to inflate the denominator of the unemployment rate in rural areas when the extended definition of the labor force is used.

The results on the unemployment ratio, shown in Figure 1.6, confirm that rural unemployment has worsened considerably more than urban unemployment in this 10-year period, especially for males. Figure 1.7, which breaks down unemployment by region, reveals that most of the increase in unemployment in rural areas occurred in Lower Egypt. Male unemployment ratios there increased by a factor of 4, compared to only a 50 percent increase in rural Upper Egypt. Similarly, female unemployment ratios in rural Lower Egypt more than doubled, whereas female ratios in rural Upper Egypt declined. Urban Lower Egypt did not fare much better. The unemployment ratios of both males and females increased there, with female ratios increasing significantly more to nearly 8 percent. This is the highest ratio of unemployment in the country. The only region to experience falling unemployment ratios among both males and females was Greater Cairo.[5]

Figure 1.5: Unemployment Rate by Gender and Urban/Rural Location, 1988–98. Extended Labor Force, Job Search Required

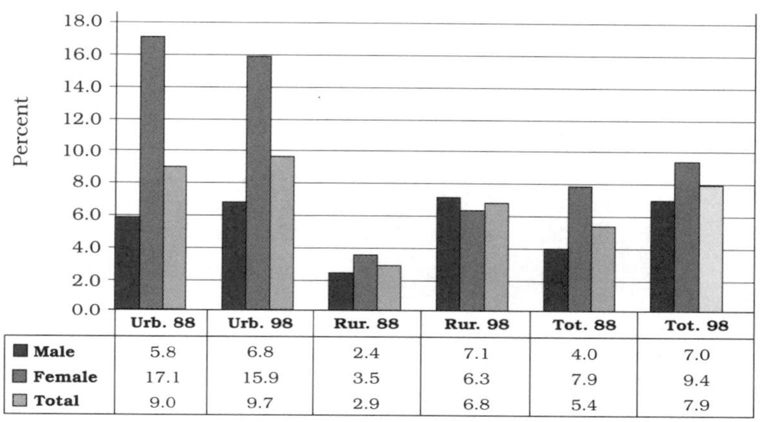

	Urb. 88	Urb. 98	Rur. 88	Rur. 98	Tot. 88	Tot. 98
Male	5.8	6.8	2.4	7.1	4.0	7.0
Female	17.1	15.9	3.5	6.3	7.9	9.4
Total	9.0	9.7	2.9	6.8	5.4	7.9

Figure 1.6: Unemployment Ratio by Gender and Urban/Rural Location, 1988–98. Job Search Required

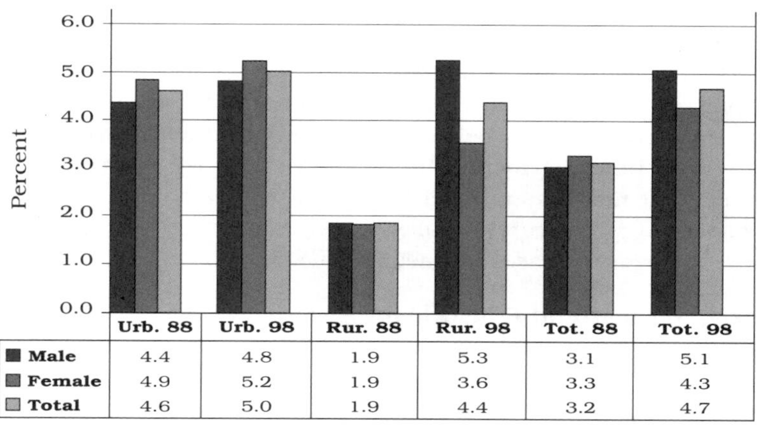

	Urb. 88	Urb. 98	Rur. 88	Rur. 98	Tot. 88	Tot. 98
Male	4.4	4.8	1.9	5.3	3.1	5.1
Female	4.9	5.2	1.9	3.6	3.3	4.3
Total	4.6	5.0	1.9	4.4	3.2	4.7

Figure 1.7: Unemployment Ratio by Region and Gender, 1988, 1998

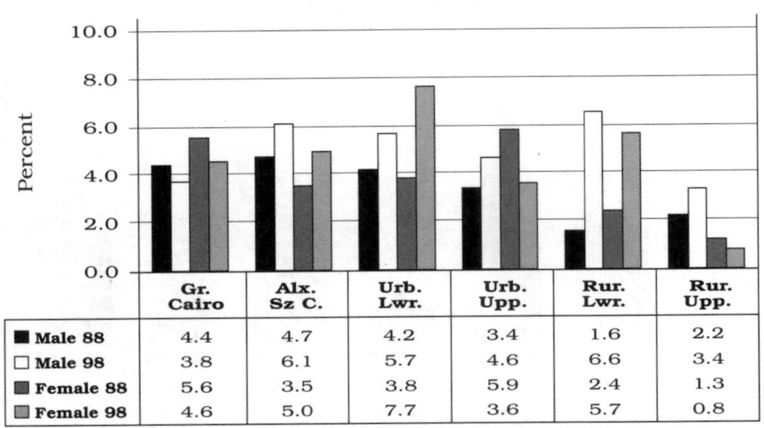

	Gr. Cairo	Alx. Sz C.	Urb. Lwr.	Urb. Upp.	Rur. Lwr.	Rur. Upp.
Male 88	4.4	4.7	4.2	3.4	1.6	2.2
Male 98	3.8	6.1	5.7	4.6	6.6	3.4
Female 88	5.6	3.5	3.8	5.9	2.4	1.3
Female 98	4.6	5.0	7.7	3.6	5.7	0.8

3.3 The Age Profile of Unemployment

A disaggregation of unemployment rates by age reveals that unemployment among youth, the group most likely to be unemployed, has worsened for both males and females, but much more so in rural areas. As shown in Figure 1.8 and Appendix Table A1.5, young rural males have experienced the greatest increase in unemployment. The least change occurred among young urban males. The decline in overall unemployment for urban females is the result of an apparent decline in unemployment among older women (a decline on which I cast some doubt below). Young urban women—who experience extremely high unemployment rates, in the vicinity of 50 percent—are actually faring worse now than in 1988. There is also a sizeable increase in unemployment among young rural females. Among youth, only young urban males were spared major increases in unemployment.

3.4 Unemployment and Educational Attainment

An examination of unemployment rates by education level tells a similar story. As shown in Figure 1.9 and Appendix Table A1.6, there is hardly any change in unemployment rates among urban males at any educational level. On the other hand, the unemployment rate of educated rural males has increased significantly, especially at the intermediate and above-intermediate levels of education. A similar pattern is apparent for rural females, but the increases are much smaller and less consistent than for males. Among urban females, there was no change in unemployment for those with intermediate education and above-intermediate education, but there was a significant decline for those with less-than-intermediate education.

Figure 1.8a: Unemployment Rates by Age, Gender, and Urban/Rural Location, 1988, 1998

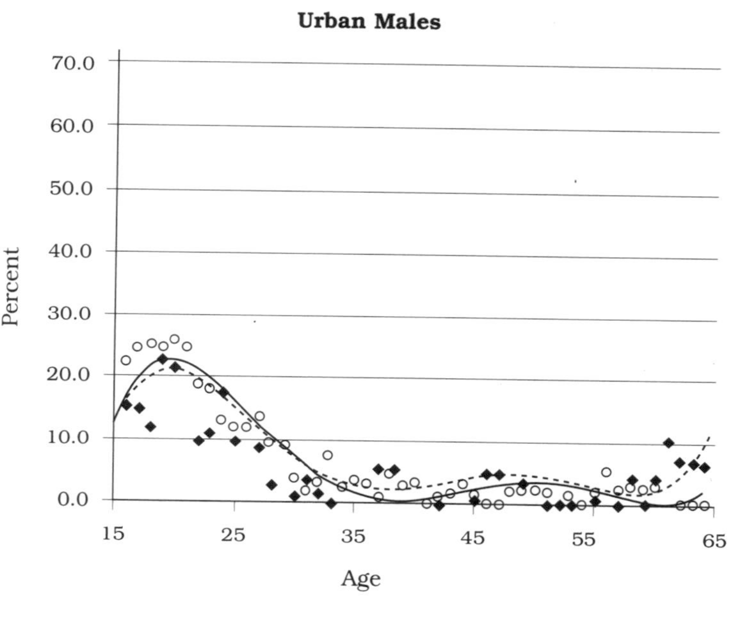

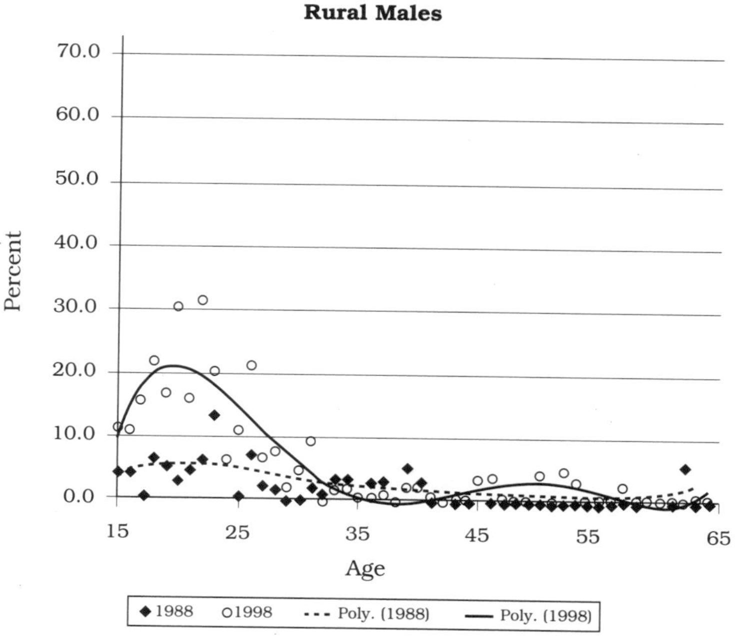

Figure 1.8a: Unemployment Rates by Age, Gender, and Urban/Rural Location, 1988, 1998

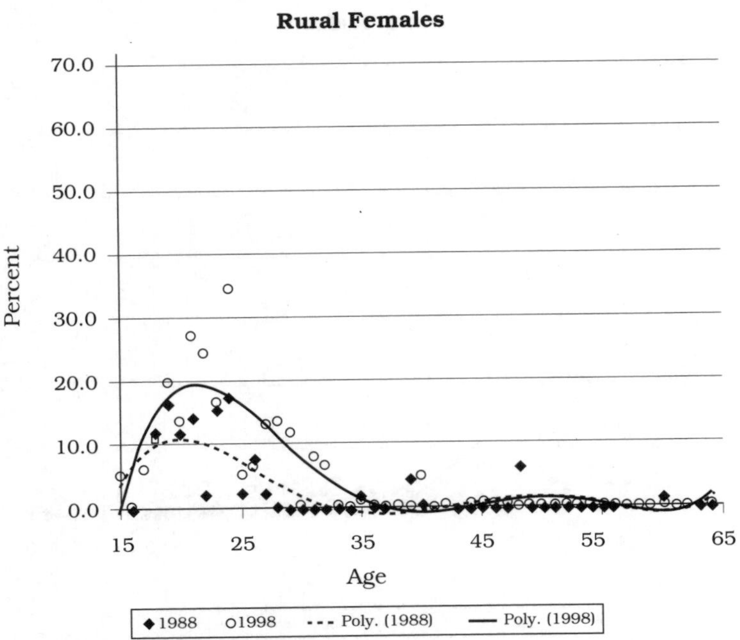

Figure 1.9a: Unemployment Rates by Educational Attainment, Gender and Urban/Rural Location, Ages 15–64; 1988, 1988; Extended Labor Force Definition, Active Search Required

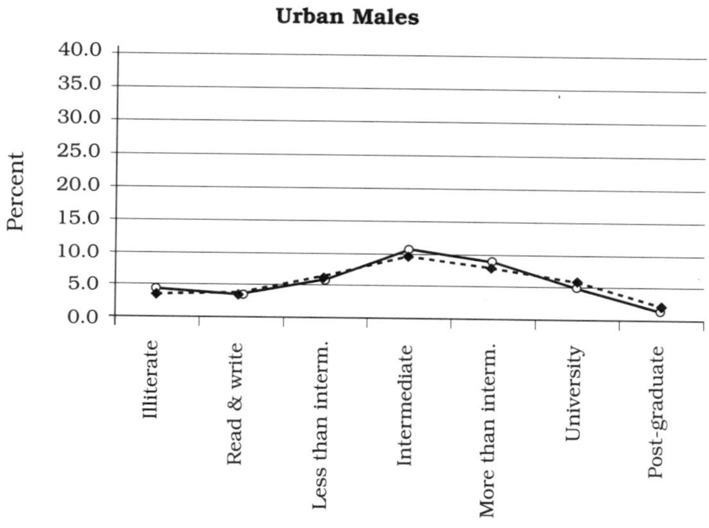

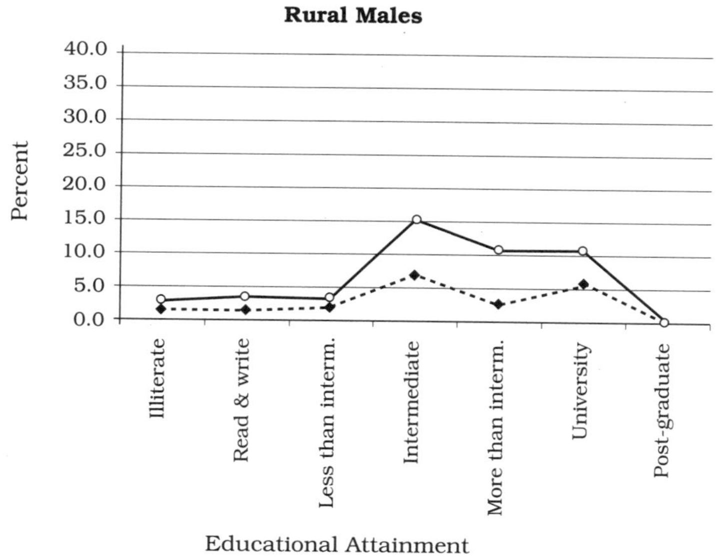

Figure 1.9b: Unemployment Rates by Educational Attainment, Gender and Urban/Rural Location, Ages 15–64; 1988, 1988; Extended Labor Force Definition, Active Search Required

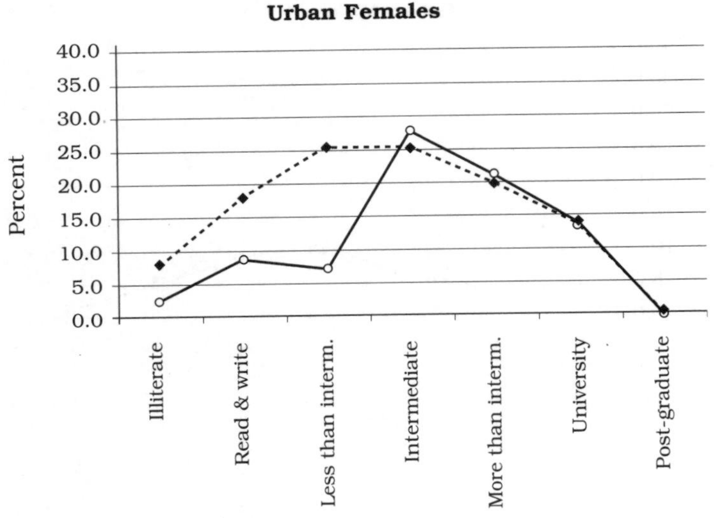

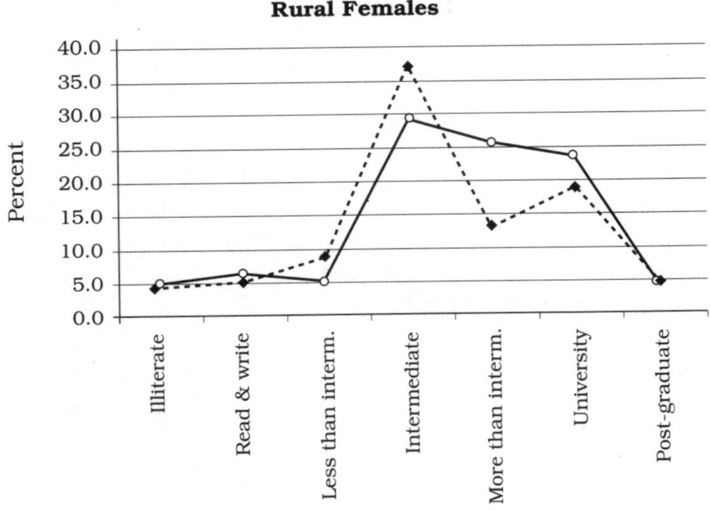

The latter result, combined with the drop of unemployment among older urban women, is intriguing enough to justify going to other data sources to confirm it. An earlier study (Assaad, 1997b), estimates unemployment rates by educational level calculated from data derived from the regular LFSS of 1991 and 1995. These estimates show a pattern of female unemployment by educational attainment that is virtually identical to the pattern shown for 1998, and quite different from the pattern for 1988. Unemployment rates for urban females with lower-than-intermediate education are well below 10 percent in 1991, 1995, and 1998, but well above 10 percent in 1988. The main explanation for this discrepancy is that in 1988, the question about job search was not limited to a specific reference period, as specified in international recommendations, but included any search during the entire duration of unemployment. On the other hand, in 1998 it was limited to a three-month reference period, except for the case of registration in the Manpower Office. This makes it easier to meet the search criterion in 1988 than in 1998.

3.5 The Proportion of New Entrants among the Unemployed

We now examine the proportion of new entrants among the unemployed to determine the extent to which unemployment continues to be concentrated among those who are entering the labor force for the first time. Figure 1.10 and Appendix Table A1.6 shows that the percentage of new entrants among the unemployed has increased from 58.2 percent in 1988 to 70.3 percent in 1998. There was an across-the-board increase in both sexes and in urban and rural areas. The highest proportion of new entrants in both 1988 and 1998 was among rural females. As seen earlier, these are educated females, most of whom are probably waiting for government employment. The high proportion of new entrants among them is basically the result of the absence of socially acceptable employment opportunities for educated rural females outside the government.

The highest increase in the proportion of new entrants is observed among rural males, where the proportion increased from 38 percent in 1988 to 63 percent in 1998. This increase underscores the deteriorating labor market prospects for the rapidly growing number of educated male youths in rural areas.

3.6 Concluding Remarks on Unemployment

To conclude, open unemployment in Egypt continues to be concentrated among educated youths under the age of 30, with the highest unemployment rates being experienced at the intermediate levels of education. Unemployment rates seem to have remained fairly stable in urban areas among both males and females, but have increased significantly among educated youths in rural areas, especially in rural Lower Egypt, and among males. Rural males with secondary educations have seen their unemployment rates more than double, from 7 percent to more than 15 percent. While rural females with secondary educations fared better—with their very high unemployment rates dropping from 36 percent to 27 percent—rural females with post-secondary and university education, like their male counterparts, experienced significant increases in unemployment.

Figure 1.10: Proportion of New Entrants Among the Unemployed by Gender, and Urban/Rural Location, 1988, 1998

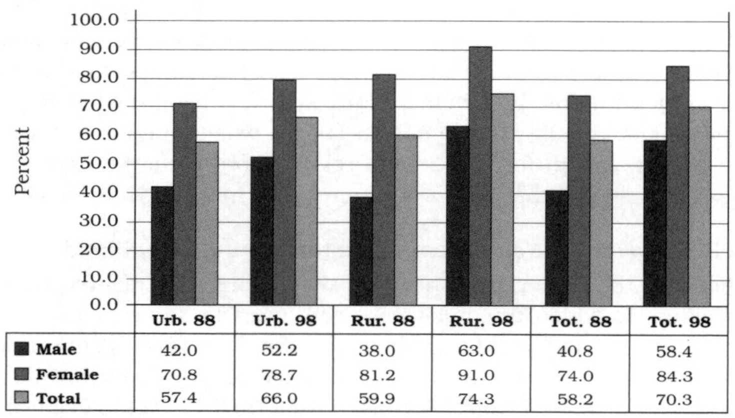

	Urb. 88	Urb. 98	Rur. 88	Rur. 98	Tot. 88	Tot. 98
Male	42.0	52.2	38.0	63.0	40.8	58.4
Female	70.8	78.7	81.2	91.0	74.0	84.3
Total	57.4	66.0	59.9	74.3	58.2	70.3

Unemployment in rural areas appears to be the result of continued demographic pressures on the labor market. Rural labor supply is still outpacing the job-creation capacity in rural areas, and migration has been too limited to transfer the labor surplus to urban areas. The cohort of people ages 10–19 in 1998—which constitutes 28.1 percent of the population and is by far the largest, historically, in rural areas—will complete its transition into the labor market over the next decade. After this, labor supply pressures will subside as the smaller cohort, currently under the age of 10 (23.5 percent of the rural population), reaches the age of labor market entry. Although urban areas also experienced demographic pressures, they were less intense due to the earlier onset of fertility declines there. The 15–19 cohort, although also at historical highs, was relatively smaller at 24 percent of the urban population, and is followed by an even smaller cohort (18 percent of the urban population).

Because of the increasing educational attainment of new entrants, it is now more likely than in previous decades for demographic pressures to translate into open unemployment. Educated workers are much more likely than their uneducated counterparts to remain unemployed while holding out for regular wage employment. As we will see in the following section, labor surplus for uneducated workers generally translates into underemployment, rather than open unemployment.

4. Underemployment and Discouraged Unemployment

As shown in the previous section, open unemployment in Egypt reveals the extent of employment inadequacy among a specific segment of the Egyptian labor market, namely educated new entrants looking for their first regular jobs. A more encompassing measure of underemployment is necessary to capture employment inadequacy among less-educated workers whose regular job prospects are limited.

Table 1.8: Underemployment Ratio by Gender, Urban/Rural Location, 1988, 1998 as Share of Working-Age Population 15–64

		Urban		Rural		Total	
Education		**1988**	**1998**	**1988**	**1998**	**1988**	**1998**
Male	U	4.4	4.9	1.9	5.3	3.1	5.1
	DU	0.4	0.8	0.3	0.9	0.3	0.8
	IPT	4.3	1.9	8.0	5.0	6.3	3.6
	Total	9.0	7.6	10.2	11.2	9.6	9.6
Female	U	4.9	5.3	1.9	3.6	3.3	4.3
	DU	0.8	0.8	0.5	0.6	0.7	0.7
	IPT	0.7	0.2	2.8	0.6	1.8	0.4
	Total	6.3	6.3	5.1	4.7	5.7	5.4
Total	U	4.6	5.1	1.9	4.5	3.2	4.7
	DU	0.6	0.8	0.4	0.7	0.5	0.8
	IPT	2.5	1.1	5.4	2.8	4.0	2.0
	Total	7.7	6.9	7.6	7.9	7.6	7.5

Notes: U = Open unemployment; DU = Discouraged unemployment; IPT = Involuntary part-time, available.

Source: Author's calculations based on data from LFSS 88 and ELMS 98.

The underemployment ratio we present below is just such a measure. It consists of three components, each of which is expressed as a proportion of the working-age population (15–64): (1) the openly unemployed, as defined in the previous section; (2) the visibly underemployed, i.e., those involuntarily working part-time (less than 40 hours per week) while being available for more work;[6] and (3) the discouraged unemployed, i.e., those who have not worked at all during the reference week, are available and ready to work, but have not actively searched for work in a three-month reference period.

Because of the difficulty in operationalizing the concept of "invisible underemployment" using data from a household survey, it is excluded from this broader measure of underemployment. Invisible underemployment comprises individuals who are working full-time but at productivity or earning levels below a certain norm.

Table 1.8 shows the underemployment ratio and its three constituent components by sex and urban/rural location for 1988 and 1998. Most notably, the overall underemployment rate has not changed much, with approximately 7.5 percent of the working-age population underemployed in both years. While open unemployment has gone up, the proportion of those engaged in involuntary part-time work has been cut in half. So, as educational levels have increased, the weight of underemployment has shifted from involuntary part-time work in 1988 to open unemployment in 1998. Discouraged unemployment has gone up from 1988 to 1998, but it remains a fairly insignificant part of overall underemployment in Egypt.

The contrasting trends observed earlier for open unemployment in urban and rural areas are present in the case of underemployment, as well, but the difference is much less stark. Underemployment fell slightly in urban areas and rose slightly in rural areas. The sharp increase in open unemployment in rural areas was counteracted by a drop in involuntary part-time work, resulting in a small drop in overall underemployment. The disaggregation by gender reveals that men are much more likely to be involuntary part-time workers than women are, in part because they are much more likely to be casual wageworkers. The substantial drop in involuntary part-time work among men in both urban and rural areas indicates that casual workers, who are strongly represented among the poor, were able to find more work to keep them fully occupied in 1998 than in 1988. Young educated workers who are seeking regular employment, on the other hand, are facing a tougher labor market.

Discouraged unemployment appears to have increased among males and remained stable among females in both urban and rural areas. In either case, it constitutes a small fraction of underemployment in 1998. A large proportion of women in rural areas work part-time (38 percent in 1988 and 45 percent in 1998), but, because the rest of their time is usually fully occupied in non-economic activities, they do not declare themselves to be available for more work.

Figure 1.11 shows the pattern of underemployment by educational attainment. We notice immediately that the pattern differs considerably from that of open unemployment for males, but is quite similar for females. Uneducated males are more likely to be casual wageworkers, and therefore experience most of the underemployment in the form of involuntary part-time work. With this broader measure, their underemployment is as high as that of educated males. A further indication of the strength of labor market conditions in urban areas relative to rural areas is that underemployment ratios for uneducated urban male workers have fallen significantly, while they have remained constant for their rural counterparts. For more educated workers, the underemployment ratio reflects the open unemployment pattern fairly closely.

A broader measure of underemployment that includes involuntary part-time work and discouraged unemployment does a better job capturing employment inadequacy among uneducated male workers. The results indicate that these workers are seeing improved conditions in urban areas, but no improvements in rural areas. The broader measure fails to provide an adequate measure of the availability of productive employment opportunities for uneducated females because it still assumes that inadequately employed individuals would be seeking to increase their workload, which is not the case for many of these women.

5. Employment

As in the case of labor force, I adopt the extended definition of employment, which includes those engaged in subsistence agriculture, to be able to undertake comparisons with data from LFSS 88. However, to isolate the effect of subsistence agriculture on the results, I separate out agriculture from nonagricultural activities in the ensuing analysis.

By the same token, since the nonagricultural jobs taken up by rural dwellers can be either in the rural areas themselves or in nearby cities, I abstract from the urban/rural distinction, focusing instead on the agricultural/nonagricultural distinction. All the analysis that follows applies to employment among the working-age population ages 15–64.

5.1 The Pattern of Employment Growth

According to the extended definition of economic activity, employment has grown from 15.7 million in 1988 to 20.0 million in 1998.[7] This implies an increase of 4.3 million jobs in 10 years, an average rate of 430,000 jobs per year—or a 2.5 percent average annual growth rate.

Again, these aggregate rates mask considerable variations by gender, by sector, and by employment status. Table 1.9 shows employment growth along these three dimensions, expressed as the share of the change accruing to each labor market segment and the annual average rate of growth in each segment.[8]

Figure 1.11a: Underemployment Ratio by Educational Attainment, Gender, and Urban/Rural Location; 1988, 1998

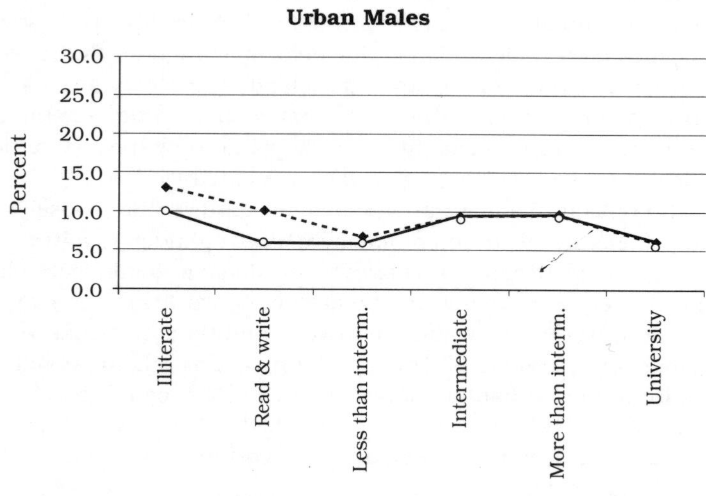

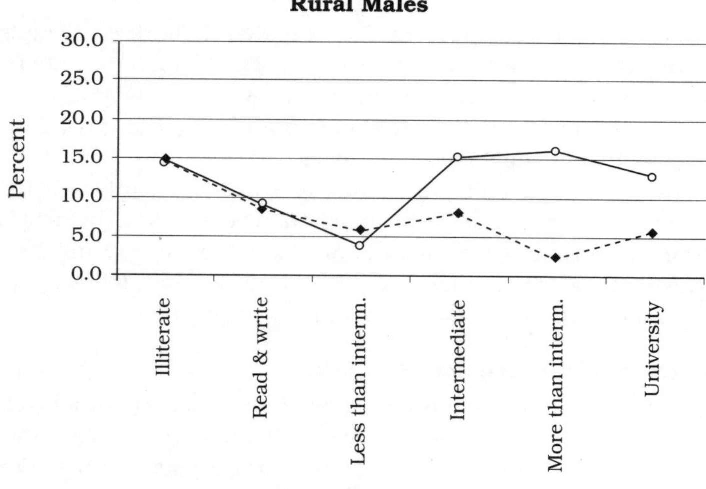

Figure 1.11b: Underemployment Ratio by Educational Attainment, Gender, and Urban/Rural Location; 1988, 1998

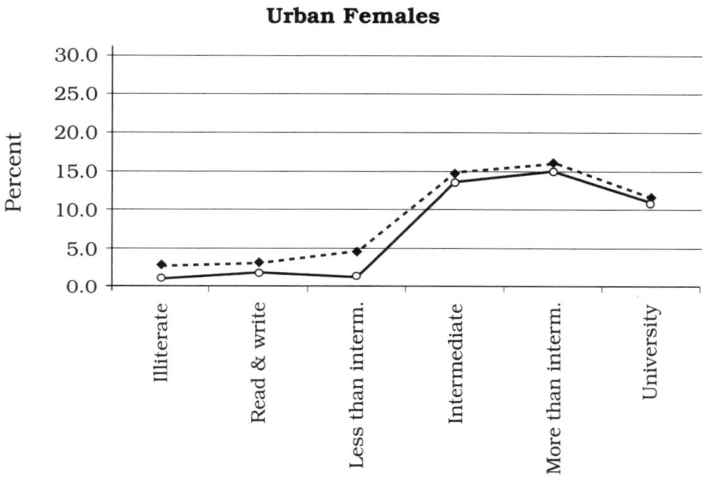

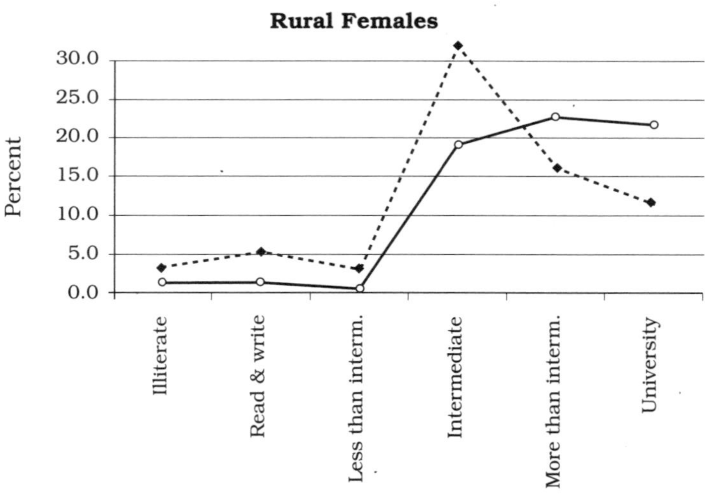

Despite years of reductions in the share of public spending and structural adjustment, the fastest-growing segment and the largest contributor to employment growth in Egypt continues to be the government. Government employment grew at 4.8 percent per annum, nearly twice as fast as total employment, and contributed 42 percent of net job creation during the 10-year period. Because the state-owned enterprise sector contracted by 2.6 percent per year, the share of the public sector, broadly defined, in employment creation was somewhat lower, at 35 percent of net employment growth. Even with the contraction of the state-owned enterprise employment, the public sector as a whole increased its share of total employment, from 27.6 percent to 29.1 percent.[9] Government employment grew rapidly for both males and females, with somewhat more rapid growth rates for females. On the whole, the public sector labor force is becoming feminized due to the higher share of females in the government and the rising share of government in the public sector.

Table 1.9: Employment Growth in the Egyptian Economy by Gender, 1988–98

	Male		Female		Total	
	Share of Growth	Ann. Rate of Growth	Share of Growth	Ann. Rate of Growth	Share of Growth	Ann. Rate of Growth
Public Sector:						
Government	55.6	4.5	28.1	5.4	41.8	4.8
State-owned enterprise	-11.2	-2.3	-2.9	-4.1	-7.0	-2.6
Subtotal Public sector	44.4	2.6	25.2	4.3	34.7	3.0
Private Agriculture:						
Wage work	2.7	0.6	-3.5	-6.3	-0.4	-0.2
Nonwage work	-28.6	-3.1	82.4	4.4	27.4	1.9
Subtotal priv. agriculture	-25.9	-1.9	78.9	4.1	26.9	1.6
Private Nonagriculture:						
Wage work	61.0	4.7	2.6	1.6	31.6	4.3
Nonwage Work	20.5	2.6	-6.8	-2.7	6.7	1.3
Subtotal priv. nonagric.	81.5	3.9	-4.1	-1.0	38.3	3.0
Total	**100.0**	**1.9**	**100.0**	**3.4**	**100.0**	**2.5**

Source: Author's calculations based on data from LFSS 88 and ELMS 98.

Agricultural employment grew at a significantly slower rate than other sectors and contributed approximately 27 percent of employment growth (Table 1.9). The share of agriculture in total employment fell from 42 percent in 1988 to 39 percent in 1998 (Appendix Table A1.7). Unlike the public sector, where male and female trends in employment are similar, gender differences in the evolution of agricultural employment are striking. Male agricultural employment declined at a rate of 1.9 percent per annum, whereas female agricultural employment increased at 4.1 percent per annum. Most of the change, for both males and females, occurred among nonwage workers. It appears, therefore, that there is wide-scale substitution of female labor for male labor on family farms. However, this is not likely to be the case for several reasons. First, with the strict gender division of labor in agriculture in Egypt, it is not easy for females to undertake male agricultural tasks. Second, most women who are engaged in nonwage employment in agriculture (93 percent in 1998) are producing exclusively for purposes of household consumption, with most of them engaged in animal husbandry or raising poultry. Men who work on family farms, on the other hand, mostly engage in the production of marketable crops, fruits, and vegetables. Further investigation is needed, however, to test the hypothesis of substitution of female for male labor in agriculture at the household level.

Wage employment in agriculture grew very slowly for males and, although it declined rapidly for females, it contributed very little to the change in overall female employment. The dominant contributions of agriculture to employment change are happening in agricultural nonwage employment, which contributed 82.4 percent of net female employment growth, and a reduction in male employment growth equal to 29 percent of net male employment growth.

The growth in private sector nonagricultural employment was fairly healthy at 3 percent per annum, but it is exclusively limited to the male portion of the population. Female private nonagricultural employment actually declined by about 1 percent per annum. Unlike agriculture, where nonwage work among women is growing, nonwage work outside agriculture is responsible for the entire decline in female private nonagricultural employment. Female wage work in this sector has, in fact, grown, albeit rather slowly. Among males, the growth is mostly accounted for by the growth in wage labor. The growth in wage labor in the private nonagricultural sector has even outpaced the growth of male employment in the fast-growing government sector. This indicates considerable dynamism in the private sector, but unfortunately, this dynamism seems to be limited to males. It appears that a variety of barriers to entry have prevented females from sharing in the growth of private sector employment opportunities.

5.2 The Growth of Government Employment

The rapid growth of government employment at a time of significant cuts in public expenditures and what appears to be a dramatic slowdown in hiring requires further investigation. First, I examine the age and education profile of the government workforce to determine the source of government employment growth, and then I examine the change in the occupational distribution of the government workforce.

Figure 1.12a: Ratio of Employment in Government by Age, Gender, and Urban/Rural Location; 1988, 1998

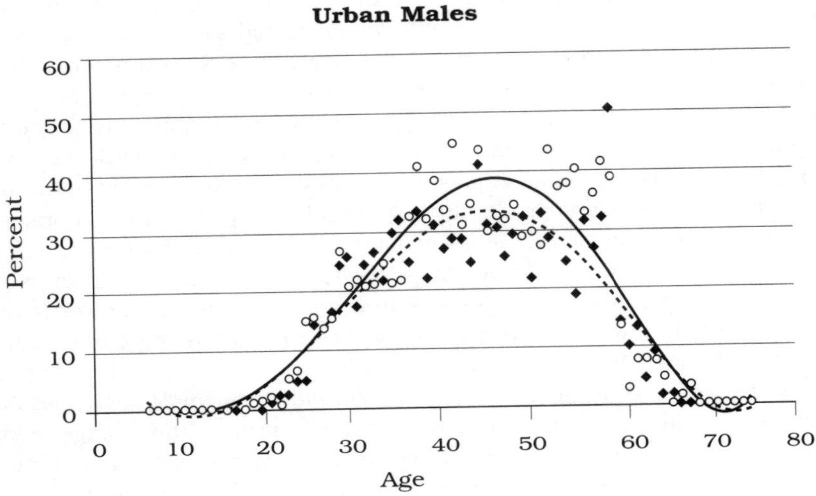

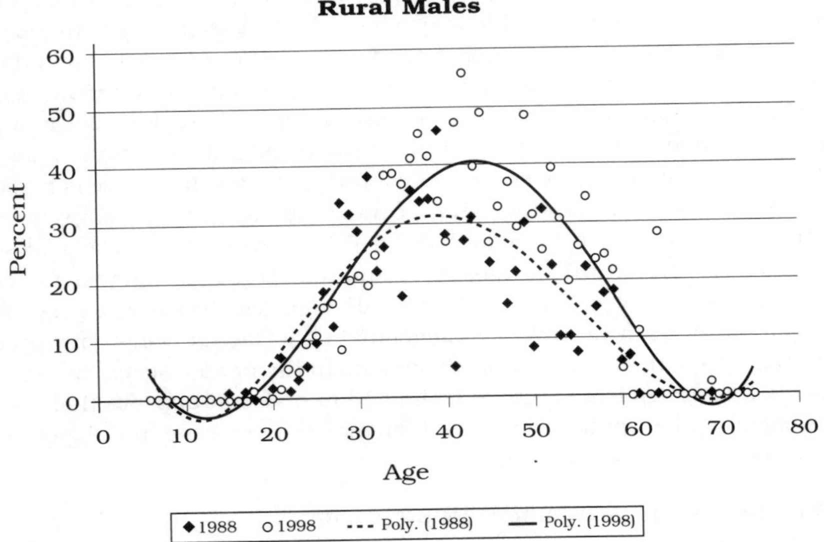

Figure 1.12b: Ratio of Employment in Government by Age, Gender, and Urban/Rural Location; 1988, 1998

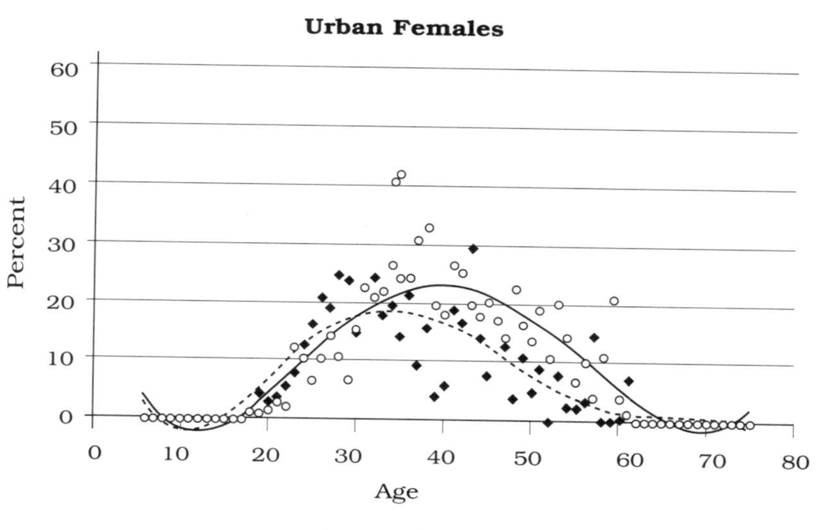

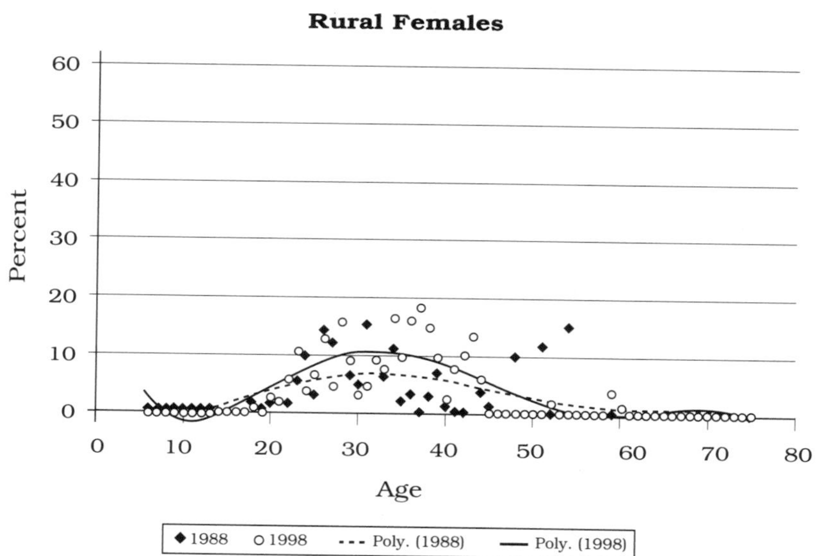

The previous Figure 1.12 shows the ratio of government employment to population by age for various subgroups of the population. As before, the black diamonds and white circles indicate the proportion of government employees to the total population by age for the relevant subgroup in 1988 and 1998, respectively. The dashed-and-black curves are a 5th order polynomial fit through these points. The figure shows that among 3 of the 4 subgroups of the population we are considering, government employment ratios among people under 30 have either declined or remained constant from 1988 to 1998. The exception is the rural female subgroup, whose rate of government employment was quite low to start with, and where the increase reflects the substantial improvements in education experienced by the rural female population. We see significant increases in government employment among older workers. This is due, in part, to the lengthening of the queues for government employment, so that people now enter the government at an older age. But in the case of women, it is also due to delayed withdrawal from the government workforce. Women who would have left government employment after marriage are now holding on to these jobs. Thus, the increase in the relative size of the government workforce is not so much due to an acceleration of hiring, but to a failure to reduce hiring sufficiently to make up for the greater persistence of government employees, especially female employees, on public payrolls.

The failure to slow down the growth of government employment may also be the result of growth in the ranks of those who are eligible for the public employment guarantee, i.e., those with intermediate or above-intermediate education. So even if the rate of hiring within that group is reduced, the pressure to continue providing "graduates" with employment, even at reduced rates, could have fueled the expansion. Table 1.10 shows the rate of government employment to the population of each subgroup by education level. Although some educational levels have seen an increase in the rate of government employment from 1988 to 1998, such as university graduates, the increases are not sufficient to account for the increase in the overall rate of government employment among all subgroups.

What accounts for the increase, therefore, is the shift in the composition of the population toward the more educated groups, who have much higher government employment rates. For instance, among rural females, the rates of government employment have declined significantly at every educational level where there is significant government employment, but the overall rate has nearly doubled, indicating significant shifts in composition over the years under study. For nearly every demographic subgroup, secondary-school graduates have had a significant decline in the likelihood of government employment. But since this is the group that is growing the fastest, these reduced rates of employment did not manage to slow down government hiring significantly.[10]

Table 1.10: Government Employment Ratios by Educational Level, Gender, and Urban/Rural Location, 1988, 1998. Ages 15–64

		Urban		Rural	
		1988	1998	1988	1998
Male					
	Illiterate	6.8	7.7	6.2	7.2
	Read & write	13.8	12.8	17.2	20.0
	Less than intermediate	8.1	8.7	7.0	10.0
	Intermediate	18.4	17.4	25.7	21.6
	More than intermediate	35.2	38.9	64.1	51.3
	University	34.8	41.1	54.3	55.5
	Post-graduate	66.9	63.2	-	-
	All	16.6	19.0	14.0	17.4
Female					
	Illiterate	0.8	0.9	0.1	0.2
	Read & write	0.5	1.2	1.0	0.8
	Less than intermediate	1.1	1.3	0.8	0.7
	Intermediate	22.9	17.2	27.6	13.4
	More than intermediate	50.2	39.3	74.0	53.8
	University	38.6	46.6	47.9	41.6
	Post-graduate	74.6	73.7	-	-
	All	9.8	12.5	2.7	4.4

Note: '-' indicates that cell contains fewer than 20 observations.
Source: Author's calculations based on data from LFSS 88 and ELMS 98.

Continued growth in government hiring can therefore be attributed to greater persistence in government employment of older female civil servants, and to government's inability to slow the rate of hiring sufficiently to counteract the dramatic growth of those eligible for the public employment guarantee.

We turn to examining the kind of work people hired in the government are doing. Table 1.11 shows the contribution of a number of occupational groups to the growth of government employment, and the rate of growth of each group. The occupational groups were selected to highlight occupations that are likely to be important in the government, including educators, health professionals, and clerical workers.

The most noteworthy occupational groups are those that grew rapidly and contributed significant proportions to the growth of government employment. It is clear from the table that teachers were not only the fastest-growing occupational group, but also contributed more than one-third of government employment growth. Nearly half of almost 650,000 females who joined the government workforce over the decade became teachers.

Teachers constituted the fastest-growing and largest growth contributor among men, as well. This reflects the major commitment the government has had to expand educational opportunities over the past decade, which can be seen in the major gains achieved in enrollment rates.

The second largest contributor to government employment growth—and the third-fastest growing category—was clerical workers. This category contributed nearly a quarter of male employment growth in the government and 30 percent of female employment. The growth among clerical workers cannot be associated as easily with a growth in government output as in the case of educators. This appears to be the result of continued pressures to hire graduates, even though the graduate employment guarantee system is effectively suspended.

Table 1.11: Growth in Government Employment by Occupation and Gender, 1988–98

	Male		Female		Total	
	Share of Growth	Ann. Rate of Growth	Share of Growth	Ann. Rate of Growth	Share of Growth	Ann. Rate of Growth
Scientific/ Technical	9.9	5.3	-0.2	-0.3	6.6	4.6
Health professionals	-1.1	-1.4	4.3	2.6	0.7	0.7
Educators	28.3	7.2	46.1	7.5	34.1	7.3
Other professionals	1.8	1.3	13.4	7.6	5.6	3.6
Managers	6.2	8.2	1.4	3.0	4.7	7.0
Clerical	25.4	6.5	29.4	4.9	26.7	5.8
Services/Sales	23.5	5.6	3.4	7.2	16.9	5.6
Production/ transport	6.0	2.3	2.0	9.7	4.7	2.6
Total	**100.0**	**5.1**	**100.0**	**5.8**	**100.0**	**5.3**

Source: Author's calculations based on data from LFSS 88 and ELMS 98.

5.3 Private Nonagricultural Wage Employment

Given that private nonagricultural wage employment is the second-fastest growing segment of the labor market after government—and given the importance of this sector in national policy making—it is worth investigating the composition of its employment growth.

Again we start with the change in the age profile of workers in this sector (Figure 1.13). As before, the figure shows the proportion of private nonagricultural wageworkers to the total population by age for the relevant subgroup. Although employment ratios in the private non-agricultural sector for young urban males under the age of 20 have declined somewhat, they have increased significantly for those 20–50. The increase in nonagricultural wage employment among rural males is dramatic. It is occurring at all ages, but is largest among young males ages 20–35.

Many of the jobs rural males are getting are actually located in urban areas. There appears to be an increasing tendency among rural males to commute to jobs away from their villages.[11] It is not surprising that much of the increase in nonagricultural wage employment among rural males is occurring at the expense of agricultural employment, which is declining precipitously (see Table 1.9).

The situation among females could not be more different. Ratios of nonagricultural wage employment among urban females are not only much lower than among males, but they have hardly changed over the decade (Figure 1.13). Nonagricultural wage employment for this group peaks at about age 25 and then declines rapidly. By age 40, most females have left the sector. While there was a similar peaking at that age for males, the peak has shifted as the cohort of young men entering that sector has aged. No similar aging pattern is apparent among females, indicating that women are entering and leaving the sector at the same rate in the 1990s as in the 1980s. Among rural females, the rates of private nonagricultural wage employment are so low that it is hard to discern a trend. There appears to be an increase from 1988 to 1998, but the ratios still remain very low.

Next we examine how private nonagricultural wage employment varies with education (Table 1.12). First, we note the inverse relationship with education among males. In general, the higher the education, the less likely a male would be employed for wages in the private sector. This may be slowly changing, however. As public sector employment opportunities are dwindling, educated males are forced to enter the private sector in greater numbers. In fact, the rates of increase in the employment ratios between 1988 and 1998 appear to be higher for educated males than for their uneducated counterparts. In rural areas, very few males were employed in the nonagricultural private sector in 1988, but by 1998, their rates of employment had converged to a large extent toward those of their urban counterparts.

Again we note the stark contrast between the situation of males and females. First, there is a positive rather than a negative relationship between education and private sector nonwage employment. The only subgroup to have a ratio of more than 10 percent is urban, university-educated females. Second private nonagricultural wage employment among females is declining at nearly all education levels. It is even declining among university graduates, who were the only ones to have made some inroads into the private sector. The declining probability of employment at higher educational levels seems to have counteracted the increase in the number of females at these levels. The nonagricultural private sector appears to be increasingly closed to women at all levels of education, at the same time as it is becoming a significant source of employment for men.

Figure 1.13a: Ratio of Wage Employment in the Private Nonagricultural Sector by Age, Gender, and Urban/Rural Location; 1988, 1998

Urban Males

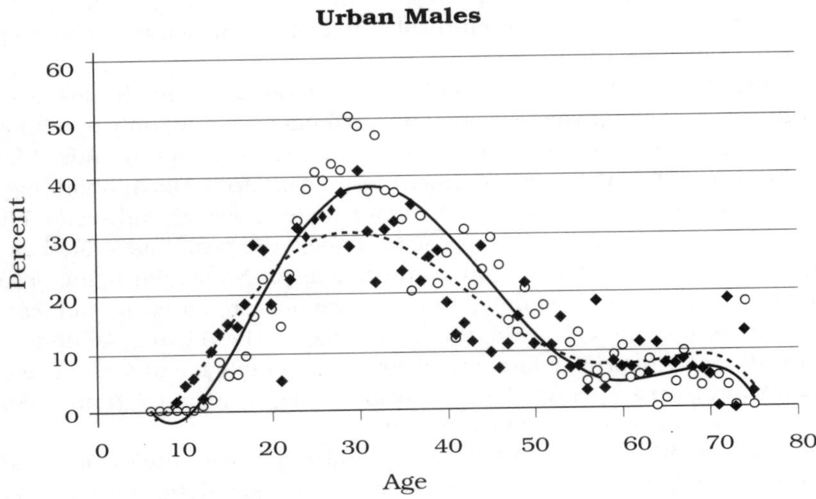

Rural Males

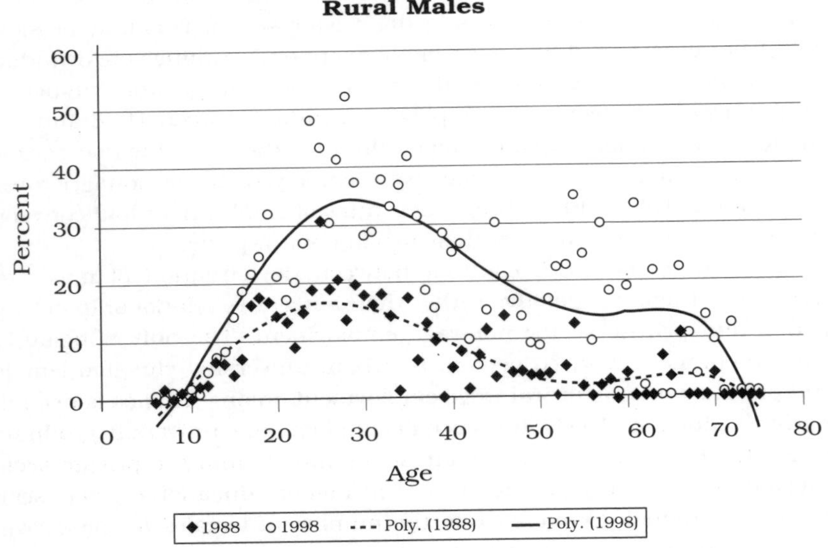

Figure 1.13b: Ratio of Wage Employment in the Private Nonagricultural Sector by Age, Gender, and Urban/Rural Location; 1988, 1998

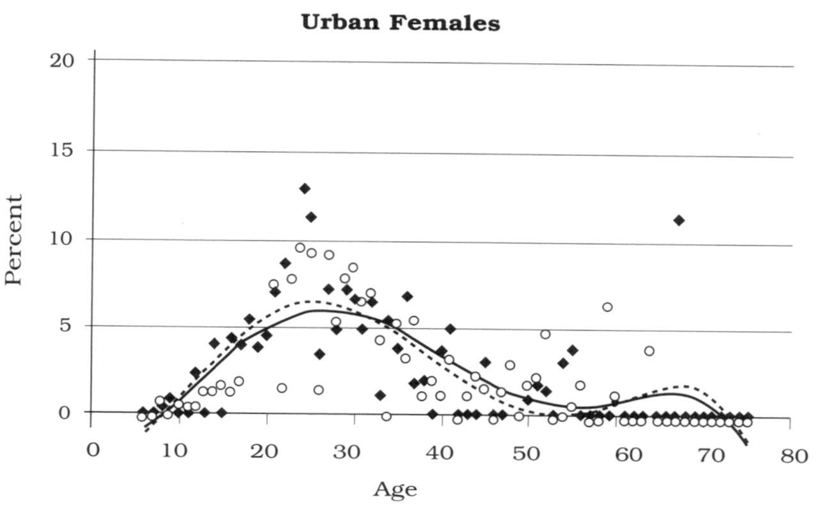

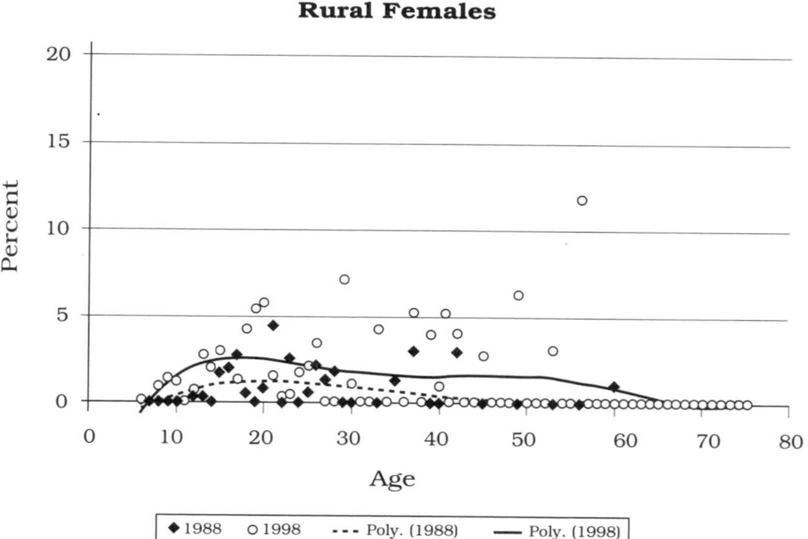

Table 1.12: Nonagricultural Private Sector Wage Employment Ratios by Educational Level, Gender, and Urban/Rural Location, 1988, 1998. Ages 15–64

	Urban		Rural	
	1988	**1998**	**1988**	**1998**
Male				
Illiterate	30.4	31.1	11.9	20.3
Read & write	25.7	29.2	16.5	22.7
Less than intermediate	17.8	21.7	8.5	14.1
Intermediate	18.1	21.0	10.4	14.7
More than intermediate	20.2	18.5	4.0	14.1
University	16.5	20.1	3.9	5.7
Post-graduate	6.7	14.7	-	-
All	21.4	22.7	11.3	16.4
Female				
Illiterate	2.6	2.0	0.7	0.6
Read & write	3.0	1.6	0.9	1.3
Less than intermediate	2.8	1.6	1.1	1.1
Intermediate	5.6	3.9	2.2	2.3
More than intermediate	6.9	6.9	0.0	0.0
University	12.1	10.4	3.2	1.5
Post-graduate	8.7	-	-	-
All	4.1	3.5	0.8	1.0

Note: '-' Indicates that a cell contains fewer than 20 observations.

Source: Author's calculations based on data from LFSS 88 and ELMS 98.

We now turn to the industrial composition of employment growth in the private nonagricultural sector. Table 1.13 breaks down employment growth in the private nonagricultural sector by industry division and gender. By far the fastest growth occurred in finance, insurance, and real estate, a sector that was opened up to private investment in recent years. Despite its rapid growth, this is still a small industry division, which contributed only 5.5 percent of total employment growth. The second-fastest growing industry division was transport, storage, and communications, which contributed 11.6 percent of employment growth. Manufacturing, which was the largest contributor to growth in the private sector with its 37 percent increase in job creation, was a close third. The remaining industry divisions grew at lower-than-average rates of wage employment in the private nonagricultural sector, which means that their employment share declined.

As usual, gender is an important determinant of the pattern of growth. First, male employment is not only growing at nearly three times the rate of female employment, but it is also more evenly distributed across industries. Female wageworkers in the private nonagricultural sector are heavily concentrated in three sectors—manufacturing, trade, and services (see Appendix Table A1.9). Female employment in manufacturing grew three times faster than average private nonagricultural female wage employment and contributed nearly 67 percent of female employment growth. This is to be compared to its 20 percent share of private nonagricultural wage employment in 1988. Trade maintained its share of female employment over time, and services saw a reduction in its share from 42 percent to 34 percent. Service was the only sector where females were highly represented in the first place and then lost employment. Most of these women were probably working as domestic servants, an occupation that is contracting in absolute terms, at least among Egyptian nationals.

Table 1.13: Growth in Private Sector Nonagricultural Wage Employment by Industry Division and Gender, 1988–98

	Male		Female		Total	
	Share of Growth	Ann. Rate of Growth	Share of Growth	Ann. Rate of Growth	Share of Growth	Ann. Rate of Growth
Manuf., mining & utilities	35.3	4.9	67.2	4.7	36.9	4.9
Construction	19.2	3.7	-	-	18.8	3.7
Trade, restaurants & hotels	18.1	4.6	33.1	2.0	18.7	4.2
Transp., storage & communic.	12.4	5.4	-	-	11.6	5.1
Finance, insur. & real estate	4.5	9.0	-	-	5.5	9.1
Public and personal services	10.7	4.6	-13.9	-0.6	9.7	3.0
Total	**100.0**	**4.6**	**100.0**	**1.6**	**100.0**	**4.3**

Note: '-' indicates that a cell contains fewer than 20 observations.
Source: Author's calculations based on data from LFSS 88 and ELMS 98.

Women appear to be somewhat over-represented in the finance, insurance, and real estate industry division, but the scope of this sector is such that the sample sizes are too small to make accurate inferences. All other sectors of the economy appear to be virtually closed to women. Women constituted a very small percentage of the private labor force in the construction and transportation sectors in 1988, and continued to be absent in 1998.

We now look at the type of wage jobs that were created in the private nonagricultural sector in terms of the degree of protection that they have and the regularity of employment that they provide. Table 1.14 shows the distribution of employment growth in the private non-agricultural wage sector along these two dimensions. Jobs are classified as protected or unprotected on the basis of whether or not they are covered by a legal employment contract. Permanent and temporary jobs are classified as "regular," and jobs that are either intermittent or seasonal are classified as "irregular." Virtually all irregular jobs are not protected by contracts.

Table 1.14: Growth of Private Sector Nonagricultural Wage Work by Protection Status and Gender, 1988–98

	Male		Female		Total	
	Share of Growth	Ann. Rate of Growth	Share of Growth	Ann.Rate of Growth	Share of Growth	Ann.Rate of Growth
Protected/ Regular	18.1	5.6	15.0	1.1	17.9	4.8
Unprotected/ Regular	64.4	7.5	92.5	3.6	65.8	7.0
Irregular	17.6	3.5	-6.3	-1.4	16.4	3.3
Total	**100.0**	**5.9**	**100.0**	**2.3**	**100.0**	**5.5**

Source: Author's calculations based on data from LFSS 88 and ELMS 98.

It is clear that by far the majority of jobs created in the 1988–98 decade were unprotected by a legal employment contract. Irregular wage employment appears to be declining as a share of total employment for both males and females, but unprotected regular employment has grown very fast. Employers are simply avoiding the job security restrictions of the labor law by not giving new workers legal contracts. Fewer than one in five new workers got such contracts in the 10-year study period. The rate of growth of protected wage work has been significantly slower for females than males, since legal contracts impose on employers even higher costs for females in the form of paid and unpaid maternity leave, as well as other mandates on child care for large employers. Irregular employment among females, which constituted only 12 percent of female private nonagricultural wage employment in 1988, is declining in both relative and absolute terms, but the vast majority of new female jobs in the private sector are unprotected, even though they are regular jobs.

6. Conclusion

Our analysis has revealed that the Egyptian labor market is highly gendered. In nearly every aspect of the labor market we have analyzed, whether labor force participation, unemployment, underemployment, or employment, the clearest contrasts can be found along gender lines. Not only does gender matter, it appears to matter more over time. We have seen that while male labor force participation rates are declining, female rates are increasing by similar magnitudes. Moreover, much of the change appears to be occurring among older males and females, rather than new entrants. We have also seen that although female unemployment rates are higher, especially when corrected for educational attainment, male unemployment appears to be worsening more in rural areas. Visible underemployment, or involuntary part-time work, is primarily a male phenomenon. Because of their heavy domestic burdens, women who work short hours almost never declare themselves as being available for more work.

Unemployment in rural areas appears to be the result of continued demographic pressures on the labor market. Rural labor supply is still outpacing the job-creation capacity in rural areas, and migration has been too limited to transfer the labor surplus to urban areas. The cohort of people ages 10–19 in 1998—which was by far the largest, historically, in rural areas—will complete its transition into the labor market over the next decade. After this, labor supply pressures will subside as the smaller cohort, currently under the age of 10, reaches the age of labor market entry. Although urban areas also experienced demographic pressures, they were less intense due to the earlier onset of fertility declines there. The 15–19 cohort, although also at historical highs, was relatively smaller than its rural counterpart and is followed by an even smaller cohort.

The contrast between males and females is strongest when it comes to the structure of employment. While male nonwage workers in agriculture have left the sector in droves, that type of female employment increased significantly in the 1990s. Conversely, while nonagricultural nonwage work increased among males, it declined among females. In the public sector, both male and female employment declined in state-owned enterprises, but female employment declined more rapidly. The only sector where both male and female employment seems to have increased rapidly is the government.

Perhaps the most worrisome trend is the gender differential in private sector nonagricultural wage employment. At a time when the share of females in the labor force is increasing significantly, their share in this crucial sector is declining. Outside manufacturing, finance, and to a lesser extent trade and services, the private sector appears to be virtually closed to women. Women appear to be opting out of domestic service work, but these jobs are not necessarily being substituted for by other wage-paying jobs in the private sector. For educated women, the options seem to be limited to the still-fairly-small finance sector and the government. Educated women in rural areas have basically only government employment as an option, since they cannot typically commute to urban areas for other types of wage jobs. If it were not for the continued rapid growth of government employment, female unemployment rates would have probably increased sharply.

Notes

1 The structure of the LFSS 1988 is described in Fergany (1990) and the results of the main employment characteristics are analyzed in Fergany (1991).

2 See Williamson and Yousef (2000) and Tunali (1998) for further discussion of the economic and labor market implications of the "demographic window of opportunity" brought about by the declining fertility stage of the demographic transition.

3 See Anker (1990) for further discussion of problems relating to applying the international recommendation, especially as they relate to the measurement of female employment.

4 According to international recommendations, members of the armed forces should be included among persons in paid employment. However, the long-term practice in

Egypt is to classify them as "out of the labor force" if they are not working at the same time in the civilian labor force.

5 Unemployment rates (as opposed to ratios) indicate a similar regional pattern of unemployment (see appendix Table A6). The highest unemployment rates in the country are for females in the Alexandria and Suez Canal region and urban Lower Egypt.

6 An individual was considered available for more work if s/he responded to a question about why s/he worked less than 40 hours per week by saying that s/he either could not find work opportunities the rest of the time or that the pay was not adequate. Those who responded that work conditions require it or that official working hours are less than 40 were not considered available for more work.

7 Of these 15.2 million were employed in 1998 based on the "market work" definition of employment. No estimate of "market" employment is available for 1988.

8 For the distribution of employment by labor market segment, see Appendix Table A1.7.

9 The question of the extent to which the contraction of state-owned enterprise (SOE) employment is the result of the transfer of some of these units to the private sector through privatization or the result of downsizing in existing SOEs needs to be further investigated.

10 Data from the two surveys indicates that the population of those holding secondary school certificates and above grew at a rate of 6.8 percent p.a. compared to a 0.9 percent p.a. growth rate for those with less than a secondary school certificate.

11 According to Wahba (in this volume), 7.7 percent of rural males have changed job location from rural to urban in the 1990s compared to 4.3 percent in the 1980s. ELMS 1998 data also show that 30 percent of rural males work in a district other than the one in which they live.

Appendix

Table A1.1: Distribution of Population by Age, Gender and Urban/Rural Location, 1988–98

	Urban				Rural				Total			
	1988		1998		1988		1998		1988		1998	
	'000s	%	'000s	%	'000s	%	'000s	%	'000s	%	'000s	%
Males												
0–4	1086	10.2	1092	8.6	2073	14.7	2053	11.6	3159	12.8	3145	10.3
5–9	1357	12.7	1263	9.9	2157	15.3	2206	12.5	3514	14.2	3469	11.4
10–14	1255	11.8	1459	11.4	2021	14.3	2537	14.3	3276	13.2	3996	13.1
15–19	1185	11.1	1537	12.0	1576	11.2	2437	13.8	2761	11.1	3974	13.1
20–24	1056	9.9	1357	10.6	1328	9.4	1726	9.8	2384	9.6	3083	10.1
25–29	923	8.7	901	7.1	939	6.7	1123	6.4	1862	7.5	2024	6.6
30–34	678	6.4	775	6.1	702	5.0	976	5.5	1380	5.6	1751	5.8
35–39	611	5.7	785	6.2	741	5.2	825	4.7	1352	5.5	1610	5.3
40–44	541	5.1	691	5.4	494	3.5	793	4.5	1035	4.2	1484	4.9
45–49	426	4.0	653	5.1	482	3.4	850	4.8	908	3.7	1503	4.9
50–54	425	4.0	633	5.0	356	2.5	600	3.4	781	3.2	1233	4.1
55–59	374	3.5	504	3.9	424	3.0	417	2.4	798	3.2	921	3.0
60–64	305	2.9	403	3.2	323	2.3	408	2.3	628	2.5	811	2.7
65+	425	4.0	708	5.5	500	3.5	729	4.1	925	3.7	1437	4.7
Total	**10,647**	**100.0**	**12,761**	**100.0**	**14,116**	**100.0**	**17,680**	**100.0**	**24,763**	**100.0**	**30,441**	**100.0**

(TableA1.1 continued)

Females												
0–4	1062	10.0	1151	9.0	2131	15.1	2063	12.0	3193	12.9	3214	10.7
5–9	1326	12.5	1143	8.9	2142	15.2	1894	11.0	3468	14.0	3037	10.1
10–14	1245	11.7	1664	13.0	1871	13.2	2311	13.4	3116	12.6	3975	13.2
15–19	1103	10.4	1410	11.0	1516	10.7	2303	13.4	2619	10.6	3713	12.4
20–24	1018	9.6	1162	9.1	1170	8.3	1475	8.6	2188	8.8	2637	8.8
25–29	883	8.3	838	6.5	1058	7.5	1135	6.6	1941	7.8	1973	6.6
30–34	761	7.1	855	6.7	717	5.1	1046	6.1	1478	6.0	1901	6.3
35–39	722	6.8	824	6.4	762	5.4	1015	5.9	1484	6.0	1839	6.1
40–44	528	5.0	851	6.6	600	4.2	768	4.5	1128	4.6	1619	5.4
45–49	492	4.6	717	5.6	500	3.5	808	4.7	992	4.0	1525	5.1
50–54	492	4.6	675	5.3	434	3.1	731	4.2	926	3.7	1406	4.7
55–59	353	3.3	482	3.8	371	2.6	441	2.6	724	2.9	923	3.1
60–64	312	2.9	427	3.3	398	2.8	402	2.3	710	2.9	829	2.8
65+	351	3.3	629	4.9	466	3.3	827	4.8	817	3.3	1456	4.8
Total	**10,648**	**100.0**	**12,828**	**100.0**	**14,136**	**100.0**	**17,219**	**100.0**	**24,784**	**100.0**	**30,047**	**100.0**
All												
0–4	2148	10.1	2243	8.8	4204	14.9	4116	11.8	6352	12.8	6359	10.5
5–9	2683	12.6	2406	9.4	4299	15.2	4100	11.7	6982	14.1	6506	10.8
10–14	2500	11.7	3123	12.2	3892	13.8	4848	13.9	6392	12.9	7971	13.2
15–19	2288	10.7	2947	11.5	3092	10.9	4740	13.6	5380	10.9	7687	12.7
20–24	2074	9.7	2519	9.8	2498	8.8	3201	9.2	4572	9.2	5720	9.5
25–29	1806	8.5	1739	6.8	1997	7.1	2258	6.5	3803	7.7	3997	6.6
30–34	1439	6.8	1630	6.4	1419	5.0	2022	5.8	2858	5.8	3652	6.0
35–39	1333	6.3	1609	6.3	1503	5.3	1840	5.3	2836	5.7	3449	5.7
40–44	1069	5.0	1542	6.0	1094	3.9	1561	4.5	2163	4.4	3103	5.1
45–49	918	4.3	1370	5.4	982	3.5	1658	4.8	1900	3.8	3028	5.0
50–54	917	4.3	1308	5.1	790	2.8	1331	3.8	1707	3.4	2639	4.4
55–59	727	3.4	986	3.9	795	2.8	858	2.5	1522	3.1	1844	3.0
60–64	617	2.9	830	3.2	721	2.6	810	2.3	1338	2.7	1640	2.7
65+	776	3.6	1337	5.2	966	3.4	1556	4.5	1742	3.5	2893	4.8
Total	**21,295**	**100.0**	**25,589**	**100.0**	**28,252**	**100.0**	**34,899**	**100.0**	**49,547**	**100.0**	**60,488**	**100.0**

Source: LFSS 88 and ELMS 98.

Table A1.2: Distribution of Population Aged 15–64 by Educational Attainment, Gender, and Urban/Rural Location, 1988–98

	Urban				Rural				Total			
	1988		1998		1988		1998		1988		1998	
	'000s	%	'000s	%	'000s	%	'000s	%	'000s	%	'000s	%
Males												
Illiterate	1362	20.9	973	11.9	3191	43.3	2727	26.9	4553	32.8	3700	20.2
Read & write	1015	15.6	683	8.3	1201	16.3	1155	11.4	2216	16.0	1838	10.0
Less than intermediate	1531	23.5	2318	28.2	1480	20.1	2801	27.7	3011	21.7	5119	27.9
Intermediate	1373	21.0	2312	28.2	1051	14.3	2523	24.9	2424	17.5	4835	26.4
More than intermediate	256	3.9	509	6.2	134	1.8	311	3.1	390	2.8	820	4.5
University	852	13.1	1333	16.2	302	4.1	565	5.6	1154	8.3	1898	10.4
Post-graduate	134	2.1	81	1.0	6	0.1	38	0.4	140	1.0	119	0.6
Total	**6,523**	**100.0**	**8,209**	**100.0**	**7,365**	**100.0**	**10,120**	**100.0**	**13,888**	**100.0**	**18,329**	**100.0**
Females												
Illiterate	2826	42.4	2242	27.3	6019	80.0	5640	55.9	8845	62.3	7882	43.1
Read & write	713	10.7	598	7.3	302	4.0	632	6.3	1015	7.2	1230	6.7
Less than intermediate	1131	17.0	1852	22.5	679	9.0	1888	18.7	1810	12.8	3740	20.4
Intermediate	1245	18.7	2188	26.6	388	5.2	1464	14.5	1633	11.5	3652	20.0
More than intermediate	186	2.8	442	5.4	67	0.9	234	2.3	253	1.8	676	3.7
University	518	7.8	868	10.6	72	1.0	222	2.2	590	4.2	1090	6.0
Post-graduate	43	0.6	29	0.4	0	0.0	4	0.0	43	0.3	33	0.2
Total	**6,662**	**100.0**	**8,219**	**100.0**	**7,527**	**100.0**	**10,084**	**100.0**	**14,189**	**100.0**	**18,303**	**100.0**

(TableA1.2 continued)

All												
Illiterate	4188	31.8	3215	19.6	9210	61.8	8367	41.4	13398	47.7	11582	31.6
Read & write	1728	13.1	1281	7.8	1503	10.1	1787	8.8	3231	11.5	3068	8.4
Less than intermediate	2662	20.2	4170	25.4	2159	14.5	4689	23.2	4821	17.2	8859	24.2
Intermediate	2618	19.9	4500	27.4	1439	9.7	3987	19.7	4057	14.4	8487	23.2
Higher than intermediate	442	3.4	951	5.8	201	1.3	545	2.7	643	2.3	1496	4.1
University	1370	10.4	2201	13.4	374	2.5	787	3.9	1744	6.2	2988	8.2
Post-graduate	177	1.3	110	0.7	6	0.0	42	0.2	183	0.7	152	0.4
Total	**13,185**	**100.0**	**16,428**	**100.0**	**14,892**	**100.0**	**20,204**	**100.0**	**28,077**	**100.0**	**36,632**	**100.0**

Source: LFSS 88 and ELMS 98.

Table A1.3: Labor Force Participation Rates (percent) by Urban/Rural Location, Gender, and Age, 1988–98, Age 6+ (Extended Labor Force Definition)

	Urban		Rural		Total	
Age	**1988**	**1998**	**1988**	**1998**	**1988**	**1998**
Males						
06–11	3.5	1.0	8.5	1.4	6.5	1.3
12–14	14.4	5.4	25.4	11.9	21.3	9.5
15–19	35.5	25.3	52.8	38.8	45.4	33.6
20–29	65.2	65.4	68.7	71.2	67.1	68.6
30–39	97.9	98.1	99.2	96.9	98.5	97.5
40–49	97.1	94.7	96.9	97.3	97.0	96.1
50–59	94.0	87.4	96.1	87.5	95.0	87.4
60–64	63.0	41.7	89.2	64.7	76.5	53.3
=>65	28.0	19.7	56.7	32.7	43.5	26.3
Total	**55.7**	**53.2**	**57.5**	**52.6**	**56.7**	**52.8**
Females						
06–11	1.5	1.4	11.1	7.9	7.4	5.4
12–14	6.8	3.5	28.2	19.9	20.0	12.9
15–19	16.0	13.4	40.1	38.6	30.0	29.0
20–29	38.9	37.6	55.9	60.2	48.1	50.4
30–39	35.7	45.7	60.7	67.1	48.2	57.5
40–49	28.6	38.5	60.9	61.9	45.3	50.2
50–59	17.0	30.1	56.2	58.2	36.1	44.3
60–64	5.3	14.1	39.2	57.8	24.3	35.3
=>65	3.7	9.9	12.8	23.0	8.9	17.4
Total	**21.5**	**24.9**	**40.8**	**43.4**	**32.1**	**35.3**
All						
06–11	2.6	1.2	9.8	4.5	7.0	3.3
12–14	10.7	4.4	26.8	15.7	20.6	11.2
15–19	26.1	19.6	46.6	38.7	37.9	31.4
20–29	52.3	52.4	62.3	65.9	57.7	60.0
30–39	64.6	70.9	79.7	81.0	72.4	76.4
40–49	61.9	64.4	77.8	80.0	70.0	72.6
50–59	54.4	58.5	75.8	71.8	64.9	65.0
60–64	33.8	27.5	61.6	61.3	48.8	44.2
=>65	17.0	15.1	35.5	27.6	27.3	21.8
Total	**38.6**	**39.0**	**49.1**	**48.1**	**44.4**	**44.1**

Source: LFSS 88 and ELMS 98.

Table A1.4: Labor Force Participation Rates (percent) by Urban/Rural Location, Educational Attainment, and Gender, (Extended Labor Force Definition), Ages 15–64

	Urban		Rural		Total	
Education	**1988**	**1998**	**1988**	**1998**	**1988**	**1998**
Males						
Illiterate	86.8	82.2	90.7	86.0	89.5	85.0
Read & write	87.4	83.5	92.1	88.8	89.9	86.9
Less than intermediate	50.7	52.8	48.9	49.8	49.8	51.1
Intermediate	66.0	65.0	66.9	72.9	66.4	69.1
More than intermediate	82.6	89.1	82.8	96.3	82.7	91.9
University	89.4	89.7	86.0	91.1	88.5	90.1
Post-graduate	95.7	92.0	100.0	100.0	95.9	94.6
All	74.4	70.8	78.8	73.6	76.7	72.3
Females						
Illiterate	18.4	26.1	55.1	60.3	43.4	50.6
Read & write	12.7	16.2	46.9	57.5	22.9	37.4
Less than intermediate	12.0	10.5	27.0	36.6	17.7	23.6
Intermediate	49.0	41.1	73.0	60.4	54.7	48.9
More than intermediate	75.9	63.6	83.7	85.0	78.0	71.0
University	69.8	73.7	70.7	75.8	69.9	74.1
Post-graduate	83.3	78.0	--	100.0	83.3	80.6
All	28.5	33.0	53.5	56.6	41.8	46.0

Source: LFSS 88 and ELMS 98.
Note: -- Too few observations in the sample.

Table A1.5: Unemployment Rate (percent) by Urban/Rural Location, Age, and Gender, 1988–98 (Extended Labor Force Definition and Search Required)

	Urban		Rural		Total	
Age	**1988**	**1998**	**1988**	**1998**	**1988**	**1998**
Males						
15–19	14.6	21.8	4.4	16.1	7.8	17.7
20–29	11.4	14.9	4.5	15.3	7.6	15.1
30–39	2.6	3.3	1.5	1.9	2.0	2.6
40–49	2.5	1.4	0.9	1.2	1.7	1.3
50–59	0.9	2.1	0.0	1.9	0.5	2.1
60–64	6.6	1.0	1.1	0.0	3.3	0.4
Total	**5.8**	**6.8**	**2.4**	**7.1**	**4.0**	**7.0**
Females						
15–19	46.8	29.4	7.6	8.4	16.4	12.1
20–29	26.9	39.6	7.0	16.3	14.4	23.9
30–39	5.1	9.1	0.6	1.6	2.2	4.3
40–49	3.6	1.1	0.3	0.9	1.3	1.0
50–59	3.3	0.3	0.0	0.0	0.8	0.1
60–64	0.0	0.0	0.7	0.0	0.7	0.0
Total	**17.1**	**15.8**	**3.5**	**6.3**	**7.8**	**9.4**
All						
15–19	24.1	24.3	5.7	12.3	11.1	15.2
20–29	17.1	23.2	5.6	15.8	10.4	18.6
30–39	3.3	5.2	1.1	1.8	2.1	3.2
40–49	2.7	1.3	0.6	1.1	1.5	1.2
50–59	1.3	1.7	0.0	1.1	0.6	1.4
60–64	6.0	0.7	1.0	0.0	2.6	0.2
Total	**9.0**	**9.7**	**2.9**	**6.8**	**5.4**	**7.9**

Source: LFSS 88 and ELMS 98.

Table A1.6: Proportion of New Entrants Among Unemployed (percent) by Educational Attainment, Urban/Rural Status, and Gender 1988–98

	Urban		Rural		Total	
Education	**1988**	**1998**	**1988**	**1998**	**1988**	**1998**
Males						
Illiterate	7.5	9.1	19.4	35.2	13.2	26.5
Read & write	10.6	21.7	28.3	15.7	16.2	17.8
Less than intermediate	36.3	18.3	48.3	45.0	38.9	28.9
Intermediate	61.0	74.4	52.4	70.4	57.9	71.8
More than intermediate	69.1	48.9	0.0	80.4	58.8	62.9
University	60.9	71.1	51.3	94.2	58.4	82.2
Total	**42.0**	**52.2**	**38.2**	**63.0**	**40.8**	**58.4**
Females						
Illiterate	51.0	51.4	0.0	100.0	38.3	79.0
Read & write	67.5	42.7	100.0	100.0	69.7	71.4
Less than intermediate	62.1	63.2	74.9	50.0	64.7	58.9
Intermediate	75.6	85.1	89.9	91.5	81.3	88.3
More than intermediate	67.4	70.4	100.0	100.0	72.8	83.6
University	81.8	76.2	100.0	76.8	84.4	76.4
Total	**70.8**	**78.7**	**81.2**	**91.0**	**74.0**	**84.3**
All						
Illiterate	28.3	21.3	14.6	48.9	23.0	39.1
Read & write	29.1	27.8	33.3	31.4	30.2	30.0
Less than intermediate	46.8	25.4	58.7	45.6	49.4	33.2
Intermediate	70.1	80.9	77.7	80.0	73.1	80.4
More than intermediate	68.0	61.5	64.6	91.9	67.5	75.0
University	72.0	74.1	68.2	87.4	71.3	79.2
Total	**57.4**	**66.0**	**59.9**	**74.3**	**58.2**	**70.3**

Source: LFSS 88 and ELMS 98.

Table A1.7: Distribution of Employment by Major Labor Market Segment, and Gender, 1988–98

	Male		Female		Total	
'000s	**1988**	**1998**	**1988**	**1998**	**1988**	**1998**
Column Percent						
Government	20.8	26.8	15.7	19.2	19.0	23.9
State-owned enterp.	11.4	7.4	3.5	1.6	8.6	5.2
Subtotal public sector	32.1	34.3	19.1	20.9	27.6	29.1
Priv. agric. wage work	8.7	7.7	3.0	1.1	6.7	5.2
Priv. agric. nonwage work	22.4	13.5	60.4	66.7	35.7	33.9
Subtotal agriculture	31.1	21.2	63.4	67.8	42.4	39.0
Priv. nonagric. wage work	21.8	28.6	6.1	5.1	16.3	19.7
Priv. nonagric. Nonwage work	14.9	15.9	11.4	6.2	13.7	12.2
Subtotal private Nonagriculture	36.7	44.5	17.5	11.3	30.0	31.8
Total	**100.0**	**100.0**	**100.0**	**100.0**	**100.0**	**100.0**

Source: LFSS 88 and ELMS 98.

Table A1.8: Government Employment by Occupation and Gender, 1988–98

	Male		Female		Total	
'000s	**1988**	**1998**	**1988**	**1998**	**1988**	**1998**
Column Percent						
Scien./Technical	9.4	9.6	4.3	2.4	7.9	7.4
Health prof.	5.3	2.7	11.3	8.2	7.0	4.4
Educators	17.9	22.1	32.3	38.3	22.2	27.1
Other prof.	8.9	6.1	9.3	11.1	9.0	7.6
Managers	3.2	4.4	3.1	2.4	3.2	3.8
Clerical	18.7	21.4	36.2	33.2	23.8	25.0
Serv/Sales	21.1	22.0	2.5	2.9	15.7	16.2
Product/Transp.	15.4	11.7	1.0	1.4	11.2	8.5
Total	**100.0**	**100.0**	**100.0**	**100.0**	**100.0**	**100.0**

Source: LFSS 88 and ELMS 98.

Table A1.9: Distribution of Private Nonagricultural Wage Employment by Industry Group and Gender, 1988–98

	Male		Female		Total	
'000s	**1988**	**1998**	**1988**	**1998**	**1988**	**1998**
Column Percent						
Manuf, mining & util.	33.1	33.9	21.1	27.8	32.5	34.0
Construction	25.5	23.2	1.9	3.3	22.4	21.2
Trade, rest., & hotels	18.4	18.3	25.3	26.5	19.3	19.1
Transp., storage & communic.	10.3	11.1	3.2	1.8	9.4	10.1
Finance, insur. & real estate	1.8	2.8	2.9	6.4	2.0	3.2
Public & personal services	10.8	10.8	42.3	34.1	14.9	13.1
Undefined	0.1	0.0	3.3	0.0	0.6	0.0
Total	**100.0**	**100.0**	**100.0**	**100.0**	**100.0**	**100.0**

Source: LFSS 88 and ELMS 98.

2 A Decade of Rising Wage Inequality? Gender, Occupation, and Public-Private Issues in the Egyptian Wage Structure

Mona Said

Introduction

According to widely held opinion, income inequalities and wage differentials are much lower in public-sector-led socialist models than in private-sector-led market economies. This is presumably due to the presence of a large public sector that allows for a high degree of centralization of wage-setting—by decree in the public sector, and by demonstration in the private sector—which, in turn, ensures a degree of equality unattainable in more decentralized models. Moreover, the concern with the welfare of the lower- and middle-income strata in more socialist-leaning state-led economies often leads to a process of wage compression between workers with different skills and education levels.

The findings of this chapter show that this decade—which witnessed further liberalization of the Egyptian economy and the implementation of stabilization and privatization programs—has been, on average, one of real wage erosion and overall wage compression. It witnessed declining real wages, devaluation of work experience in wage-setting, falling educational wage premiums for most groups and a narrowing of white-collar/blue-collar wage differentials.

The legacy of the public sector employment guarantee continues, in the sense that the public sector still offers the highest rewards for experience and education in the labor market. This is true particularly for females, though the category of female white-collar vocational-school graduates witnessed large declines in their government advantages. Compared to the private sector, government (public) workers are now, in general, in a weaker position in the labor market. The male wage disadvantage increased, and the female advantage decreased. In contrast, the remaining workers in the public enterprise sector are in a relatively better position, in that they earn larger wage premiums than they did in 1988.

Unexplained gender gaps remain most compressed—almost non-existent—in the government sector during the period under study. They also remained the same (at 25 percent) in the private sector, whereas in public enterprises they doubled from 12 percent to 24 percent. Also, the union-wage differential has hardly changed over this period. But this reflects two opposing trends: a rise in the public sector, and a fall in the private sector.

In short, wage inequality in Egypt over the past decade has declined for males and risen for females. For both, the change in observed characteristics—including the shift to a larger share of the private sector in total employment—has had an increasing impact on wage inequality. For males, this has been sufficiently counteracted by the decline in returns to education and experience to the extent that overall inequality has declined. For females, overall inequality still increased due to a large differentiation in actual female characteristics (such as education experience, etc.) that counteracted the impact from decreasing returns to such characteristics.

The findings of this study point to the need for several directions of future research. These include: the impact of the slowing of the graduate guarantee on wage outcomes in the government; public enterprise relative wage changes during privatization; causes and implications of decline in returns to experience and education; channels of gender-based discrimination in the private sector; and reasons for changes in wage and earnings inequality.

In many ways, Egypt in 1988 still followed the above model of a public-sector-led economy. Despite 14 years of "open-door policies," the public sector (defined to include both the government and public enterprises) dominated almost one-third of total employment. In the markets for workers with intermediate and higher-than-intermediate educations, and for females, the public sector played an even more dominant role, thanks to more than 25 years of a graduate public sector employment guarantee in the economy. In fact, aside from the informal sector and international migration, the public sector has still led employment absorption, particularly of educated labor. The main legacy of partial liberalization policies since the mid-1970s has not been a diminution in the employment contribution of the public sector, but rather a large erosion in real wages in the government, a slight prolonging of the waiting period for appointment of graduates under the guarantee, and a slowing down of employment growth in public enterprises. These resulted after the Egyptian government opted out of the centralized manpower allocation system in 1978. Nevertheless, nonwage benefits—especially lifetime job security in government jobs—remained untouched.

The period from 1988 to 1998 witnessed several important changes in the labor market, as the pace of liberalization rose and the economy shifted more quickly toward a market private-sector-led model. The public sector employment guarantee, although not yet officially abrogated, came almost to a complete halt. From 1987–95, there were no announcements by the Ministry of Manpower and Vocational Training of hiring full graduate classes of applicants, and in 1995, there was only a partial hiring of the 1982–83 class—a full 12 years after graduation. After more than 20 years of debate, privatization became a reality. Since 1996, schemes for early retirement and compensation for retrenched workers have been introduced in several public enterprises selected to be privatized. As a result, for the first time since the creation of public enterprises, there was an absolute decline in the number of their employees. Moreover, a recently proposed labor law would significantly decrease the job-security guarantees of public enterprise and private sector workers, in return for their gain of a limited right to strike.

I investigate the distributional and structural developments of hourly wages and quarterly earnings in Egypt between 1988 and 1998, based on the LFSS 88 and ELMS 98 labor force sample surveys. This period corresponds to the developments outlined above in the context of the implementation of various stabilization and structural-adjustment programs under the auspices of the World Bank and the International Monetary Fund (IMF). Official agreements on such programs were officially signed in 1991, but some incomplete stabilization measures were also taken beginning in 1987.

Although the economy cannot be described as having already undergone the complete transition to a capitalist economy, it is interesting to study the change in the pattern of wage inequality as the country proceeds further in this transition process. In addition to looking at the occupational, industrial, and educational distribution of wages, four axes will be highlighted to measure wage differentials. These include: gender (male/female); sector (government-private/public enterprise- private); broad occupational (white collar versus blue collar); and union (unionized versus non-unionized). The chapter is structured as follows: following the Introduction, Section 1 summarizes the main developments in real average hourly wages; real quarterly earnings; public/private and male/female wages; and earnings ratios across occupations, levels of education, and other classifications. In Section 2, empirical wage functions are estimated for different sector/gender groups over the 10-year period, and the changes in returns to skills and wage premiums are calculated and compared for 1988–98. Section 3 assesses the implications for overall measured inequality in hourly wages, and breaks this down into inequality within and between important socio-economic groups, as well as "explained" and "unexplained" components in terms of changes in observed characteristics. Section 4 summarizes the main findings of the paper and identifies directions for future research.

1. The Distribution of Average Wages and Earnings, 1988–98

It is interesting to examine the changes in average hourly wages and quarterly earnings across important socio-economic groups (gender, occupations, industries, levels of education, and sectors of ownership). It is also useful to look at a combination of attributes that are indicative of labor market status. In particular, we examine the developments of average wages of unionized white-collar or blue-collar workers versus the non-unionized; regular (permanent or temporary) blue-collar workers versus the irregular (casual or seasonal); and blue-collar workers working inside establishments versus those working outside over the period under study.

To facilitate comparability, all 1988 wages are inflated to 1998 using the Consumer Price Index, so that everything is in 1998 Egyptian pounds. In addition to hourly wages, which can be thought of as the "unit price of labor," we also look at quarterly earnings, which constitute a measure of "income from labor," and are calculated as the sum of wages earned from all primary and secondary jobs in the three months reference period. The difference in the pattern of these earnings to hourly wages captures the ability of a particular group to supplement income by working extra hours, changing primary jobs, or holding additional (secondary) jobs.

This section also examines wage and earnings ratios between 1988 and 1998 in government/private, public enterprise/private, and male/female workers. In commenting on these patterns, it is useful to distinguish between developments for higher-paid segments and lower-paid segments in the labor market. Higher-paid segments traditionally include males, white-collar workers (especially in managerial and professional occupations), higher-educated workers, unionized workers, regular workers, and workers inside establishments. Lower-paid segments traditionally include females, blue-collar workers, lower-educated workers, non-unionized workers, irregular workers, and workers outside establishments.

1.1 Real Average Hourly Wages and Quarterly Earnings

Developments in real average hourly wages are presented in Appendix Tables A2.1, A2.2, and A2.3, and in Figures 2.1 and 2.2. Together, these reveal that wages have significantly declined in real terms over this period for almost all groups. It is interesting, however, that the sharpest real-wage falls were found in some of the traditionally higher-paid segments of the labor market.

For example, males' wages fell sharper than female wages, and so did public sector managers, private sector professionals, and technical workers' wages compared to other occupations. Moreover, sharper wage falls were also witnessed for those with secondary education or higher (compared to lower education levels), unionized white-collar workers (compared to non-unionized workers), and for regular workers and those inside establishments (compared to irregular workers and those outside establishments). In general, blue-collar workers (including those in agriculture), casual workers, and those outside establishments witnessed the least real wage declines. Thus, based on average wages, there appears to have been a process of compression of the distribution of wages, which is likely to be reflected in a decline in overall measured wage inequality. (Section 3 studies the issue of wage inequality in more detail).

Figure 2.1: Real Average Hourly Wage Ratios By Gender/Occupation (1998/1988) (1998 prices)

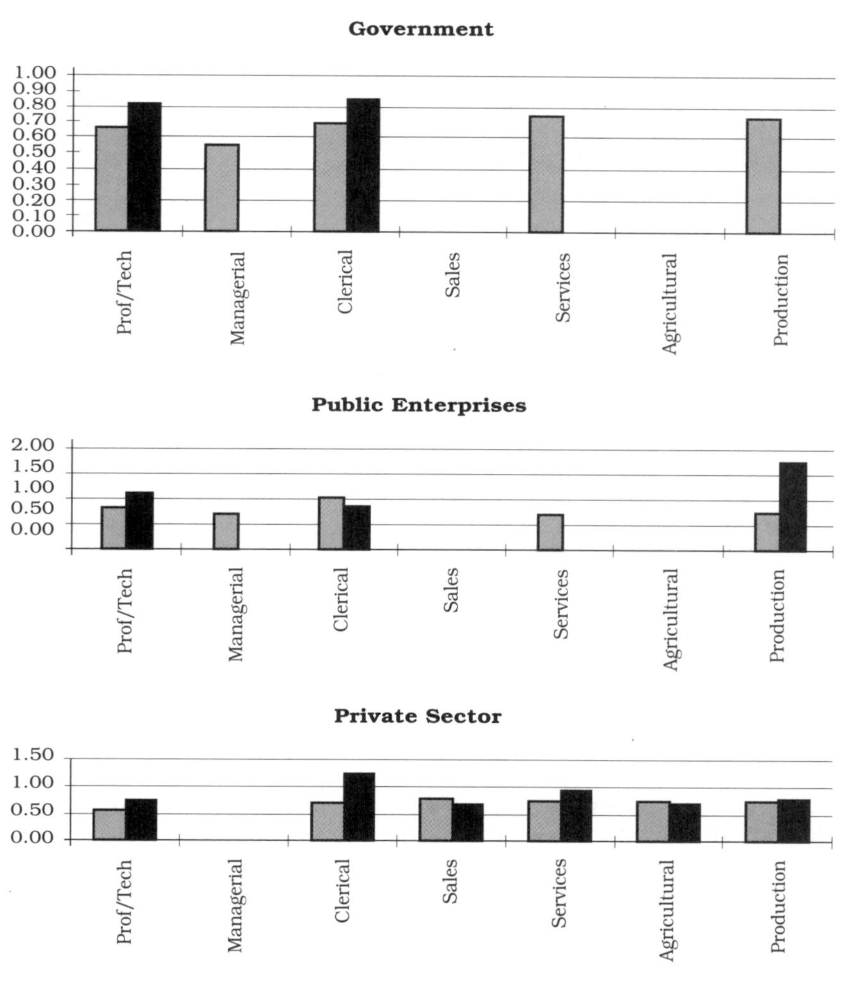

The trends in real average earnings are very similar, implying that workers who witnessed the sharpest fall in real hourly wages were unable to counteract this by working more hours, changing jobs, or working in secondary jobs. In fact, irregular blue-collar workers and those outside establishments in services were the only categories that witnessed a slight real wage and earnings improvement over this period.

Figure 2.2: Real Average Hourly Wage Ratios By Education and Labor Market Status (1998/1988) (1998 prices)

A. By Education (Private Sector Males)

1.00
0.80
0.60
0.40
0.20
0.00
Illitrate
Read & write
Primary
Preparatory
Blue collar secondary
White collar secondary
Higher than intermediate
University

B. By Labor Market Status

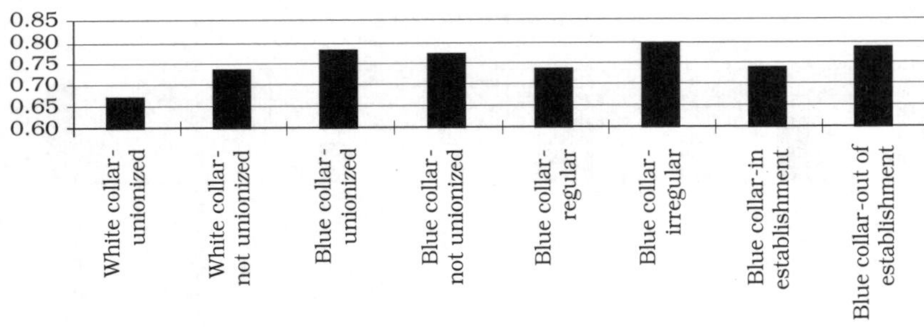

1.2 Male/Female Wage Ratios

Compared to 1988, gender gaps appear to have narrowed, especially in the private sector (see Appendix Tables A2.1–A2.3 and Figure 2.3). Whether this conclusion still holds after we correct for male-female differences in productivity-related factors is examined in Section 2. The average figures still show that in 1998, male/female wage ratios remained lower in the public sector (government and public enterprises) than in the private sector. Moreover, since 1988, male/female wage ratios have been falling in almost all occupations in the government and public enterprises. In the private sector, the incidence of the highest gender-based average hourly wage differentials are in the traditionally lower-paid segments of the labor market (blue-collar occupations, workers with lower-than-intermediate levels of education, irregular workers, and workers outside establishments). In all sectors, the gender gaps in quarterly earnings are much higher than those in hourly wages, reflecting the greater ability of males to supplement their incomes by working longer hours, changing primary jobs, and/or holding secondary jobs.

Figure 2.3: Average Male/Female Hourly Wages Ratios (1988-98)

A. Across Sectors

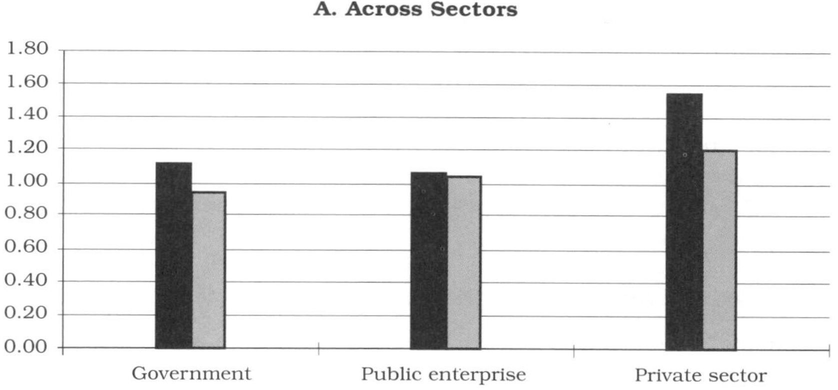

B. Private Sector (Across Occupations)

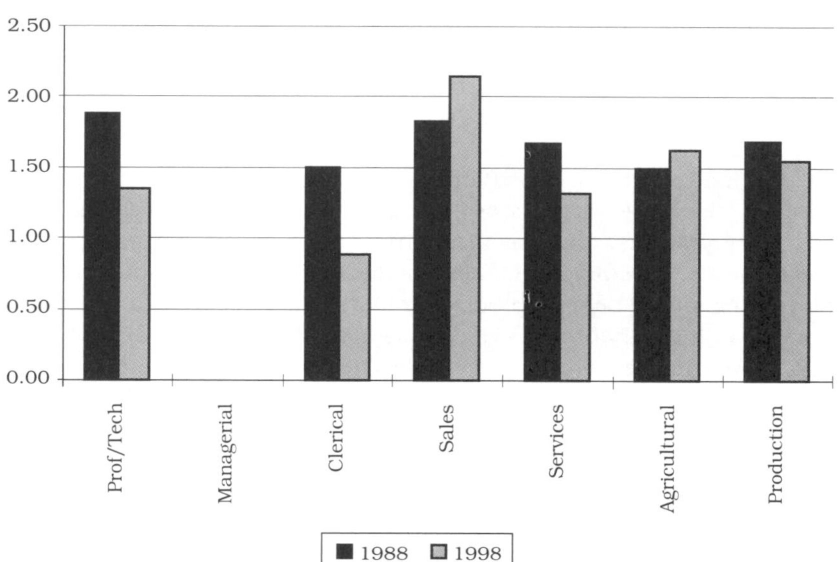

1.3 Public/Private Wage Ratios

Examination of average public/private wage ratios across occupations (see Appendix Tables A2.1–A2.3 and Figure 2.4) reveals that, over the period under study, these ratios remained broadly constant in the government sector, representing an average government disadvantage of 6–36 percent for males. Comparison across educational levels (see Appendix Table A2.2) shows that the greatest public sector disadvantages are for government male workers with lower levels of education (those who are illiterate and those who can only just read and write).

As for females, the government wage premium increased slightly in professional and technical occupations, but was reversed for clerical workers, who now earn premiums in the private sector. Both males and females (especially with higher levels of education) witnessed an increase in public enterprise wages relative to the private sector ones.

In summary, the average wage figures indicate that the relative position of government workers has remained the same or has deterio-rated slightly over the period under study, whereas that of public enterprise workers has improved.

2. Estimating Hourly Wage Differentials Using Wage Equations

Although informative about general patterns, the above wage compari-sons do not take account of differences in productivity-related factors in workers. For example, we may be comparing workers with very different levels of experience and educational attainment, and hence such factors must be corrected for. Using multivariate regression analysis (i.e. regression with more than one explanatory variable), twelve wage equations were estimated for males and females in 1988 and 1998, across the three sectors of ownership: government, public enterprises, and the private sector. In each case, the dependent variable is log hourly wage.

In addition to levels of educational attainment, experience, and square of experience, the wage regressions also include controls for regions of residence, marital status, and unionization; working on an irregular (casual or seasonal) basis, in outside establishments, or in large establishments (50 employees or more); being a blue-collar worker (as opposed to white-collar); or working in industry or services (versus agriculture). Appendix Tables A2.4 and A2.5 present the means and standard deviation of these variables for the years 1988 and 1998, respectively. These summary statistics confirm the importance of correcting for differences in these characteristics in undergoing yearly, sector, and gender wage comparisons. For example, the average levels of experience and educational attainment are higher in the 1998 sample (average years of experience are 17.4 in 1998, compared to 15.1 in 1988; and 58 percent of the 1998 sample have intermediate or higher education,

Figure 2.4: Public/Private Hourly Wages Ratios Across Occupations (1988-98)

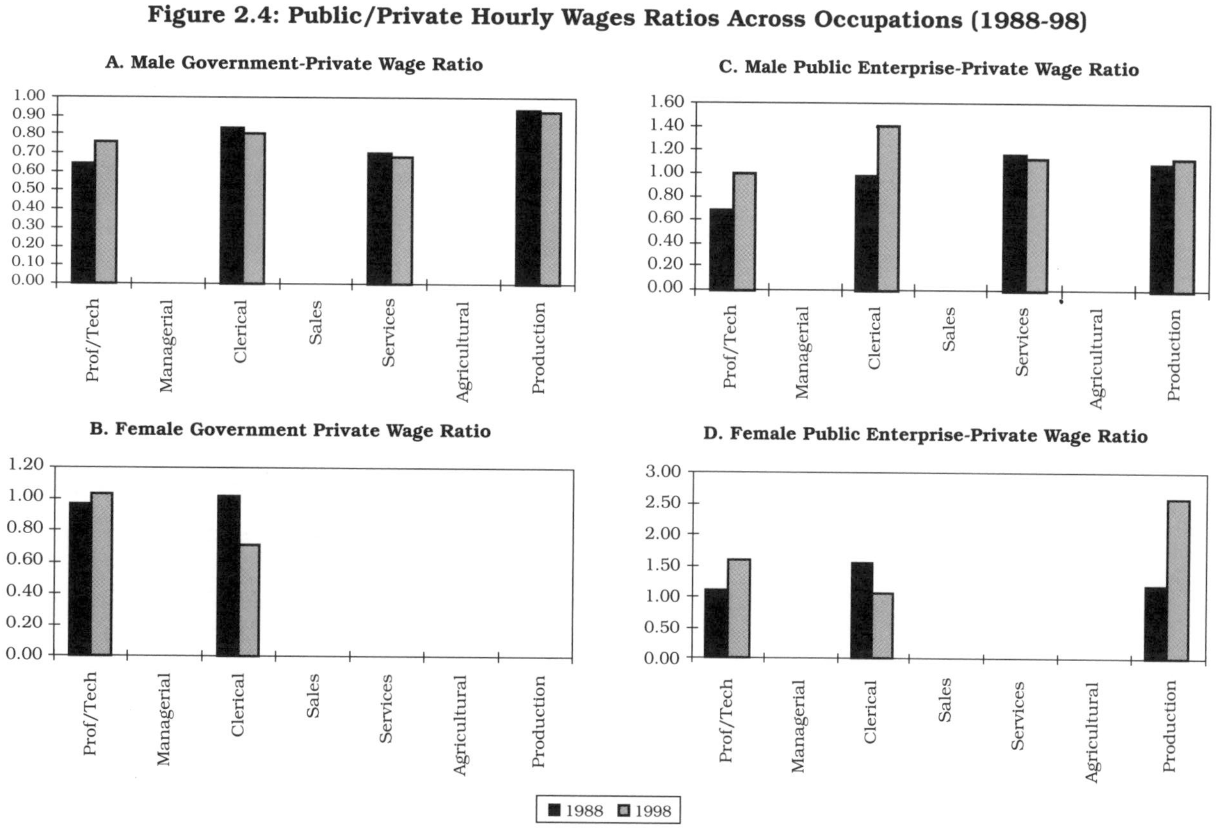

compared to 42 percent in 1988). The 1998 sample also has a higher concentration of white-collar, public sector, unionized, regular, and inside-establishment workers. As for sector comparisons, in both 1988 and 1998, the government and public enterprises had a higher concentration of all these attributes than did the private sector. Also, in both years the male sample was more experienced and unionized, but less-educated, than the female sample, and was more dominated by white-collar, regular, and inside-establishment workers. All such factors would, therefore, be very important to correct for in undergoing sector and gender comparisons.

2.1 Estimation Results

Table 2.1 calculates returns to different levels of education, in total and by sector and gender, based on the wage equation estimates reported in the appendix. It also plots wage-experience profiles for the reference worker (with a secondary-school certificate) across gender and sector groups. The results indicate that the period between 1988 and 1998 witnessed a devaluation of work experience in wage-setting and falling education wage premiums for both males and females. The decline in returns to education took place for all but the lowest end (those who can only just read and write or who have finished only primary school) and the highest end (those completing higher institute and university levels) of the educational ladder.

A more detailed look at the experience variables parameter estimates and implied wage-experience profile reveals that the devaluation in returns to experience between 1988 and 1998 were strongest in the private sector. In that sector, we can still witness an inversely U-shaped wage-experience profile (which has more curvature than in the public sector), consistent with following a human-capital model of wage-setting over the life cycle, whereby wages increase with experience, peak at mid-career or so, and then decline again close to retirement. For both males and females, the returns to experience are highest (or wage-experience profile steeper) in the public sector.

Also, the returns for each year of experience for females are higher than those for males in the public sector, whereas males' returns are higher in the private sector.

The figures in Table 2.1 show that in 1998 returns to education, like returns to experience, were higher for females than males in the government sector. In addition, except at the university level, they were higher in the public sector than in the private sector. Also of note are the returns for education at the entry level for those eligible for the public sector employment guarantee (i.e., blue-collar and white-collar secondary-school certificate holders). The estimates in the table show that the drop in returns for education were higher for white-collar secondary certificates than for blue-collar ones. The decline was particularly dramatic for females with white-collar certificates in the government.

Table 2.1: Proportionate Returns To Different Levels of Education by Sector and Gender

	Male						Female						Total	
	Govern.		Public Enterp.		Private		Govern.		Public Enterp.		Private			
	88	98	88	98	88	98	88	98	88	98	88	98	88	98
Read and write	7.7	-	7.4	-	-	7.2	-	-	-	-	-	-	3.8	4.5
Primary	4.5	3.7	-	4.9	2.6	2.2	-	-	-	-	-	-	2.8	3.1
Preparatory	3.6	1.2	6.1	2.0	4.3	1.3	-	-	-	-	-	-	4.6	1.6
Blue-collar secondary	3.8	5.4	11.0	9.1	7.9	4.3	8.6	6.4	8.2	-	-	-	6.8	5.9
White-collar secondary	6.5	5.4	12.1	8.3	6.6	4.8	12.6	3.6	4.5	-	-	-	8.8	5.8
Higher institute	6.3	7.0	8.3	10.0	-2.6	5.8	2.2	10.2	-	-	-	13.3	3.5	8.5
University	7.4	10.5	10.0	10.6	11.3	11.4	6.9	11.5	4.3	12.0	19.4	20.2	8.5	11.1

Notes: Returns to education were not calculated for the general secondary and above university and wherever '-' appears, due to small cell size and/or insignificant estimates on underlying parameters. The above calculations are based on the assumptions that reaching the read and write level requires two years of education compared to the illiterates. The primary level requires an extra six years, then an additional three for secondary certificates, then two for higher institutes or four for university.

To sum up, the results on changes in returns to experience and education from 1988 to 1998 confirm that the legacy of the predominance of the public sector as an employer, and the impact of the public sector employment guarantee, continues in the labor market in Egypt. The public sector in general, and the government in particular, still offers the highest rewards for experience and education, particularly for females. However, females with vocational/secondary-school (white-collar) certificates witnessed large declines in returns to this level of education in the government sector in the 1990s.

Attributes that tend to increase private sector wages include marriage, membership in trade unions, irregular jobs, work outside establishments, work in large establishments, and work in the industrial or services sectors. Unlike the results obtained by looking at average figures in Section 1 above, the premium for working on an irregular basis and outside establishments had not increased in 1998. The premium for working in the service sector of economic activity has, however, significantly increased, reflecting the importance of these activities in the private sector. Another change in 1998 was an increase in the married-worker premium for both males and females in the private sector.

As for regional controls, living outside greater Cairo is associated with a wage disadvantage for all sector and gender groups. This is greatest for rural Upper Egypt, the notoriously poorest governorates, or provinces. Results show that the efforts of the government to reverse these trends in 1990 have succeeded only in the government sector; the situation for public enterprise and private sector workers worsened.

2.2 Sector and Gender Wage Differentials

Gender and sector wage differentials were calculated based on the results mentioned above (see Table 2.2). These represent the component of the observed wage gaps that are unexplained by productivity-related characteristics.

Comparison of 1988 and 1998 estimates show that the government/private sector male wage disadvantage has increased from 6 percent to 14 percent over the 10-year period, and the female government-sector premium decreased by half, from 36 percent to 18 percent. For public enterprises, an opposite trend took place, with the public enterprise premium (relative to the private sector) increasing for both males and females. We can conclude, then, that civil service reform and privatization had a divergent impact on labor market outcomes in the public sector relative to the private sector. Government workers are now in a weaker position, whereas workers in the public enterprise sector are in a better position than they were in 1988.

As for unexplained gender wage gaps, they are still highest in the private sector and most compressed—almost non-existent—in the government. In fact, they hardly changed in these two sectors from 1988 to 1998. It is in public enterprises that the most notable change took place, with a doubling

Table 2.2: Gender, Sector, Broad Occupational and Union Wage Differentials, 1988–98
(in log hourly wages)

	1988	1998
Sector wage differentials		
Males		
Government-private	-0.062	-0.142
Public enterprise-private	-0.023	0.097
Females		
Government-private	0.357	0.175
Public enterprise-private	-0.113	0.168
Gender wage differentials (Female-Male)		
Government	-0.003	-0.016
Public enterprise	-0.118	-0.238
Private sector	-0.254	-0.247
Broad occupational wage differentials (blue collar - white collar)		
Total	-0.055**	0.012
Males		
Government	-0.107**	-0.129**
Public enterprise	0.047	0.092
Private sector	-0.074	0.073
Females		
Government	0.182	0.270 **
Public enterprise	0.309	-0.314
Private sector	-0.007	0.344*
Union wage differentials (unionized- non-unionized)		
Total	0.143 **	0.144**
Males		
Government	0.129**	0.133**
Public enterprise	0.112**	0.132**
Private sector	0.149**	0.143**
Females		
Government	0.142**	0.069
Public enterprise	-0.025	0.079
Private sector	0.278	0.129

*Note: Sector wage differentials are calculated as the difference between predicted log hourly wages for public sector employees using the public sector wage equation and their predicted log hourly wages using the private sector equation (expressed as a proportion of the former). Similarly, gender wage differentials are the difference between predicted female wages using the female equation and their predicted wages using the male equation. Broad occupational and union wage differentials are the estimated parameter for blue collar and unionized status in the wage equations (see appendix 1). For these, * denotes significance at the 10% level and ** denotes significance at the 5% level.*
Source: Calculated from log hourly wage regressions based on the LFSS 88 and ELMS 98 (see appendix1).

of gender gaps from 12 percent to 24 percent, almost the same level as in the private sector. This trend is expected, as these enterprises moved away from institutional and uniform wage-setting to more decentralized and private sector-like compensation practices. Also, the centralized compensation policy of the government sector has not been changed, so we can expect gender gaps to remain as compressed in 1998 as they were in 1988.

It is less obvious why gender wage gaps have not been affected by the changes that took place in the private sector. One can suggest that there might have been opposing forces at work over this period, resulting in no significant changes. Or one can question whether or not the changes that took place reflect patterns of occupational segregation not captured in the present estimates. Such questions can best be answered by using decomposition techniques of gender gaps that help identify different channels of gender-gap discrimination in the labor market

2.3 Broad Occupational and Union Wage Gaps

As for broad occupational and union wage gaps, the slight disadvantage of blue-collar workers observed in 1988 has disappeared in 1998, and there is no significant difference between blue-collar and white-collar workers in the public enterprise and private sectors—consistent with falling educational premiums in these two sectors. The union wage differential has hardly changed over the period, which reflects two opposing trends. On one hand, there was a rise of that premium in the public sector, which is consistent with the perception of increased involvement of public sector unions in wage setting, perhaps to elicit their support during times of privatization. On the other hand, there was a fall in the union premium in the private sector. This may be indicative of a weakening of bargaining power of workers in wage setting in the private sector, despite a nominal increase in total membership recorded over this period.

3. Changes in Average Hourly Wage and Quarterly Earnings Inequality

In this section, we turn to an analysis of the implications of the above changes in wage differentials to the overall observed inequality (or dispersion) of hourly wages and quarterly earnings. This constitutes a direct test of the hypothesis outlined in the introduction: Has wage inequality increased over the past decade of stabilization and structural adjustment in Egypt?

Table 2.3 presents several standard statistical measures of inequality of both wages and earnings, calculated separately for males and females. The results for hourly wages are presented separately for the government, public enterprise, and private sectors. In each case, an attempt was made to decompose measured inequality into a component attributable to changes "within" and "between" important socio-economic groups (i.e., occupation, industry, education, and experience).

Before summarizing the results in the table, it is important to clarify the differences between the various measures of inequality. The most commonly reported statistical measure of inequality is usually "the standard deviation," which is a measure of how far each observation is from the mean. It is not, however, a good measure of inequality—if everyone's income doubles, or if there is inflation, the standard deviation will also double. However, if the standard deviation is standardized by dividing it by the mean of the distribution, we obtain the second measure, namely "the coefficient of variation," which does not have this limitation. A third measure is the Gini coefficient, which is defined graphically as the area between the Lorenz curve (which graphs the cumulative fraction of income versus the cumulative fraction of the population, arranged in ascending order) and the line of perfect equality in income distribution. Intuitively, the Gini coefficient can be given the interpretation that if one randomly drew two people from the population, the expected wage difference between them as a proportion of the average wage is twice the Gini coefficient. However, a problem with each of these three measures is that as they take into account all observations, they are sensitive to errors or real changes at the tails of the distribution. It is therefore also useful to report the decile ratio (the ratio of the 90th percentile of the wage distribution to the 10th percentile), which is not sensitive to outliers or extreme observations at either end of the distribution.

In this chapter, the estimated measures of inequality include the coefficient of variation, the decile ratio, and the Gini coefficient. Another measure calculated is half the square of the coefficient of variation. This is a member of the general entropy (GE) indices, which have the desirable property of being additively decomposable into com-ponents within and between groups. In other words, we can use this index to measure inequality both between and within certain classifications or groups. The groups considered are level of work experience (5 groups), education (10 groups), occupation (7 groups), and industry (9 groups).

The results in Table 2.3 show that both hourly wage and quarterly earnings inequality have declined for males in the sample over the observation period (1988 to 1998). Although quarterly earnings inequality has also declined for females, hourly wage inequality has increased. For both males and females, the results have been driven by changes in the government and private sectors. Thus, an examination of whether or not inequality has been increasing in Egypt shows that it has not increased for the male subsample, and it has increased for the female subsample.

The decomposition of the GE index shows that most of the observed inequality for males and females in the three sectors is within (as opposed to between) groups. Over this period, however, for both males and females in the private sector there was some decline in inequality between educational groups and occupations—consistent with declining educational and white-

Table 2.3: Measures of Inequality of Hourly Wages: Within and Between Groups

Var.		Coeficient of variation	Decile ratio	Gini coeficient	General Entropy Index									
					Total	Edu.		Experience group		Occupation		Industry	
						With.	Bet.	With.	Bet.	With.	Bet.	With	Bet.
Hourly Wages													
Males													
Total	88	1.13	5.38	0.40	0.74	0.66	0.08	0.73	0.01	0.64	0.10	0.72	0.00
	98	0.86	4.87	0.36	0.37	0.33	0.04	0.35	0.02	0.33	0.04	0.36	0.01
Government	88	1.14	4.51	0.38	0.65	0.52	0.13	0.63	0.02	0.58	0.07	0.64	0.01
	98	0.76	4.85	0.35	0.28	0.23	0.05	0.26	0.02	0.24	0.05	0.28	0.01
Public enter.	88	0.88	4.56	0.36	0.39	0.31	0.06	0.38	0.01	0.29	0.09	0.35	0.03
	98	0.80	5.45	0.37	0.33	0.27	0.06	0.31	0.02	0.25	0.08	0.31	0.02
Private sector	88	1.40	6.74	0.41	0.97	0.91	0.05	0.96	0.01	0.80	0.16	0.92	0.05
	98	0.91	4.50	0.36	0.42	0.39	0.03	0.41	0.01	0.38	0.04	0.40	0.01
Females													
Total	88	0.83	6.42	0.38	0.34	0.27	0.07	0.28	0.06	0.26	0.07	0.30	0.04
	98	1.06	6.80	0.42	0.56	0.50	0.05	0.49	0.06	0.52	0.04	0.54	0.02
Government	88	0.69	4.21	0.33	0.23	0.20	0.03	0.17	0.05	0.20	0.02	0.22	0.01
	98	1.02	4.82	0.38	0.52	0.48	0.04	0.46	0.06	0.49	0.02	0.49	0.02
Public enter.	88	0.90	8.02	0.43	0.42	0.35	0.06	0.25	0.17	0.28	0.14	0.28	0.14
	98	0.76	6.70	0.39	0.29	0.21	0.07	0.17	0.10	0.18	0.11	0.27	0.02
Private sector	88	0.83	6.83	0.39	0.35	0.23	0.11	0.33	0.02	0.29	0.05	0.27	0.07
	98	1.26	7.44	0.47	0.79	0.69	0.09	0.85	0.04	0.68	0.12	0.72	0.07
Quarterly Earnings													
Males													
Total	88	1.01	5.36	0.39	0.51	0.44	0.06	0.49	0.02	0.41	0.10	0.48	0.03
	98	1.27	4.88	0.36	0.31	0.27	0.03	0.29	0.02	0.27	0.03	0.29	0.01
Females													
Total	88	0.90	6.02	0.37	0.40	0.36	0.04	0.30	0.08	0.35	0.05	0.38	0.02
	98	0.74	4.91	0.36	0.27	0.24	0.03	0.21	0.06	0.24	0.04	0.25	0.02

Note: Coefficient of Variation=Standard of Deviation/mean; Decile Ratio=90th percentile/10th percentile; Due to rounding off error, the within and between components of the Generalized Entropy Index might not add up exactly to the total. Source: LFSS 88 and 98; own calculation.

collar premiums reported in the wage regression results above. Comparison of measures of inequality across sectors in 1998 also reveals that hourly wages are most compressed or equalized in the government sector, and most dispersed in public enterprises for men and the private sector for women.

These results, especially concerning the changes in inequality between 1988 and 1998, warrant further analysis. In particular, one needs to ascertain how much of the observed changes can be explained (in terms of changes in observable characteristics) and how much remains unexplained. Following the seminal work of Juhn, Murphy, and Pierce (1993), we break down the changes in male and female wage inequality between 1988 and 1998 into three components: a characteristics effect, which describes changes in inequality emanating from changes in the composition of characteristics such as experience, education, or sector over time; a coefficient effect, which describes changes in inequality due to changes in labor market characteristics; and a residual effect, which describes the changes in equality due to changes in the composition, or effects, of unobserved characteristics.

These effects can be calculated by comparing the distribution of the following variables:

$$y_{88,i} = \hat{\beta}_{88} x_{i,88} + \hat{\sigma}_{88} \hat{\varepsilon}_{88} \qquad (1)$$

$$y_{1,i} = \hat{\beta}_{88} x_{i,98} + \hat{\sigma}_{88} \hat{\varepsilon}_{98} \qquad (2)$$

$$y_{2,i} = \hat{\beta}_{88} x_{i,98} + \hat{\sigma}_{88} \hat{\varepsilon}_{98} \qquad (3)$$

$$y_{2,i} = \hat{\beta}_{88} x_{i,98} + \hat{\sigma}_{88} \hat{\varepsilon}_{98} \qquad (4)$$

Where ε = a standardized residual with mean 0 and variance 1, and σ = residual standard deviation of log hourly wages.

The characteristics effect is the difference between (1) and (2); the coefficient effect is the difference between (2) and (3); and the residual effect is the difference between (3) and (4). The results from this exercise for males and females separately are presented in Table 2.4. They confirm that the forces in the Egyptian labor market in the past decade had a different impact on male and female inequality.

For males, the overall change in inequality as measured by the decile ratio shows a decline in inequality. This is driven by an even larger decline in returns to coefficients (particularly returns to education and experience, as discussed in the above section). It was partially counteracted by the change in observed characteristics, which has an increasing impact on inequality. This is presumably due to the increasing share of private sector employment, where wage inequality measured by the decile ratio is much higher than in the public sector (see Table 2.4).

Table 2.4: Decomposition of Change in Wage Inequality

	Male		Female	
	1988	**1998**	**1988**	**1998**
Decile ratio	5.38	4.87	6.42	6.80
Change in decile ratio (1988–98)	-0.51		0.38	
Charateristics effect	0.32		2.94	
Coefficients effect	-0.68		-0.06	
Residual effect	-0.15		-2.50	

For females, on the other hand, the observed increase in overall inequality was driven by the underlying change in observed characteristics. The impact of the revaluation of coefficients was negligible. The change in the composition or effect of unobservables, as captured in the residuals effect, had also a strong decreasing effect on inequality, and tended to counteract (but not eliminate) the effect of changes in characteristics.

To sum up, the change in observed characteristics—including the shift to a larger share of the private sector in total employment—had an increasing impact on wage inequality over the past decade. For males, this has been sufficiently counteracted by the impact of devaluation in coefficients—mainly a decline in returns to education and experience—such that overall inequality has declined. For females, overall inequality still increased, because the large increase due to the characteristics effect was not sufficiently eroded by the decreasing impact from devaluation of coefficients or changes in unobservables (the residual effect).

Some questions remain: What are those unobservable characteristics that tended to equalize wages among females over the past decade, regardless of their observable personal and job attributes? Are wages equalized across jobs and individuals because of a perception among employers that females are costly or insufficiently attached to the labor force? Or is it a change in females' tastes or preferences for certain jobs or occupations that, by a clustering effect, tend to reduce wage dispersion among them? Answering these and other questions regarding recent developments in female wages, perhaps in comparison to that of males, constitutes an important direction for future research on the Egyptian labor market.

Conclusion

This chapter investigates the distributional and structural developments of hourly wages and quarterly earnings in Egypt between 1988 and 1998 on the basis of two nationwide labor force sample surveys, the LFSS 88 and the ELMS 98. The results highlight several important changes in the wage structure in Egypt over this decade, which witnessed further liberalization of the economy and the implementation of stabilization and privatization programs. These can be summarized as follows:

Wages have significantly declined in real terms over this period for almost all groups. The sharpest real-wage falls were for some of the traditionally higher-paid segments of the labor market, which implies a compression of the overall wage structure in Egypt over the past decade.

In line with this story of compression, there was a trend of devaluation of work experience in wage setting, and falling educational wage premiums for both males and females. The decline in returns to education took place for all but the lowest end (basic reading and writing skills or a primary-school education) and the highest end (study completion at a higher institute or at the university level) of the educational ladder. This also led to the narrowing of white-collar/blue-collar wage differentials.

The legacy of the public sector employment guarantee—and the predominance of the public sector as an employer—continues in the sense that the public sector still offers the highest rewards in the labor market for experience and education. This is particularly true for females, although the category of female white-collar vocational-school graduates witnessed large declines in returns to this level of education in the government sector in the 1990s.

Relative to the private sector, government workers are now in a weaker position in the labor market (the male wage disadvantage increased, and the female wage advantage decreased). In contrast, workers in the public enterprise sector are in a better relative position than they were in 1988, earning larger wage premiums.

Unexplained gender gaps are most compressed—almost non-existent—in the government. This has hardly changed from 1988 to 1998, which is consistent with the fact that the centralized compensation policy of the government has remained intact. Gender wage gaps remained the same in the private sector (at 25 percent), whereas in public enterprises they doubled (from 12 to 24 percent), reaching almost the same level as in the private sector. Again, the change in public enterprises is expected as they move away from institutional and uniform wage setting to more decentralized and private sector-like compensation practices. However, more research is needed to ascertain whether standard methods yield underestimates of unexplained gender gaps in the private sector, and whether the channels through which discrimination takes place there might have changed in recent years.

The union-wage differential has hardly changed over this 10-year period, which reflects two opposing trends: a rise in the public sector, consistent with attempts to elicit union support during privatization; and a fall in the private sector, indicative of a weakening in the bargaining power of organized workers, despite the recorded increase in total union membership.

Finally, the answer to whether or not wage inequality has been rising over the past decade in Egypt is negative for males and positive for females. Most of the observed inequality is within, as opposed to between, occupational, industrial, educational, and experience groups. Decomposition of observed inequality shows that for both males and females, the change in observed characteristics—including the shift to a larger share of the private sector in total employment—had an increasing impact on wage inequality over the past decade. For males, this has been sufficiently counteracted by the impact of devaluation in coefficients (mainly a decline in returns to education and experience), such that overall inequality has declined. For females, overall inequality still increased, because the large increase due to the characteristics effect was not sufficiently eroded by the decreasing impact from the devaluation of coefficients or changes in unobservables (residual effect).

It is worth stressing that not much can be inferred from the above results in terms of the incidence of poverty and the change in income distribution in Egypt over the past decade. For one thing, labor market surveys, like the two underlying the present study, tend to capture very few observations at both ends of the wage-distribution spectrum. Moreover, the decile ratio, our main chosen measure of inequality (on account of robustness to the presence of some extreme observations or outliers), by definition does not include the top and bottom 9 percent of the wage distribution. Finally, the data used only measures one type of income—wage income. Even setting aside problems of under-reporting of wages typical in labor force surveys, such surveys do not provide information on various transfers (usually important for lower-income groups) and capitalist income (important for higher-income groups).

With these caveats in mind, the main findings of the present study of wage-distribution changes in Egypt over the past decade can be stated as follows: Compared to 1988, there has been a tendency in the labor market for wageworkers toward an equalization of hourly wage outcomes at a lower standard of living (or real wages) for males. Females experienced less real-wage declines than their male counterparts and a higher dispersion, rather than a compression, of wages. As males constitute the majority of wage-workers, the past decade of stabilization and structural adjustment in Egypt can be said to have been, on average, one of real wage erosion and overall wage compression.

The findings of the paper point to several areas of possible future research on the topic of wage and earnings structure in Egypt:

One is to examine peculiarities in the pattern of adjustment in the government or civil service; the extent to which the legacy of the guarantee still influences wage setting; the favorable position of women there; and reasons for the weakening of wages relative to comparable private sector workers.

A second area worth examining is that of public enterprise workers during times of privatization. Why have their wage premiums increased, gender gaps widened, and male blue-collar wages improved relative to white-collar wages? What role, if any, have public sector unions played in these processes?

A third area relates to the reasons for, and implications of, the fall in returns to experience and education in all sectors in the economy. How did this affect skill and blue-collar/white-collar differentials? Why were the declines in returns to education limited to the preparatory and secondary levels? And how does this relate to the slowing down of the graduate public sector employment guarantee?

A fourth direction of research is to look at gender-related issues. These issues include the reasons for the apparent constancy of gender gaps in the private sector over the past decade; the different channels through which discrimination can take place (such as differences in returns to characteristics, payment of a pure rent component to males, occupational segregation, differences in pace of promotion, etc.); and factors responsible for increasing dispersion in female wages and their lower pay in the private and public enterprise sectors. The issue of wage versus earnings inequality deserves more detailed study in order to understand why wage inequality has declined for males, but not for females; why earning inequality has declined for both genders; and what accounts for the unexplained component of inequality changes.

Appendix

Table A2.1: Distribution of Real Average Hourly Wages and Quarterly Earnings Across Sectors and Occupations, 1988–98 (LE 1998 Prices)

Sector/ Occupation	Employment Occupational Distribution (%)				Wage and Earnings Ratios											
	Male		Female		1988/1998				Male/Female				Public/Private Hourly Wage			
	1988	1998	1988	1998	Real Hourly Wage		Real Quarterly Earnings		Real Hourly Wage		Real Quarterly Earnings		Male		Female	
					Male	Female	Male	Female	88	98	88	98	88	98	88	98
Government	**100.00**	**100.00**	**100.00**	**100.00**	**0.74**	**0.88**	**0.75**	**0.86**	**1.12**	**0.94**	**1.33**	**1.16**	**1.16**	**1.10**	**1.61**	**1.41**
Professional/ Technical	41.19	40.54	57.12	60.15	0.66	0.82	0.72	0.80	1.25	1.00	1.29	1.16	0.64	0.76	0.96	1.03
Managerial & Administrative	3.20	4.41	3.11	2.38	0.55	-	0.49	-	-	-	-	-	-	-	-	-
Clerical	18.57	21.35	36.06	33.14	0.70	0.86	0.71	0.86	1.23	1.00	1.47	1.22	0.83	0.80	1.02	0.71
Sales	0.54	0.75	0.49	0.00	-	-	-	-	-	-	-	-	-	-	-	-
Services	20.51	21.28	2.04	2.91		0.74	-	0.74	-	-	-	-	-	0.70	0.69	-
Agricultural workers	2.70	1.97	0.29	0.67	-	-	-	-	-	-	-	-	-	-	-	-
Production workers	13.30	9.70	0.89	0.76	0.73	-	0.72	-	-	-	-	-	0.93	0.93	-	-
Public Enterprise	**100.00**	**100.00**	**100.00**	**100.00**	**0.87**	**0.89**	**0.88**	**0.81**	**1.06**	**1.04**	**1.21**	**1.31**	**1.30**	**1.45**	**1.91**	**1.68**
Professional/ Technical	20.26	21.89	15.06	27.78	0.82	1.10	0.82	1.12	1.17	0.87	1.51	1.12	0.67	1.00	1.09	1.57
Managerial & Administrative	5.62	6.04	9.96	6.20	0.71	-	0.80	-	-	-	-	-	-	-	-	-
Clerical	12.71	12.63	38.98	37.88	1.03	0.85	0.92	0.84	0.97	1.18	1.19	1.30	0.99	1.40	1.53	1.05
Sales	3.72	4.17	6.59	3.14	-	-	-	-	-	-	-	-	-	-	-	-
Services	10.46	9.78	1.49	6.92	0.73	-	0.76	-	-	-	-	-	1.16	1.13	-	-
Agricultural workers	0.91	0.54	27.93	18.07	-	-	-	-	-	-	-	-	-	-	-	-
Production workers	46.31	44.94	-	-	0.76	1.76	0.77	1.23	1.56	0.68	1.70	1.06	1.08	1.12	-	-

(TableA2.1 continued)

Private Sector	**100.00**	**100.00**	**100.00**	**100.00**	**0.78**	**1.01**	**0.79**	**0.95**	**1.56**	**1.20**	**1.77**	**1.49**	-	-	-	-
Professional/ Technical	4.84	6.98	14.07	19.34	0.55	0.77	0.62	0.72	1.88	1.36	2.23	1.91	-	-	-	-
Managerial & Administrative	0.71	0.79	0.00	1.13	-	-	-	-	-	-	-	-	-	-	-	-
Clerical	1.40	2.32	8.29	11.61	0.72	1.23	0.67	0.99	1.50	0.88	1.46	0.99	-	-	-	-
Sales	7.74	9.02	8.30	11.37	0.78	0.66	0.78	0.88	1.83	2.16	2.62	2.32	-	-	-	-
Services	6.83	7.17	13.60	13.10	0.75	0.95	0.73	0.82	1.66	1.32	1.88	1.67	-	-	-	-
Agricultural workers	30.28	21.58	42.12	21.94	0.76	0.70	0.97	2.05	1.49	1.63	3.04	1.44	-	-	-	-
Production workers	48.19	52.13	13.61	21.50	0.73	0.80	0.83	0.77	1.69	1.55	1.53	1.67	-	-	-	-
All Sectors					0.69	0.88	0.72	0.80	1.24	0.98	1.40	1.25	-	-	-	-

Notes: '-' denote small sample sizes (less than 30 observations) All figures are averages of observations in the sample weighted by sample weights. 1988 figures are inflated to 1998 prices using the CPI (inflation factor from 1988 to 1998 is 3.19). Hourly wages are in 1998 LE/hour and quarterly earnings are the sum of wages from all primary and secondary jobs over the reference three months (in 1998 LE/3 reference months).

Source: LFSS 88 and ELMS 98 and IMF International Financial Statistics, for CPI: own calculation.

Table A2.2: Distribution of Real Average Hourly Wages and Quarterly Earnings Across Sectors and Levels of Education, 1988–98 (LE 1998 Prices)

Sector/ Education Level	Employment Occupational Distribution (%)				Wage and Earnings Ratios											
	Male		Female		1988/1998				Male/Female				Public/Private Hourly Wage			
	1988	1998	1988	1998	Real Hourly Wage		Real Quarterly Earnings		Real Hourly Wage		Real Quarterly Earnings		Male		Female	
					Male	Female	Male	Female	88	98	88	98	88	98	88	98
Government	**100.00**	**100.00**	**100.00**	**100.00**	-	-	-	-	-	-	-	-	-	-	-	-
Illiterate	13.96	8.26	3.66	2.29	0.74	-	0.72	-	-	-	-	-	0.71	0.78	-	-
Read & write	16.14	9.72	0.81	0.90	0.65	-	0.69	-	-	-	-	-	0.91	0.65	-	-
Primary	7.10	10.07	0.90	1.07	0.63	1.23	0.64	1.18	3.07	1.57	3.12	1.68	1.15	0.89	0.47	0.83
Preparatory	3.79	4.49	1.97	1.58	0.67	1.25	0.73	1.15	1.28	0.68	1.56	0.99	1.20	0.89	0.91	1.05
Blue-collar secondary	11.44	14.78	3.32	4.88	0.72	0.79	0.74	0.82	1.34	1.22	1.48	1.35	0.76	0.98	3.19	-
White-collar secondary	9.53	11.99	37.49	28.76	0.72	0.73	0.74	0.79	0.97	0.96	1.18	1.09	0.59	0.95	0.95	-
General secondary	2.71	0.95	0.98	1.02	0.84	1.11	0.82	1.08	1.13	0.85	1.32	1.00	1.06	0.86	1.20	-
Higher than intermediate	8.59	10.88	18.03	21.57	0.67	0.74	0.80	0.68	1.08	0.98	0.96	1.14	0.77	0.86	-	-
University	21.93	26.37	28.74	36.31	0.74	0.88	0.72	0.89	1.22	1.02	1.52	1.24	0.62	0.86	0.81	0.95
Post-graduate	4.81	2.49	4.09	1.62	0.49	-	0.59	-	-	-	-	-	-	-	-	-

(TableA2.2 continued)

Public Enterprise	**100.00**	**100.00**	**100.00**	**100.00**	-	-	-	-	-	-	-	-	-	-	-	-
Illiterate	18.74	8.73	5.29	3.58	0.59	-	0.71	-	-	-	-	-	1.13	0.98	-	-
Read & write	22.51	17.35	3.09	0.00	0.68	-	0.68	-	-	-	-	-	1.16	0.87	-	-
Primary	9.45	14.71	7.76	4.82	0.87	-	0.81	1.00	1.22	0.98	1.25	1.01	1.22	1.30	1.06	1.12
Preparatory	7.98	8.30	5.45	10.19	0.85	-	0.82	0.41	4.54	-	1.62	3.19	1.19	1.12	1.17	1.00
Blue collar secondary	13.42	21.09	4.35	2.76	0.75	-	0.71	0.83	1.40	-	1.41	1.21	1.12	1.50	1.84	-
White-collar secondary	5.29	4.84	43.71	42.61	0.67	-	0.67	0.41	1.46	-	0.76	1.23	0.98	1.47	2.06	-
General secondary	2.56	1.59	5.58	2.33	-	-	-	-	0.99	1.23	1.12	2.09	1.15	1.98	1.21	-
Higher than intermediate	2.92	5.94	3.38	6.53	0.78	-	0.80	-	-	-	-	-	1.19	1.53	-	-
University	15.59	16.50	21.39	27.17	-	-	-	-	-	-	-	-	-	-	-	-
Post-graduate	1.55	0.95	0.00	0.00	0.86	-	0.87	-	-	-	-	-	0.84	1.35	-	-
Private Sector	**100.00**	**100.00**	**100.00**	**100.00**	-	-	-	-	-	-	-	-	-	-	-	-
Illiterate	42.26	33.32	55.90	38.48	0.69	0.76	0.84	0.86	1.73	1.56	1.75	1.71	-	-	-	-
Read & write	17.94	13.71	7.59	6.20	0.92	-	0.80	-	-	-	-	-	-	-	-	-
Primary	11.97	16.03	5.89	8.48	0.81	0.70	0.76	0.89	1.26	1.46	2.11	1.82	-	-	-	-
Preparatory	9.34	6.39	4.13	1.25	0.90	1.08	0.96	0.68	0.98	0.81	1.78	2.52	-	-	-	-
Blue-collar secondary	6.12	14.40	2.31	4.91	0.56	-	-	0.62	5.59	-	1.42	-	-	-	-	-
White-collar secondary	3.97	5.23	9.24	16.55	0.45	-	-	0.95	1.57	-	1.61	-	-	-	-	-
General secondary	2.09	0.63	2.16	0.00	-	1.27	-	1.58	-	-	-	-	-	-	-	-
Higher than intermediate	1.69	3.15	1.99	6.05	0.60	-	0.77	-	-	-	-	-	-	-	-	-
University	4.37	6.85	10.19	18.06	-	-	-	-	-	-	-	-	-	-	-	-
Post-graduate	0.26	0.30	0.61	0.00	0.54	0.75	0.56	0.76	1.58	1.13	1.71	1.26	-	-	-	-

Notes: '-' denote small sample sizes (less than 30 observations). All figures are averages of observations in the sample weighted by sample weights. 1988 figures are inflated to 1998 prices using the CPI (inflation factor from 1988 to 1998 is 3.19). Hourly wages are in 1998 LE/hour and quarterly earnings are the sum of wages from all primary and secondary jobs over the reference three months (in 1998 LE/3 reference months).
Source: LFSS 88 and ELMS 98 and IMF International Financial Statistics, for CPI: own calculation.

Table A2.3: Real Average Hourly Wages and Quarterly Earnings By Broad Occupational and Sector of Economic Activity, 1988–98 (LE 1998 Prices)

	Distribution of Employment (in %)							
	Agriculture		Industry		Services		Total	
	1988	1998	1988	1998	1988	1998	1988	1998
White collar	5.8	7.58	21.92	22.12	64.94	67.19	40.98	46.84
Blue collar	94.2	92.42	78.08	77.88	35.06	32.81	59.02	53.16
White collar	100.00	100.00	100.00	100.00	100.00	100.00	100.00	100.00
Union	49.83	67.77	64.81	50.14	52.40	56.88	54.38	56.16
Not unionized	50.17	32.23	35.19	49.86	47.60	43.12	45.62	43.84
Blue collar	100.00	100.00	100.00	100.00	100.00	100.00	100.00	100.00
Union	4.47	4.67	20.88	9.49	26.33	18.25	17.79	11.66
Not unionized	95.53	95.33	79.12	90.51	73.67	81.75	82.21	88.34
Regular	11.04	26.34	63.77	67.28	87.41	90.47	55.70	67.14
Irregular	88.96	73.66	36.23	32.72	12.59	9.53	44.30	32.86
In establishment	5.81	9.96	70.26	65.18	80.53	79.88	54.74	58.99
Out of establishment	94.19	90.04	29.74	34.82	19.47	20.12	45.26	41.01

(TableA2.3 continued)

	1988/1998 Ratios							
	Agriculture		Industry		Services		Total	
	Hourly Wages	Quarterly Earnings	Hourly Wages	Quarterly Earnings	Hourly Wages	Quarterly Earnings	Hourly Wages	Quarterly Earnings
White collar	0.71	0.92	0.72	0.72	0.70	0.70	0.69	0.70
Blue collar	0.77	0.98	0.71	0.78	0.79	0.76	0.76	0.78
White collar								
union	0.79	1.01	0.76	0.77	0.66	0.68	0.67	0.68
Not unionized	0.46	0.58	0.76	0.74	0.73	0.72	0.73	0.73
Blue collar								
union	0.76	1.00	0.76	0.76	0.82	0.84	0.78	0.80
Not unionized	0.77	0.99	0.73	0.86	0.80	0.76	0.77	0.82
Regular	0.77	0.79	0.73	0.78	0.75	0.77	0.73	0.77
Irregular	0.77	0.79	0.68	0.79	1.16	1.20	0.79	0.82
In establishment	0.77	0.77	0.77	0.77	0.71	0.70	0.74	0.74
Out of establishment	0.77	1.20	0.60	0.98	1.05	1.03	0.78	1.03

Source: 1988 Labor Force Sample Survey and 1998 Egyptian Labor Sample Survey and IMF International Financial Statistics, for CPI: own calculation.

Table A2.4a: Means and Standard Deviations of Variables by Sector and Gender, 1988

Variable	Male							
	Government		Public Enterprise		Private		Total	
	Mean	SD	Mean	SD	Mean	SD	Mean	SD
Hourly wage	0.72	0.76	0.81	0.68	0.62	0.83	1.68	1.59
Log hourly wage	-0.58	0.66	-0.43	0.62	-0.81	0.83	0.28	0.68
Quarterly earnings	381.72	329.51	478.72	328.58	396.08	506.77	954.80	752.40
Experience	19.43	11.98	20.57	11.33	13.52	12.98	17.42	12.81
Experience2	520.97	547.25	551.29	513.69	351.21	614.90	467.56	583.91
Illiterate	0.13	0.33	0.19	0.39	0.41	0.49	0.16	0.37
Read and write	0.16	0.36	0.24	0.43	0.18	0.39	0.09	0.28
Primary	0.07	0.25	0.10	0.30	0.12	0.33	0.11	0.32
Preparatory	0.04	0.20	0.08	0.27	0.10	0.30	0.05	0.23
Blue-collar secondary	0.12	0.33	0.13	0.34	0.06	0.24	0.14	0.34
White-collar secondary	0.09	0.29	0.06	0.23	0.04	0.19	0.12	0.33
General secondary	0.03	0.17	0.03	0.16	0.02	0.14	0.01	0.10
Higher institute	0.08	0.28	0.03	0.17	0.02	0.13	0.09	0.28
University	0.22	0.41	0.14	0.35	0.04	0.20	0.20	0.40
Above university	0.05	0.22	0.01	0.11	0.00	0.05	0.01	0.11
Greater Cairo	0.23	0.42	0.38	0.49	0.27	0.44	0.22	0.41
Alexandria and Canal cities	0.08	0.27	0.20	0.40	0.09	0.29	0.13	0.34
Urban Lower Egypt	0.15	0.35	0.14	0.34	0.14	0.34	0.16	0.37
Urban Upper Egypt	0.18	0.38	0.05	0.21	0.08	0.27	0.19	0.39
Rural Lower Egypt	0.22	0.41	0.17	0.37	0.23	0.42	0.19	0.39
Rural Upper Egypt	0.15	0.36	0.07	0.25	0.19	0.39	0.11	0.32
Married	0.83	0.38	0.82	0.39	0.43	0.50	0.65	0.48
Blue collar	0.35	0.48	0.59	0.49	0.85	0.36	0.48	0.50
Agriculture	0.04	0.21	0.02	0.15	0.27	0.44	0.09	0.28
Industry	0.06	0.24	0.73	0.44	0.42	0.49	0.29	0.45
Services	0.89	0.31	0.25	0.43	0.32	0.46	0.63	0.48
Unionized	0.55	0.50	0.64	0.48	0.10	0.30	0.37	0.48
Out of establishment	0.00	0.00	0.00	0.00	0.53	0.50	0.19	0.39
Large establishment	0.00	0.00	0.00	0.04	0.05	0.22	0.06	0.24
Irregular worker	0.00	0.07	0.01	0.10	0.54	0.50	0.15	0.36
Government							0.45	0.50
Public enterprises							0.10	0.30
Private enterprise							0.45	0.50
Female							0.22	0.41
Sample size	1166		594		1847		4837	

Note: With the exception of hourly wages, quarterly earnings, and the experience variables, all variables in the above table are dummies, therefore the mean refers to the percentage of the relevant variable in the sample.

Table A2.4b: Means and Standard Deviations of Variables by Sector and Gender, 1988

Variable	Female							
	Government		Public Enterprise		Private		Total	
	Mean	SD	Mean	SD	Mean	SD	Mean	SD
Hourly wage	0.64	0.45	0.76	0.67	0.40	0.33	1.68	1.59
Log hourly wage	-0.63	0.62	-0.59	0.83	-1.20	0.78	0.28	0.68
Quarterly earnings	287.28	212.09	396.87	328.38	223.26	247.14	954.80	752.40
Experience	10.10	8.46	11.94	8.77	8.48	10.11	17.42	12.81
Experience2	173.32	259.81	218.72	255.92	173.94	387.61	467.56	583.91
Illiterate	0.04	0.19	0.07	0.25	0.55	0.50	0.16	0.37
Read and write	0.01	0.10	0.03	0.17	0.08	0.27	0.09	0.28
Primary	0.01	0.08	0.09	0.28	0.06	0.24	0.11	0.32
Preparatory	0.02	0.14	0.06	0.24	0.04	0.20	0.05	0.23
Blue-collar secondary	0.03	0.17	0.04	0.19	0.03	0.16	0.14	0.34
White-collar secondary	0.36	0.48	0.43	0.50	0.09	0.29	0.12	0.33
General secondary	0.01	0.12	0.06	0.24	0.02	0.14	0.01	0.10
Higher institute	0.17	0.37	0.03	0.17	0.02	0.15	0.09	0.28
University	0.27	0.44	0.20	0.40	0.09	0.29	0.20	0.40
Above university	0.03	0.18	0.00	0.00	0.01	0.08	0.01	0.11
Greater Cairo	0.30	0.46	0.53	0.50	0.28	0.45	0.22	0.41
Alexandria and Canal cities	0.16	0.36	0.21	0.41	0.10	0.30	0.13	0.34
Urban Lower Egypt	0.22	0.42	0.15	0.35	0.09	0.28	0.16	0.37
Urban Upper Egypt	0.16	0.36	0.02	0.14	0.03	0.17	0.19	0.39
Rural Lower Egypt	0.14	0.35	0.04	0.19	0.38	0.49	0.19	0.39
Rural Upper Egypt	0.03	0.16	0.05	0.22	0.12	0.33	0.11	0.32
Married	0.68	0.47	0.59	0.49	0.29	0.45	0.65	0.48
Blue collar	0.04	0.20	0.32	0.47	0.70	0.46	0.48	0.50
Agriculture	0.03	0.16	0.01	0.10	0.44	0.50	0.09	0.28
Industry	0.01	0.12	0.64	0.48	0.14	0.35	0.29	0.45
Services	0.96	0.19	0.35	0.48	0.42	0.49	0.63	0.48
Unionized	0.55	0.50	0.50	0.50	0.07	0.26	0.37	0.48
Out of establishment	0.00	0.00	0.00	0.00	0.56	0.50	0.19	0.39
Large establishment	0.00	0.00	0.00	0.00	0.07	0.25	0.06	0.24
Irregular worker	0.00	0.00	0.00	0.00	0.50	0.50	0.15	0.36
Government							0.45	0.50
Public enterprises							0.10	0.30
Private enterprise							0.45	0.50
Female							0.22	0.41
Sample size	515		103		309		4837	

Note: With the exception of hourly wages, quarterly earnings, and the experience variables, all variables in the above table are dummies, therefore the mean refers to the percentage of the relevant variable in the sample.

Table A2.5a: Means and Standard Deviations of Variables by Sector and Gender, 1998

	Male							
Variable	**Government**		**Public Enterprise**		**Private**		**Total**	
	Mean	**SD**	**Mean**	**S.D.**	**Mean**	**SD**	**Mean**	**SD**
Hourly wage	1.69	1.32	2.24	1.84	1.54	1.55	1.68	1.59
Log hourly wage	0.31	0.63	0.57	0.66	0.20	0.66	0.28	0.68
Quarterly earnings	915.15	663.82	1342.99	1023.36	1003.30	822.00	954.80	752.40
Experience	21.06	11.99	23.26	12.12	15.76	13.60	17.42	12.81
Experience2	587.20	563.10	687.50	587.86	433.06	655.71	467.56	583.91
Illiterate	0.07	0.26	0.09	0.29	0.28	0.45	0.16	0.37
Read and write	0.07	0.26	0.14	0.35	0.13	0.33	0.09	0.28
Primary	0.09	0.28	0.14	0.35	0.17	0.38	0.11	0.32
Preparatory	0.05	0.21	0.08	0.28	0.07	0.25	0.05	0.23
Blue-collar secondary	0.15	0.35	0.20	0.40	0.16	0.36	0.14	0.34
White-collar secondary	0.12	0.32	0.06	0.24	0.06	0.23	0.12	0.33
General secondary	0.01	0.11	0.02	0.14	0.01	0.08	0.01	0.10
Higher institute	0.11	0.32	0.07	0.26	0.03	0.18	0.09	0.28
University	0.29	0.46	0.17	0.38	0.08	0.27	0.20	0.40
Above university	0.03	0.16	0.01	0.11	0.00	0.06	0.01	0.11
Greater Cairo	0.17	0.38	0.27	0.45	0.22	0.41	0.22	0.41
Alexandria and Canal cities	0.10	0.29	0.26	0.44	0.12	0.33	0.13	0.34
Urban Lower Egypt	0.17	0.38	0.13	0.33	0.15	0.35	0.16	0.37
Urban Upper Egypt	0.24	0.43	0.13	0.34	0.14	0.35	0.19	0.39
Rural Lower Egypt	0.21	0.41	0.10	0.30	0.22	0.41	0.19	0.39
Rural Upper Egypt	0.11	0.31	0.11	0.31	0.15	0.36	0.11	0.32
Married	0.81	0.39	0.82	0.39	0.49	0.50	0.65	0.48
Blue collar	0.29	0.45	0.51	0.50	0.78	0.41	0.48	0.50
Agriculture	0.02	0.15	0.02	0.14	0.17	0.38	0.09	0.28
Industry	0.06	0.23	0.75	0.44	0.45	0.50	0.29	0.45
Services	0.92	0.27	0.23	0.42	0.38	0.48	0.63	0.48
Unionized	0.58	0.49	0.49	0.50	0.11	0.31	0.37	0.48
Out of establishment	0.00	0.00	0.00	0.00	0.44	0.50	0.19	0.39
Large establishment	0.00	0.00	0.00	0.00	0.12	0.33	0.06	0.24
Irregular worker	0.00	0.07	0.00	0.05	0.36	0.48	0.15	0.36
Government							0.45	0.50
Public enterprises							0.10	0.30
Private enterprise							0.45	0.50
Female							0.22	0.41
Sample size	1433		433		1932		4837	

Note: With the exception of hourly wages, quarterly earnings, and the experience variables, all variables in the above table are dummies, therefore the mean refers to the percentage of the relevant variable in the sample.

Table A2.5b: Means and Standard Deviations of Variables by Sector and Gender, 1998

Variable	Female							
	Government		Public Enterprise		Private		Total	
	Mean	SD	Mean	SD	Mean	SD	Mean	SD
Hourly wage	1.80	1.85	2.16	1.73	1.28	1.70	1.68	1.59
Log hourly wage	0.35	0.65	0.50	0.76	-0.15	0.83	0.28	0.68
Quarterly earnings	796.82	529.34	1026.56	624.81	674.00	658.79	954.80	752.40
Experience	14.44	9.75	17.16	10.66	7.61	9.66	17.42	12.81
Experience2	303.25	347.60	406.13	402.61	150.86	346.14	467.56	583.91
Illiterate	0.02	0.13	0.04	0.19	0.30	0.46	0.16	0.37
Read and write	0.01	0.09	0.00	0.00	0.04	0.21	0.09	0.28
Primary	0.01	0.09	0.02	0.13	0.09	0.29	0.11	0.32
Preparatory	0.02	0.13	0.09	0.29	0.02	0.13	0.05	0.23
Blue-collar secondary	0.05	0.21	0.04	0.19	0.06	0.25	0.14	0.34
White-collar secondary	0.29	0.45	0.44	0.50	0.20	0.40	0.12	0.33
General secondary	0.01	0.08	0.04	0.19	0.00	0.00	0.01	0.10
Higher institute	0.18	0.39	0.07	0.26	0.07	0.25	0.09	0.28
University	0.37	0.48	0.27	0.45	0.20	0.40	0.20	0.40
Above university	0.02	0.13	0.00	0.00	0.00	0.00	0.01	0.11
Greater Cairo	0.22	0.41	0.50	0.50	0.41	0.49	0.22	0.41
Alexandria and Canal cities	0.14	0.35	0.23	0.43	0.10	0.30	0.13	0.34
Urban Lower Egypt	0.21	0.41	0.13	0.33	0.14	0.34	0.16	0.37
Urban Upper Egypt	0.28	0.45	0.05	0.23	0.10	0.30	0.19	0.39
Rural Lower Egypt	0.12	0.33	0.04	0.19	0.15	0.36	0.19	0.39
Rural Upper Egypt	0.03	0.18	0.05	0.23	0.10	0.30	0.11	0.32
Married	0.75	0.44	0.66	0.48	0.26	0.44	0.65	0.48
Blue collar	0.04	0.18	0.20	0.40	0.52	0.50	0.48	0.50
Agriculture	0.01	0.10	0.00	0.00	0.13	0.33	0.09	0.28
Industry	0.02	0.13	0.64	0.48	0.27	0.45	0.29	0.45
Services	0.97	0.17	0.36	0.48	0.60	0.49	0.63	0.48
Unionized	0.64	0.48	0.46	0.50	0.13	0.33	0.37	0.48
Out of establishment	0.00	0.00	0.00	0.00	0.22	0.41	0.19	0.39
Large establishment	0.00	0.00	0.00	0.00	0.20	0.40	0.06	0.24
Irregular worker	0.00	0.04	0.02	0.13	0.17	0.37	0.15	0.36
Government							0.45	0.50
Public enterprises							0.10	0.30
Private enterprise							0.45	0.50
Female							0.22	0.41
Sample size	764		56		219		4837	

Note: With the exception of hourly wages, quarterly earnings, and the experience variables, all variables in the above table are dummies, therefore the mean refers to the percentage of the relevant variable in the sample.

Part II. The Role of the Informal Sector

3 The Labor Absorption Capacity of the Informal Sector in Egypt

Alia El Mahdi

Introduction

The immediate implications of Egypt's Economic Reform and Structural Adjustment Program on the labor market can be summed up in the following points: First, the public sector which until then had the highest employment-absorptive capacity, compared to both the private nonagricultural and the agricultural sectors, experienced a declining growth rate (El Mahdi, 1997), thereby affecting the overall employment growth rate in Egypt. Second, the real wages in the beginning of the 1990s were declining steadily in the public sector, to the extent that they became less than two-thirds of the real wage levels at the end of the 1970s. Third, new graduates entering the labor market encountered severe difficulties finding jobs. Because of this, unemployment rates started to increase, particularly among those 20 to 30 years old.

Finally, female graduates faced a more difficult situation, since the public sector had been their major job provider since the 1960s. Data shows that the private sector was unable to compensate for the diminishing role of the public sector, especially in the area of providing work for female new entrants to the labor market. The intensity of the obstacles facing females in the labor market is expected to increase with the continuation of the privatization process, and the tendency to reduce public sector hiring. This new trend towards the reduction of public hiring will have a strong negative impact on female employment as the majority of female workers have usually been employed in the government and public sectors. Furthermore the privatized companies tend to try to reduce the female workforce among their ranks by offering them different early retiring schemes.

1. The Interest in Informal Sector Activities

Ever since the International Conference of Labor Statisticians (ILO) became concerned with the role and magnitude of the informal activities—especially in less-developed countries—scholars have been increasingly eager to study and understand the dynamics of this sector, its interrelationships, and its work conditions.

Only a few studies on informal employment have been conducted in Egypt, but they lacked coordination, continuity, and coverage of a wide geographical area. These traits distinguish this current study from its predecessors. Since the 1998 Egypt Labor Market Study (ELMS 98) was conducted exactly 10 years after the 1988 Labor Force Sample Survey (LFSS 88) with almost exactly the same sets of questions, it enables us to examine the different aspects of change over a time span that witnessed significant structural adjustments. We can therefore attempt to assess the impact of change on the labor market especially on its informal segment.

Our primary focus is on the ways the private informal sector responded to these structural changes. Was it able to absorb an increasing number of workers, and therefore, serve as a sufficient replacement to the diminishing role of the public sector? Or did the private formal sector fulfill this role successfully, and thus succeed in replacing the declining role of public hiring?

2. Objectives of the Study

The aim is to investigate the changing role of the informal sector in providing work opportunities to Egypt's growing labor force between 1988 and 1998. To analyze the impact of the informal sector, we will study two types of participants in the labor market who appear in the household data as either: a) wageworkers, whether in the formal or informal sector; or b) employers and the self-employed.

Several questions are raised in this context:

1. To what extent was the informal sector able to absorb labor in the Egyptian market? Compared to 1988, did the magnitude of absorption increase or decrease by the end of 1998?
2. To what extent are the informal entrepreneurs and the informal workers represented in the groups of self-employed and employers, and of employees, respectively?
3. Are the informal or small-scale enterprises examples of family enterprises, where the majority of the workers are members of the household (whether paid or nonpaid)? Or do they employ outsiders and pay them according to market rules?
4. Are the informal enterprises concentrated in certain economic activities? Or are they spread over the same activities as the formal ones?

5. Are informal enterprises characterized by their limited capital, in comparison to formal enterprises? Do informal enterprises face special difficulties in acquiring their starting capital?
6. Is the limitation of capital reflected in the size of enterprise as measured in terms of number of workers? Or is it in the productivity of labor and in the wage levels?
7. How are the informal enterprises connected dynamically to the other sectors of the economy? What kind of economic ties exist between the informal sector and the rest of economy?
8. Do informal entrepreneurs and workers hold second jobs in the formal sectors? Were they previously engaged in work in those sectors?

These and other questions were posed at the beginning of this study. It is important to note, as we explore changes in the informal sector, that the literature on the informal economy pinpoints certain realities—based on empirical research—which pervade and characterize it:

(a) The informal sector is the sector of the poor. The definition of poverty could now very well expand to include new aspects in addition to low income, such as modest skills, quality of products or services, living conditions, and education.
(b) Employment in the informal sector is mostly of a temporary nature; the turnover rate of informal workers is high.
(c) Work conditions are poor in the informal sector in the sense that workers are not socially or medically insured, employers are not bound by a contract with their workers, and the work environment is usually not safe.
(d) Due to the regulatory constraints imposed by the government which make it difficult for the small enterprises to register or function on a formal basis, the informal enterprises usually remain small in size (in terms of labor and capital), and their ability to expand is limited unless they can become formal units.

Given the previous assumptions—which are based on findings from previous empirical research in several developing countries—and the questions raised by the researcher, this study aims to test the above-mentioned assumptions and to provide answers to those questions. The main intent is to draw a profile of the informal economy in Egypt and to understand how it has responded to the structural changes that have taken place over the last 10 years

3. Methodology

Every individual in the household (six years or older) who was either self-employed, an employer, or a worker in the private or public sector have been included in the following two sections. Individuals engaged in agricultural, subsistence, or home-based activities are not included in the analysis. In addition, only individuals who proved to have worked within the last three months before the survey, for more than 25 hours per week, are included in the following analysis and comparisons.

Part 1 will be concerned with the employees or workers. The aim is to distinguish formal and informal workers to see whether there are: a) changes in their numbers between the two surveys; b) clear differences in their educational backgrounds, experience, the settings in which they are working, and their earnings.

As to the distinction between formal and informal workers, two criteria are considered essential: contract availability and social security coverage of the employees. Accordingly, if the two conditions, or at least the availability of a contract, were satisfied, the employee is considered formally employed.

Part 2 will deal with the formal and informal self-employed or employer (SE/E). The objective of the study is to understand the main characteristics of the informal enterprises, their links, and their inherent dynamics.

The distinction between the formal and informal self-employed or employer in the ELMS 98 study depends on the compliance of the enterprise to certain rules that imply formality, namely the availability of a license, the commercial or industrial register (in case they are required), and the regular keeping of accounts. If these conditions have all been met, the enterprise is considered formal in nature, while the partial compliance with or the disregard of these conditions would indicate a state of informality.

4. The Growing Pool of Informal Workers

Egypt's working population was estimated at 16.1 million in October 1998, with an increase above the LFSS 88 figure (14.26 million) of nearly 1.88 million workers (13.2 percent). Table 3.1 shows the distribution of the economically active population according to employment status in 1988 and 1998.

It is clear that within the last 10 years, the relative proportion of wage-workers grew from 45.7 percent of the workforce in 1988 to 52 percent of the workforce in 1998. On the other hand, the share of non-paid family workers has remained in the range of 30–32 percent in those two years. As to the self-employed and employers category, it is clear that its relative proportion declined between the two years (from 24.2 percent in 1988 to 15.7 percent in 1988).

The changes that took place show that the workforce has been growing in the direction of more wageworkers and stable non-paid family workers, with a decline in the share of the self-employed and employers. This change could indicate that being an entrepreneur is becoming increasingly difficult, especially in an open and competitive market.

Table 3.1: Distribution of the Work Force According to Employment Status

Employment Status	1998			1988		
	Male Col%	Fem. Col%	Tot. Col%	Male Col%	Fem. Col%	Tot. Col%
Wageworkers	68.9	25.3	52.0	56.7	26.0	45.7
Employers	13.4	0.9	8.5	18.9	7.3	14.7
Self-employed	9.6	3.4	7.2	6.8	14.6	9.5
Non-paid family workers	8.1	70.4	32.2	17.7	52.2	30.0
	100.0	100.0	99.9	100.1	100.1	100.0
Total	**4456**	**1210**	**5666**	**4164**	**1208**	**5372**

The data used in Section 4 is that of the nonagricultural workers who proved to be working in their basic jobs during the last three months before the beginning of the ELMS 98 study.

The number of nonagricultural wageworkers (NAWW) in 1998 was estimated at nearly 9.8 million (see Table A3.1). Within this number, 34.7 percent of the NAWW (3.4 million) work on an informal basis, and 20.3 percent (2 million) are females.

Among NAWW in 1998, the private sector's employment was estimated at 4 million workers, representing 41 percent of the total NAWW. In contrast, the 1988 figures were estimated to be 2.79 million, though the percentage of private workers to the total NAWW was nearly the same (41.4 percent of the total NAWW).

Furthermore, private informal employment represented 80.8 percent of the total private NAWW in 1998, indicating a very slight decrease in their share of total private NAWW, as compared to the 1988 data, where the informal NAWW represented 81.3 percent of the total private NAWW.

The following subsections will include a more detailed discussion of the main characteristics and differences of the formal/informal dichotomy of the Egyptian labor market.

4.1 The Age and Gender of the NAWW

Table 3.2 summarizes several major features of NAWW in Egypt: (i) The percentage of formal NAWW is evidently higher (65.4 percent) than that of the informal workers, which could be explained by the still-dominant role of the government in the nonagricultural labor market; (ii) the representation of female workers within the group of formal employment (25.8 percent) is clearly higher than in informal employment, where female workers do not exceed 10 percent.

Children between the ages of 6 and 14 who are NAWW cannot be observed in the formal workers group, but their percentage rose close to 3.2 percent of the total informal workers. Girls younger than 15 represent 7.8 percent of the total informal female workers, while boys who work on an informal basis do not exceed more than 2.8 percent of the total informal male workers.

Table 3.2: Distribution of Workers According to Formality, Gender, and Age Groups in 1998

Age Group	Male			Female			Total		
	F Col%	IF Col%	%F of Total Row	F Col%	IF Col%	%F of Total Row	F Col%	IF Col%	%F of Total Row
06–11	0.0	0.1	0.0	0.0	1.7	0.0	0.0	0.2	0.0
12–14	0.0	2.7	0.0	0.0	6.1	0.0	0.0	3.1	0.0
15–19	0.6	19.2	4.8	1.1	21.1	19.8	0.7	19.4	6.7
20–29	17.3	37.7	41.6	21.1	44.8	69.6	18.2	38.4	47.2
30–39	29.8	22.4	67.5	40.2	18.1	91.6	32.5	21.9	73.7
40–49	30.7	10.8	81.6	25.5	2.8	97.8	29.3	10.0	84.7
50–59	19.9	4.8	86.5	11.3	4.9	91.9	17.7	4.8	87.4
60–64	1.6	1.1	69.0	0.8	0.6	86.5	1.4	1.1	71.1
=>65	0.1	1.2	15.9	0.0	0.0	0.0	0.1	1.1	15.9
	100.0	100.0		100.0	100.0		100.0	100.0	65.4
Total	**2086**	**1254**		**851**	**150**		**2937**	**1404**	

If the following figures are compared to those found in the LFSS 88, a few relevant changes are noticeable (see Table A3.2). In summary, (i) the number of NAWW increased from 6.7 million workers in 1988 to 9.8 million workers in 1998; (ii) the increase in the number of formal workers in 1998 (55 percent) over those counted in the LFSS 88 study is larger than that of the informal workers (30.7 percent); (iii) the main increase in the female workforce was in the formal sector, just as it was for the male workers; (iv) the percentage of children participating in the informal workforce in 1988 was 10.7 percent; it dropped to 3.2 percent in 1998. This change indicates a clear trend toward limiting the engagement of children (6 to 14 year-olds) in the informal labor market.

4.2 Educational Attainment

The available data confirms that the informal sector has provided a convenient market for those individuals with less chances of finding work in the public sector, primarily those with low levels of education. Table 3.3 shows the distribution of workers according to different levels of education.

Table 3.3: Distribution of Workers According to Formality and Educational Attainment in 1998

Education	Male			Female			Total		
	F Col%	IF Col%	%F of Total Row	F Col%	IF Col%	%F of Total Row	F Col%	IF Col%	%F of Total Row
Illiterate	7.1	30.0	27.0	2.0	31.2	23.9	5.8	30.1	26.7
Read & write	11.4	14.2	55.6	0.7	5.8	35.7	8.6	13.4	55.0
Less than intermediate	16.7	26.9	49.2	4.0	12.5	60.9	13.4	25.5	49.9
Intermediate	28.7	21.8	67.3	38.5	31.6	85.6	31.3	22.8	72.2
Higher than intermediate	9.9	2.5	86.2	18.5	6.8	93.0	12.1	2.9	88.8
University	24.2	4.4	89.5	35.0	12.1	93.4	27.0	5.2	90.8
Post-graduate	2.0	0.2	93.4	1.4	0.0	0.0	1.9	0.2	94.6
	100.0	100.0		100.0	100.0		100.0	100.0	65.5
Total	**2085**	**1247**		**851**	**149**		**2936**	**1396**	

The distinction between formal and informal workers is clear in the following areas:

Education. The formal workers have visibly higher educational levels than the informal workers. Whereas the percentage of illiterates in formal employment does not exceed 6 percent, it rises to 30 percent of the total informal workers. Conversely, those workers with university or higher degrees represent nearly 29 percent of formal workers. For informal workers, it is only a fraction of that percentage (5.4 percent).

Female education. Within the group of formal workers, females are better-educated. There is a smaller percentage of illiterates and a higher percentage of university graduates in formal employment. This phenomenon is not visible with informal workers. This could be explained by the fact that employment opportunities were available for female high school and university graduates, especially in the government and the public sector—at least until the beginning of the 1990s. This means that education was a necessary condition for hiring females in a formal way, while it was less important in the case of male applicants.

Female university graduates. The informal market provided work for a significantly higher percentage of female university graduates by the end of the 1990s. One possible explanation for this high percentage of female graduates working on an informal basis is the difficulty they had accessing the formal market when they needed work. By the end of the 1990s, the public sector was no longer providing jobs to the majority of educated women who were compelled to seek work in the informal sector.

Educational attainment. When we compare the ELMS 98 data with the LFSS 88 findings in educational attainment (see Table A3.3), we see a trend toward improvement. The educational levels of workers (males and females) have improved within the last 10 years. This change is especially accentuated in the case of informal workers, where the illiterates constituted 33.6 percent of workers in 1988 and declined to 30 percent in 1998. In addition, the informal illiterate female workers in 1988 represented 37 percent of the total informal female workers, dropping to 32 percent in 1998. A similar change occurred with male informal workers during this decade.

In light of this, we can conclude that state educational policies are clearly reflected in the characteristics of the workers, which could also have an impact on workers' abilities to acquire knowledge and become more productive. As has been shown, the educational levels of the informal workers are improving due to provision of free education. However, the inability of the government to hire as many workers in its ranks as before contributed to the increasing percentage of educated workers in informal employment.

4.3 Economic Sector of Employment

Being formally or informally employed does not necessarily reflect a worker's affiliation to a certain economic sector. Accordingly, a worker could be hired on an informal basis in the private sector or the government/public sector and vice versa.

Table 3.4: Distribution of Workers According to Formality and Economic Sector of Employment

Sector	Male			Female			Total		
	F Col%	IF Col%	%F of Total Row	F Col%	IF Col%	%F of Total Row	F Col%	IF Col%	%F of Total Row
Government	67.2	1.3	98.8	85.6	10.1	97.6	72.0	2.2	98.4
Public enterprise	18.7	0.3	98.9	7.3	1.1	97.0	15.7	0.4	98.7
Private	11.5	97.7	15.5	6.1	88.2	25.2	10.1	96.7	16.5
Joint-stock companies	2.2	0.3	92.9	0.5	0.0	100.0	1.7	0.2	93.3
Foreign	0.3	0.0	96.7	0.0	0.0	0.0	0.3	0.0	96.7
Other	0.1	0.4	31.3	0.5	0.6	79.1	0.2	0.4	47.8
	100.0	100.0		100.0	100.0		100.0	100.0	65.4
Total	**2086**	**1254**		**851**	**150**		**2937**	**1404**	

A look at Table 3.4 reveals that:

1. The government and the public sector have been the main sectors to provide formal employment (87.7 percent) for the Egyptian NAWW. The role of the private sector in hiring workers on a formal basis is strictly limited

to 12.3 percent of the formal NAWW, which shows a slight decline over its contribution (12.6 percent) in 1988 (see Table A3.4).

2. Although it would have been expected that informal workers would be engaged in work only in the private sector, the table shows that they represent 2.6 percent of workers in the government and the public sector. This trend of hiring individuals on a temporary basis in the government and the public sector is a relatively new phenomenon that started in the mid-1980s and continues to be a feature of public sector hiring.
3. Females seem to prefer working in the government and the public sector, either formally or informally. It is possible that these sectors are the main areas where females could find employment. As to those females who were working in the private sector, they were mostly employed on an informal basis.

4.4 The Relation to the Employer and the Workplace

Within the group of formal NAWW, the question of a worker's relationship to the employer was of no importance. This is in contrast to the informal wage-workers, of whom a significant proportion (39.2 percent) was somehow related to enterprise owners, either as household members, relatives, or friends, or lived in the same village or town. Therefore, having connections with the entrepreneur seems to facilitate the issue of finding work. This confirm sociologist Mark Granovetter's argument that economic theory has not fully taken into account the embeddedness of economic behavior and organizational contacts in a network of social relationships (Granovetter, 1985). These relationships can be essential in providing access to opportunity.

Table 3.5: Workers' Relationships to the Employers

Relationship to employer	Male col%	Formal female col%	Total col%	Male col%	Informal female col%	Total col%
Member of HH	0.1	0.0	0.1	2.3	0.4	2.1
Relative outside HH	0.7	0.0	0.5	11.2	4.8	10.5
Neighbors/ friends	0.3	0.1	0.3	11.4	11.5	11.4
From same village/town	0.1	0.0	0.1	16.2	7.4	15.2
Not related to the owner	98.8	99.8	99.1	58.9	75.8	60.8
Total	**100**	**100**	**100**	**100**	**100**	**100**

Although most of the work was conducted within the boundaries of an establishment, nearly 38 percent of workplaces were "outside establishments." "Inside establishment" work locations include offices, buildings, shops, and factories, whereas "outside establishments" include fields or farms, itinerant workers, street vendors, and taxi drivers, among others.

Table 3.6: Different Types of Workplaces

Place of work	Formal %	Informal %
Shop	0.7	20.1
Office/flat/building	87.5	15.4
Garage/factory	10.4	24.3
Mobile worker	0.0	25.5
Van	0.0	2.8
Taxi	0.0	5.5
Other	1.4	5.6
Total	**100**	**100**

Table 3.6 indicates that the most prevalent type of work location is the office/building, which is consistent with the fact that both the government and the public sector are the major providers of jobs related to provision of services.

4.5 Economic Activity

The distribution of workers according to type of economic activity indicates that:

1. Within the group of formal workers, services represent by far the most important economic activity, followed by manufacturing.
2. Informal workers, on the other hand, are more evenly distributed among the different economic activities, with a more pronounced role in manufacturing, construction, trade, and services activities.
3. The distribution pattern of formal female workers among the various economic activities reveals a concentration in the service sector, in comparison to formal male workers. Informal female workers are less evenly distributed, but with a marked concentration in services and manufacturing. This pattern of concentration implies that female work is confined to a certain limited number of activities, while male workers have a greater ability to access different economic activities.

A comparison between 1998 and 1988 shows that certain structural changes have been taking place in the Egyptian economy over the decade (see Table A3.5). First, formal workers in 1998 show a clear tendency toward concentration in the services sector, which they did not display in 1988. Second, informal workers have shifted toward manufacturing, construction, and trade in the late 1990s. Third, female informal workers seem to have moved toward manufacturing activities over the past decade.

Table 3.7: Distribution of Workers According to Economic Activity

Activity	Male			Female			Total		
	F Col%	IF Col%	%F of Total Row	F Col%	IF Col%	%F of Total Row	F Col%	IF Col%	%F of Total Row
Mining	0.5	0.5	62.3	0.0	0.0	0.0	0.4	0.4	62.3
Mfg.	20.3	28.5	52.6	6.1	30.5	49.5	16.6	28.7	52.3
Electronics	2.8	0.0	100.0	1.0	0.0	100.0	2.3	0.0	100.0
Construction	3.4	25.8	17.2	0.9	2.5	64.0	2.8	23.5	18.3
Trade	4.6	18.2	28.3	2.1	24.6	29.8	4.0	18.8	28.5
Trans.	7.3	12.1	48.5	2.7	0.5	96.4	6.1	10.9	51.4
Finance	2.9	1.6	73.8	4.1	5.0	80.0	3.2	1.9	75.7
Services	58.2	13.4	87.1	83.1	37.0	91.6	64.6	15.7	88.6
	100.0	100.0		100.0	100.0		100.0	100.0	65.4
Total	**2086**	**1254**		**851**	**150**		**2937**	**1404**	

4.6 Job Stability and Informality

Another obvious area of discrepancy between formal and informal workers is in the degree of stability or permanency in a job. Data in Table 3.8 shows that workers who were formally employed enjoyed a far higher degree of job stability than informal workers. Whereas 97 percent of formal workers had permanent jobs, this did not exceed 55.4 percent in the case of informal workers.

Table 3.8: Degree of Job Stability of the NAWW

Stability	Male			Female			Total		
	F Col%	IF Col%	%F of Total Row	F Col%	IF Col%	%F of Total Row	F Col%	IF Col%	%F of Total Row
Permanent	97.7	54.8	73.5	95.1	60.7	88.4	97.0	55.4	76.8
Temporary	2.2	13.2	20.4	4.9	28.8	45.1	2.9	14.8	26.8
Seasonal	0.0	0.8	6.8	0.0	2.5	0.0	0.0	0.9	5.1
Casual	0.1	31.3	0.7	0.0	8.0	0.0	0.1	28.9	0.7
	100.0	100.0		100.0	100.0		100.0	100.0	65.4
Total	**2086**	**1254**		**851**	**150**		**2937**	**1404**	

Casual workers seemed to constitute a relatively high proportion of informal workers (29 percent) especially in the male workforce. However, if we compare this figure with that of 1988 (26 percent), it becomes clear that the proportion of casual workers has increased over time (see Table A3.6).

For female informal workers, temporary versus casual work was a widespread and growing phenomenon in the late 1990s. Nearly 29 percent of female informal workers were currently employed in temporary work.

Despite the relative proportion of casual and temporary work among informal workers, more than 99.5 percent of both formal and informal workers had been in the same job during the last three months before the surveys. This phenomenon reflects certain stability in the labor market.

4.7 Work Conditions and the Size of the Firm

For purposes of analysis, we'll exclude government and public sector enterprises in this section in order to look more closely at the private sector's legal status and size. This will help us better understand the day-to-day work setting and lifestyle of private sector workers.

Table 3.9: Legal Status of Private Firms

Legal Body	Formal			Informal		
	Male Col%	Fem Col%	Tot. Col%	Male Col%	Fem Col%	Tot. Col%
Individual	31.5	35.7	32.1	84.6	81.8	84.3
Partnership	33.9	29.9	33.3	10.3	14.5	10.9
Corporation company	24.1	20.9	23.7	1.8	1.5	1.8
Limited liability co.	0.6	0.0	0.5	0.1	0.0	0.1
Not known	9.9	13.4	10.4	3.1	2.2	3.0
	100.0	100.0	100.0	100.0	100.0	100.0
Total	**267**	**708**	**975**	**47**	**113**	**160**

Table 3.9 points out one of the distinctive features of informal employment. From a legal perspective, informal employment tends to be primarily "individual" enterprises or partnerships, while formal employment tends to offer workers different legal status, in the form of partnerships, individual enterprises, or large corporations.

As to the size of enterprises, measured in terms of number of workers, it is clear that enterprises hiring workers on a formal basis tended to be larger firms—in terms of number of workers—than those providing informal employment.

Table 3.10 shows that while 2.1 percent of formal workers were concentrated in microenterprises (those with 4 workers or less), 60 percent of informal workers worked in the same microsized economic units (EUs).

Enterprises employing 50 workers or more offered work opportunities to 60 percent of formal workers. The interesting observation is that 5.7 percent of the informal NAWW were hired by large enterprises. This result reflects a reality that is apparent in large formal enterprises, where owners try to reduce costs (social security contributions and fiscal responsibilities for a large number of contract workers) by hiring workers on an informal basis.

Table 3.10: Size of Enterprises Employing Formal and Informal Workers in 1998

Number of workers	Formal			Informal		
	Male Col%	Fem Col%	Tot. Col%	Male Col%	Fem Col%	Tot. Col%
0–4–	2.0	2.7	2.1	60.5	54.3	60.0
5–9	5.6	5.5	5.6	20.5	13.9	19.8
10–29	15.7	17.9	16.0	8.4	12.6	8.8
30–49	10.7	12.6	11.0	1.9	4.3	0.0
50+	61.1	53.7	60.1	4.9	13.6	5.7
Not Specified	4.9	7.5	5.2	3.8	1.4	3.6
	100.0	100.0	100.0	100.0	100.0	97.9
Total	**279**	**51**	**330**	**1216**	**138**	**1354**

The differences between enterprises employing formal and informal workers do not stop at the legal body or size of the firm, but extend to several other aspects of the work process. Data indicates that both the number of workdays per week or work hours per day seemed to be relatively higher for informal workers.

One of the interesting results is the obvious difference between the daily wage levels earned by informal workers compared to formal workers. Comparisons between formal and informal wage levels will include the basic wages as well as all extras, such as bonuses, incentives, rewards, and distributed profits.

Table 3.11a shows the distribution of wages for both the formal and informal NAWW, whether they worked in the private or public sector. The results indicate that the informal workers appeared to be in a disadvantaged position. The fraction of informal workers in the lowest wage category (< LE5) was double that of the formal sector. In addition, the percentage of informal workers earning daily wages equal to or higher than LE20 did not exceed 5.1 percent of the total informal workers, while it reached 10 percent in the case of formal workers.

If public sector and government workers—formal or informal—are eliminated, the differences between the formal and informal wage structures become more distinct, because the government and public sector wages helped keep the gap smaller. Table 3.11b sheds light on the pattern of wage distribution between the private formal and informal workers. One could conclude from the results that wage levels in the private formal sector are generally higher than in all other sectors. The main constraint is that private formal employment in 1998 represented only one-third of the total private NAWW. However, comparisons with LFSS 1988 data points out an important fact: that private formal employment grew over the decade at a faster rate (48.6 percent) than private informal employment (43.6 percent).

Table 3.11a: Total Daily Wage Rate for Formal and Informal Workers in 1998

Total Daily	Formal			Informal		
wage [LE]	Male Col%	Fem Col%	Tot. Col%	Male Col%	Fem Col%	Tot. Col%
0–<5	26.5	63.3	33.2	15.3	21.1	16.8
5–<10	43.8	29.4	41.1	42.5	48.0	43.9
10–<20	24.3	3.7	20.5	31.2	24.1	29.4
20–<50	5.4	3.6	5.1	9.9	6.5	9.1
50–<100				0.9	0.2	0.7
100–>				0.1	0.1	0.1
Total	**100**	**100**	**100**	**100**	**100**	**100**

Table 3.11b: Total Daily Wages for Private Sector Wageworkers in 1998

Total Daily Wage	Formal			Informal		
[LE] Col%	Male Col%	Fem Col%	Tot. Col%	Male Col%	Fem Col%	Tot. Col%
0–<5	26.7	60.6	32.1	7.2	23.1	9.6
5–<10	42.4	29.5	40.4	37.1	40.3	37.6
10–<20	25.3	5.0	22.1	38.7	23.5	36.4
20–<50	5.6	4.8	5.45	15.8	11.4	15.2
50–<100				0.8	1.6	0.9
100–>				0.3		0.3
Total	**100**	**100**	**100**	**100**	**100**	**100**

Another notable point is the clear gender-related wage gap in both formal and informal employment. The exclusion of government and public sector workers' wages from the two studies indicates a negative change in the females' wage structure, which means that the government and public sectors provided females with better wage levels than did the private sector.

Conclusion

Informal workers represent 35 percent of the total nonagricultural workforce in 1998, which means that the informal labor market largely parallels the formal one. The relative proportion of informal employment to total employment in 1998 has declined as compared to the 1988 levels (38 percent of the total nonagricultural workforce). The share of informal employment in the total private NAWW has also decreased slightly, from 81.7 percent in 1988 to 80.8 percent in 1998. However, the role of the informal labor market is expected to continue being relatively important with the receding role of the government as an employment provider.

In fact, the current data reveals an unexpected phenomenon, namely that both the government and the public sector are employing some of their workers on an informal basis, which allows them to eliminate new employees easily, at any time. This practice was a characteristic of the private sector in the past, but happened very rarely in public sector agencies.

However, being informally employed entails certain advantages as well as several disadvantages. The main advantages are the provision of employment opportunities, which are fairly stable, at wage levels that are relatively higher than in formal employment—at times when public employment is becoming a rare possibility. The informal employee usually gains his or her training and experience within the boundaries of the private, usually informal, sector.

But the drawbacks of informal employment are numerous. First, workers face insecurity regarding their futures due to the lack of social security coverage or any binding contract with their employers. Without contracts, informal workers could be terminated anytime, without any obligations from their employers.

Second, informal female workers find it difficult to get jobs at acceptable wage levels—equivalent to that of males with similar educational backgrounds and experience. Some type of "female employment-encouraging programs" should be devised to address the difficulty females face finding jobs.

Third, the ongoing social security scheme proved to be a failure. It is a burden on both the employer and the employee because of the high percentage of wages that should be cut and directed to cover the social security subscription. A revision of the social security laws is a necessity to widen the scope of coverage. In addition, a positive intervention from the government to partially subsidize the social security subscription should be considered.

Fourth, all the laws and decrees governing the relationship between the employer and the employee (labor law) should be revised and eventually modified to become more agreeable to both workers and employers.

Fifth, although 55 percent of informal labor is hired to work on a permanent basis, there is still another 45 percent of the informal workers who are working either on a casual, temporary, or seasonal basis. This relatively large segment of informal workers is working primarily in construction, manufacturing, and trade. The majority of both seasonal and casual workers have achieved modest, or less-than-intermediate, levels of education.

Sixth, additional work opportunities and specialized training programs should be implemented to target informal workers through the concerned public and private organizations and their "employment-generating programs."

Finally, the structure of the present labor market is witnessing continuous change. The private sector will definitely play a greater role in the coming years. Without introducing positive and structural changes to the institutional framework that governs and organizes the workings of the private sector entities, the growing labor force could face great difficulties getting any jobs.

5. The Role of Informal Enterprises in a Changing Reality

The purpose of this section is to describe the main features of informal enterprises in Egypt in 1998: the role they played in employment creation; the sources of funding for their activities; their ability to survive; and the problems they encountered in their daily transactions. This chapter intends first to examine the primary characteristics of small enterprises, both formal and informal, and second, to trace the changes that took place over the last 10 years. The objective of this comparison is to help assess changes in the role of small enterprises during a period of structural adjustment—especially in light of the important goal of the new economic policy to strengthen the role of private enterprises.

However, the last target, namely the comparison with the 1988 data, is difficult, and to some extent inaccurate, simply because the definition used to distinguish between formal and informal units in 1998 is not applicable on the data set and variables of 1988. The definition used in ELMS 98 to differentiate between units according to the formality status is based on the availability of three criterion: license, commercial/industrial register (when required), and regular bookkeeping. Accordingly, if an economic unit complies to the three procedures, it is considered as functioning on a formal basis, whereas if the EU does not abide totally or partially by any of these three procedures, it is considered an informal unit.

Naturally, informal economic units will not be of a homogeneous nature, since some of the owners (employers or self-employed) will be abiding by one or two procedures while others will be ignoring these procedures completely. Table 3.12 could help shed light on the degrees of formality within the SE/E community in 1998.

As can be seen in Table 3.12, a high percentage of EUs (31.7 percent) do not comply to any of the three procedures, and only 18 percent of EUs do. Using the information available in this table, we divide the EUs into two groups: the formal EUs (18 percent) and the informal EUs (82 percent).

In the LFSS 88, both the enterprise workers and owners were asked in the questionnaire forms to declare whether the enterprises they worked in or owned were registered or had a license or not. Their answers are summarized in Table 3.13.

According to the logic of the LFSS 88, an EU could have either a register or a license. The existence of either would imply formality. But in reality, in Egypt the EUs could be required to comply with the two procedures (the license and the commercial or industrial register)—especially if it is an establishment—to become a formal unit. However, having a license is an absolute necessity to all entrepreneurs (inside or outside establishment), while the industrial or commercial register is an additional requirement in fewer cases. As is evident, the classification of enterprises in 1988 is different from the one applied in 1998.

Table 3.12: Economic Units Distributed According to Compliance by Legal Procedures in 1998

Number of procedures	Sample Frequency	Population Percent
0	474	31.66
1	207	13.83
2	547	36.54
3	269	17.97
Total	**1497**	**100.00**

Table 3.13: Economic Units Distributed According to Compliance by Procedures in 1988

Formality	Sample Frequency	Population Percent
No R or L required	161	4.81
Official registration	2024	60.42
Official license	584	17.43
None present	293	8.75
Do not know	288	8.60
Total	**3350**	**100.00**

Table 3.14: Three Degrees of Formality Among Small Enterprises in 1988

Formality	Percent of EUs (%)
Totally informal	17.4
Semi-informal	60.4
Formal	22.2
Total	**100.0**

Therefore, and in light of the importance of the license, despite its limitation as a sole criteria of distinction, the LFSS 88 data will be used to assess and assign a state of formality. Accordingly, a unit that has a license will be considered as complying with the minimum level of formality, and will therefore be designated as formal. Those units with only a commercial or industrial register are complying with one of the essential legal procedures, but still don't have official licenses or permits to operate. So we will consider as totally informal all cases where it was reported that: 1) no registration or license is required; 2) none present; or 3) do not know. Thus, according to this categorization, one could distinguish between three main levels of formality.

If the results in Tables 3.12 and 3.14 are compared, a few changes can be observed:

First, the inflow of small EUs into the Egyptian labor market was accompanied by a growth in informality. A comparison of totally informal enterprises in the two studies shows that the percentage to the total number of EUs was 17.4 percent in 1988, and increased to 31.7 percent in 1998. Second, at the same time, it becomes clear that those EUs working on a totally formal basis constituted 22.2 percent in 1988, and declined to 18 percent in 1998.

More details concerning the characteristics of the EUs and their owners will be discussed in the following sections. Before we go into these details, it must be clear that the analysis in the next sections will focus only on those who were described as economically active during the last three months before the beginning of the survey and those who worked more than 25 hours per week. All subsistence and agricultural activities are excluded.

This definition limits the number of economic units—both formal and informal—to 3.3 million in 1998. Of these units, 80.9 percent were owned by male entrepreneurs, while the rest were female-owned. In addition, data indicates that 19 percent of these EUs were working on a formal basis, while the rest were considered informal units.

Small-scale economic units in 1988 were estimated at 2.934 million units, the informal units representing 83 percent of this figure, close to the percentage of units in 1998. The male-owned EUs were estimated at 82.9 percent of the total EUs. These results point to the fact that there has beeen no obvious change in the relative percentage of the informal units within the total number of small-scale enterprises, and that the informal units represent the great majority of the small EUs (see Table A3.7).

5.1 Geographical Distribution and Age of the Economic Unit

The ELMS 98 data indicates that there has been a continuous increase in the percentage of small enterprises located in rural areas. This phenomenon is more emphasized in informal units.

This development could be due to the long, ongoing trend of net internal migration from rural to urban areas, which has nearly ceased to be of any significance. In fact, the new Census 1996 indicates that the percentage of urban to total population is witnessing a slight decline. Given that the population growth rate is higher in rural than in urban areas, and that the agricultural land has been unable to provide the labor force with growing work opportunities, it becomes understandable that small-scale activities—usually based on the manufacturing, services, trading, or transporting of agricultural products—start to increase in number.

Another factor could be the growing interest of the government and semi-governmental organizations—e.g., the Social Fund for Development (SFD), the Shorouk Rural Development Project, the Ministry of Social Affairs' (MOSA) Productive Families Project, and nongovernmental organizations (NGO)—that are working to develop small-scale economic activities, especially in rural areas.

Table 3.15a: Geographical Distribution of Small EUs According to Formality in 1998

Urban/Rural	Formal			Informal		
	Male Col%	Fem Col%	Tot. Col%	Male Col%	Fem Col%	Tot. Col%
Urban	67.9	85.1	70.1	49.0	48.8	48.9
Rural	32.1	14.9	29.9	51.0	51.2	51.1
Total	**100**	**100**	**100**	**100**	**100**	**100**

Table 3.15b: Geographical Distribution of Small EUs According to Formality in 1988

Urban/Rural	Formal			Informal		
	Male Col%	Fem Col%	Tot. Col%	Male Col%	Fem Col%	Tot. Col%
Urban	71.2	86.7	74.4	71.3	59.3	69.3
Rural	28.7	13.2	25.6	28.6	40.6	30.6
Total	**100**	**100**	**100**	**100**	**100**	**100**

As to the age of the economic units measured according to the year they began operation, it is clear that some of the EUs were more than 50 years old. This phenomenon applies to both the formal and informal EUs, and is evident in both the ELMS 98 and LFSS 88 results. One of the conclusions that could be drawn from this is that small enterprises have a relatively long life. Therefore, informality should not necessarily indicate temporality. Actually, there is no perceivable difference between the two types of EUs in this respect.

Table 3.16 reflects three additional features:

1. Small-scale EUs have, in general, grown in numbers over the last decade.
2. Female entrepreneurs seem to have increased in number more quickly than male entrepreneurs, particularly from 1990–98.

3. Formal enterprises have grown in number over the last decade, compared to informal units.

Table 3.16: The Beginning Date of Small EUs Distributed According to Formality and Gender of the Entrepreneur in 1998

Start Date	Formal			Informal		
	Male Col%	Fem Col%	Tot. Col%	Male Col%	Fem Col%	Tot. Col%
Before 1952	2.1	0.0	1.7	3.6	2.2	2.9
1952–59	2.9	1.9	2.8	4.6	2.9	3.8
1960–69	5.7	2.4	5.3	8.2	8.4	8.3
1970–79	15.8	8.6	14.9	19.4	18.1	18.8
1980–89	29.4	22.9	28.6	27.5	30.5	28.8
1990–98	44.0	64.1	46.5	36.4	37.0	36.7
Do not know	0.0	0.0	0.0	0.2	0.7	0.4
Total	**100**	**100**	**100**	**100**	**100**	**100**

5.2 Age and Gender of the Entrepreneurs

In looking at the age and gender distribution of small-enterprise owners in 1998, some primary features of informality become clear, as shown in Table 3.17:

Table 3.17: Distribution of the SE/Es According to Formality, Age, and Gender in 1998

Age Group	Formal			Informal		
	Male Col%	Fem Col%	Tot. Col%	Male Col%	Fem Col%	Tot. Col%
06–11	0.0	0.0	0.0	0.1	0.3	0.1
12–14	0.0	0.0	0.0	1.3	1.1	1.3
15–19	10.9	9.9	10.8	8.8	4.2	7.9
20–29	20.3	23.1	20.6	***22.9***	20.2	***22.3***
30–39	16.3	***30.8***	18.2	***22.9***	***34.3***	***25.1***
40–49	***28.3***	***24.4***	***27.7***	21.3	21.7	21.4
50–59	15.3	6.1	14.2	14.0	13.3	13.8
60–64	4.23	5.7	4.4	3.6	2.1	3.3
=>65	4.6	0.0	4.1	5.0	2.7	4.5
Total	**100**	**100**	**100**	**100**	**100**	**100**

First, the formal self-employed and employers are 15 years or older, while informal workers can be younger. Therefore, we see few entrepreneurs ages 6–14 working as informal SE/Es, while we find no formal entrepreneurs in these age categories.

Second, female representation is still quite limited within both the formal and informal SE/Es. Their percentage amidst the formal entrepreneurs was 15.2 percent, while it grew to 20 percent among the informal SE/Es.

Third, the formal entrepreneurs were mainly concentrated in a higher age bracket (40 to 49 year-olds), while the informal SE/Es were more prevalent in younger age brackets (20 to 39 year-olds). This result is understandable. Becoming a formal agent requires more capital, connections in the market, experience, and familiarity with the regulations. These credentials are usually acquired with time.

While it is easier for informal SE/Es to access the labor market, since less capital is usually needed, the market connections develop with time, and experience is not a necessity—at least at the beginning of work. Furthermore, being familiar with the rules and regulations is of no importance to this group, since they are likely to work informally, like their peers.

However, if the results of ELMS 98 are compared to those of LFSS 0.38 (see Table A3.8), one could notice that some changes took place.

First, the highest concentration of SE/Es in 1988 was witnessed at a younger age bracket (15 to 19 year-olds) in the case of both formal and informal entrepreneurs.

Second, children's participation was much more limited in 1988 (.38 percent of the formal SE/Es, and 0.89 percent of the informal SE/Es), compared to 1.4 percent of the total informal SE/Es in 1998.

Third, female participation within the formal SE/E was 21 percent in 1988 and dropped to 15.2 percent in 1998, while their participation within the informal entrepreneurs grew between the two study periods (17 percent in 1988, and 20 percent in 1998).

5.3 Educational Attainment

Levels of educational attainment have been improving significantly over the last decade. This is reflected in changes to the educational levels of the formal entrepreneurs in 1998, as compared to 1988. This change affected both males and females.

Accordingly, one can detect a strong correlation between the formality status of the entrepreneur and his or her education, especially in ELMS 98 results. This relation was not as clear in the results of 1988. Formal entrepreneurs are now better educated and illiterates are far fewer, in comparison to the informal entrepreneurs or to the results of LFSS 88.

As to the informal entrepreneurs in 1998, the data show that the highest percentage of SE/Es were illiterate, but that some improvement in their educational status had occurred since 1988.

Illiteracy is and has been highest among female informal SE/Es. Nearly half of the informal female SE/Es in 1998 were illiterate, while 26 percent of them had intermediate levels of education (general or technical secondary school). However, nearly 14.5 percent of the informal female SE/Es had completed their university studies, a higher percentage than informal male entrepreneurs who had university-level educations or higher. The previous results indicate: a) the notion of the existence of a correlation between informality and low levels of educational attainment, especially among female entrepreneurs; and b) that with time, more of the highly educated females will seek work in the informal sector.

Table 3.18a: Distribution of SE/Es According to Formality, Gender, and Educational Attainment in 1998

Age Group	Formal			Informal		
	Male Col%	Fem Col%	Tot. Col%	Male Col%	Fem Col%	Tot. Col%
Illiterate	6.74	8.76	***6.99***	***21.70***	***41.20***	***25.50***
Read & write	6.85	2.92	6.35	15.60	5.35	13.60
Less than intermediate	28.60	7.03	25.80	21.00	12.60	19.40
Intermediate	25.50	21.20	25.00	23.70	18.10	22.60
Higher than intermediate	6.55	7.31	6.65	5.86	8.17	6.31
University & higher	25.70	52.70	***29.10***	***12.00***	***14.50***	***12.50***
Total	**100**	**100**	**100**	**100**	**100**	**100**

Table 3.18b: Distribution of SE/Es According to Formality, Gender, and Educational Attainment in 1988

Education	Formal			Informal		
	Male Col%	Fem Col%	Tot. Col%	Male Col%	Fem Col%	Tot. Col%
Illiterate	29.80	24.30	***28.69***	***29.16***	***49.19***	***32.49***
Read & write	19.50	6.6	16.90	21.70	12.03	20.10
Less than intermediate	18.60	12.5	17.40	24.80	13.40	22.90
Intermediate	13.80	18.2	14.70	13.70	18.50	14.50
Higher than intermediate	2.10	5.6	2.80	2.40	1.50	2.20
University & higher	15.90	32.6	***19.30***	***8.01***	***5.30***	***7.60***
Total	**100**	**100**	**100**	**100**	**100**	**100**

5.4 Economic Activities

The distribution of formal enterprises according to economic activity is quite different from that of informal ones. Whereas the formal EUs were mostly concentrated in trade (55 percent), manufacturing (18 percent), and services (17 percent), informal EUs were more evenly distributed among trade (38 percent), services (31 percent), and manufacturing (19 percent) activities.

Table 3.19: Distribution of Small Enterprises According to Formality, Gender, and Economic Activity

Economic Activity	Formal			Informal		
	Male Col%	Fem Col%	Tot. Col%	Male Col%	Fem Col%	Tot. Col%
Mining	0.23	0.00	0.20	0.03	0.00	0.03
Manufacturing	20.20	2.97	18.05	19.84	15.80	19.04
Electricity	0.23	2.46	0.51	0.57	0.00	0.45
Construction	2.03	0.00	1.78	5.92	0.00	4.76
Trade	59.60	22.85	55.01	35.56	49.59	38.32
Transport	2.80	2.97	2.82	5.93	0.34	4.83
Finance	3.93	5.48	4.12	2.12	0.65	1.83
Services	10.98	63.27	17.50	30.03	33.62	30.74
Total	**100**	**100**	**100**	**100**	**100**	**100**

The female entrepreneurs, whether working formally or informally, seemed to be active primarily in two major activities—trade and services. The formal male entrepreneurs preferred to work mainly in trade, manufacturing, and services activities. Informal entrepreneurs, who are more evenly distributed among the different economic activities, were mostly engaged in trade, services, and manufacturing.

5.5 Invested Capital and the Sources of Finance

One of the variables that could help draw a dividing line between formal and informal EUs is the present value of the invested capital. As mentioned before, informal units have an easy entry into the labor market because they usually rely on a limited or negligible amount of capital. Table 3.20 helps confirm this notion.

Table 3.20: Distribution of the SE/Es According to Size of Capital

Capital	Formal			Informal		
	Male Col%	Fem Col%	Tot. Col%	Male Col%	Fem Col%	Tot. Col%
None	0.32	1.12	0.42	3.61	4.04	3.70
less than LE100	0.00	0.00	0.00	5.60	12.20	6.90
LE100–499	3.75	0.00	3.28	11.70	20.40	13.40
LE500–999	7.50	4.80	7.20	14.90	12.80	14.50
LE1000–4999	12.80	8.70	12.30	20.00	19.00	19.80
LE5000–9999	14.40	22.30	15.40	11.70	10.40	11.50
LE10 000 or more	58.70	61.10	***58.90***	30.30	20.10	***28.30***
Do not know	2.50	1.90	2.40	1.90	0.80	1.70
Total	**100**	**100**	**100**	**100**	**100**	**100**

It is evident that the formal EUs tended to invest using a more sizeable capital. Nearly 59 percent of the formal EUs had a value of capital equal to or greater than LE10,000, while informal EUs with the same values of capital constituted 28 percent of the total informal EUs. In addition, the EUs that had a capital value equal to zero or higher, to the limit of LE999, made up 10.5 percent of the formal EUs and 38.7 percent of the informal EUs. The EUs with a capital value between LE1000<10,000 represented 28 percent of the formal EUs and 31 percent of the informal EUs.

Formal female SE/Es fared better than their male counterparts in terms of the size of their capital. A substantial percentage of formal female entrepreneurs (61. percent) had capital valued at LE10,000 or more. On the contrary, informal female SE/Es in the same high-capital category represented only 20 percent of the total informal female SE/Es, whereas male SE/Es in this category made approximately 30 percent of the total informal male SE/Es.

In examining the ways small entrepreneurs financed their economic projects, several strategies were observed: self-finance, partnerships with others, support from religious organizations (mosques or churches) or from philanthropists, the Rotating Savings and Credit Association (ROSCA, or *Gameya* in Arabic), loans from the different financial institutions, businessmen associations, the Social Fund for Development (SFD), non-governmental organizations (NGOs), the Shorouk Rural Development Project or Productive Families project, or the Credit Guarantee Corporation. Due to the possibility of multiple financial resources, the SE/Es were allowed to mention their three most important means of financing.

Table 3.21 summarizes the major financial resources for SE/Es. The results revealed in this table ascertain an important phenomenon, namely that small enterprises relied almost completely on informal sources, such as self-finance, for their funding. Self-finance could indicate several things, such as dependence on previous savings, inheritance, or the support of spouses or family members. The role of formal financial institutions is nearly invisible and, therefore, quite insignificant.

The second major source of finance was joining other individuals in partnerships. This was more prevalent among the formal SE/Es than among informal entrepreneurs. The NGOs played a minor role in providing funds to small enterprises. The small loans obtained by SE/Es were nearly split between fixed-capital investments and working-capital needs. Most of the EUs did not get any technical or training assistance. Those that did, received it primarily from machine suppliers.

In light of this, one question arises: If the small enterprises were able to manage their affairs and survive despite their inability to access the formal financial market, why are the international and national institutions concerned with providing finances to the small entrepreneurs?

Table 3.21: Sources of Finance for the Formal and Informal SE/Es

Source of Finance 1st mean	Formal			Informal		
	Male Col%	**Fem Col%**	**Tot. Col%**	**Male Col%**	**Fem Col%**	**Tot. Col%**
Self-finance	83.9	84.8	84.1	93.70	91.70	93.30
Partnership	12.1	10.2	11.8	3.81	3.94	3.84
Religious org.	0.0	0.0	0.0	0.27	0.00	0.20
ROSCA	0.0	0.0	0.0	1.03	1.20	1.10
Nasser Social Bank	1.5	0.0	1.3	0.40	1.20	0.60
Indust. Devel. Bank	0.3	1.9	0.5	0.00	0.00	0.00
SFD	1.5	0.0	1.3	0.20	0.30	0.20
Commercial banks	0.3	0.0	0.3	0.20	0.00	0.20
Agricultural Credit Bank	0.0	0.0	0.0	0.31	1.63	0.56
NGOs	0.4	2.9	0.7	0.00	0.00	0.00
Total	**100**	**100**	**100**	**100**	**100**	**100**

The interest in small enterprises is partially derived from their ability to provide employment opportunities at a relatively limited cost, in terms of size of capital per worker. Increasing the size of the EUs depends on the availability of funds. Therefore, relieving the financial constraint that confronts the small entrepreneur becomes a necessity to help him or her expand operations and employ more workers.

Table 3.22: Relationship Between Present Value of Invested Capital and Number of Workers in the EUs (1998)

Value of current capital	Number of EUs in each labor group					
of EUs	**1–4**	**5–9**	**10–29**	**30–49**	**50–99**	**Total**
None	***48***	-	-	-	-	48
Less than LE100	***62***	-	-	-	-	62
LE 100–499	***174***	-	-	-	-	174
LE 500–999	***160***	***7***	-	-	-	167
LE 1000–4999	***277***	***11***	-	-	-	288
LE 5000–9999	***166***	***2***	-	-	-	168
LE10,000 or more	***430***	***93***	***31***	**5**	***2***	***561***
Total	***1317***	***113***	**31**	**5**	**2**	**1468**

Table 3.22 shows the distribution of EUs according to capital and number of workers. As is evident, the majority of the EUs (88 percent) were concentrated in a category that ranges from 1–4 workers. Only 2.1 percent of the EUs employed 10 workers or more. Those EUs were the ones with capital value equal to or greater than LE10,000. Increasing the value of capital does not necessar-

ily lead to an increase in labor. The ability to increase the size of the EUs in terms of employment depends on the ability to raise the size of capital invested. However, if the size of the EU is measured in terms of the number of its workers, it becomes clear that informal units are predominantly small-scale.

Table 3.23 reveals that 95 percent of the informal EUs employed less than 5 workers, whereas the formal units that employed the same number of workers represent 75 percent of the total formal EUs.

Table 3.23: Small-Scale EUs Distributed According to Formality Status and Number of Workers

No. of workers	Informal	%	Formal	%	Total	%
1–4	1146	***94.6***	195	***74.6***	1341	91.3
5–9	66	4.6	48	16.4	114	6.5
10–29	11	0.6	22	6.9	33	1.6
30–49	2	0.1	3	1.1	5	0.3
50–99	1	***0.1***	1	***0.8***	2	0.2
Total	**1226**	**100**	**269**	**100**	**1495**	**100**

However, the formal enterprises were not much larger than the informal units, since the second largest concentration of formal EUs (16.4 percent) was in the range of 5–9 workers, and only 9 percent of the formal EUs employed more than 10 workers.

5.6 Small-Scale and Other Related Aspects

When small enterprises become the subject of analysis, several issues come to mind. Small-scale should not be measured or perceived in terms of the size of employment or capital alone. Other aspects should be considered, such as productivity, type and quality of products, main users of the products, forward and backward linkages, type of technical assistance available, the kind of problems confronted, and ability to survive, expand, and develop.

Some of these points were tackled in "the Household Projects" module (ELMS 98), but others were not. By reviewing the primary findings of these issues, some relevant conclusions can be made that could help shed light on the framework within which small enterprises operate.

First, only a meager percentage (6.2 percent) of the EUs was offered technical or training assistance from the numerous agencies and NGOs in Egypt. Surprisingly, one of the primary technical assistance providers proved to be machine suppliers. Other agencies, such as the SFD and the NGOs, were of minor influence in this respect.

Second, the main users of the goods and services produced by the small EUs were the consumers (77 percent) and the retail and wholesale traders (13 percent). Links with both large and small enterprises or with other economic sectors were strictly limited. This phenomenon reflects the inability of small entrepreneurs to cultivate stronger linkages, or to serve as suppliers of production inputs for other producers.

Third, there were signs of growth and movement between small-scale enterprises and the other sectors, as well as incessant in- and out-flows of workers. However, the results point out that only 10.4 percent of the EUs witnessed an increase in the number of workers, as compared to three years ago. The rest of the EUs either kept the number of workers constant (79.5 percent) or decreased them (5.06 percent). In the cases where change occured, the number of workers who either joined or left the EUs did not usually exceed two.

Several points can be drawn from the previous analysis of small enterprises:

1. The number of small economic units increased between the two years of comparison, especially the informal units.
2. The number and relative percentage of the economic units working on a totally informal basis increased significantly by the end of the 1990s.
3. Informal activities are growing at a rapid pace in rural areas.
4. The average age of formal and informal entrepreneurs tended to be higher in the 1990s than in the 1980s. This change could be taken as an indicator of a growing difficulty in accessing even the informal market.
5. Although the educational attainment levels of formal entrepreneurs have improved significantly, there was only a slight change for informal entrepreneurs in this respect—especially female entrepreneurs, who were still burdened with high illiteracy rates.
6. The informal economic unit is clearly smaller than the formal unit, whether measured in terms of number of workers or value of capital.
7. The problems of small enterprises differ according to their state of formality, though some problems are common to both formal and informal units. All small units shared difficulty marketing their products, purchasing raw materials or equipment, and dealing with labor, customers, and various government authorities.
8. Informal entrepreneurs faced three main problems: limited income, marketing, and taxes. Only 4 percent of entrepreneurs felt that obtaining finance was a difficulty they faced.
9. The main concerns of formal entrepreneurs were taxes, marketing, and limited income or financing, respectively.
10. Limited financing was only a minor problem for small entrepreneurs, though its weight was felt more by the formal unit owners, compared to informal owners. However, the positive result was that 28 percent of the informal entrepreneurs and 26 percent of the formal entrepreneurs declared that they had no problems whatsoever.

Conclusion

The previous analysis aimed to answer the questions raised at the beginning of this chaper. The main goal was to pinpoint the role played by the informal labor market during the last decade (1988–98), and identify the kind of changes that occurred as a response to the structural transformation that took place in the Egyptian economy starting in the 1990s. The outcome suggests the following:

First, the informal labor market and the informal sector are definitely growing over time, and with the current economic changes. Both the informal workers and entrepreneurs are increasing in numbers and relative weight in the labor market.

Second, although temporality could be the nature of work for nearly half the informal workers, (work for nearly half the informal workers could have been characterized by being of temporary nature), it was not a characteristic of the small economic unit. As has been shown before, most of the informal units have been working for more than 10 years, regardless of their status inside or outside establishment.

Third, it is difficult to assess whether or not the informal labor market is the sector of the poor. If wages of informal labor are compared to those of formal workers, then the former group is faring better than the latter. Wages in the informal market seem to be higher. But if other dimensions are considered—such as medical, industrial, and social security coverage, stability in work and educational backgrounds of informal participants—then poverty could be a main feature of a large segment of informal workers and economic units.

Fourth, poverty is basically a dominant characterist'c of female informal workers and unit owners. This group deserves considerable attention due to its vulnerability, the need to work to support family' income, and the government's continued withdrawal as a major job provider.

Fifth, as data indicates, the ability of small enterprises to grow and expand is still hampered by an environment which is not enabling. Though the majority of economic units have been active for more than 10 years, most of them are still small in terms of employment and capital. This does not mean that all small units are incapable of growing. The data set of ELMS 98 does not offer information about those small enterprise owners who developed into medium or large producers, or the ways in which they did so.

Finally, the coming years will certainly witness a growth in the role of the private informal sector. Understanding more about this sector is crucial, not just to satisfy "academic curiosity," but to help design appropriate policies for the present and the future.

Appendix

Table A3.1: Distribution of NAWW By Gender and Formality 1988

Distribution of NAWW, 1988

	Formal			Informal			GTM	GTF	Grand Total
	Male	Female	Total	Male	Female	Total			
	3,103,575	1,036,015	4,139,590	2,274,519	329,812	2,604,331	5,378,094	1,365,827	6,743,921

Distribution of NAWW, 1998

	Formal			Informal			GTM	GTF	Grand Total
	Male	Female	Total	Male	Female	Total			
	4,764,183	1,657,305	6,421,488	3,063,238	340,732	3,403,970	7,827,421	1,998,037	9,825,458
% Change	53.5	60.0	55.1	34.7	3.3	30.7	45.5	46.3	45.7

Distribution of Private NAWW in 1988

	Formal			Informal			GTM	GTF	Grand Total
	Male	Female	Total	Male	Female	Total			
	416,466	103,843	520,309	2,019,201	253,232	2,272,433	2,435,667	357,075	2,792,742

Distribution of Private NAWW in 1998

	Formal			Informal			GTM	GTF	Grand Total
	Male	Female	Total	Male	Female	Total			
	664,542	108,459	773,001	2,961,415	302,541	3,263,956	3,625,957	411,000	4,036,957
% Change	59.6	4.4	48.6	46.7	19.5	43.6	48.9	15.1	44.6

Table A3.2: Distribution of Workers According to Formality, Gender and Age Groups, 1988

Age group	Male			Female			Total		
	F Col%	IF Col%	F Row%	F Col%	IF Col%	F Row%	F Col%	IF Col%	F Row%
06–11	0.0	2.7	0.0	0.0	1.0	0.0	0.0	2.5	0.0
12–14	0.2	8.7	2.7	0.0	5.0	0.0	0.1	8.2	2.5
15–19	1.5	21.8	8.7	1.6	17.5	22.6	1.5	21.2	10.4
20–29	19.8	34.2	44.2	41.1	43.7	74.7	25.1	35.4	53.1
30–39	35.4	18.6	72.2	37.2	18.7	86.2	35.9	18.6	75.4
40–49	24.7	7.5	81.8	15.8	6.9	87.8	22.5	7.4	82.8
50–59	16.5	4.2	84.4	4.1	5.2	71.1	13.4	4.3	83.2
60–64	1.6	1.3	62.2	0.2	1.3	27.9	1.2	1.3	59.9
=>65	0.2	1.1	22.5	0.0	0.6	0.0	0.2	1.0	21.1
Total	**100.0**	**100.0**		**100.0**	**100.0**		**100.0**	**100.0**	**61.4**
	1778	**1327**		**616**	**190**		**2394**	**1517**	

Table A3.3: Distribution of Workers According to Formality and Education Attainment, 1988

Education	Male			Female			Total		
	F Col%	IF Col%	F Row%	F Col%	IF Col%	F Row%	F Col%	IF Col%	F Row%
Illiterate	15.4	33.1	39.1	3.9	37.6	24.8	12.6	33.6	37.4
Read & write	18.1	19.1	56.6	1.5	5.5	46.5	14.0	17.4	56.3
Less than intermediate	12.6	25.5	40.4	4.7	15.1	49.6	10.6	24.2	41.3
Intermediate	23.3	16.0	66.7	46.4	24.6	85.7	29.1	17.1	73.2
Higher than intermediate	6.5	2.1	80.8	13.7	4.7	90.2	8.3	2.4	84.4
University	20.5	3.8	88.0	26.7	12.1	87.5	22.1	4.9	87.9
Post-graduate	3.5	0.4	93.1	3.1	0.4	0.0	3.4	0.4	93.9
	100.0	**100.0**		**100.0**	**100.0**		**100.0**	**100.0**	**61.6**
Total	**1778**	**1316**		**616**	**187**		**2394**	**1503**	

Table A3.4: Distribution of Workers According to Formality and Economic Sector, 1988

Economic Sector	Male			Female			Total		
	F Col%	IF Col%	F Row%	F Col%	IF Col%	F Row%	F Col%	IF Col%	F Row%
Government	56.3	7.3	91.4	73.8	17.3	93.0	60.7	8.5	91.9
Public enterprise	30.3	4.0	91.3	16.1	5.9	89.6	26.7	4.2	91.0
Private	9.8	87.4	13.3	7.9	75.8	24.8	9.3	86.0	14.7
Joint-venture	2.9	0.7	84.2	0.9	0.0	100.0	2.4	0.7	85.6
Foreign	0.3	0.5	44.2	0.4	0.0	0.0	0.3	0.4	53.6
Other	0.4	0.1	80.3	0.8	0.9	72.0	0.5	0.2	76.8
	100	**100**		**100**	**100**		**100**	**100**	**61.4**
Total	**1778**	**1327**		**616**	**190**		**2394**	**1517**	

Table A3.5: Distribution of Workers According to Formality, Gender, and Economic Activity, 1988

Economic Activity	Male			Female			Total		
	F Col%	IF Col%	F Row%	F Col%	IF Col%	F Row%	F Col%	IF Col%	F Row%
Mining	0.5	0.5	56.2	0.4	0.0	0.0	0.5	0.0	62.8
Manufact.	25.1	29.8	53.5	11.4	21.5	62.6	21.7	28.7	54.5
Electr.	3.8	0.5	91.9	0.7	0.0	100.0	3.0	0.4	92.3
Const.	5.0	23.9	22.0	1.4	2.9	59.6	4.1	21.3	23.3
Trade	5.5	19.0	28.1	4.7	23.7	38.2	5.3	19.6	29.9
Trans	9.8	8.5	61.1	3.8	2.4	83.3	8.3	7.7	63.0
Finance	3.9	0.6	89.2	4.6	3.4	80.8	4.1	1.0	86.6
Service	46.5	17.2	78.7	73.0	46.0	83.3	53.1	20.8	80.2
	100.0	100.0		100.0	100.0		100.0	100.0	61.4
Total	**1778**	**1327**		**3105**	**616**		**4883**	**1943**	

Table A3.6: Distribution of Workers According to Formality and Stability in NAWW, 1988

Stability	Male			Female			Total		
	F Col%	IF Col%	F Row%	F Col%	IF Col%	F Row%	F Col%	IF Col%	F Row%
Permanent	97.6	52.0	71.9	98.3	66.3	82.4	97.8	53.8	74.3
Temporary	1.8	6.8	26.1	1.7	16.5	24.4	1.7	8.0	25.7
Seasonal	0.0	13.0	0.0	0.0	6.1	0.0	0.0	12.1	0.0
Casual	0.6	28.2	3.0	0.0	11.2	0.0	0.5	26.1	2.8
	100.0	100.0		100.0	100.0		100.0	100.0	61.4
Total	**1778**	**1327**		**3105**	**616**		**4883**	**1943**	

Table A3.7: Number of Small Economic Units in the Formal and Informal Sector in 1988 and 1998

Year	Formal			Informal			Total		
	Male	Female	Total	Male	Female	Total	Male	Female	Total
1988	400,985	101,340	502,325	2,031,219	401,303	2,432,522	2,432,204	502,643	2,934,847
1998	477,459	68,986	546,445	2,231,121	544,910	2,776,031	2,708,580	613,896	3,322,476

Table A3.8: Distribution of Employers According to Age, Formality, and Gender in LFSS 88

	Formal						Informal					
Age	Male		Female		Total		Male		Female		Total	
Group	Count	Col %	Count	Col %	Count	Col %	Count	Col %	Count	Col %	Count	Col %
06–11		0.00		0.00	0	0.00		0.00		0.00		0.00
12–14	2	0.49		0.00	2	0.38	19	0.92	3	0.71	22	0.89
15–19	121	29.44	25	22.73	146	28.08	594	28.81	207	49.05	801	32.23
20–29	82	19.95	7	6.36	89	17.12	444	21.53	50	11.85	494	19.88
30–39	75	18.25	17	15.45	92	17.69	512	24.83	59	13.98	572	23.02
40–49	57	13.87	20	18.18	77	14.81	281	13.63	76	18.01	357	14.37
50–59	9	2.19	6	5.45	14	2.69	49	2.38	6	1.42	55	2.21
60–64	58	14.11	35	31.82	93	17.88	152	7.37	20	4.74	172	6.92
=>65	7	1.70		0.00	7	1.35	11	0.53	1	0.00	12	0.48
Total	**411**	**100.00**	**110**	**100.00**	**520**	**100.00**	**2062**	**100.00**	**422**	**99.76**	**2485**	**100.00**

4 Informalization of Labor in Egypt

May Moktar and Jackline Wahba

Introduction

From the 1960s to the 1980s, the Egyptian government was the main generator of jobs and the preferred sector for many workers. In the 1990s, reforms have constrained the public sector in terms of the number of new employment opportunities it can generate (i.e., public-sector employment is still increasing, but at a declining rate). Given the limited prospects of new government jobs, the start of privatization of public enterprises, and the relative limitations of the private formal sector absorbing the growing labor force, one would expect to see an increase in the proportion and numbers of workers drawn into informal employment. Thus, it seems important to find out whether, and to what extent, labor has become informalized in the Egyptian labor market during the 1990s.

In this chapter, we will attempt to answer the following questions: Have informal arrangements in the labor market increased in the 1990s? What are the characteristics of informal employment in Egypt? Who are the informal workers? Are workers moving from the public sector to informal employment? Are new workers overly drawn to informal employment in the 1990s?

The study uses the Egypt Labor Market Survey 1998 (ELMS 98) to assess whether or not there is any evidence of the Egyptian labor market being increasingly characterized by informal labor arrangements (Assaad and Barsoum, 1999). It is important to underscore the fact that this study deals with informal employment and workers and is not attempting to estimate the actual size of the informal sector. Thus, we have adopted the International Conference of Labor Statisticians' (ILO) 1993 definition of informality activity—that is, activity unregulated by the formal institutions and regulations of society, such as contract, labor laws, registration, and taxation (ILO Web). Also, given that the focus of the paper is on workers' mobility between formal and informal employment, we limit our analysis to those ages 18–64 (i.e., those who are independent to move on their own).

The structure of the chapter is as follows: Section 1 describes the data; Section 2 provides descriptive statistics of the features of informal employment and informal workers; Section 3 presents the transition patterns of individuals to and from informal employment between 1990 and 1998; Section 4 examines the changes in the pattern of employment of new entrants to the labor market; and Section 5 concludes by summarizing the main findings.

1. The Data and Methodology

This paper uses the labor mobility module survey of the ELMS 98 for details on the labor mobility module), which benefits from having an elaborate vector of employment characteristics about which individuals were asked (Wahba, in this volume). The respondents provided employment characteristics for a specific point in time—August 1990, the time of Iraq's invasion of Kuwait—and gave information about the last two changes in all of their employment characteristics and locations of residence.

1.1 Description of Informality

In order to be able to study the extent to which labor has become informalized during the 1990s, we construct two samples. The first consists of those ages 18–64 who were economically active in the labor market in 1990. The second sample consists of those ages 18–64 who were economically active in the labor market in 1998.

1.2 Mobility Patterns

We also examine labor mobility patterns between August 1990 and November 1998. This enables us to compare the status of an individual before the implementation of economic reforms in 1990 against his or her status in 1998, the time of the survey. It is important to note here that one of the problems with using two fixed dates is that it understates the number of movers—it does not take into account individuals who have moved more than once, or those who have moved but returned to their original status. In this part of the study, we limit the analysis to those who were at least 18 years old in 1990, and those who were less than 65 years old in 1998.

2. Informality in the 1990s

This section describes informal employment and the characteristics of informal workers in the 1990s. First, the notion of informality is discussed.

2.1 ILO Definition of Informality

The ILO 1993 definition of the informal sector of employment has become recognized and accepted internationally. The "informal sector" covers small-scale income-generating activities that take place outside the official regulatory framework. These activities typically utilize a low level of capital, technology, and skills, while providing low incomes and unstable employment. "Informality" denotes activity that is unregulated by the formal institutions and regulations of society, such as labor laws, registration, and taxation—which govern similar activities in the formal sector. The ILO identified three main groups of informal workers: owners or employers of microenterprises, own-account workers (self-employed), and dependent workers. The third group encompasses wage laborers engaged in full-time or casual employment, generally without a formal contract, and working on a regular or casual basis, and unpaid workers, including family members and apprentices. In our analysis, we study all workers, not just those earning wages. In other words, we include those self-employed or employing others as well as unpaid workers.

Workers engaged in informal activities are for the most part unregistered and unrecorded in official statistics. They tend to have little or no access to organized markets, to credit institutions, to formal education and training institutions, or to many public services and amenities. They are not recognized, supported, or regulated by the government. They are often compelled by circumstances to operate outside the framework of the law (so their activities are not registered or recorded). Even when they are registered and respect certain aspects of the law, they are almost invariably beyond social protection, labor legislation, and protective measures at the workplace. They generally do not have access to many of the benefits that workers in the formal sector receive, such as old-age pensions, health and invalidity (disability) insurance, limits on regular working hours, payments for overtime, paid leave, maternity protection, and priority access to subsidized goods and services.

2.2 Extent of Informality

In this section, we study and compare the extent of informal employment in 1990 and 1998, based on the 1993 ILO definition. Given that "informal workers" refers to those engaged in activity that is unregulated by the formal institutions and regulations of society—such as labor laws, registration, and taxation—we use different indicators to explore the various dimensions of informality.

First, we consider all workers, but limit our analysis to those aged 18–64 at each period (Table 4.1, Column 1). We report the share of workers in the labor force who had: (1) no job contracts, (2) no social security coverage, (3) no contracts and no social security, (4) no contracts and no regular jobs, and

(5) no social security and no regular jobs. Half of all workers had no job contracts, and slightly less than half had no social security coverage in 1998. Between 1990 and 1998, the proportion of workers with no contracts increased by 2.4 percent, and those with no social security increased by 2.9 percent. The proportions of workers who had no contracts and no regular jobs, no social security and no regular jobs, or no contracts and no social security coverage had all increased by 3.2 percent between 1990 and 1998. In other words, whether informality is defined as the absence of a job contract, the lack of social security coverage, or both, it seems that informality among all workers has increased by 2–3 percent in the 1990s.

Table 4.1: Informality of Workers in 1990 & 1998, Ages 18–64 (%)

	All Workers	Nonagricultural Workers
No contracts		
1990	51.99	39.02
1998	54.38	44.34
No social security		
1990	44.24	30.00
1998	47.11	35.93
No contracts and no social security		
1990	43.32	28.93
1998	45.36	33.98
No contracts and no regular jobs		
1990	52.57	39.74
1998	55.78	46.04
No social security and no regular jobs		
1990	45.10	31.01
1998	48.33	37.39

Note: Age limit (18 to 64 years-old) applies in both 1990 and 1998.

To get a better picture of informality, we consider only nonagricultural workers. Column 2 in Table 4.1 displays the percentage of nonagricultural workers who were 18–64 years old during each study. In 1998, 44 percent of nonagricultural workers had no contracts and 36 percent had no social security coverage. Excluding agricultural workers reduces the proportion of workers engaged in informal activities, relative to the total nonagricultural workers (e.g. 44 percent of nonagricultural workers have no contracts, compared to 54 percent of all workers in 1998). However, it also underscores the fact that between 1990 and 1998, informality increased among nonagricultural workers more than among all other workers. The proportion of nonagricultural workers who had no contracts increased by 5.3 percent, and those with no social security increased by 5.9 percent. In addition, the proportion of those with no regular jobs and no contracts increased by 6.3 percent, while those with no regular jobs and no social security increased by 6.4 percent. Using any one of these measures shows that informality has increased among nonagricultural workers by 5–6 percent in the 1990s.

2.3 Characteristics of Nonagricultural Workers

We use different indicators of informality to examine the characteristics of informal workers, to compare them to formal workers, and to point out any changes in those characteristics that might have occurred between 1990 and 1998. Here we focus only on nonagricultural workers. Table A4.1 displays the characteristics of nonagricultural workers ages 18–64.

Gender

In 1990, 22 percent of nonagricultural female workers had no job contracts. By 1998, the share increased to 31 percent. Although the share of nonagricultural male workers who had no contracts also increased, it was only by 4 percent. In 1998, almost half of the nonagricultural male workers and one-third of the nonagricultural female workers were non-job-contract holders. Also, in the 1990s, the share of nonagricultural female workers with no social security increased by 10 percent, while the proportion among males increased by 5 percent. Any definition of informality shows that both genders have experienced an increase in participation in informal activities, but females have witnessed the biggest increase (10 percent compared to 5 percent for males). This implies that female workers felt the brunt of reforms more than male workers. This is due to the fact that females tend to face more disadvantages in informal employment, such as the lack of maternity protection, paid leave, and other benefits.

Age

In 1998, two-thirds of those ages 18–29 had no contracts and no social security, while one-third of nonagricultural workers ages 30 and up had no contracts and no social security. In other words, the majority of young people have been engaged in informal employment. And while the share of nonagricultural workers with no contracts and no social security coverage increased among all age groups, the increase was most significant for those under 30. In 1990, 52 percent of workers ages 18–29 had no contracts. By 1998, 64 percent had no contracts. Also, the proportion of young nonagricultural workers with no social security increased from 47 percent in 1990 to 62 percent in 1998. Thus, the share of young workers engaged in informal employment has increased substantially in the 1990s. Section 4 discusses how, in the 1990s, the proportion of young workers starting at informal jobs has reached an unprecedented high.

Education

Participation in informal employment is negatively correlated with education—those with less education are more likely to have informal jobs. In 1998, 81 percent of illiterates had no contracts, compared to17 percent of university graduates. However, all educational groups experienced an increase in the share of workers who had no job contracts. Those with less-than-intermediate and intermediate levels of education seem to have experienced the highest increase in participation in jobs with no contracts (10 percent for less-than-intermediate and 11 percent for intermediate education). In comparison, the share of most-highly-educated workers with no job contracts increased by only 4 percent. In short, higher participation in informal employment in the 1990s has been experienced by all educational groups, especially those with less-than-intermediate and intermediate levels of education.

Urban/Rural Residence

Between 1990 and 1998, the share of job-contract holders increased by 4 percent among urban residents and 6 percent among rural dwellers. In 1998, 48 percent of nonagricultural workers living in rural areas and 42 percent of those in urban areas had no job contracts. Other measures of informality also show that half of the nonagricultural workers living in rural areas were engaged in informal employment.

Summary

Between 1990 and 1998, the share of nonagricultural workers engaged in informal employment increased by 5–6 percent. However, some groups experienced a greater increase. The share of female workers and young workers (18 to 29 year-olds) in informal employment has increased significantly. Also, it is worth noting that whether informality is measured by a lack of job contracts or a lack of social security coverage, the results seem to indicate the same trends.

2.4 Wage Status of Informal Nonagricultural Workers

More than half of the nonagricultural workers who had no job contracts were wageworkers in 1998. Also, one-fifth of non-contract holders were self-employed and 16 percent were employers. The share of wageworkers increased among non-contract holders between 1990 and 1998. The same trend is also seen among those workers who have no social security coverage. Two-thirds of workers who had no social security were wageworkers in 1998. The share of employers and self-employed among workers not covered by social security was 8 percent and 19 percent, respectively, in 1998. It is worth noting here that the shares of employers and self-employed workers engaged in informal employment have fallen in the 1990s.

Table 4.2: Wage Status of Informal Workers (%)

	No Contract		No Social Security Coverage	
	1990	**1998**	**1990**	**1998**
Wageworker	53.84	56.26	61.66	65.29
Employer	16.82	15.61	10.00	8.35
Self-employed	24.24	21.30	22.55	18.84
Unpaid family worker	5.10	6.82	5.80	7.53
Total	**100.00**	**100.00**	**100.00**	**100.00**

Another finding is that 31 percent of waged nonagricultural workers had no contracts in 1998, compared to 26 percent in 1990. Also, 29 percent of nonagricultural wageworkers had no social security coverage, compared to 23 percent in 1990. To sum up, more wageworkers in absolute number and as a share of the nonagricultural workers have become informalized in the 1990s. This implies that fewer workers are becoming entrepreneurs, and more wageworkers are being hired on an informal basis.

2.5 Composition of Jobs

It is interesting to compare the composition of informal jobs to formal employment. In this section, the lack of job contracts is used as a measure of informality. Jobs held by nonagricultural workers ages 18–64 are studied here.

The field of informal employment is dominated by males. However, a comparison of figures gathered in 1990 and 1998 shows that female informal employment has risen by 3 percent, while male informal employment has fallen by 3 percent. Female formal employment has not risen over the same period.

Table 4.3: Formal and Informal Jobs by Gender (%)

	1990			1998		
	Formal Jobs	**Informal Jobs**	**Total Jobs**	**Formal Jobs**	**Informal Jobs**	**Total Jobs**
Male	75.08	89.00	80.52	74.56	85.73	79.51
Female	24.92	11.00	19.48	25.44	14.27	20.49
Total	**100.00**	**100.00**	**100.00**	**100.00**	**100.00**	**100.00**

The age composition of workers in formal employment seems to be slightly different from those in informal employment. In 1990, the majority of formal workers were between 30–45 years old, while those between 30–45 and 18–29 were equally represented in informal employment (approximately 40 percent). In 1998, the majority of workers in informal employment were less than 30 years old. During the 1990s, the time spent waiting for public-sector jobs was longer than ever, with some people waiting for employment for as long as 10 years after their graduation. This is one reason why the share of younger people in formal employment fell by 5 percent between 1990 and 1998.

Table 4.4: Formal and Informal Jobs by Age (%)

	1990			1998		
	Formal Jobs	Informal Jobs	Total Jobs	Formal Jobs	Informal Jobs	Total Jobs
18–29	24.11	40.12	30.36	18.72	41.04	28.62
30–45	53.73	41.46	48.94	52.64	37.69	46.01
46–64	22.17	18.42	20.70	28.63	21.27	25.37
Total	**100.00**	**100.00**	**100.00**	**100.00**	**100.00**	**100.00**

Table 4.5: Formal and Informal Jobs by Educational Level (%)

	1990			1998		
	Formal Jobs	Informal Jobs	Total Jobs	Formal Jobs	Informal Jobs	Total Jobs
Illiterate	8.72	36.82	19.68	5.76	30.50	16.71
Read & write	10.68	17.59	13.37	8.40	12.96	10.42
Less than intermediate	13.93	21.20	16.76	12.86	23.41	17.54
Intermediate	29.65	14.91	23.90	31.48	21.62	27.11
Higher than intermediate	10.27	3.46	7.61	12.05	3.87	8.43
University & higher	26.76	6.01	17.35	29.45	7.63	19.79
Total	**100.00**	**100.00**	**100.00**	**100.00**	**100.00**	**100.00**

The educational composition of informal employment seems to have altered between 1990 and 1998. This, in part, reflects the changes in the educational composition of the total working population. The proportion of workers with no education, or those in the working population who can just read and write, have fallen, as have their proportions in informal employment. But, in 1998, there were 3 percent more workers with an intermediate education in the working population and 7 percent more in informal employment. The proportion of workers with higher-than-intermediate, university, and higher education has increased slightly in the total working population and in informal employment.

Table 4.6: Formal and Informal Jobs by Urban/Rural Region of Work (%)

	1990			1998		
	Formal Jobs	Informal Jobs	Total Jobs	Formal Jobs	Informal Jobs	Total Jobs
Urban	75.66	50.13	65.68	73.55	46.88	61.72
Rural	24.14	21.53	23.12	26.44	23.73	25.24
Mobile	0.20	28.34	11.20	0.01	29.40	13.04
Total	**100.00**	**100.00**	**100.00**	**100.00**	**100.00**	**100.00**

Table 4.7: Formal and Informal Jobs by Occupation (%)

	1990			1998		
	Formal Jobs	Informal Jobs	Total Jobs	Formal Jobs	Informal Jobs	Total Jobs
Technical & scientific	37.11	4.49	24.37	41.36	5.66	25.53
Management	3.92	0.06	2.41	4.33	0.26	2.53
Clerical	24.08	2.03	15.47	22.15	1.71	13.09
Sales	1.69	29.74	12.64	2.40	31.66	15.37
Services	13.79	7.85	11.47	14.23	8.88	11.86
Production	19.42	55.83	33.64	15.53	51.82	31.62
Total	**100.00**	**100.00**	**100.00**	**100.00**	**100.00**	**100.00**

Table 4.8: Formal and Informal Jobs by Economic Activity (%)

	1990			1998		
	Formal Jobs	Informal Jobs	Total Jobs	Formal Jobs	Informal Jobs	Total Jobs
Agriculture	2.25	0.50	1.57	1.77	0.35	1.14
Mining	0.49	0.34	0.43	0.38	0.32	0.35
Manufacturing	19.59	24.18	21.38	16.23	22.82	19.15
Utilities	2.46	0.09	1.53	2.25	0.00	1.25
Construction	2.08	16.81	7.83	2.72	15.93	8.58
Trade	3.63	35.57	16.10	4.66	37.21	19.09
Transport	6.47	9.92	7.82	5.96	9.59	7.57
Finance	2.93	1.82	2.50	3.23	2.15	2.75
Services	60.11	10.77	40.85	62.80	11.63	40.11
Total	**100.00**	**100.00**	**100.00**	**100.00**	**100.00**	**100.00**

The distribution of the location of informal jobs by urban and rural areas has changed between 1990 and 1998. The proportion of informal jobs located in urban areas has fallen by 3 percent, while informal employment in rural areas has risen by 2 percent. This reflects the increase in rural nonagriculture employment during the 1990s. However, the change in the proportion of informal jobs that were mobile (not located in a certain region) was not significant.

The distribution of informality among occupations, excluding agriculture, reveals an increase in informality in all occupations except for production. However, production still accounts for half of all informal jobs. It is also worth noting that the sales sector seems to be predomi-nantly informal. Table 4.7 shows that informal employment is comprised mainly of production, sales, and services jobs.

Table 4.8 shows the distribution of informal jobs by economic activity. (Agriculture here refers to activities that come under that economic activity or industry but do not refer to agriculture as occupation.) Mining and utilities (electricity) sectors are the two economic areas where there is no informal employment. The trade sector accounted for more than one-third of all informal employment in 1998. Construction also offers primarily informal employment.

Summary

In 1998, informal jobs—jobs without contracts—were held primarily by males. Thirty percent of those jobs were filled by uneducated workers; only 8 percent were filled by the most-educated workers. Production, trade, and services are the three dominant informal job occupations. Construction and trade sectors are also predominantly informal. And the majority of informal jobs are located in urban areas.

3. Transition Patterns among Formality States

3.1 Transition Patterns of Nonagricultural Workers

Here we examine the transition patterns of workers who were employed in nonagriculture activities in both 1990 and 1998, and who were at least 18 years old in 1990 and less than 65 years old in 1998. Table 4.9 presents patterns of transition of nonagricultural workers between holding and not holding job contracts in 1990 and 1998. The proportion of workers who moved from jobs with contracts to jobs without contracts is very similar to the proportion of workers who moved in the opposite direction. However, in terms of absolute numbers, almost twice as many workers moved from jobs with no contracts to jobs with contracts, versus those who went from jobs with contracts to ones without contracts.

Table 4.9: Transitions of Nonagricultural Workers Between Contract Statuses: 1990–98

Contract Status in 1990	Contract Status in 1998: Contract	No Contract	Total
Contract	2049.00	75.00	2124.0
	93.40	5.96	100.0
No Contract	145.00	1188.00	1333.0
	6.60	94.04	100.0
Total	**2194.00**	**1263.00**	**3457.0**
	63.46	**36.54**	**100.0**

Note: In each entry, the top bold-face figure gives the absolute number; the second figure is the % of the row.

This is also reflected in the total share of workers holding contracts in 1998. Among those who had contracts in both 1990 and 1998—and who were at least 18 years old in 1990 and less than 65 years old in 1998—63.5 percent had contracts in 1998, compared to 61 percent in 1990. Although the share of job-contract holders rose by 2 percent over the same period, as seen in Table 4.9, the share of job-contract holders in the labor force fell (Table A4.1). This fall is due to new entrants in the labor market who were drawn into jobs with no contracts. Among those workers who entered the labor market between 1990 and 1998, only 34 percent had contracts, while 66 percent had jobs without contracts.

Table 4.10: Transitions of Nonagricultural Workers Between Social Security Coverage Statuses: 1990–98

Contract Status in 1990	Social Security Coverage Status in 1998: Social Security	No Social Security	Total
Social Security	2404.00	41.00	2445.0
	92.88	4.77	100.0
No Social Security	184.00	828.00	1012.0
	7.12	95.23	100.0
Total	**2588.00**	**869.00**	**3457.0**
	74.87	**25.13**	**100.0**

Note: In each entry, the top bold-face figure gives the absolute number; the second figure is the % of the row.

Table 4.10 presents transition patterns of nonagricultural workers between jobs with and without social security coverage, in both 1990 and 1998. (It shows a pattern similar to the one in Table 4.9). In terms of absolute numbers, four times as many workers moved from jobs without social security coverage to jobs with social security coverage than the other way around.

Summary

Patterns among those employed in 1990 and 1998 are similar, even when we allow for different age ranges. In other words, informality has fallen among those already employed. Next we examine the mobility patterns to and from informal employment, by both those who were employed and those who were not.

3.2 Transition Patterns of Individuals

In this section, we use the existence of a job contract as a measure of formality. Tables A4.2–A4.7 provide summary data on transitions between formal and informal employment by tabulating the conditional probability of finding an individual in one category in 1998 when they began in another in 1990. The row percentage sums to 100 percent, and the totals at the bottom represent the share of workers to be found in each category in 1998. The diagonal figures are the percentages of nonmovers in each group.

In these tables we study all individuals, including the unemployed, housewives, and those out of the labor force. We include individuals who were at least 18 years old in 1990 and less than 65 years old in 1998. We distinguish between four types of employment: 1) informal jobs (nonagricultural private); 2) formal public jobs; 3) formal private jobs; and 4) agriculture. We also study individuals who were not working: those unemployed, housewives, students, and others (primarily Army). These groups are useful in showing the different patterns of mobility of those who were not working in 1990, and their location and employment status in 1998. We also highlight those who were overseas in 1990—a group that reflects the pattern of behavior of return migrants and their choices between formal and informal employment.

Table A4.2 presents the transition patterns of individuals from 1990 to 1998. Over that period, formal public workers had the highest stay rate (85 percent); formal private workers had the lowest stay rate (76 percent); and the stay rate of informal workers was 79 percent. In 1990, 3 percent of formal public employees moved to informal jobs by 1998, while 6 percent of informal employees moved to formal public employment by 1998. The number of workers who moved from informal to formal public jobs is 30 percent more than the number who moved the opposite way. This goes against expectations: we did not anticipate more movement from public to informal employment as a result of downsizing the public sector. However, when we limit age ranges in our comparisons, we find that only younger workers mirror the movement from informal to formal jobs. Also, in percentage terms and in absolute numbers, more workers moved from informal jobs to formal private ones than they did from formal private to informal employment. The probability of agricultural workers moving out of agriculture and into other sectors is higher than the probability of nonagricultural workers moving into agriculture. However, more agricultural workers moved to formal public jobs than to informal ones.

It is also important to track the movement of individuals not employed in 1990 to their current standing in 1998. Among those who were unemployed in 1990, half were drawn into formal employment, and only a quarter were drawn into informal employment by 1998. Among those who were full-time students in 1990, 23 percent had informal jobs, 40 percent had formal public jobs, and 13 percent had private formal jobs by 1998. Among those who had been overseas in 1990, 32 percent had moved to informal employment by 1998 and 38 percent had moved to public formal jobs. Only 9 percent had moved to formal private employment.

The group that stands out as being disproportionately drawn into informal employment is that of housewives. From 1990 to 1998, 29 percent moved to informal jobs, compared to 10 percent who moved to formal public jobs and 2 percent who moved to formal private employment. There are several explanations for women being drawn more into informal employment. First, the public sector has served as the main employer of women in the past. But with fewer jobs being created in the 1990s, the chances of getting a public sector job decreased. Also, female workers find it much easier to become engaged in informal jobs than in private formal employment—our data shows that four times as many women had informal jobs than formal private employment. Finally, those who were in the Army in 1990—the majority of the "Others" category—were more likely to move into informal employment than into formal employment.

There are many differences as well as similarities in the transition patterns of males and females. However, female workers displayed very little mobility, and thus, given the sample size, we discuss only the significant mobility patterns we found. Three patterns of mobility among females appear: First, female workers who in 1990 were out of the labor force—either unemployed or students—were more likely to be drawn into formal public employment than into informal jobs by 1998. Second, housewives were more likely to move into informal jobs than into public formal employment, though only 10 percent of housewives joined public formal jobs. And third, female workers are more likely to quit informal jobs to become housewives than they are to quit formal public jobs. This reflects the benefits of public formal employment: females get maternity leave and unpaid leave, which they do not receive in informal employment. In many cases, the absence of these benefits would cause female workers to quit their jobs.

Male workers tend to be more mobile than females. Table A4.3 shows the transition pattern of males from 1990 to 1998. Male workers had similar stay rates in all jobs: 81 percent in informal employment and agriculture, 82 percent in formal private, and 84 percent in formal public employment. Public employees were still the least mobile (see Table A4.3). As many unemployed males moved to informal jobs as into public jobs, which differs from the pattern seen among females.

Another important dimension of job transition involves age. In general, younger individuals tend to be more mobile. Thus, in an attempt to control for the age effect, we distinguish between two age groups: young—those 40 years old or less in 1998; and old—those older than 40 in 1998 (see Table A4.4 and A4.5). Among the younger individuals, four times as many moved from informal employment to formal public jobs than from formal public employment into informal jobs. However, among the older individuals, more than twice the number of workers moved from public formal to informal employment than from informal to formal public jobs. In terms of absolute numbers, more older workers moved out of formal jobs and into informal ones than did younger workers. This confirms our expectation that downsizing the public sector would cause more older public workers to move to informal jobs.

Table A4.6 presents a summary of the mobility patterns discussed above: the likelihood of workers leaving the public sector and moving to informal jobs is lower than the probability of informal workers moving to the public sector. Workers in the public sector or in informal employment are equally likely to move to the agricultural sector. More informal workers are likely to become unemployed than formal public workers. A greater number of agricultural workers moved to the public sector than into informal jobs. More unemployed workers were absorbed into the public sector than into informal employment. Two-thirds of females who were housewives joined informal jobs, and less than a quarter of them moved into the public sector. More students were absorbed in the public sector than in both private formal and informal employment. The biggest share of workers returning from abroad went back to public sector employment (a good number of them may have been on sabbatical or unpaid leave).

The final table of transition patterns (see Table A4.7) distinguishes between types of formality and informality without controlling for the economic sector (i.e., private, public, or agricultural fields). We distinguish between three types of informal workers: waged, self-employed and employers, and unpaid family. We also study waged formal workers and compare them to other formal workers (employers and unpaid). The first four columns and rows represent waged informal, nonwaged informal, waged formal, and nonwaged formal. The rest of the table displays individuals who are not working (in Egypt): those unemployed, housewives, students, those who were working abroad, and others (primarily Army workers). Among those employed, unpaid family workers are the most mobile, while employers and those self-employed are the least mobile. Among wageworkers, those with informal jobs are more mobile than those with formal employment. More formal workers became self-employed and employers than became waged informal workers (their waged informal counterparts). Four times as many workers moved from waged informal jobs to waged formal jobs than moved in the other direction. However, twice as many self-employed workers and employers moved into waged formal employment than into waged informal jobs. Among those unemployed, twice as many got waged formal jobs than waged informal jobs. Half of those who were students got waged formal jobs, while the proportion of students who became waged informal workers was almost equal to the proportion of those who became employers and self-employed.

Summary

More workers moved from informal jobs to formal (private and public) employment than from formal to informal jobs. Among younger individuals—those less than 40 years old—four times as many moved from informal employment to formal public jobs than from formal public jobs into informal jobs. However, among the older population, more than twice the number of workers moved from public formal to informal employment than from informal to formal public jobs. As a result of structural adjustment, one would expect movement of workers out of public employment and into informal jobs. This has been witnessed among older workers. The younger workers, however, tend to stay in informal employment until they are able to move into public sector jobs.

4. Patterns of Employment of New Entrants

While Section 3 shows that more nonagricultural workers moved from informal jobs to formal employment than the other way around, Section 2 shows that the number and share of nonagricultural workers engaged in informal employment has risen. This suggests that the rise in informality is due to new entrants being disproportionately drawn into informal jobs. Therefore, we examine the percentage of new entrants to the labor market during the last three decades or so, between 1969 and 1998, to get a clear picture of the time trend. We distinguish between four types of jobs: informal, formal public, formal private, and agriculture. We use the existence of job contracts as a measure of informality in this part of the analysis. And we base our analysis on those workers 18 or more years old.

Figure 4.2 shows the annual percentage of new workers—new entrants to the labor market—who were drawn into different jobs between 1969 and 1998. In 1969, 74 percent of new workers were drawn into formal public employment and 20 percent into informal jobs. Since 1993, informal employment has been absorbing more workers than formal public employment. By 1998, 69 percent of new workers were drawn into informal employment and only 19 percent into formal public jobs. The relative share of formal private employment has doubled: in 1969 it was 5 percent; in 1998 it was 10 percent. It is worth noting that the share of agriculture absorbing new entrants seems to be relatively small because workers who join agriculture do so at an early age (Figure 4.1). In Figure 4.1, where all entrants are included (i.e., not just those 18 or more years old), agriculture was absorbing 40 percent of the new entrants in 1969, but by 1998, only 12 percent were starting in agriculture.

Figure 4.1: Percent of New Entrants into Formal and Informal Employment

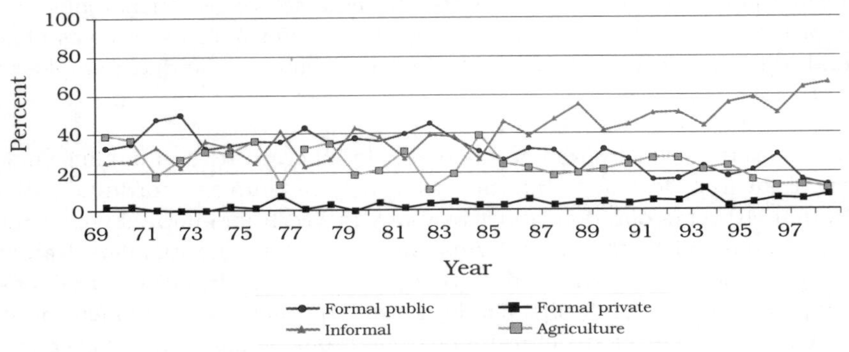

Figure 4.2: Percent of New Entrants to Formal and Informal Employment: 18 or More Years Old

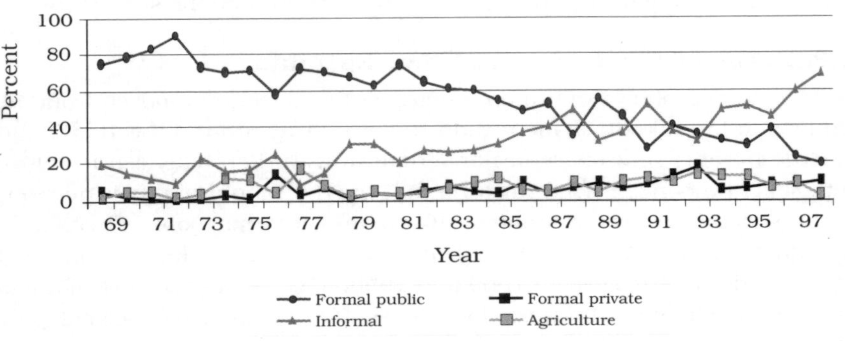

Figure 4.3: Percent of Male New Entrants to Informal and Formal Employment: 18 Years or Older

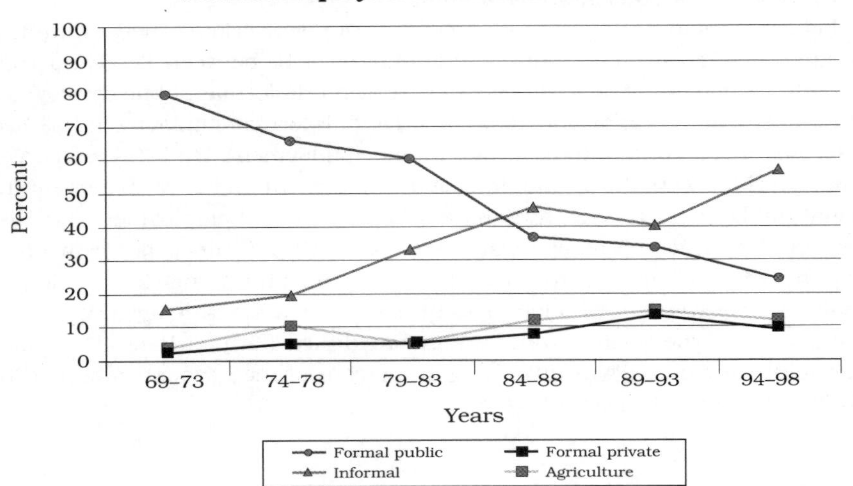

Figure 4.4: Percent of Female New Entrants to Informal and Formal Employment: 18 Years Old or Older

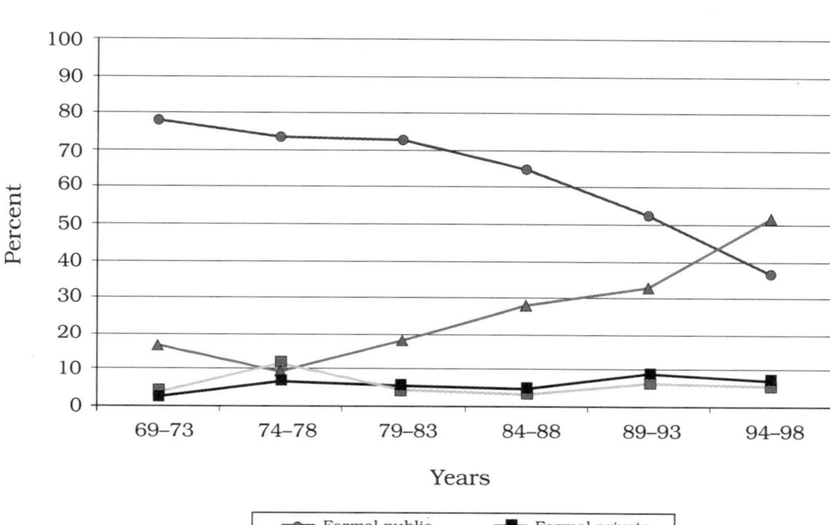

Table 4.11: Age at Start of First Job (18–40)

Start of First Job		Formal Workers	Informal Workers	Total Workers
1974–81	**Mean**	23.26	22.71	23.12
	Std Dev	3.01	4.44	3.43
	N	434.00	147.00	581.00
	t-statistics	1.38		
1982–90	**Mean**	23.34	22.31	22.95
	Std Dev	3.19	4.59	3.81
	N	597.00	356.00	953.00
	t-statistics	3.75*		
1991–98	**Mean**	23.86	21.95	22.79
	Std. Dev.	3.82	4.39	4.26
	N	532.00	683.00	1215.00
	t-statistics	8.12**		

*Note: Mean of age, standard deviation, and number of observations. *The t-statistics test whether the difference in the mean age of formal and informal workers at each period is equal, i.e., whether the mean of age of formal workers is equal to the mean age of informal workers. ** Significant at the 10% level. *** Significant at the 5% level.*

We examine these trends for males and females separately, but given the sample size, we average over a four-year-period. It is clear from Figures 4.3 and 4.4 that since the mid-1980s, male workers have been drawn disproportionately into informal jobs. This only started to take place for females in the early 1990s.

We also compare the mean age of starting formal and informal jobs over time. We include individuals who started their first jobs between the ages of 18 and 40. Table 4.11 shows that the mean age of people starting formal jobs is greater than that of those starting informal jobs, which is not surprising. Individuals who start formal jobs tend to be slightly older than those who start informal ones, since they are more likely to be better educated. This means they would have spent more years studying and having to queue for public jobs before being offered employment. However, the difference between the two age means has been increasing over time. Between 1974 and 1980, the difference in age was not significant. In contrast, in the two later periods, the difference has increased significantly. This reflects the growing queues for public jobs in the 1990s.

Conclusion

The main findings point to the shift from formal, or public, employment to informal employment as a result of economic and social change in Egypt during the 1990s. The proportion of nonagricultural workers (18 years and older) engaged in informal jobs—whether measured as a lack of job contracts or social security coverage—has increased by 5–6 percent in the 1990s. In 1998, 54 percent of the working labor and 44 percent of nonagricultural workers were engaged in jobs without any contracts. Also, 47 percent of all workers and 36 percent of nonagricultural workers were employed without social security coverage. Some groups have experienced a greater increase in informality than have others; female workers and both men and women 18–29 years old have experienced a substantial rise in their participation in informal employment. In addition, the share of wageworkers engaged in informal employment as nonagricultural workers has increased, while the shares of employers and the self-employed have fallen.

Among those who were already employed in 1990, and in terms of absolute numbers, more workers moved from informal to public jobs than in the opposite direction. However, this is only true for the young workers (18–40 years old), who tend to use informal jobs as a "waiting place" until they move into public jobs. More older workers (41–64 years old) moved from the public sector to informal jobs than from informal jobs to the public sector. This supports our expectations that as a result of economic reforms in Egypt, more workers would move from public to informal employment.

Another interesting finding is that new entrants to the labor market in the 1990s have been overly drawn into informal employment. In the early 1970s,

20 percent of workers began their working lives with informal jobs; by 1998, 69 percent of new workers started out in informal employment. In short, the Egyptian labor market has experienced an increase in the informalization of new workers in the 1990s.

In summary, economic reforms in Egypt have led to a significant movement of older workers from the public sector to informal employment. But the main impact of these reforms has been felt by new entrants to the labor market. Given the limited new opportunities in the public sector, new workers have to begin their careers in informal jobs. And while in the past many workers took informal employment while waiting for public sector jobs, the last few years of reforms have pushed the proportion of workers starting in informal employment higher than it has even been before.

Appendix:

Table A4.1: Characteristics of Nonagricultural Workers Using Different Definitions of Formality and Informality, 18–64 Years Old (%)

	Total	Gender		Age			Urban/Rural Residence		Educational Levels					
	Sample	Male	Female	18–29	30–45	46–64	Urban	Rural	Illiterate	Read & write	<interm	intermediate	>interm	University & higher
Contract														
1990	60.98	56.86	77.95	48.43	66.95	65.26	62.76	58.03	27.05	48.65	50.68	75.67	82.46	87.42
1998	55.66	52.19	69.11	36.41	63.67	62.82	58.43	52.05	19.19	44.91	40.88	64.69	79.66	82.92
No contract														
1990	39.02	43.13	22.05	51.57	33.05	34.74	37.24	41.97	72.95	51.35	49.32	24.33	17.54	12.58
1998	44.34	47.81	30.89	63.59	36.33	37.18	41.57	47.95	80.81	55.09	59.12	35.31	20.34	17.08
Social security														
1990	70.00	67.83	78.99	53.17	77.13	77.84	73.46	64.35	37.55	67.45	63.91	80.73	88.03	90.61
1998	64.07	62.79	69.03	37.89	72.06	79.12	69.61	56.86	30.06	61.02	53.59	69.88	79.93	89.30
No social security														
1990	30.00	32.17	21.01	46.83	22.87	22.16	26.54	35.65	62.45	32.55	36.09	19.27	11.97	9.39
1998	35.93	37.21	30.97	62.11	27.94	20.88	30.39	43.14	69.94	38.98	46.41	30.12	20.07	10.70
Contract and social security														
1990	59.91	55.77	76.97	46.64	66.27	64.60	61.86	56.70	26.61	48.18	49.76	74.24	81.78	85.43
1998	53.71	50.51	66.11	31.94	62.49	53.71	54.96	33.92	18.93	43.41	39.03	62.15	74.27	81.48
Contract or social security														
1990	71.07	68.92	79.97	55.14	77.81	78.50	74.36	65.68	37.99	67.92	64.84	82.16	88.72	92.61
1998	66.02	64.48	72.02	42.36	73.24	79.62	71.34	59.10	30.33	62.52	55.44	72.43	85.33	90.74
No contract and no social security														
1990	28.93	31.08	20.03	44.86	22.19	21.50	25.64	34.32	62.01	32.08	35.16	17.84	11.28	7.39
1998	33.98	35.52	27.98	57.64	26.76	20.38	28.66	40.90	69.67	37.48	44.56	27.57	14.67	9.26

(TableA4.1 continued)

Contract & regular job														
1990	60.26	56.24	76.84	46.80	66.61	65.00	62.25	57.00	26.46	48.37	50.57	74.35	81.91	86.42
1998	53.96	50.95	65.65	32.11	62.86	62.47	56.89	50.15	18.45	43.92	40.28	62.22	74.62	81.55
Social security and regular job														
1990	68.99	66.75	78.24	51.61	76.41	76.95	72.53	63.20	36.23	66.47	62.95	79.30	87.17	90.32
1998	62.61	61.35	67.48	34.93	70.86	78.85	67.94	55.67	28.98	59.42	51.83	68.10	79.18	87.96

Table A4.2: Mobility Patterns of Individuals, 18–64 Years Old: 1990–98

Employment	Employment Status in 1998							
Status in 1990	Formal public	Formal private	Informal	Agriculture	Unemployed	Housewife	Others	Total
Formal public	1718	17	59	20	16	15	169	2013
	85.38	0.87	2.91	1.00	0.78	0.69	8.37	100
Formal private	10	149	11	1	7	5	15	197
	5.25	75.54	5.63	0.12	3.56	2.49	7.42	100
Informal	89	45	1098	18	49	27	58	1386
	6.43	3.24	79.27	1.33	3.55	1.97	4.20	100
Agriculture	63	3	47	781	23	14	36	968
	6.54	0.36	4.85	80.71	2.37	1.44	3.74	100
Unemployed	48	10	28	4	19	3	3	115
	41.81	8.98	24.09	3.27	16.47	2.73	2.65	100
Housewife	28	4	79	5	2	154	0	274
	10.33	1.62	29.03	1.67	0.79	56.57	0.00	100
Student	120	38	70	24	20	11	13	299
	40.15	12.62	23.47	8.13	6.68	3.64	4.36	100
Out of Egypt	56	13	46	10	8	1	10	145
	38.41	9.22	31.83	7.22	5.36	0.96	7.00	100
Others	61	15	100	30	8	0	63	278
	21.95	5.50	36.14	10.64	2.90	0.00	22.87	100
TOTAL	**2194**	**296**	**1539**	**893**	**152**	**230**	**367**	**5675**
	38.67	**5.22**	**27.12**	**15.74**	**2.67**	**4.06**	**6.47**	**100**

Note: In each entry the top figure gives the absolute number; the second figure is the % of the row.

Table A4.3: Mobility Patterns of Males, 18–64 Years Old: 1990–98

Employment Status in 1990	Employment Status in 1998						
	Formal public	Formal private	Informal	Agriculture	Unemployed	Others	Total
Formal public	1216	13	55	20	13	131	1448
	83.97	0.93	3.77	1.36	0.89	9.07	100
Formal private	6	132	10	0.23	6	9	161
	3.56	81.80	6.22	0.14	2.85	5.42	100
Informal	82	43	968	18	42	56	1209
	6.77	3.57	80.08	1.49	3.44	4.65	100
Agriculture	59	3	43	680	15	35	836
	7.01	0.41	3.57	81.37	1.77	4.24	100
Unemployed	23	7	24	4	7	1	66
	34.36	11.18	35.70	5.63	11.36	1.77	100
Student	79	31	55	22	12	7	208
	37.91	14.86	26.47	10.45	5.67	3.29	100
Out of Egypt	53	13	45	10	8	9	138
	38.63	9.45	32.63	7.41	5.50	6.37	100
Others	57	15	98	29	8	50	256
	22.18	5.82	38.03	11.27	3.08	19.61	100
Total	**1574**	**258**	**1297**	**782**	**109**	**299**	**4322**
	36.41	**5.97**	**30.02**	**18.11**	**2.51**	**6.91**	**100**

Note: In each entry the top figure gives the absolute number; the second figure is the % of the row.

Table A4.4: Mobility Patterns of Individuals, 18–40 Years Old: 1990–98

Employment Status in 1990	Employment Status in 1998							
	Formal public	**Formal private**	**Informal**	**Agriculture**	**Unemployed**	**Housewife**	**Others**	**Total**
Formal public	660.00	13.00	18.00	5.00	7.00	7.00	8.00	720
	91.73	1.79	2.50	0.75	1.04	1.03	1.16	100
Formal private	10.00	77.00	7.00	1.00	5.00	3.00	3.00	105
	9.12	73.68	6.69	0.23	4.46	3.04	2.79	100
Informal	73.00	32.00	556.00	12.00	29.00	20.00	9.00	730
	9.95	4.42	76.18	1.60	3.97	2.68	1.21	100
Agriculture	46.00	2.00	28.00	360.00	8.00	4.00	3.00	453
	10.22	0.53	6.25	79.63	1.72	0.88	0.77	100
Unemployed	47.00	10.00	27.00	4.00	14.00	3.00	3.00	109
	43.56	9.59	24.42	3.50	13.19	2.92	2.83	100
Housewife	25.00	4.00	51.00	3.00	1.00	82.00	0.00	166
	15.01	2.17	30.56	2.07	0.63	49.56	0.00	100
Student	121.00	38.00	71.00	25.00	20.00	11.00	13.00	302
	40.15	12.62	23.47	8.13	6.68	3.64	4.36	100
Out of Egypt	33.00	7.00	30.00	2.00	3.00	0.00	1.00	77
	43.09	9.63	39.29	3.01	3.48	0.00	1.49	100
Others	55.00	14.00	96.00	29.00	7.00	0.00	5.00	205
	27.00	6.41	46.71	14.22	3.26	0.00	2.39	100
Total	**1070.00**	**198.00**	**884.00**	**441.00**	**94.00**	**130.00**	**46.00**	**2867**
	37.35	**6.89**	**30.84**	**15.38**	**3.28**	**4.55**	**1.60**	**100**

Note: In each entry the top figure gives the absolute number; the second figure is the % of the row.

Table A4.5: Mobiliy Patterns of Individuals, 41–64 Years Old: 1990–98

Employment	Employment Status in 1998							
Status in 1990	**Formal public**	**Formal private**	**Informal**	**Agriculture**	**Unemployed**	**Housewife**	**Others**	**Total**
Formal public	1054.00	5.00	40.00	15.00	8.00	6.00	159.00	1288
	81.89	0.36	3.13	1.14	0.63	0.50	12.34	100
Formal private	1.00	72.00	4.00	0.00	2.00	2.00	12.00	92
	0.92	77.63	4.44	0.00	2.54	1.88	12.59	100
Informal	17.00	13.00	542.00	7.00	20.00	8.00	49.00	656
	2.57	1.96	82.66	1.04	3.09	1.20	7.48	100
Agriculture	17.00	1.00	19.00	420.00	15.00	10.00	32.00	515
	3.36	0.22	3.63	81.65	2.92	1.92	6.30	100
Unemployed	1.00	0.00	1.00	0.00	5.00	0.00	0.00	7
	16.15	0.00	19.21	0.00	64.65	0.00	0.00	100
Housewife	4.00	1.00	21.00	1.00	1.00	73.00	0.00	108
	3.30	0.79	26.72	1.05	1.02	67.12	0.00	100
Out of Egypt	22.00	6.00	16.00	8.00	5.00	1.00	9.00	68
	33.15	8.76	23.45	11.95	7.47	2.03	13.19	100
Others	6.00	2.00	5.00	1.00	1.00	0.00	58.00	73
	7.99	2.98	6.89	0.73	1.91	0.00	79.50	100
Total	**1122.00**	**99.00**	**657.00**	**452.00**	**58.00**	**100.00**	**319.00**	**2808**
	39.98	**3.54**	**23.39**	**16.09**	**2.07**	**3.57**	**11.37**	**100**

Note: In each entry the top figure gives the absolute number; the second figure is the % of the row.

Table A4.6: Mobility Patterns of Individuals, 18–64 Years Old: 1990–98: Normalized

Employment	Employment Status in 1998							
Status in 1990	Formal public	Formal private	Informal	Agriculture	Unemployed	Housewife	Others	Total
Formal public	0.00	17.00	59.00	20.00	16.00	15.00	169.00	295
	0.00	5.93	19.90	6.85	5.31	4.72	57.29	100
Formal private	10.00	0.00	11.00	1.00	7.00	5.00	15.00	48
	21.45	0.00	23.00	0.49	14.54	10.19	30.32	100
Informal	89.00	45.00	0.00	18.00	49.00	27.00	58.00	288
	31.00	15.65	0.00	6.42	17.14	9.52	20.27	100
Agriculture	63.00	3.00	47.00	0.00	23.00	14.00	36.00	187
	33.90	1.88	25.12	0.00	12.27	7.46	19.37	100
Unemployed	48.00	10.00	28.00	4.00	0.00	3.00	3.00	97
	50.06	10.75	28.83	3.92	0.00	3.27	3.17	100
Housewife	28.00	4.00	79.00	5.00	2.00	0.00	0.00	119
	23.80	3.72	66.84	3.84	1.81	0.00	0.00	100
Student	120.00	38.00	70.00	24.00	20.00	11.00	13.00	298
	40.54	12.74	23.69	8.21	6.74	3.67	4.40	100
Out of Egypt	56.00	13.00	46.00	10.00	8.00	1.00	10.00	145
	38.41	9.22	31.83	7.22	5.36	0.96	7.00	100
Others	61.00	15.00	100.00	30.00	8.00	0.00	0.00	214
	28.46	7.13	46.85	13.79	3.76	0.00	0.00	100
Total	**478.00**	**148**	**441**	**112.00**	**133.00**	**76.00**	**305.00**	**1693**
	28.21	**8.72**	**26.10**	**6.61**	**7.87**	**4.48**	**18.01**	**100**

Note: In each entry the top figure gives the absolute number; the second figure is the % of the row.

Table A4.7: Mobility Patterns of Individuals 18–64 Years Old Using Wage Status: 1990–98

Employment Status in 1990	Employment Status in 1998							
	Waged Informal	**Self-empl. & employers Informal**	**Nonwaged Informal**	**Waged Formal**	**Unemployed**	**Housewife**	**Others**	**Total**
Waged informal	762.00	73.00	5.00	141.00	59.00	26.00	67.00	1131
	67.33	6.44	0.43	12.45	5.23	2.26	5.66	100
Self-empl. and								
employers	12.00	849.00	0.00	25.00	9.00	7.00	27.00	927
Informal	1.32	91.36	0.00	2.67	1.00	0.71	2.93	100
Nonwaged	15.00	50.00	153.00	29.00	4.00	9.00	12.00	273
Informal	5.60	18.46	55.97	10.74	1.37	3.30	4.40	100
Waged Formal	31.00	57.00	2.00	1893.00	20.00	19.00	190.00	2213
	1.38	2.59	0.10	85.58	0.92	0.85	8.58	100
Unemployed	25.00	4.00	2.00	58.00	19.00	3.00	4.00	115
	21.33	3.54	2.08	50.46	16.47	2.73	3.40	100
Housewife	23.00	48.00	13.00	33.00	2.00	155.00	0.00	274
	8.44	17.36	4.89	11.95	0.79	56.57	0.00	100
Student	36.00	39.00	18.00	159.00	20.00	11.00	14.00	299
	11.93	12.93	6.01	53.12	6.68	3.64	4.75	100
Out of Egypt	31.00	20.00	1.00	67.00	8.00	1.00	12.00	140
	22.28	14.03	0.60	47.59	5.55	0.71	8.95	100
Others	87.00	29.00	13.00	79.00	10.00	0.00	81.00	300
	29.00	9.67	4.33	26.33	3.33	0.00	27.00	100
Total	**1021.00**	**1169.00**	**2484.00**	**207.00**	**152.00**	**230.00**	**408.00**	**5675**
	18.01	**20.60**	**43.77**	**3.65**	**2.67**	**4.06**	**7.18**	**100**

Note: In each entry the top figure gives the absolute number; the second figure is the % of the row.

Part III. Special Groups

5 Women and Work in Egypt: A Decade of Change

Safaa El-Kogali

Introduction

The status of women in the labor market is not a new topic or area of study. For decades, various models have been developed and numerous arguments made on the position of women in the economy. In Egypt, women figured prominently in studies on the labor market, especially during the past decade, with the introduction of economic reforms and structural adjustment policies. But the study of women's labor in Egypt has been hampered by a serious measurement problem. While there is a rich body of data on various aspects of female labor dating back decades, due to the variety of methods used in defining the labor force and economic activity, comparability across time is not possible (Assaad, 1997). The Egypt Labor Market Survey (ELMS 98) offers a unique opportunity to measure changes in the labor market in general and the status of women in particular during the past 10 years—a decade of major reforms and structural changes in the Egyptian economy.

The ELMS 98 was conducted in October 1998. This nationally representative survey at the regional level consists of 5000 households and is rich with information on women in the labor market. It was closely designed to match the 1988 Special Round of the Labor Force Sample Survey (LFSS 88) and was undertaken at exactly the same time, ten years later. The survey was designed in a manner to capture as much female activity as possible, especially wage work.[1]

Based on data from the ELMS 98 and LFSS 88, this study aims to observe changes in female wage work in Egypt between 1988 and 1998—a time of major structural changes in the economy. By no means is the report an attempt to measure the impact of these changes on women's position in the labor market. Other than the fact that causality would be difficult to establish, this is a task that would require more sophisticated methodology and deeper analysis—both of which are beyond the limited scope of this paper. The aim here is to simply shed some light on the changes in the status of women in the labor market—especially female wageworkers, during this 10-year period.

This chapter is organized as follows: section one defines the major concepts, section two gives an overview of labor force participation in Egypt, section three observes changes in wage work for women during the decade, section four discusses changes in working conditions of female wageworkers in the private sector. Finally, some concluding remarks are made.

1. Definitions

Definitions used in this report correspond to definitions used in both the ELMS 98 and LFSS 88.

The labor force constitutes men and women ages 15–64 who were economically active during the reference period. The reference period used in this study is one week—i.e., the focus is on the "currently" active. Economic activity includes any work in the production of a good or service, including wage work, self-employment, and unpaid family work. Subsistence work in the primary sectors is also included in this definition.

The labor force consists of employed and unemployed persons. Employment is determined on the basis of participation in an economic activity for at least one hour during the reference week. There are two definitions of unemployment used in this study. One definition is that of open unemployment, whereby a person between the ages of 15 and 64 desires work and is ready for it, but did not participate in any economic activity during the reference week. The second definition adds a search requirement to the first definition—that is, a person desires work, is prepared for it and is actively searching for employment. This is the definition commonly used in Egypt and is used in this study. There is also visible underemployment, in which a person is working less than 40 hours a week, and discouraged unemployment, where a person declared himself/herself as not working and available for work but did not actively search for employment. In this study, those were classified as being out of the labor force.

2. Overview of Women in The Labor Market in Egypt[2]

Female labor force participation rates vary widely with the definition of the labor force. Using the broad definition that includes subsistence work, there were 8.5 million Egyptian women between the ages of 15 and 64 in the labor force in 1998. Between 1988 and 1998, the female labor force grew 3.6 percent per annum, increasing their share of the total labor force from 35.7 percent in 1988 to 38.7 percent in 1998. The female labor force participation rate increased from 41.8 percent in 1988 to 46.3 percent in 1998. This rate reflects the high female subsistence activities in agriculture. Male participation rates have dropped by more than three percentage points during the 10-year period, from 76.7 percent in 1988 to 73.3 percent in 1998. Because men make up the bulk of the labor force, the decline in male rates cancelled out the increase in female rates, making the overall labor force participation rate stable at around 59 percent during the decade.

Labor force participation rates are higher in rural areas than in urban areas for both women and men. Between 1988 and 1998 participation rates for women increased more in urban areas than in rural areas, reducing the urban/rural gap.

Table 5.1: Labor Force Participation, Employment, and Unemployment Rates by Gender, Egypt, 1988, 1998

Labor Force Participation	1988		1998		Growth Rate per Annum	
	%	'000s	%	'000s	%	'000s
Total	59.1	16,595	59.8	21,982	2.8	539
Male	76.7	10,653	73.3	13,483	2.4	283
Female	41.8	5931	46.3	8503	3.6	257
Unemployment						
Total	5.4	896	7.9	1737	6.6	84
Male	4.0	426	7.0	944	8.0	52
Female	7.9	469	9.4	799	5.3	33
Employment						
Total	94.6	15,699	92.1	20,245	2.5	455
Male	96.0	10,227	93.0	12,539	2.0	231
Female	92.2	5469	90.6	7704	3.4	223

Source: LFSS 88, ELMS 98.

Moreover, the increase in the rate of participation for women and the decrease in the male rate reduced the gender gap in the labor market. Using the ratio of female-to-male participation to measure the gender gap (on a scale of zero to one, whereby zero denotes total inequality and one denotes total equality), the gender gap decreased by about 17 percent, from 0.5 in 1988 to 0.6 in 1998. The gender gap was much narrower in rural areas than in urban areas. That is, the difference in participation rates between men and women were smaller in rural areas than in urban areas. However, the increase in urban female participation has substantially narrowed the gap in urban areas over the past decade, further reducing the urban/rural gap in participation.

In terms of education, the lowest participation rates in 1988 and 1998 were among women with less-than-intermediate level education. However, during that decade labor force participation increased the most among those women with less that intermediate level education, and dropped among those with intermediate and above education. This is likely due to the fact that girls who reach that level in schooling usually continue their education. Starting from intermediate-level education, labor force participation rates among women increased with education. Between 1988 and 1998, participation rates increased significantly for women with less-than-intermediate level of education and dropped for women with intermediate and secondary schooling.

Women in 1998 entered the labor force later and stayed in it longer than they did in 1988, as shown by the drop in participation rates among girls ages 19 and younger and the rise in participation among 60 to 64 year-old women. Participation rates increased for women between the ages 20 and 64, with the highest rate among women ages 60–64 (from a low base) and 30–34. Over half of all women of working age are out of the labor force, and about three quarters of them stay at home. Increasingly, younger women are staying out of the labor force to attend school. Between 1988 and 1998, school enrollment of young women ages 15–24 increased 40 percent. This may explain the drop in participation rates for younger women and the delayed entry into the labor force.

There were 1.7 million unemployed persons in Egypt in 1998. The open unemployment rate (using the definition that includes searching for work as a requirement) grew from 5.4 percent in 1988 to 7.9 percent in 1998. Unemployment is higher among women than men, and increased for both during the decade. For men, unemployment increased from 4.0 percent in 1988 to 7.0 percent in 1998, at an annual rate of 8 percent. Female unemployment grew at a much lower pace during the same period, from 7.8 percent in 1988 to 9.4 percent in 1998—a 5.3 percent annual increase.[3] Dropping the search criterion from the definition shows unemployment rates for both men and women increased by one-and-a-half percentage points. The variation, given the search requirement, may suggest discouraged unemployment among men and women. That is, given the high unemployment rates, many may stop searching for work. Using the market-based definition of economic activity, i.e., excluding subsistence work, the unemployment rate in 1998 becomes 11.7 percent—a 48 percent increase from the rate determined through the broader definition. While the male rate remains constant, the female unemployment rate increases to 27.6 percent—more than three times the rate determined through the narrow definition.

Unemployment is highest among young new entrants into the labor force. The survey shows that 85.5 percent of women who were unemployed in 1998 had never worked before. In 1998, 30.4 percent of young women ages 20–24 were unemployed. However, it was women ages 30–34 who suffered the highest growth in unemployment during the decade—from 1.6 percent in 1988 to 6.0 percent in 1998. The rise in female unemployment is primarily among women with above-intermediate levels of education. Unemployment dropped significantly among women with intermediate and less-than-intermediate levels of education.

The majority of women and men cited the unavailability of work opportunities as the reason for their unemployment. Other reasons cited by women were unavailability of work that corresponds to their qualifications and no available work with a suitable location. More men and women cited the scarcity of work opportunities as a main reason for their unemployment in 1998 than in 1988, and less cited other reasons, such as unsuitable location or pay. This may suggest that work opportunities have become scarcer in 1998, and that the reason for unemployment is the lack of availability of jobs rather than a lack of suitability. On average, women remained unemployed for four years before finding a job or stopping their search. The average duration of unemployment for men was two years.

Unemployed men and women used various formal and informal channels to search for jobs. The majority relied on the assistance of family and friends. Women tended to also depend heavily on the government for employment, registering at government employment offices and/or entering competitions for government jobs. Men depended less on government channels; they tended to seek assistance from acquaintances, inquire at work locations, contact contractors or employers directly, and wait at assembly points in search of jobs. Between 1988 and 1998, men and women increasingly searched for jobs through more formal channels, such as employment offices and hiring competitions.

Employment grew at an average rate of 455,000 jobs annually during the 10-year study period—an annual growth rate of 2.5 percent. Female employment grew at an annual rate of 3.4 percent, or 223,000 jobs per annum, while employment for men grew at an annual rate of 2.0 percent. Female employment is concentrated in unpaid work in the private sector, mostly in subsistence agriculture. Unpaid agricultural work increased significantly for women between 1988 and 1998, from 66.8 percent to 97.3 percent, respectively.

3. Women and Wage Work in Egypt, 1988–98

Half of the economically active population in Egypt was engaged in wage work in 1998—a quarter of women and two-thirds of men. Between 1988 and 1998, three million waged jobs were created. The share for women was 550,000 jobs, which increased the number of female wageworkers from 1.5 million in 1988 to 2.1 million in 1998—a 3 percent annual growth rate.

Table 5.2: Distribution of Female Wage Workers by Sector, Egypt, 1988, 1998

Female Wage Work	1988		1998		Growth Rate per Annum	
	%	'000s	%	'000s	%	'000s
Government	56.3	870	71.3	1493	5.4	62
Public sector enterprises	12.5	193	6.0	126	-4.3	-7
Private						
Agricultural wage work	10.3	159	4.2	88	-5.9	-7
Nonagricultural wage work	20.9	323	18.5	387	1.8	6
Total female wage work	100.0	1545	100.0	2094	3.0	55

Source: LFSS 88, ELMS 98.

In 1998, women constituted 19 percent of wageworkers in Egypt. The majority are married and live in urban areas. On average, they are between the ages of 27 and 37, with younger women more concentrated in the private sector than older women. The majority of female wageworkers have intermediate and above-intermediate levels of education. Between 1988 and 1998, the proportion of illiterate female wageworkers dropped significantly, from 19.4 percent in 1988 to 9.2 percent in 1998, reflecting the advances in education achieved during the decade.

Figure 5.1: Government Jobs for Women, Egypt, 1988, 1998

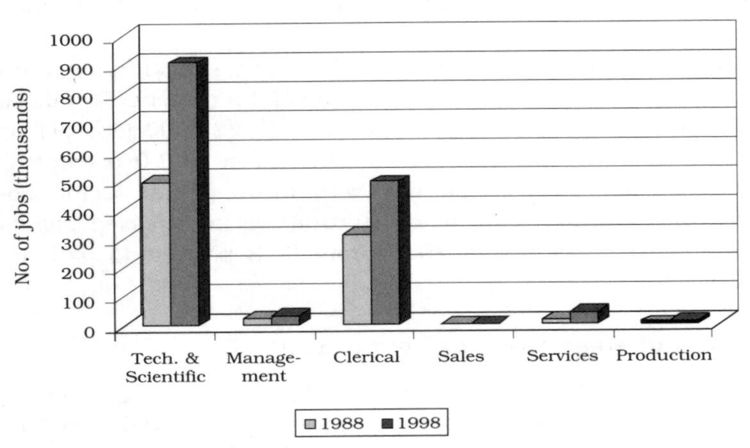

Source: LFSS 88, ELMS 98.

Government employment has traditionally constituted the largest share of female wage work in Egypt. The increase in wage work for women was primarily in government employment, which grew at an average annual rate of 5.4

percent, or 62,000 jobs per annum increasing the share of government employment for female wageworkers from 56.3 percent in 1988 to 76.3 percent in 1998. Female employment in public sector enterprises dropped significantly—4.3 percent annually—such that 70,000 jobs were lost during these 10 years. This is due to the privatization efforts that Egypt began during the 1980s, and which escalated during the 1990s. It is remarkable that the largest increase in female wage work is in government employment despite the massive efforts for structural adjustment and economic reforms during the decade.

Two-thirds of the new jobs for women in the government were in technical and scientific occupations—i.e. teaching and nursing—and almost one-third were clerical occupations. This is due to the major efforts undertaken during the decade to expand health and education services, especially in Upper Egypt.

In the private sector, agricultural wage work for women dropped significantly during the 10-year period, at an annual rate of 5.9 percent. Nonagricultural private sector waged employment grew for women at an annual rate of 1.8 percent, resulting in 60,000 new jobs, mostly in manufacturing, trade, and finance. Services, which was the leading economic activity for women in private sector wage work, declined. The net effect of employment growth for women in the private sector is negative, because of the large decline in agricultural work. Given that most women in the private sector are engaged in agricultural work, the share of private sector wage work among working women dropped between 1988 and 1998.

Table 5.3: Distribution of Female Wage Workers in Nonagriculture Private Sector by Occupation, Egypt, 1988, 1998

Female Private Nonagri. Wage Work	1988		1998		Growth Rate per Annum	
	%	'000s	%	'000s	%	'000s
Mining	0.8	2	0.0	0	0	-0.2
Manufacturing	22.4	72	28.6	111	4.2	3.8
Construction	2.0	6	3.4	13	7.2	0.7
Trade	26.4	85	27.2	105	2.1	2.0
Transport	3.4	11	1.9	7	-4.2	-0.4
Finance	3.0	10	6.6	26	9.5	1.6
Services	42.0	136	32.4	125	-0.8	-1.0
Total private nonagri. Wage work	100.0	323	100.0	387	1.8	6.4

Source: LFSS 88, ELMS 98.

Job opportunities for women emerged mostly in private sector sales, clerical and production occupations which grew at an annual rate of 4.2, 3.8, and 3.4 percent, respectively. Technical and scientific jobs also increased in the private sector but at a much slower pace than in the government and other nonagriculture private sector occupations. Nevertheless, technical and scientific occupations still constitute over a quarter of jobs in nonagriculture private sector. Services, which presented the second leading occupation in 1988, dropped tremendously at an annual rate of 3.3 percent—constituting only 13.7 percent of the occupational distribution. Occupations in production comprise the largest share of female occupations in the private sector at 26.7 percent.

4. Conditions of Work

The literature is replete with arguments about increases in female activity in the private sector being accompanied by longer working hours, less stability, and fewer benefits (see for example Standing, 1989 and Mogadham, 1998). In this section, the changes in working conditions are measured by employment stability, incidence of a contract, hours of work, social security, and medical insurance. The analysis will apply to the private sector since, by default, public-sector work is formal and permanent, and contains a benefits package.

In general, nonagricultural private-sector wage work for women is permanent. However, the share of women engaged in nonagricultural private-sector wage work declined during the 10-year period, from 75.3 percent in 1988 to 69.5 percent in 1998, while temporary work almost doubled, from 12.3 percent to 21.7 percent, respectively.

If we take the incidence of a contract among wageworkers as an indication of formality, then the greater part of private sector wage work is informal. Almost all of the women engaged in agricultural wage activity have no contracts, while approximately one-third of those working in nonagricultural private work do have contracts. Between 1988 and 1998, the proportion of women in nonagricultural private wage work with contracts declined from 32.2 percent to 28.5 percent, respectively.

Women in private sector wage work in Egypt are working longer days today than they did a decade ago. The average number of working hours per week in private sector wage work increased from 44 hours in 1988 to 50 hours in 1998. In agricultural employment, women worked on average 10 hours more per week than they did in 1988. In nonagricultural activity, the average number of hours per week increased from 45 to 49 over the 10-year period.

Social security and medical insurance are also indicators of the quality of jobs. Less women enjoyed these benefits in 1998 than in 1988. The incidence of social security for women in private nonagricultural work declined from 38.1 percent in 1988 to 28.7 percent in 1998. Similarly, the proportion of women in nonagricultural private wage work with medical insurance dropped from 21 percent in 1988 to 19 percent in 1998.

Hence, it appears that while women made some gains in labor force participation and in wage work, working conditions in the private sector deteriorated during the decade. Working conditions did not improve for men either. Work became less stable and less formal, with longer hours and fewer benefits. It is no surprise that when women wageworkers were asked whether they would work if they did not need the income, 57.8 percent of those working in the private sector responded "No" (compared to 41.6 percent in the public sector). Of married women working in the private sector, 54.9 percent have children less than six years old, whom they leave with their own mothers, mothers-in-law, or daughters for childcare while they work. While 80 percent of women in the public sector worked during their latest pregnancy, only 39.8 percent of those in the private sector did. Of those women in the private sector who did work during their pregnancy, 53.3 percent did not get paid maternity leave. These statistics suggest that the majority of women working in the private sector must work during pregnancy because they need the income.

Answers to the survey's questions on the use of income show that 83 percent of women wageworkers in the private sector contribute to their household budgets; 48.8 percent contribute all their income, especially if they are married women (or are divorced or widowed). For 61.8 percent of the women, their contributions constitute between one-quarter and one-half of their total monthly household budgets. And 5.4 percent of female wageworkers provide all of their household income. Younger women tend to keep most of their salaries for their own use. Also, 52.5 percent of single women and 82.5 percent of legally married women whose marriages are legal on paper, but who have not yet moved in with their husbands, keep their entire salaries for their own use—usually to prepare for their "*jihaz*" (personal and household items acquired in preparation for marriage).

5. Conclusion

This study provided an overview of changes in female wage work in Egypt between 1988 and 1998—a period of major structural adjustments in the Egyptian economy. Female labor force participation increased during this decade, and although unemployment among women increased, it was at a slower pace than among men. The unavailability of work was the main reason cited by both women and men for their unemployment. Women stayed unemployed on average for four years—twice as long as men. Employment for women increased, but mostly in unpaid subsistence agriculture. Waged employment also increased, but primarily in the public sector. It is interesting that despite a decade of economic reforms in Egypt, the government not only remains the dominant employer for women, but has actually grown at a remarkably fast pace. However, privatization efforts appear to have been more successful in the significant reduction of public enterprise employment.

Nonagricultural wage work for women in the private sector has also grown, but by very little, and mostly in informal activities. It has been noted that in many developing countries, the informal sector has been the absorber of new entrants into the labor market and has offered alternative employment for those who were released from the public sector during economic reforms. Some argue that in Egypt, the informal sector will be the "engine of growth" for future development, and the limited growth in private sector work has been accompanied by longer working hours, more temporary work, and fewer benefits. For the majority of women working in these conditions, their incomes form a major contribution to their households, especially married women. Younger single women need the income to prepare for their marriages.

These results have serious policy implications. The growth of the government sector at such a fast pace cannot be sustained. Growth of the private sector remains slow, despite a decade of private sector development efforts and various policy incentives put in place for local and foreign investors. The formal private sector remains closed for women, and opportunities seem to be emerging only in informal activity, where working conditions are poor and unregulated. Regulations—such as the Labor Code, which aims to protect women against poor working conditions—have to a large extent deterred employers from hiring women, due to the strict requirements associated with hiring them. Regulations and policy incentives need to be revisited to be more aligned with the demands of the private sector, to foster growth, and to offer equitable access for men and women alike.

Notes

1 See Assaad, R. and G. Barsoum, 1999 on details of survey design.

2 See Assaad, R. "The Transformation of the Egyptian Labor Market: 1988–98" in this volume for greater details on changes in participation patterns.

3 Previous studies show female unemployment rates rising faster than male rates. Assaad explains that this result may be due to a lower denominator of the unemployment rate in the 1988 data due to a "declining effort overtime to detect female employment in agriculture and informal activities" (See Assaad, R., "The Transformation of the Egyptian Labor Market" in this volume).

Appendix

Table A5.1: Labor Force Participation Rates of Men and Women Ages 15 to 64 by Gender, Egypt, 1988, 1998

	Male	Female
Age 15–64		
Including search criteria		
1988	76.7	41.8
1998	73.3	46.3
Age 15–64		
Without search criteria		
1988	77.7	42.9
1998	74.4	47.2
Age 15–64		
Excluding subsistence, 1998		
With search	73.2	21.4
w/o search	74.4	22.5

Notes: N = number of observations.
Source: LFSS 88, ELMS 98.

Table A5.2: Labor Force Participation Rates of Ages 15 to 64, by Urban/Rural Location, Egypt, 1988, 1998

	1988			1998		
	Urban	**Rural**	**Total**	**Urban**	**Rural**	**Total**
Male	74.4	78.8	76.7	71.5	74.8	73.3
Female	28.5	53.5	41.8	33.3	56.9	46.3
Total	51.2	66.0	59.1	52.4	65.8	59.8
N	8837	6896	15733	9610	5022	14632
Female/Male Ratio	0.38	0.68	0.54	0.47	0.76	0.63

Source: LFSS 88, ELMS 98.

Table A5.3: Labor Force Participation Rates by Gender and Age, Egypt, 1988, 1998

Age	Male		Female		Female/Male Ratio	
	1988	1998	1988	1998	1988	1998
05–09	4.1	0.4	5.4	2.3	1.32	5.23
10–14	17.2	6.7	16.3	11.7	0.95	1.75
15–19	45.4	33.9	30.0	29.1	0.66	0.86
20–24	49.5	55.9	46.2	50.1	0.93	0.90
25–29	89.5	90.3	50.2	51.3	0.56	0.57
30–34	98.2	97.9	48.8	59.1	0.50	0.60
35–39	98.9	98.8	47.6	56.2	0.48	0.57
40–44	97.6	98.5	47.4	50.1	0.49	0.51
45–49	96.3	95.2	43.0	50.9	0.45	0.53
50–54	96.7	92.2	35.4	48.6	0.37	0.53
55–59	93.4	85.3	37.1	39.2	0.40	0.46
60–64	76.5	56.5	24.3	36.7	0.32	0.65
15–64	76.7	73.3	41.8	46.3	0.54	0.63
N	7777	7320	7956	7312		

Source: LFSS 88, ELMS 98.

Table A5.4: Labor Force Participation Rates by Gender and Educational Level, Egypt, 1988, 1998

Education Level	Male		Female		Female/Male Ratio	
	1988	1998	1988	1998	1988	1998
Illiterate	89.5	89.1	43.4	51.1	0.48	0.57
Read & write	89.9	88.3	22.9	37.9	0.25	0.43
Less than intermediate	49.8	51.4	17.7	23.8	0.36	0.46
Intermediate	66.4	69.2	54.7	48.9	0.82	0.71
Higher than intermediate	82.7	92.1	78.0	71.0	0.94	0.77
University	88.5	90.2	69.9	74.1	0.79	0.82
Post-graduate	95.9	94.6	83.3	80.6	0.87	0.85
Total	76.7	73.4	41.8	46.4	0.54	0.63
N	7777	7290	7956	7288		

Source: LFSS 88, ELMS 98.

Table A5.5: Unemployment Rates by Gender, Egypt, 1988, 1998

Unemployment Rates	1988	1998
With search criteria		
Male	4.0	7.0
Female	7.9	9.4
Total	5.4	7.4
Female/Male Ratio	2.0	1.3
Without search criteria		
Male	5.2	8.4
Female	10.2	10.9
Total	7.0	9.4
Female/Male Ratio	2.0	1.3
Excluding subsistence and with search criteria		
Male	N.A.	7.0
Female	N.A.	27.6
Total	N.A.	11.7
Female/Male Ratio	N.A.	3.9

Note: N.A.: not available as 1988 definition of labor force includes subsistence work.
Source: LFSS 88, ELMS 98.

Table A5.6: Unemployment Rates by Gender and Urban/Rural Location, Egypt, 1988, 1998

	1988			1998		
	Urban	**Rural**	**Total**	**Urban**	**Rural**	**Total**
Male	5.8	2.4	4.0	6.8	7.1	7.0
Female	17.1	3.5	7.8	15.8	6.3	9.4
Total	9.0	2.9	5.4	9.7	6.8	7.9
Female/Male Ratio	2.9	1.5	2.0	2.3	0.9	1.3

Source: LFSS 88, ELMS 98.

Table A5.7: Unemployment Rates by Gender and Age, Egypt, 1988, 1998

	Male		Female		Female/Male Ratio	
	1988	1998	1988	1998	1988	1998
15–19	7.8	17.7	16.4	12.1	2.10	0.68
20–24	10.6	19.9	21.2	30.4	2.00	1.53
25–29	5.6	10.7	7.4	15.3	1.32	1.43
30–34	1.5	3.3	1.6	6.0	1.07	1.82
35–39	2.5	1.8	2.9	2.4	1.16	1.33
40–44	1.8	1.2	1.6	1.7	0.89	1.42
45–49	1.5	1.4	1.0	0.2	0.63	0.14
50–54	0.3	2.4	1.4	0.1	4.52	0.06
55–59	0.6	1.6	0.0	0.0	0.00	0.00
60–64	3.3	0.4	0.7	0.0	0.20	0.00
15–64	4.0	7.0	7.8	9.4	1.95	1.34
N	5922	5335	3236	3152		

Source: LFSS 88, ELMS 98.

Table A5.8: Unemployment Rates by Gender and Educational Level, Egypt, 1988, 1998

	Male		Female		Female/Male Ratio	
	1988	1998	1988	1998	1988	1998
Illiterate	2.1	3.3	1.4	0.8	0.67	0.25
Read & write	2.5	3.5	7.5	3.6	3.00	1.03
Less than intermediate	4.3	4.7	13.6	2.3	3.16	0.49
Intermediate	8.7	13.6	28.8	27.6	3.31	2.03
Higher than intermediate	6.2	9.9	16.9	22.1	2.73	2.23
University	5.8	6.9	14.2	15.3	2.45	2.22
Post-graduate	2.0	1.0	0.0	0.0	0.00	0.00
Total	4.0	7.0	7.8	9.4	1.95	1.34
N	5922	5323	3236	3146		

Source: LFSS 88, ELMS 98.

Table A5.9: Distribution of Female Wage Workers in Government Work by Occupation, Egypt, 1988, 1998

Occupations	1988		1998		Growth per Annum	
	%	'000s	%	'000s	%	'000s
Technical & Scientific	57.3	499	60.8	908	6.0	41.0
Management	3.2	28	2.4	36	2.6	0.8
Clerical	36.1	314	33.0	493	4.5	17.9
Sales	0.5	4	0.0	0.0	0.0	-0.4
Services	2.1	18	3.0	44	8.9	2.6
Production	0.8	7	0.8	11	4.8	0.4
Total Govt. Work	100.0	870	100.0	1493	5.4	62.0

Source: LFSS 88, ELMS 98.

Table A5.10: Distribution of Female Wage Workers in Nonagricultural Private Sector Work, by Economic Activity, Egypt, 1988, 1998

	1988		1998		Growth per Annum	
	%	'000s	%	'000s	%	'000s
Mining	0.8	2	0.0	0		-0.2
Manufacturing	22.4	72	28.6	111	4.2	3.8
Construction	2.0	6	3.4	13	7.2	0.7
Trade	26.4	85	27.1	105	2.1	2.0
Transport	3.4	11	1.9	7	-4.2	-0.4
Finance	3.0	10	6.6	26	9.5	1.6
Services	42.0	136	32.4	125	-0.8	-1.0
Total	100.0	323	100.0	387	1.8	6.4

Source: LFSS 88, ELMS 98.

Table A5.11: Average Number of Hours Worked Per Week for Female Wage Workers in the Private Sector, by Agriculture and Nonagriculture Activity, Egypt, 1988, 1998

	1988	1998
Agriculture	42	52
Nonagriculture	45	49
Total	44	50

Source: LFSS 88, ELMS 98.

Table A5.12: Incidence of Contract for Female Wage Workers in the Private Sector, by Agriculture and Nonagriculture Activity, Egypt, 1988, 1998

	1988	1998
Agriculture		
Yes	4.1	2.4
No	95.9	97.7
Total	100.0	100.0
N	73	19
Nonagriculture		
Yes	32.2	28.5
No	67.9	71.5
Total	100.0	100.0
N	162	176

Source: LFSS 88, ELMS 98.

Table A5.13: Incidence of Social Security for Female Wage Workers in the Private Sector, by Agriculture and Nonagriculture Activity, Egypt, 1988, 1998

	1988	1998
Agriculture		
Yes	0.8	2.4
No	99.2	97.7
Total	100.0	100.0
N	82	19
Nonagriculture		
Yes	38.1	28.7
No	61.9	71.3
Total	100.0	100.0
N	116	176

Source: LFSS 88, ELMS 98.

Table A5.14: Incidence of Medical Insurance for Female Wage Workers in the Private Sector, by Agriculture and Nonagriculture Activity, Egypt, 1988, 1998

	1988	1998
Agriculture		
Yes	0.8	2.4
No	99.2	97.7
Total	100.0	100.0
N	82	19
Nonagriculture		
Yes	21.0	19.0
No	79.0	81.0
Total	100.0	100.0
N	116	176

Source: LFSS 88, ELMS 98.

Table A5.15: Employment Stability for Female Wage Workers in the Private Sector, by Agriculture and Nonagriculture Activity, Egypt, 1988, 1998

	1988	1998
Agriculture		
Permanent	5.8	9.2
Seasonal	21.8	45.3
Casual	72.4	45.6
Total	100.0	100.0
N	87	19
Nonagriculture		
Permanent	75.3	69.5
Temporary	12.3	21.7
Seasonal	2.6	2.2
Casual	9.8	6.7
Total	100.0	100.0
N	169	176

Source: LFSS 88, ELMS 98

6 Gender Differentials in Children's Work Activities: 1988–98

Nadia Zibani

Introduction

There has been, in recent years, a growing interest in the issue of child labor among academics, professionals, and the media. Though the International Conference of Labor Statisticians' estimates on labor force participation rates for children ages 10- to 14-years-old show a declining trend, in absolute terms, the size of the child labor force is and will continue to be large enough to be a serious concern. Child labor does constrain a child's ability to benefit fully from schooling and education, possibly condemning him or her to perpetual poverty and low wage employment.

However, in recent years there has been a rapidly expanding literature on child labor.[1] While some of these studies (Knight, 1980) discuss mainly qualitative features of child labor, the recent literature has focused attention on the quantitative aspects taking advantage of the increasing availability of good quality data on child employment. Within the empirical literature on child labor, there has been a shift in emphasis from mere quantification to an econometric analysis of its determinants. This has coincided with the widespread realization that simply banning child labor is unlikely to eradicate this phenomenon, and may even be counterproductive.

The main objective of the paper is to investigate the relationship between school attendance and early employment among children at the household level, using data from the 1988 Labor Force Sample Survey (LFSS 88) and the 1998 Egypt Labor Market Survey (ELMS 98). The novelty of this study is to focus particularly on children's activities and, more specifically, on gender differentials by giving special attention to domestic work in examinations of children's work. The intent of this research is to pinpoint changes in the Egyptian labor market over the period of economic reform and structural adjustment that began in the early 1990s.

This study is divided into two sections. The first section is a descriptive analysis to assess the major changes in school enrollment and labor force participation among Egyptian children (ages 6–14) between 1988 and 1998. The data in it is drawn from the LFSS 88 and ELMS 98 surveys. This section raises the issue of measurement problems related to the definition of participation in economic activity. Moreover, it provides a brief overview on trends in labor force participation and on school enrollment among Egyptian children (ages 6–14) between 1988 and 1998. In the second section, the factors that influence the schooling and work status, at the household level, are examined. First, the relationship between work and school are discussed, followed by a more detailed analysis of the three definitions of work (market work, subsistence, and domestic work, successively) among children (ages 6–14). Then results on participation rates based on two separate definitions of work (the standard versus the broad labor force definition) are discussed. Finally, a descriptive analysis based on preliminary results in children's activities takes into consideration the characteristics of the child, the parents, and the socioeconomic background of the household.

Overall, the data across the two surveys has clearly shown that children's work is declining quite significantly in Egypt, concomitant with an increase in school enrollment among children ages 6–14. In Egypt, over the past decade, the enrollment rates of children in the 6–11 age group increased from 85 percent in 1988 to 89 percent in 1998. The eldest group (ages 12–14) experienced a much higher increase, from 71 percent to 89 percent, respectively. In the meantime, participation rates of children ages 6–14 fell from 18.5 percent to 7.1 percent. Among children ages 12–14, the participation rates fell from 32 percent to 13 percent between 1988 and 1998.

In the literature on child labor, the link between child labor and basic education is increasingly and consistently recognized. Even though the relationship between school and work is complex, there is still a persistent belief that schooling is the best antidote to children's work. While some believe compulsory education is the single most important instrument leading to the elimination of children's work, others argue that changes in the perceived roles of children and the increase in family income play a more decisive role.

The nature of child labor force participation responds to long–run changes related to the structural transformation of economies. Factors such as technological change, urbanization, enforcement of legislative laws, and formal education may eliminate incentives to employ children, on both the supply and demand side. Child labor force participation has both long- and short-term consequences on individual, family, and social welfare. Many of these consequences may be summarized in terms of the effect they have on educational attainment. Families tend to allocate their children's time between a variety of activities, including school attendance, study time, leisure, household work, and market work. The latter is likely to compete with the time that children would spend on educational activities. Still, it is possible that the added income from the labor force participation of children could facilitate school attendance among families that are constrained in terms of income (i.e., if a child's combination of work and school helped finance their school-related expenses or allow siblings to go to school). Further, some skills learned in the labor market may be complementary to formal education (Becker, 1993).

In considering the relationship between school and work, certain assumptions are usually made. School and work are usually considered mutually exclusive categories to researchers and in official data. The important link between child work and schooling—that is, its non-exclusive nature—is given important status in the second section of this analysis. In this study, we propose to analyze children's activities at the household level using the household microdata from ELMS 98. More specifically, we are interested in understanding the impediments to studying, which have implications for educational attainment. We hypothesize that both early employment and household responsibilities affect children's ability to attend or progress in school. In particular, we consider four categories of activity status for girls and boys separately: (1) in school, (2) both attending school and working, (3) only working, or (4) doing neither. One of the main aims of this research is to emphasize the need to take into account domestic work in the role of child labor, despite the fact that housework[2] does not fall within the standard definition of employment. These research findings are relevant in highlighting the undercounting of children's work in relation to their whole sphere of daily activities.

While school dropout and early entry into the labor force are not necessarily coincidental, there is still an important relationship between the two. School enrollment rates have increased dramatically in the past decade in Egypt, especially among rural girls. As many as 1.4 million children ages 6–14 (11 percent) were not attending school in 1998. Of these children, approximately 863,000 (7.1 percent) were regularly working in the labor force. Restricting the definition of work to include only market-based activities, more than 417,000 children ages 6–14 were in the labor force in 1998. With the inclusion of participation in subsistence agriculture, animal husbandry, and home-based work—most of which is undertaken by girls—the number of child workers exceeds 3 million.

Unlike most other household surveys in Egypt, ELMS 98 covered a comprehensive set of issues, including detailed employment characteristics and earnings of children, whether or not they were enrolled in school. In Egypt, as in most developing countries, one factor that plays a consistent role in educational decisions is gender: girls usually attain lower levels of education and have lower enrollment rates than do boys.

Section One

1. Concept of Economic Activity and Measurement Problems

In this section, we will draw attention to certain measurement problems intrinsic to the nature of the phenomenon under study here (i.e., children's work).

1.1 Methodological Considerations in Measuring Children's Work

Official estimates of children's participation in the labor force are very often underestimated in Third World countries. The following discussion concentrates on some of the factors that usually contribute to this underestimation:

First, the difficulty of measuring a phenomenon that is by definition illegal leads us to believe that official estimates of working children are often underestimated. In spite of the Egyptian labor regulation that forbids children under the age of 15 to work—and also the law requiring children to fulfill basic education requirements—these laws are not strictly enforced. This is evident in official statistics on children's employment in Egypt gathered as far back as the census of 1917.[3] What is the level of reliability and/or accuracy of the data collected, considering the fact that child labor is a phenomenon prohibited by law? Also, in this situation parents of the working children are most likely to report "politically correct" answers to interviewers who come knocking at their door.

Second, if in reality some children do combine school with work, censuses and labor force surveys are not currently capable of capturing this information accurately. In such a situation, which one of the two activities is more likely to be considered a primary activity and, consequently, reported as such by the person interviewed? And on what criteria will they base their decisions? Will people be influenced by the social expectation that children should be at school rather than working and, therefore, most frequently report their children as being enrolled at school?

Third, the child labor force is sensitive to a number of factors related to its measurement, including questionnaire design, how questions are asked, and which field work techniques are used to collect this data.

Fourth, people interviewed for surveys can, unfortunately, not be those targeted by a questionnaire. Responses from people other than intended interviewees can skew the data, since they may not respond as the targeted population would.

Fifth, the last—and probably most complicated—issue relates to the definition of economic activity among children. Official labor statistics usually count as workers only those children who are engaged in economically productive work, whether they are paid or not, at any time of the day, within or outside of the family. Thus, studies on child labor have shown that activities related to wage or salary employment and market-oriented activities engage mostly boys. Evidence from several studies indicates that the participation of girls in subsistence agriculture is substantial. Also important, more girls than boys are engaged in domestic activities. Despite the increasing recognition of the essential participation of female children in carrying out household maintenance activities—defined as cooking, washing clothes, housecleaning, and childcare, among other tasks—the "invisible" contribution of girls to domestic chores has often been overlooked, since female respondents do not consider household work to be productive. The relevant questions here are: What is the economic significance of non-market household activities? Is "housework" actually work?

By keeping in mind these problems related to measuring child labor, it is more likely that the actual size of the working child population can be determined.

1.2 Differences between the Two Surveys

Some Egyptian labor market specialists have described the LFSS 88 survey as the richest and most valuable source of individual and household-level information about the Egyptian labor market to date. The fact that the ELMS 98 survey has replicated as closely as possible the design and methodology used in the October 1988 round enhances the comparability of data across the 10-year period. Nevertheless, we would like to point out some minor differences that exist between these two national labor market surveys.

The LFSS 88 questionnaire included, for the first time in Egypt's labor surveys, a separate module on paid child work.[4] In this specific module, detailed questions were administered to children who reported working for wages during the reference week or at any time during the reference year. These questions were focusing particularly on the conditions of work, such as the number of working hours per day, the overtime work, the regularity of daily breaks, the control over their salaries, etc. In contrast, the ELMS 98 questionnaire did not have any specific module on child labor. In fact, it had three separate questionnaires: 1) the household questionnaire, 2) the individual questionnaire, and 3) the family enterprise questionnaire. The data for the individual questionnaire included modules on parents' characteristics, education, employment during the reference week, unemployment, characteristics of employment during the reference three months, work histories, and earnings from work for wageworkers only. Information was collected from every household member age 6 and over.

With regard to children's activities—whether school, market work, subsistence agriculture, or domestic activities—ELMS 98 questions seem, to a certain extent, more comprehensive than those in LFSS 88. For instance, among school-aged children who have never been to school or who have dropped out of school, specific questions were asked regarding their reasons for not going to school and for dropping out from school, as well. Concerning the latter category of children, questions were also asked about the age they left school and the last stage and year of schooling they attended. For those at school during the time of the survey, questions focused more on the quality of schooling, such as the type of school, the number of school shifts during primary education, the number of hours spent at school each day of the past week, whether a child has private tutoring and/or a help group, and the costs involved. Moreover, important information on a community level was gathered, such as the availability of primary and preparatory schools in the immediate surrounding community, as well as the distance and means of transportation between home and school.

It is well documented that the burden of household duties in Egypt falls largely upon the female child. A unique aspect to the employment section of ELMS 98 is that for the first time, the importance of domestic work was directly addressed to women and young girls (ages 6 and up). The questions focused on the types of household activities—defined as cooking, getting water, childcare, washing clothes, cleaning, and other tasks—in which mothers and/or their daughters devote some of their time, and the amount of time spent daily in these activities.

1.3 Definition of Child Labor Force Activity

The measure of "human resources" is population size. However, not every member of the population can engage in economic activity. The exclusion of the very young, the very old, and the disabled leaves a population that is defined as "manpower." The actual labor availability is measured by the size of the labor force, i.e., the number of those who are engaged within a relatively short reference period (usually one week). Members of the labor force can be either employed or unemployed. While the amount of manpower is determined by demographic considerations, the size of the labor force—relative to population or manpower—is a socioeconomic phenomenon expressing participation in economic activity.

In LFSS 88, the term "economic activity"[5] was used for market exchange and home production for own consumption (subsistence activities in agriculture), without any separate differentiation. The distinction between economic and non-economic activities for many subsistence activities has been questioned. In the case of children—and in particular, girls living in rural areas—it is clear that such a distinction is fundamental in measuring both the "currently active population" (those active in a short reference period of one week) and the "usually active population" (those in the labor force during the reference three months and past year). The basic rationale underlying the concept of the extended labor force (defined as both market work and subsistence activities) is the usefulness of having data on the satisfaction of basic needs and of broadening the definition of "economic" activity beyond the often arbitrary distinctions made in the United Nations system of national accounts statistics (Goldschmidt-Clermont, 1987).

Inversely, in ELMS 98, a distinction was made between the market labor force (based only on market production) and the extended labor force (including subsistence agriculture). Consequently, the comparison between the results of our two surveys is only available for the extended labor market definition—which includes both market exchange and home production for own consumption—for both the currently active population and the usually active population among children ages 6–14. Thus, in the first section of this study, when comparing activity rates among children (ages 6–14) between both surveys, only the extended definition of labor force is used, for both reference periods: the last week prior to the survey and the past three months.

2. Trends of Population and Labor Force Participation among Children, from 1988–98

2.1 Population of Children

In 1998, the population of children ages 6–14 was 12.8 million, representing approximately one-fifth of the Egyptian civilian population of 60.4 million. The overall share of children less than 15 years old in the total Egyptian population was nearly 35 percent in 1998, a decrease of nearly 5 percentage points in the 10-year period between the two surveys.

Between 1988 and 1998, among the overall child population, the proportion of each of the two age groups (6–11 and 12–14) remained relatively the same, with the youngest group counting for almost two-thirds in 1998. However, results across surveys show that the older age group has gained 4 percentage points between 1988 and 1998. The distribution of this population between urban and rural areas has, remarkably, remained the same, with the biggest share for rural children representing 61 percent of children ages 6–14.

As shown in Table 6.1, the population growth rate of the group of children ages 6–14 has increased steadily by 1.1% per year between 1988 and 1998, almost the same rate for both sexes, and in both urban and rural locations. Nevertheless, this relative stability masks some differences between the two age groups, and urban and rural areas. In fact, the second age group, 12–14, has grown at a much higher rate (2.4 percent per year) than the youngest one (0.4 percent per year), reflecting the fertility decline that occurred in Egypt in the mid-1980s. For instance, the average family size of 7.4 persons in 1988 decreased to 6.2 in 1998 (still remaining high). Here, one can wonder if in

Egypt the recent fertility decline has played a role in the decrease in child labor over the past decade.

Table 6.1: Population Annual Growth Rate by Age Group, Gender, and Urban/Rural Location, 1988–98

Age/Sex		Urban	Rural	Egypt
6–11	Boys	-0.1	1.1	0.7
	Girls	0.1	0.3	0.2
	All	0.0	0.7	0.4
12–14	Boys	1.8	2.4	2.1
	Girls	3.9	2.0	2.7
	All	2.8	2.2	2.4
6–14	Boys	0.6	1.5	1.2
	Girls	1.4	0.8	1.1
	All	1.0	1.2	1.1

Source: Author's calculations using LFSS 88 and ELMS 98 data.

2.2 Market Versus Extended Labor Force Definitions

In this section, we examine how sensitive children's employment rates are according to the labor force definitions, using the two reference periods across both surveys. Table 6.2 shows the activity rates for both sexes and age groups, using the market and extended definitions, during the reference-week period. An interesting finding is that the activity rates of children ages 6–14 have declined significantly, by nearly half, at an annual rate of -5.8 percent over the past 10 years. Furthermore, it appears that the annual rate of decline of male children is much higher by far than that of female children (-9 percent and -3.4 percent per year, respectively). Also, it is worth noticing that, using the extended definition, the activity rates among children ages 6–14 remained the same for both sexes in 1988 (almost 11.5 percent). In contrast, the girls' participation rate in 1998 is 4 percentage points higher than that of boys.

Among the youngest age group, ages 6–11, the activity rates decreased at a higher rate of –7.2 percent per year more among boys than girls (-14 percent and -3.3 percent per year, respectively), in comparison to their oldest counterparts (-5.8 percent per year). This contrasts with the population growth rate of 0.4 percent per year between 1988 and 1998 for the group ages 6–11. In both age groups, the decrease of activity rates remains much slower for girls than for boys. In particular, urban girls seemed to experience a higher rate of decrease (–4.4 percent per year) than rural girls. In short, there was a significant decline of children's activity rates across both surveys, and it seems that the younger children are, the greater the decline of their activity rates—especially if they are boys.

Major differences appear across the two surveys when comparing activity rates, based on the extended definition (Tables 6.2 and 6.3). As Anker (1983) pointed out, "labor force activity using the broader definition of the labor force can be characterized by the performance of many different activities, whereas the activities that comprise the narrow definition tend to be more intensive." Consequently, there is a tendency for rates to be notably higher for the last three months, compared to the last week.

Table 6.2: Children's Labor Force Participation Rate (%) by Gender and Age Group using the Market and Extended Labor Force Definitions, 1988–98

Age/Gender	LFSS 88	ELMS 98	Annual Growth Rate
6–11			
Boys			
Market labor force	N.A.	1.4	N.A.
Extended labor force	6.8	1.5	-13.8
Girls			
Market labor force	N.A.	0.9	N.A.
Extended labor force	7.6	5.4	-3.3
All			
Market labor force	N.A.	1.2	N.A.
Extended labor force	7.2	3.4	-7.2
12–14			
Boys			
Market labor force	N.A.	9.7	N.A.
Extended labor force	21.3	9.8	-7.4
Girls			
Market labor force	N.A.	3.2	N.A.
Extended labor force	20.2	12.9	-4.4
All			
Market labor force	N.A.	6.4	N.A.
Extended labor force	20.7	11.4	-5.8
6–14			
Boys			
Market labor force	N.A.	4.4	N.A.
Extended labor force	11.5	4.5	-8.9
Girls			
Market labor force	N.A.	1.8	N.A.
Extended labor force	11.6	8.3	-3.4
All			
Market labor force	N.A.	3.1	N.A.
Extended labor force	11.6	6.3	-5.8

Note: N.A.= Not Available.
Source: Author's calculations using LFSS 88 and ELMS 98 data.

In ELMS 98, the first striking result is the close correspondence between the activity rates of children ages 6–14 in the last week (6.3 percent) and in the last three months (7.1 percent). These results contrast with the estimates obtained in LFSS 88. The activity rates are quite different in the two reference periods: 11.6 percent and 18.5 percent, respectively. As expected, these differences are most likely to occur in settings with strong seasonal variations in child labor force activities. When looking at this remarkable stability in 1998, one might consider the importance of seasonal work, especially during summer school vacations.[6] One possible explanation is the huge drop in size, between 1988 and 1998, of the seasonal work among the usually active population between the ages of 6–14. In fact, this type of employment has fallen from nearly 37 percent to 7.6 percent between the two surveys.

In the following, we examine the variations of children's participation rates based on the ELMS 98 data. As shown in Tables 6.2 and 6.3, the comparison of the market with extended labor force definitions available only in ELMS 98 reveals quite clearly that boys are predominantly engaged in market work, in both age groups and in both the current and the usually active population. In 1998, boys' participation rates for each age group remained the same when comparing the market with the extended definition. This close correspondence in rates for both definitions confirms that boys are mainly engaged in market-based activities. Moreover, child participation rates based on the market definition remain, in all cases, much higher for boys than for girls, especially for boys ages 12–14.

In contrast, results across surveys show that there are substantial differences between both definitions in girls' participation rates, confirming that girls are predominantly working as unpaid family workers, mainly in subsistence activities. It seems quite clear that the extended definition is more sensitive to the measurement of girls' employment, especially in subsistence agriculture.

In conclusion, among parents who opt for engaging their children in some form of work, it is obvious that the choice in the case of sons favored market work. The comparison of estimates across surveys, using any of the outlined definitions, highlights a strong gender bias in children's employment

2.3 Child Labor Force Participation Trends: Urban Versus Rural

In a context of a general decline in children's work, the emphasis here is placed on the disparities between urban and rural areas in terms of activity rates using the extended definition in Egypt. As is commonly known in Egypt, the child participation rates are substantially higher in the countryside than in the cities, as is shown in Table 6.4. The bulk of child labor is predominantly higher in rural areas, reflecting the biggest population size of children ages 6–14 (almost 60 percent live in rural areas). Nevertheless, the general decrease in activity rates among children masks some contrasted evolution along gender lines, between both age groups and urban and rural areas.

Table 6.3: Children's Labor Force Participation Rate (%) by Gender and Age Group Using the Market and Extended Labor Force Definitions, 1988–98

Age/Gender	LFSS 88	ELMS 98	Annual Growth Rate
6–11			
Boys			
Market labor force	N.A.	1.8	N.A.
Extended labor force	13.9	1.9	-18.0
Girls			
Market labor force	N.A.	0.9	N.A.
Extended labor force	10.6	6.0	-5.6
All			
Market labor force	N.A.	1.4	N.A.
Extended labor force	12.2	3.9	-10.9
12–14			
Boys			
Market labor force	N.A.	11.8	N.A.
Extended labor force	38.6	12.0	-11.0
Girls			
Market labor force	N.A.	3.3	N.A.
Extended labor force	24.4	13.4	-5.8
All			
Market labor force	N.A.	7.5	N.A.
Extended labor force	31.7	12.7	-8.7
6–14			
Boys			
Market labor force	N.A.	5.4	N.A.
Extended labor force	21.9	5.5	-12.9
Girls			
Market labor force	N.A.	1.8	N.A.
Extended labor force	15.0	8.8	-5.2
All			
Market labor force	N.A.	3.6	N.A.
Extended labor force	18.5	7.1	-9.1

Note: N.A. = Not Available.
Source: Author's calculations using LFSS 88 and ELMS 98 data.

Considering the variation of the proportion of working children, we can notice some patterns among the two age groups. Among the youngest, the proportion of rural boys declined at a much higher rate per year (-15 percent), in comparison to urban boys (-10 percent). In contrast, in the older age group, the number of working boys dropped more rapidly in the cities than in the countryside (-9 percent and -7 percent per year, respectively).

Regarding female children, the decline of the incidence of child work is relatively higher among girls ages 12–14 residing in urban areas (-6.8 percent per year), in comparison to their rural counterparts of both age groups (almost -3.5 percent per year).

At a much lower level than boys, working rural girls of both age groups decreased at a rate of approximately -3.5 percent per year, while for urban girls ages 12 and 13, the rate of decline was much higher (nearly –7 percent per year). One explanation is that the greater availability of schools in urban areas—and the fact that urban children are more a part of the "urban culture"—makes school enrollment more than an option for city children. Also, it is well known that Egyptian harvests attract large numbers of women and children. In brief, over the past 10 years, the situation of working boys has improved much more than that of girls in Egypt.

Table 6.4: Children's Labor Force Participation Rate (%) by Gender, Age Group and Urban/ Rural Location Using the Extended Labor Force Definition, 1988–98

Age/Gender	Urban		Rural		Annual Growth Rate		
	1988	1998	1988	1998	Urban	Rural	Egypt
6–11							
Boys	3.6	1.2	8.8	1.7	-10.3	-15.1	-13.8
Girls	1.5	1.4	11.5	7.9	-0.7	-3.6	-3.3
All	2.6	1.3	10.1	4.6	-6.4	-7.5	-7.2
12–14							
Boys	14.6	5.5	25.5	12.2	-9.2	-7.0	-7.4
Girls	7.4	3.5	28.3	19.9	-6.8	-3.5	-4.4
All	11.0	4.5	26.9	15.9	-8.6	-5.1	-5.8
6–14							
Boys	7.2	2.8	14.3	5.5	-9.0	-9.1	-8.9
Girls	3.3	2.3	16.9	12.3	-3.7	-3.2	-3.4
All	5.3	2.5	15.6	8.7	-7.1	-5.6	-5.8

Source: Author's calculations using LFSS 88 and ELMS 98 data.

2.4 Child Labor Force Participation Trends: Regional Disparities

Besides the usual urban-rural division, an examination of the variations of children's rates by region shows very distinct patterns. For the survey design of this study, Egypt is divided into six regions: Greater Cairo is entirely urban;[7] Alexandria and Suez Canal cities;[8] and the remaining part of the country—which includes Lower and Upper Egypt—is divided between urban and rural areas.

Tables 6.5 and 6.6 show that there are huge differences in the activity rates among regions. Across surveys, children's rates appear to be disproportionately represented in rural Lower and Upper Egypt. Indeed, in both surveys, rural Upper Egypt has a lower incidence of schooling and a higher incidence of work than other regions. That it is girls who are mostly working reflects the importance of their contributions in subsistence agriculture activities.

Table 6.5: Children's Labor Force Participation Rate (%) by Region, 1988

Age/ Gender	Region						
	Greater Cairo	Alex/ Suez	Urban Lower	Urban Upper	Rural Lower	Rural Upper	Total Egypt
6–11							
Boys	3.7	2.5	4.4	3.7	10.6	6.7	6.8
Girls	0.7	1.1	4.1	1.5	11.7	11.2	7.6
All	2.2	1.8	4.3	2.6	11.2	8.8	7.2
12–14							
Boys	13.4	10.7	19.7	16.7	28.1	22.6	21.3
Girls	8.8	5.1	6.6	5.2	29.5	26.8	20.2
All	11.2	7.8	12.9	11.1	28.8	24.5	20.7
6–14							
Boys	6.8	5.2	9.0	8.3	16.2	12.1	11.5
Girls	3.1	2.4	4.9	2.8	17.7	16.0	11.6
All	5.0	3.7	7.0	5.6	16.9	13.9	11.6

Note: The six regions are the following: Greater Cairo, Alexandria, and Suez Canal cities, urban Lower Egypt, urban Upper Egypt, rural Lower Egypt, and rural Upper Egypt.
Source: Author's calculations using LFSS 88 data.

Table 6.6: Children's Labor Force Participation Rate (%) by Region, 1998

Age/ Gender	Region						
	Greater Cairo	Alex/ Suez	Urban Lower	Urban Upper	Rural Lower	Rural Upper	Total Egypt
6–11							
Boys	0.4	1.2	0.8	3.0	0.8	2.7	1.5
Girls	0.3	0.0	1.7	4.6	6.4	9.6	5.4
All	0.4	0.6	1.2	3.8	3.4	6.0	3.4
12–14							
Boys	3.0	4.0	7.3	8.6	10.1	14.6	9.8
Girls	2.1	0.9	5.7	6.8	13.3	28.2	12.9
All	2.5	2.3	6.5	7.7	11.7	20.8	11.4
6–14							
Boys	1.3	2.2	3.4	4.9	4.0	7.1	4.5
Girls	1.0	0.4	3.4	5.4	9.0	16.0	8.3
All	1.2	1.3	3.4	5.1	6.4	11.3	6.3

Source: Author's calculations using ELMS 98 data.

Also noteworthy is that, in the context of the decline in child labor, only rural girls ages 12–14 living in Upper Egypt experienced an increase during the 10-year period, thought it was slight. The high incidence of child labor in the rural areas of Egypt has, until now, been considered a sign of underdevelopment, especially in Upper Egypt, where its people are also known to be more conservative than the rest of the country.

If a priori one may believe that the child labor force in agriculture declined because of the policy of compulsory school attendance, it is hard to believe that complete primary school enrollment of children would eliminate their part-time participation in agriculture.

In contrast to girls, the incidence of boys working is much more predominant in urban regions, which reinforces the assumption that boys are mainly engaged in market-based work, predominantly available in cities more than in villages.

3. Major Changes in Mass Schooling Between 1988–98

As pointed out in the previous section, the overall data suggest that children's work in Egypt fell noticeably, a trend that is concomitant in the rising school enrollment rates over the past 10 years. Whether or not the increase in school enrollment has contributed to the decline of children's work, here we would like to shed light on the link between children's work and school activities. Most educational research in developing countries has often neglected the obvious link between working children and school-absentee children (Salazar and Glasinovich, 1996). Curiously, the link between children's work and basic education is recognized more consistently in international conventions and in some national legislation than it has been in the actual policy and practice in Egypt.

In Egypt, basic education is compulsory until age 14. Basic education includes primary education, which consists of six years of schooling (from ages 6–11), followed by three years of preparatory education (from ages 12–14). In spite of compulsory school attendance laws—and labor laws prohibiting most forms of child labor before age 14[9]—in reality, many Egyptian children leave school to begin working, or begin working while continuing to go to school, during these age spans.

Access to formal education in Egypt reached a level of 89 percent in 1998 —an increase of nearly 8 percent in comparison to 1988 (Table 6.7). Moreover, and as a general pattern, girls' school enrollment lags behind boys. But there are striking differences along gender lines, between the two age groups, and between urban and rural locations, confirming the worldwide handicap of the accessibility of schooling to girls, especially in Third World countries.

Although rural enrollment rates are still significantly lower than urban rates—and girls' enrollment rates are lower than boys'—both gaps and differences began closing fast over the past 10-year period. In 1988, 74.6 percent of rural children ages 6–14 were enrolled in school; this had jumped to 86% in 1998. Urban children's enrollment rates increased from 90 percent to 94 percent. Female school enrollment rates increased considerably more than what is implied by the reduction in labor force participation rates of female children. Girls in rural areas appear to have made important strides in school enrollment, with enrollment rates increasing from 62 percent to 81 percentbetween 1988 and 1998. In comparison, rural boys' enrollment increased slightly, from 87 percent to 90.5 percent.

Table 6.7: School Enrollment Rate (%) by Gender, Age Group, and Urban/Rural Location, 1988–98

Age/Gender	Urban		Rural		Egypt	
	1988	1998	1988	1998	1988	1998
6–11						
Boys	94.6	96.4	90.0	93.6	91.8	94.6
Girls	92.6	95.4	69.1	84.8	78.3	88.9
All	93.6	95.9	79.8	89.4	85.2	89.0
12–14						
Boys	86.1	92.6	80.3	84.9	82.5	87.7
Girls	79.9	88.8	46.8	74.4	59.6	80.6
All	83.1	90.5	64.0	79.9	71.3	84.1
6–14						
Boys	91.9	95.0	86.8	90.5	88.8	92.1
Girls	88.6	92.7	61.9	81.0	72.3	85.7
All	90.2	93.8	74.6	86.0	80.7	89.0

Source: Author's calculations using LFSS 88 and ELMS 98 data.

In Egypt, the influence of the urban vis-à-vis rural disparities on school non-enrollment seems to follow the long established patterns of inequality, particularly in the rural part of the country, and especially with Lower and Upper Egypt having the lowest schooling levels. One study concluded that the largest numbers of out-of-school children were found in rural Upper Egypt—especially among girls (Fergani et al., 1994).

Considering the well-known inverse relation between age and schooling across the two surveys, it appears, as expected, that the likelihood of being in school decreases with age. This pattern seems to apply to Egyptian children—most notably female children. Although rural girls ages 12–14 appeared to be the most disadvantaged, the reduced gender gap achieved in the rural areas over the past 10 years is quite remarkable. For example, among rural children ages 12–14, the huge gender gap of 34 percentage points in 1988 is reduced to 10 percentage points in 1998. However, it seems quite clear that the gender differential in enrollment is essentially a rural phenomenon in Egypt. This is partly due to government support and efforts in building new schools in rural areas during this period.

In Egypt, the second reform initiated by the Ministry of Education (MOE) was supported through an increase in the government's budget for education expenditures from 12 percent in 1990–91 to 19 percent in 1995–96. An evaluation found that overall the government met its target of building 7500 new and rehabilitating 3500 old schools. Moreover, in the 1990s the MOE supported several innovative initiatives to enroll hard-to-reach groups and to supplement its own and USAID-supported new school construction. The two most important were the One-Classroom Schools[10] and UNICEF-supported Community Schools[11] (Rugh, 2000).

Studies suggest that parents' perceptions of the indirect opportunity costs of educating children are often unfavorable to girls' school attendance (Hill and King, 1993). Because girls' labor is valued at home, parents may withdraw their daughters from school—or never send them in the first place. And while domestic responsibilities do not always prevent girls from going to school, girls with these responsibilities who are in school generally bear a double burden of school and household work, according to the few existing studies in this area.

In Egypt, most children attend public school. In 1998, nearly 90 percent of Egyptian children were in public schools, 8.4 percent were in private schools, and 2 percent were in religious schools. On average, Egyptian children ages 6–14 spend 5.9 hours per day in school, with no gender differential. Many schools work in shifts: 42 percent of children were in schools that had more than one shift (shifts are normally in the morning and afternoon).

In this brief descriptive analysis on the decline of children's work and increase in enrollment rates between 1988 and 1998, data showed that these two activities have to be studied simultaneously. Theoretically, the direct connection between children's work and schooling activities is provided by a total time constraint. At some level of work and schooling, a child will be unable to increase time in one activity without sometimes decreasing time spent in the other activity. That is, the overall relationship between hours worked and school attendance must be negative.

Furthermore, effects of working on a child's performance can range from positive[12] to negative.[13] Time spent in school, on the other hand, can improve productivity at work (higher level of literacy), or can reduce productivity at work (fatigue). It is not possible, therefore, to establish a single direction of causality from work to school or vice-versa; indeed, it is most probable that the causality runs in both directions.

Probably the most widespread single risk children face when they work a substantial amount of time is the loss of the basic education necessary to equip them with fundamental skills required for success in life, such as literacy, numeracy, and critical-thinking ability. The relationship between education and child work is complex, and government action cannot afford to be simplistic.

In Egypt, research on both education and child labor is recent and very weak in certain important respects, making it difficult to use in the development of policy guidelines. Given the intricacy of the relationship between education and child work, the tendency for research on education and on child labor to be segregated is another major flaw. For example, the assumption of Weiner's Thesis is that education is effective against child labor because children who attend school will not be able to work, simply for lack of time. But the fact that a large proportion of children throughout the world effectively combine school and work demonstrates how the incompatibility of the two activities has been greatly exaggerated.

Section Two

The objective of this second section is to develop a solid understanding of the factors that influence the schooling and work status, at the household level, of children ages 6–14, using microdata from ELMS 98. This data set has detailed information on 5003 children in the 6–14 age range and on the 4816 households to which they belong. More specifically, we are interested in understanding the impediments to studying, which have implications for educational attainment. In particular, our focus is to examine the four categories of activity status for girls and boys separately: (1) in school, (2) both attending school and working, (3) only working, or (4) doing neither.

We address the following questions:

1. Are the various definitions of employment in measuring child labor force activity gender sensitive?
2. How does the propensity to work and the relationship between work and schooling differ for girls and boys?
3. What are the factors that influence the propensity to work and the relationship between work and schooling at the household level (e.g., a child's characteristics, household characteristics, parents' characteristics)? Are they the same for boys and girls?

1. The Relationship between School and Work

Until relatively recently, it was common to have studies on child labor that barely mentioned education. Most educational research in developing countries, moreover, has neglected the obvious link between not being in school, or performing poorly in school, and being a working child.

Among experts and policymakers, more and more attention is being directed toward the interrelationship between reducing and eventually eliminating child labor, on one hand, and the extension of compulsory education, on the other. Many education experts note, however, that making education compulsory is not necessarily the most effective way to make it accessible. Hugh Cunningham and other historians have attributed a much more complex array of factors to the historical decline of child labor in the industrialized world—economic, technological, cultural, and ideological factors. Several recent literature reviews have emphasized the complexity of the relationship between education and child labor, including the tendency for work and schooling to be combined among children living in poverty. It is important to avoid any assumption that compulsory primary education is a panacea for combating child labor (Salazar and Glasinovich, 1996). But it is equally important to acknowledge, in policymaking, the high degree to which the goals of eliminating child labor and achieving universal primary education are complementary.

Human capital theorists claim that although children who begin to work at young ages often forfeit the opportunity to attend school, these children are at least partially compensated for that loss by the corresponding increase in their on-the-job experience. Furthermore, whether or not a child goes to school affects his or her lifetime earnings (Levison, 1991). The question of how children's time is allocated, between schooling and other activities, is therefore of great relevance to policy making. Even if the relationship between school and work is complex, it is not at all certain how—or even if—the achievement of education will eliminate child labor.

2. A Redefinition of "Work": Incorporating Domestic Work into Children's Work

The concept of "work" is usually narrowly interpreted, generally referring to remunerated economic activities. In reality, a great number of children do not receive any payment for their work. In Egypt, programs to assist working children tend to be focused on the most visible forms of child work and exclude many tasks, such as domestic service, factory labor, and agricultural labor. Furthermore, the problems of defining "labor" or "work" in ways that effectively distinguish between exploitative activities and those that can actually contribute to a child's education are receiving much more attention than they did a few years ago.

The gender differences in the work activities of children pose an additional difficulty in identifying child workers. This may generate gender biases in programs directed toward working and out-of-school children, and may aggravate the overall tendency to underestimate working children.

Domestic work activities performed by women and children inside or outside their own homes, with or without remuneration, which contribute to the social reproduction of the family are defined as domestic work. As in the case of women, much of the domestic work activities performed by young girls are not registered in labor force statistics, as they are undertaken within the person's own home without remuneration and, therefore, are not conceived as an economic activity. These workers are typically registered in national census data and most other statistics as "inactive." The problem here is that these activities could interfere with a child's school attendance and performance. Further, given that most of the research uses the standard economic definition of labor force participation, home-based domestic work is usually unregistered (Knaul, 1998).

Very few quantitative studies on child labor devote particular attention to the gender differences in the work of children. In analyzing the importance of reconstructing the concept of economic activity in light of the work activities of women, Beneria (1981) highlights that the undercounting of the work of women is based on ideological bias, as well as on issues of definition. "Economic activity" is usually associated with exchanges that occur in the marketplace and involve remuneration. "Unpaid family labor" includes work undertaken to assist in an occupation, but excludes household work that is not directly associated with the production of income. These issues are equally applicable to the work of young girls, with the knowledge that children's work, even in the market, tends to be underestimated for a variety of reasons, including the fact that it is often clandestine and illegal.

While quantitative information is scarce, several recent studies differentiate between market and household work. In her study on Brazil, Levison (1991) considers gender differentials in the labor force parti-cipation rates and hours of work.[14] Knaul (1998) highlights the importance of considering home-based domestic work in the calculation of overall figures for work activity among children. A number of authors have noted that domestic work is comprised of female-specific activities that may be overlooked in the formulation of policies and programs (International Conference of Labor Statisticians (ILO), 1996; Bequele and Myers, 1995; Burra, 1989). In fact, by assigning resources and rights to occupations in which male child labor is more common, policies and laws reinforce the underevaluation of girls that is prevalent in certain societies.

In measuring child work, several factors are to be taken into consideration:

1. Parents' understanding of when a child's activity is to be counted as work (Levison, 1991).
2. Parents may misreport their children's activities due to embarrassment or shame about their poverty.
3. If parents are aware of child labor laws or compulsory education laws, they may misreport children's work of all types.

This paper gives a particular emphasis on the gender differentials in the activities of children with the inclusion of domestic work activities. If the need to use a broad definition of work activity is difficult given data limitations, the data available in ELMS 98 is unusual in this respect.

3. Differences in Using the Three Definitions of Employment in the 1998 Survey

Standard definitions of employment typically mask, and often misrepresent, the scale and nature of gender differentials among children. In this section, we examine the gender sensitivity of the various definitions of employment in measuring child labor activity among children ages 6–14, based on ELMS 98 (Table 6.8). We base this examination on three different categories of work: market work, subsistence work, and domestic work.

Table 6.8: Labor Force Participation Rate (%) by Gender Using the Three Definitions of Employment

	Boys	Girls	Total
Market work	4.68	1.72	3.24
Subsistence work	0.13	7.45	3.71
Household work	0.00	41.12	20.10
Sample size	***2545***	***2458***	***5003***

Source: Author's calculations using ELMS 98 data.

3.1 Definitions and Methodology

In ELMS 98, questions on economic activities were asked of individuals ages 6 and up. Children ages 6–14 were asked if they engaged in the production of marketable goods in economic activities that resulted in income (cash or in-kind) and if they supplied unpaid family labor for two reference periods: the week prior to the survey, and the past three months. We classified those who answered "yes" to both economic activities as having engaged in market work and engaged in subsistence work. The children who answered "no" were asked if they engaged in housework during the previous week.[15] Those who answered "yes" we classified as having engaged in home work. In fact, home-based domestic work is defined as a "residual activity." Respondents were asked if they were students or if they worked during the week prior to the survey, before being asked about undertaking housework. The terms "home-based domestic work," "housework," "household work," and "household chores" are used to refer to this form of work (Table 6.8). Based on this definition, 41 percent of female children who did not engage in market work were doing domestic work.[16]

Major gender differences in children's participation rates appear when we consider the three categories of work separately (Figure 6.1). It is to be expected that, overall, male children have higher rates of market employment than do females (using the past reference three months), across all age groups (Table 6.9). In Egypt, almost 5 percent of boys ages 6–14 are employed in market work, compared to nearly 2 percent of girls in 1998.

Figure 6.1: Labor Force Participation Rates by Gender and Categories of Work

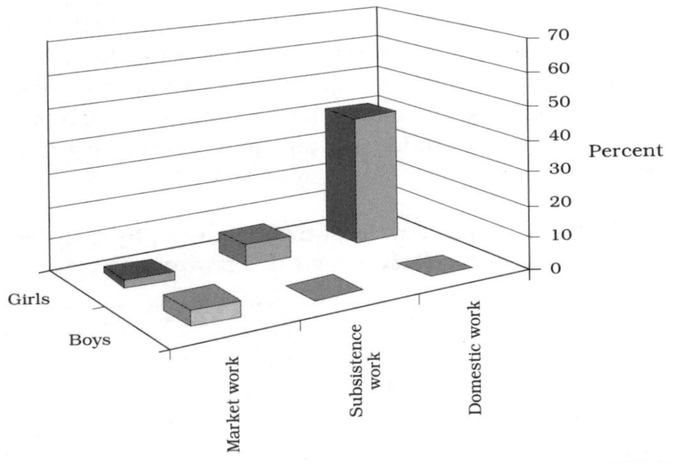

	Market work	Subsistence work	Domestic work
Boys	4.68	0.13	0.00
Girls	1.72	6.46	41.12

Table 6.9: Labor Force Participation Rate (%) by Gender, Age Group Using the Three Definitions of Employment

Age		6–8	9–10	11–12	13–14	6–14
Market	Boys	0.29	1.66	5.25	12.41	4.68
	Girls	0.62	1.32	1.37	3.64	1.72
Subsistence	Boys	0.09	0.20	0.18	0.08	0.13
	Girls	1.38	4.62	8.25	11.69	7.45
Domestic	Girls	15.89	36.77	46.84	66.21	41.12
Sample Size						
Boys	***709***	***608***	***634***	***594***	***2545***	
Girls	***661***	***536***	***650***	***611***	***2458***	

Source: Author's calculations using ELMS 98 data.

Figure 6.2 shows clearly that boys' market employment rates increase consistently with age, reaching nearly 13 percent in the group of boys ages 13–14. In fact, based on this definition, boys are predominantly engaged in market work activities (74 percent), as opposed to their female counterparts. This is a standard finding in most parts of the world, and it gives the impression that child labor is a condition suffered predominantly by working boys (UNICEF, 1997). Quite surprisingly, the number of boys working in subsistence activities is relatively negligible in Egypt.

Figure 6.2: Boys' Labor Force Participation Rates by Age Group and Categories of Work

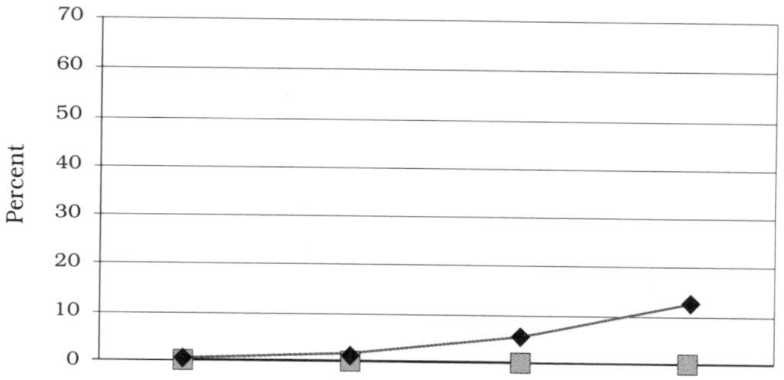

	Age 6–8	Age 9–10	Age 11–12	Age 13–14
Market	0.29	1.66	5.25	12.41
Subsistence	0.09	0.20	0.18	0.08

Age Group

Figure 6.3: Girls' Labor Force Participation Rates by Age Group and Categories of Work

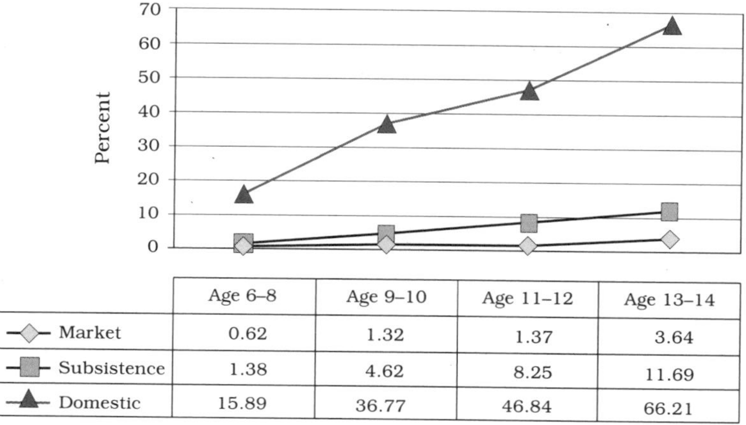

	Age 6–8	Age 9–10	Age 11–12	Age 13–14
Market	0.62	1.32	1.37	3.64
Subsistence	1.38	4.62	8.25	11.69
Domestic	15.89	36.77	46.84	66.21

Age Group

In contrast, as shown in Figure 6.3, female children ages 6–14 have much higher employment rates in subsistence work and, especially, domestic work—almost 7 percent and 41 percent, respectively. The rates are much higher for older girls. Activity rates based on the market work definition of employment differ substantially and indicate a much lower proportion of working girls than boys. ELMS 98 data corroborate the finding that market based work at an early age is less common among females.

3.2 Market Work

This section provides information on gender differentials of child employment characteristics based on the market work definition. The analysis also considers differences by gender in the following: age at entry into the labor force, hours worked, earnings, school attendance, and occupational structure.

Current versus usual

Employment statistics based on ELMS 98 are derived from a series of questions in the survey directed to all persons age 6 and up. The questions ask, "Did you participate in any employment?" and include two reference periods: the last week ending October 31 (labeled as "current"), and the last three months (labeled as "usual"). The data also included important information on hours worked last week and usual hours worked per week. Of those engaged in market work in the sample, 121 out of 153 children (80 percent) described themselves as workers in both reference periods. A priori, the number of children working at any point in time will always be less than the number of children who do work during a longer period than the three months pinpointed (designated three months period) in the survey. The activity rates obtained using the extended labor force definition for each reference period in LFSS 88 and ELMS 98 are quite different (Zibani, 1999). In LFSS 88, the activity rates are significantly different (11 percent and 18 percent), whereas in ELMS 98 they are quite similar (6 percent and 7 percent, respectively). In fact, in ELMS 98, the activity rates of children engaged in market work are relatively similar when using both reference periods (nearly 3 percent). While a slight increase is observed for boys, the girls' rates remain almost the same between these periods.

Age at first work

Work at an early age is becoming more common among children. Among children ages 6–14 engaged in market work, we find that girls begin working before the age of 9, while for boys, it is before the age of 10—that is, before finishing their primary education. Rural girls are working earlier than their urban counterparts (by nearly 3 years), while no difference is observed for boys in both urban and rural areas.

Hours worked per week

In terms of hours worked per week in market employment, children of both sexes work considerably long hours (an average of 42.4 hours per week). The gender differentials in the average number of hours spent in market work are substantial: girls engaged in market employment worked an average of 47.6 hours per week, compared to 40.7 hours for boys. Furthermore, it is interesting to note that the gender pattern is inverted when considering the location of residence. For example, rural boys spent an average of 41.8 hours per week on market work, compared to 39.5 hours for urban boys. Urban girls spent an average of 51 hours per week, while rural girls spent 45.7 hours. Note that the differentials in the average number of hours spent in market work according to location are much smaller among boys than girls. It is worth mentioning that, in addition to the long working hours of girls employed in market work, nearly 32 percent are doing household activities at home as well.[17]

Using the mean of the hours per week usually worked, the estimate for the youngest 6 to 11 year-olds is more than 38 hours per week. The gender differentials among children ages 12–14 are quite substantial; hours worked per week are higher for girls than for boys. In fact, the mean figures are 54 hours for girls and 41 hours for boys. Also, in both urban and rural locations, the hours per week usually worked is nearly similar, averaging 42 hours.

Economic activity

Sixty-five percent of all economically active children (in market employment) ages 6–14 work in agriculture. This is probably due to the fact that, among those employed in market work, 79 percent are children residing in rural areas. Aside from agriculture, the most important economic activities are services (12 percent) and manufacturing (11 percent).

Table 6.9 gives the breakdown of participation rates of working children in market work for both sexes, by age groups. The proportion of children engaged in market work increases slowly but steadily between ages 6 and 12, and registers a big jump at age 13—particularly among boys—when a majority of children complete their primary schooling. Differences by gender become evident around this time: boys ages 13–14 engaged in market work outnumber girls by a factor of 3.4. In general, market employment rates are much higher for the older age group. Nearly 13 percent of 13 to 14 year-old boys, and 4 percent of 13 to 14 year-old girls are engaged in market work.

Work stability

In terms of the work stability that differentiates between regular and irregular jobs (the latter capturing the seasonal work that children are more likely to be doing during summer school vacations), the data shows a much higher proportion of girls having regular jobs than boys, 85 percent and 65 percent, respectively. In contrast, for irregular work, boys are working more than girls during summer school vacations. One intriguing finding is that, although we would expect a higher proportion of seasonal work in rural areas, the incidence of seasonal work is the same in both urban and rural locations

Employment status

As with research on women's labor force participation, many children who do work are "unpaid"—that is, they receive no remuneration. Of those children engaged in market work, those working as wageworkers count for 51 percent, while the rest are unpaid family workers—primarily in agriculture (84 percent). This latter category implies a likelihood that those children work as family workers in a family enterprise. Regardless of the economic situation, this could also be an important determinant of whether or not a child works. Of those working as wageworkers, only 46 percent work in an establishment.

Occupation

The occupational distribution of child workers provides additional information on the gender differentials in child employment in the market labor force. In urban areas, the largest employers of male children are factory work, commerce, and services. For females, the most important sector is services. In rural areas, agricultural activities dominate the distribution, particularly amongst boys. Still, factory work, commerce, and services continue to be important employers of male children. The predominance of agricultural labor among Egyptian children—and the fact that Egyptian child labor law does not take into consideration the agricultural sector—suggests the need for further research, as well as programs targeted to these children. As suggested in Bequele and Myers (1995), agricultural work is counted among the forms of child labor that are likely to be invisible, in part because it is often carried out with the family.

Earnings

In the survey, questions on earnings were asked only of those employed as wageworkers, whether for regular or irregular jobs. Quite surprisingly, the earnings for regular wageworkers show that on a monthly basis, the salaries for girls tend to be slightly higher than for boys (LE131 against LE124). In contrast, the earnings for irregular wageworkers are much higher for boys than for girls (LE74 and LE56, respectively). These differences most likely reflect the long hours worked by girls.

School attendance

Among children ages 6–14 employed in market work, 70 percent were not attending school at the time of the survey. For working girls, this figure reaches a high of 90 percent (girls' rates are much higher across all age groups than are boys'), while for boys, the figure is 63 percent. The higher proportion of children not enrolled in school is found in the group ages 13–14, and is similar across genders. Of those who drop out of school, 78 percent do not have even the primary degree. The reasons given for children working and dropping out of school are: "repetitive failure in school" (40 percent); "the child did not want to continue school" (30 percent); and "financial reasons" (11 percent).

4. Subsistence Work

In ELMS 98, children's activity rates in subsistence work are nearly 4 percent. The bulk of children working in subsistence activities are found in agriculture/rural settings (90 percent). In contrast to results obtained on market work, the subsistence activities show a clear gender bias that favors girls; the proportion of girls working in subsistence work activities is 98 percent.

Rural families tend to use child labor in a different way than do urban families. Rural children are much more likely to engage in unpaid but productive work, such as farming and tending livestock, as well as in the greater number of household tasks necessary in a rural setting. The hypothesis is that children from subsistence economies, where the "spread of work" among family members is likely to be great, will have the highest labor force participation rates. Also, and this is to be expected, labor force participation rates across age groups increase as the age increases, reaching 12 percent for the older group.

4.1 Subsistence Work

For those children working mostly as unpaid family workers in subsistence, this type of work is clearly a regular, daily activity. Even though the number of observations is few for boys, girls spend an average of 9.6 hours per week engaged in this type of work. This relatively low number of working hours may suggest that the majority of girls are engaged in domestic activities as well. In fact, of girls engaged in subsistence activities, 93 percent are doing domestic work, as well.

4.2 School Attendance

Because many hours are required to participate in school each day, a large proportion of girls who undertake subsistence work do not currently attend school (42 percent). When we look at the reasons given as the "most important" for those not currently attending school, we find that "parents and traditions or mentality" count for more than 50 percent, and "school is expensive"—that is, financial reasons—are given for 24 percent of the children who do not attend school. Children from the less-well-off families are probably less likely to be able to afford school-related expenses, such as private tutoring, uniforms, and textbooks.

In Egypt, one of the more expensive costs of schooling is tutoring. Private tuition in after-school hours had assumed epidemic proportions by the 1980s and was becoming prohibitively expensive for many parents. Alarmed by this phenomenon, the Ministry of Education sought to ban the practice (decree no. 211/1993). By 1996, Hua (1996) found two kinds of "special" tutoring in effect: private lessons and in-school group tutoring.

Fergany (in Ridker, 1997) showed that private tutoring or in-school tutoring increased the chances of primary completion but did not significantly impact cognitive achievement. He also noted that school quality had deteriorated over time, partly as a consequence of this tutoring system. One should wonder what is the point in providing access to education opportunities if children do not learn.

5. Domestic Work among Girls

Additional survey questions address the issue of household activity: "in which of the following household chores do you spend most of your time?" and "how many hours per week?" While a large proportion of girls do housework, it is important to note that survey questions on this particular activity were asked only of girls, even if some boys are actually doing some household work as well. Previous studies indicate that the burden of household duties falls largely upon the female child. Even at a very young age, girls are substantially involved in domestic work. A significant proportion (40 percent) of girls ages 6–14 reported doing domestic work at the time of the survey (Table 6.9).

5.1 Types of Domestic Activities

The answers to the survey's question, "in what type of activities do girls spend most of their time?" are important. In general, whether living in urban or rural areas, girls engaged in domestic work have the same pattern regarding the types of activities (tasks) undertaken: "shopping" (38 percent) is by far the most important, more so in urban than in rural areas; "cleaning the house" (30 percent); "cooking" (18 percent); and "doing laundry" (10 percent). In some way, girls' involvement in housework may contribute to releasing adults for more productive and remunerative work. The average age of these girls doing domestic work is about 11 years old, in both urban and rural settings, which corresponds to the end of their primary education.

5.2 Hours Worked Per Week

It is interesting to note that young girls spend a considerable number of hours per week in home-based domestic work. Girls ages 6–14 spend an average of 18.3 hours per week doing such work. The differentials between urban and rural locations in the average number of hours spent on domestic work are important. For example, girls ages 6–14 living in urban areas spend on average 16.9 hours on home-based work, compared to 19.9 hours for those living in rural areas. The gap widens as age increases.

5.3 School Attendance

In fact, many girls who are engaged in home work continue to attend school (nearly 75 percent). There is a significant difference between rural and urban areas in the percentage of girls who are doing domestic work and are not enrolled in school—there are twice as many of these girls in rural areas than in urban areas.

Looking closely at the activity rates using the three separate categories of work shows clearly the gender differentials in children's work. Boys are predominantly engaged in market work, while girls are mostly working in subsistence and home work activities.

If we consider each category of work separately, we find that boys' market employment is more likely to be less compatible with schooling than in the two other categories of work. Regarding girls ages 6–14 engaged in housework, most of them (75 percent) declared they were currently attending school at the time of the 1998 survey. It seems obvious that doing housework is an activity that could be more easily accommodated with education and does not immediately suggest great need of money.

To better understand children's work, one should incorporate broader definitions of work and economic activity (Goldschmidt-Clermont, 1982). In this research, we seek to justify the study of the female working child as a separate category. In fact, we are attempting to bring out the differences between working girls and working boys in terms of access to education and the type of work done.

6. Labor Force Participation and Nonenrollment Rates in 1998

In order to highlight the gender differences in children's work, three definitions of child employment rates have been generated (Table 6.10). The first, and more restrictive, "narrow definition" is produced by market-based employment. The second definition, the "standard definition," is produced by adding market employment and subsistence work activities with no restrictions on the number of hours spent on either one. It is worth noting here that if, in reality, some children engaged in market work could be doing subsistence work as well, ELMS 98 would consider these two types of employment mutually exclusive. The third, and probably the most comprehensive, definition is the "broad definition," which is produced by adding to the standard definition the home work activities being done mostly by girls. Because it covers a wider range of activities undertaken by children, this definition provides a complete picture of the proportion of children who do not devote their time entirely to school. In the following analysis, the three labor force definitions are based on the usually economically active population.

6.1 Child Employment Rates

In this section, we focus on children's activity rates using the standard definition of employment that includes work undertaken inside or outside of the home, with or without remuneration, in the production of marketable goods. We compare it to the broad definition, which considers domestic work undertaken in the child's own home that does not directly lead to the production of commercial goods (Table 6.10).[18]

Table 6.10: Labor Force Participation Rate (%) by Gender, Using the Three Definitions of Employment

	Boys	Girls	Total
Narrow	4.68	1.72	3.24
Standard	4.81	8.18	6.46
Broad	4.81	42.78	23.37
Sample Size	***2545***	***2458***	***5003***

Source: Author's calculations using ELMS 98 data.

The standard definition includes both market and subsistence activities, so it means different things when talking about boys and girls. Boys are mainly engaged in market-based activities, and girls mostly in subsistence activities.

As mentioned earlier, in using the broad definition, it is important to remember that the questions on household activities were asked only of females ages 6 and up (i.e. girls only in the children 6–14 subsample). Consequently, the results obtained with the broad definition for boys are the same as the standard definition. It is also important to consider that both definitions used to assess activity rates are based on any given number of working hours declared, versus an arbitrary number (such as 8 hours per week).

In terms of policy, the implications of using the broad definition of child work are important. This definition presents a much more widespread picture of the phenomenon of child labor and shows the importance of recognizing children—girls, in particular—who devote time to activities that are likely to impair their possibilities of attending school.

Activity rates compared by sex across age groups, using the standard and the broad definitions, are highly contrasted (Table 6.11). The participation rates using the broad definition concern only girls, as mentioned previously.

6.2 Standard Definition

Based on the standard measure, girls' activity rates across age groups are much higher than those of their male counterparts, reaching 15 percent for girls in the 13–14 age group (see Table 6.11). In 1998, nearly 850,000 children ages 6–14 were working, according to the standard employment definition. Very clearly, a significant increase in children's activity rates is taking place after the ages of 11–12 (especially among boys), which corresponds to the end of primary education. While no major difference in activity rates exists among urban children, in contrast, rural girls' activity rates are twice that of boys who report working.

Table 6.11: Labor Force Participation Rate (%) by Gender and Age Group, Using the Standard and Broad Labor Force Definitions

	Age				
	6–8	**9–10**	**11–12**	**13–14**	**6–14**
Standard					
Boys	0.38	1.86	5.42	12.49	4.81
Girls	2.00	5.94	9.61	15.34	8.18
Broad					
Boys	0.38	1.86	5.42	12.49	4.81
Girls	16.45	38.05	48.01	69.90	42.78
Sample Size					
Boys	***709***	***608***	***634***	***594***	***2545***
Girls	***661***	***536***	***650***	***611***	***2458***
Total	***1370***	***1144***	***1284***	***1205***	***5003***

Source: Author's calculations using ELMS 98 data.

6.3 Broad Definition

Adding domestic activities in the child's own home to the standard measurement of labor force participation generates very high activity rates. In using this measure, the activity rate of children ages 6–14 almost quadruples, reaching nearly 24 percent in 1998 (Table 6.10). It is worth noting that with this definition, boys' activity rates are equivalent to the standard labor force definition, which includes market work and subsistence work, since domestic work information was collected only for girls. Among girls, the inclusive definition implies a multiplication by 5 of the activity rate. Overall, this suggests that child labor force participation using the broad definition is multiplied by nearly four in comparison to the rate using the standard definition. If we include girls ages 6–14 who spent time in housework, the absolute number of female children working increases from 515,000 to 2.7 million. Similarly, data suggests that the number of working children ages 6–14 is 3 million, when using the broader definition, as opposed to less than half a million, using the narrow definition (based only on market work). Evidence that a division of labor along gender lines is beginning to shape up can be seen as early as age 6 (Table 6.11).

Under the definition of household work, participation rates across age groups are high—even for young girls—in both urban and rural areas, regardless of the hours worked. It is interesting that the participation rates across age groups in both locations are similar except in the older group (13–14), where urban girls' activity rates are higher than their rural counterparts.

Here, we assume that the duration of work (i.e., the total amount of hours spent in work) directly affects schooling. A child who devotes fewer hours of work in any activity may have a higher propensity to attend school than children with greater amounts of work. The question is, what should be considered the cut-off point for the number of hours worked per week? A crucial factor in evaluating the likelihood of a child combining school with work (whether we use the standard or the broad definition of work) is the total amount of time that the child devotes to work. In this study, the cutoff point is children ages 6–14 who spend at least 14 hours per week on work.[19]

In placing a minimum of 14 hours a week in the standard definition, the estimates on children's participation rates decrease by half. This is due primarily to the decrease in the number of girls engaged in those activities.[20] As shown in Table 6.12, when using the broad definition—restricted to girls only—the activity rates drop from 43 percent (without the minimum of 14 hours) to 32 percent (with the minimum of 14 hours). Using the 14-hour cutoff, we see that a sizeable number of Egypt's nearly 2.3 million children are working—2 million of whom are girls, according to the broad definition.

Table 6.12: Labor Force Participation Rate (%) by Gender and Labor Force Definitions, with a Minimum of 14 Hours Worked Weekly

	Boys	Girls	Total
Standard 14h	4.52	2.90	3.73
Broad 14h	4.52	32.06	17.98
Sample Size	***2545***	***2458***	***5003***

Source: Author's calculations using ELMS 98 data.

Children ages 6–14 who work at least 14 hours per week, either in the market or in subsistence, are much less likely to be attending school (72 percent were not attending school at the time of the survey). As expected, the rates are much higher among girls (85 percent) than boys (65 percent). In contrast, using the broad definition with the 14-hour minimum, 37 percent of children ages 6–14 did not attend school the week prior to the survey. In fact, using the broad definition, nearly 33 percent of those children currently not attending school were girls.

The hypothesis that market work and/or subsistence activities may be less compatible with school, in comparison to home work activities, could be explained by the large number of hours worked in market employment. In fact, in recent child labor studies, many researchers implicitly assumed that the major deterrent to schooling was market work. In his research, Rosenzweig concluded that the major cost of education in less-developed countries is the opportunity cost of attending school, arguing that the primary alternative to schooling in low-income countries is labor market employment—which seems to be the case in Egypt, especially among boys (Rosenzweig, 1977).

In conclusion, the idea that there are "missing children" becomes clear when we look closer at the issue of defining children's work, especially in the case of girls. In the following section, we consider only the broader labor force definition, reflecting more of the range of children's activities while taking into account girls' domestic work.

Several authors highlight the need to develop a methodology for accounting for home-based child work. In the case of Egypt, applying as a first approximation a methodology that adds domestic work to market and subsistence work is unusual. The inclusive definition of "child" suggests not only that girls are as likely to undertake work activities as boys, but also that the phenomenon of child work is much more prevalent than suggested by estimates based on the traditional definitions of employment.

6.4 Nonenrollment Rates

It would certainly be misleading to conclude that work is the only factor preventing children from attending school. Yet the evidence alerts us to the fact that child work by and large competes with, rather than facilitates, schooling.

Previous studies of children's time spent in work or in school have shown how such activities are closely related.[21] Insofar as the failure of children in school is most often attributed to child employment—and child work is seen as the cause of under-schooling—it is important to understand the relationship between work and school.

As described in the first section of this paper, school enrollment of children in Egypt has risen dramatically from 1988 to 1998, especially in rural areas and for girls, while children's participation in the labor force has fallen substantially. For a long time, we have dealt with the relationship between work and school as "communicating vessels"—child employment diminishing with schooling because, generally speaking, the rate of child activity under the age of 15 is inversely proportional to the rate of school enrollment. Moreover, until recently, the majority of studies on child labor have classified children in the 6–14 age group into two categories: those who attend school, and active children (involved in productive and household subsistence activities).

Here we would like to assume that the children who were not attending school at the time of the survey were most likely working. In Egypt, in the children subsample, girls' non-enrollment rates were twice as high as boys' in 1998. A sizeable proportion of Egypt's 1.4 million children were not attending school during the week prior to the survey in 1998. As shown in Table 6.13, of the children ages 6–14 who were not attending school, big differences exist between both sexes and across age groups. Of those children not attending school, more than 1 million were living in rural areas. Girls count for almost two-thirds of those not attending school. And the girls' rates across age groups are much higher than their male counterparts.

Table 6.13: Children Ages 6–14 Not Attending School (%), by Gender and Age Group

	Age				
	6–8	9–10	11–12	13–14	6–14
Boys	5.05	6.02	7.28	13.67	7.86
Girls	11.02	12.22	12.15	21.74	14.26
Sample Size					
Boys	***709***	***608***	***634***	***594***	***2545***
Girls	***661***	***536***	***650***	***611***	***2458***

Source: Author's calculations using ELMS 98 data.

Child workers are much less likely than others to be in school, that is, child labor activity is directly related to levels of non-schooling attained. Based on this assumption that children who are not at school are more likely to be working, the ELMS 98 data shows clearly that there is a huge discrepancy between those who are not in school and those working. If they are not working and not going to school, what are they doing?

In reality, the relationship between school and work is more complex, and depends on how "work" is being defined. One plausible approach is to add to the two common categories of children "at school" and "at work" two additional categories where children can be identified as "both" (school and work combined) or "neither."

There are many reasons why a significant number of children ages 6–14 were not enrolled in school. In the questionnaire, 12 possible answers plus a residual "other" category were listed. If we consider here the main reasons for not sending a child to school, of interest are: "parents did not want to send the child to school"; "for reasons related to traditions and culture";[22] and "school-related expenses." Nearly 35 percent of the respondents said the children (mostly girls) did not attend school because of the so-called "tradition and mentality" reasons. An additional 11 percent said school was too expensive (textbooks, private lessons, uniforms, and school supplies are a cost to families).

Regarding these expenses, Cardiff (1997) found that school costs continued to increase in Egypt; in 1995, urban parents spent roughly 15 percent of their income on education, and rural parents about half the amount. Expenditures rose with parents' educational level and decreased by a per-head cost as the number of school-age children in the family increased. Fergany et al. (1994) found the average cost per primary child in Minya (in Upper Egypt) was LE132, while in Cairo it exceeded LE500.

Moreover, information in the survey on education allows us to differentiate between those children who have never been to school (8 percent) and those who have experienced some years of schooling (3 percent). Among children ages

6–14 not attending school at the time of the survey, a very high percentage of girls (70 percent) never went to school.

A recent national survey of adolescents in Egypt found that the three most important reasons female adolescents reported for never having attended school were the low value parents placed in education (47 percent), the low economic level of the household (44 percent), and the need for girls' help in household chores (16 percent) (Ibrahim et al., 2000). The comparable figures for boys were 15 percent, 51 percent, and 1 percent. In other words, these reports show a much lower value placed on girls' education and a higher value on their household labor, compared with boys.

Quality and quantity, as many have noted, do not need to be mutually exclusive, nor does spending on one necessarily have to lead to a deterioration in the other. Quality of schooling is also related to the length of the school day. Most Egyptian school children attend approximately 6 hours of school per day (with surprisingly few differences across regions); schools often have morning, afternoon, and evening shifts. In our sample, 57 percent of 6 to 14 year-olds were in primary schools that had one shift, and 41 percent were in schools with two shifts. Children from urban families in the highest quintile of family wealth were much more likely to attend private schools (42 percent) than children from poorer families (2 percent). (Private schools are often considered to be of higher quality than the public alternatives.)

In Egypt, there are different types of schools: public (regular or experimental); private (regular and language); and religious. In the ELMS 98 sample of 6 to 14 year-olds, 85 percent attended public schools, and 14 percent attended private schools.

Overall, the proportion of children ages 6–14 who dedicate their time exclusively to schooling declines rapidly as age increases. While some begin to work and continue to study, others may drop out and devote their time to working.

7. Children's Activities in Egypt

The information in ELMS 98 enables us to divide child activity into four groups: school only; work only; both school and work; and neither school nor work. This information is available for all individuals age 6 and over. In this section, we compare the broad labor force definition—which includes domestic work, especially among girls—with the standard definition, in order to emphasize the gender disparities in children's activities.

We have already mentioned that, in this study, we have classified children ages 6–14 into four categories. Nevertheless, these categories need some clarifications when including the minimum of 14 hours of work, regardless of the type of work.

1. *School Only:* Children attending school and reporting any work (market, subsistence, or domestic activities) for less than 14 hours per week;
2. *Work Only:* Children not attending school and reporting any work for at least 14 hours;
3. *Both:* Children attending school and reporting any work for at least 14 hours;
4. *Neither:* Children not attending school and reporting any work for less than 14 hours.

Two dependent variables that reflect the four categories of activity status of children were generated using the standard labor force definition and the broad definition. SCHWRK2H represents the school-work variable that includes the four activity statuses using the standard labor force definition and a cutoff of 14 hours per week worked. SCHWRK3H represents the school-work variable using the broad labor force definition and the cutoff of 14 hours per week worked. In both cases, the minimum of 14 hours per week is included (Table 6.14).

Until recently, survey data was not available for analyzing child work and schooling simultaneously. Furthermore, most studies have presented child work and schooling as mutually exclusive categories. Table 6.14 gives the breakdown of the activity status of children ages 6–14 by sex according to the two labor force definitions, standard and broad. The most interesting results obtained by adding housework are the very strong decrease in the rates of children categorized as "at school" and "neither," compensated by the increase in the rates of those classified as "at work" and "both," which vary considerably across gender.

Table 6.14: School and Work: Mutually Exclusive Categories of Child Activities (%) by Gender, Using the Standard and Broad Labor Force Definitions with a Minimum of 14 Hours Worked Per Week

		Boys	Girls	Total
Standard (SCHWRK2H)				
	At school	90.55	85.30	87.98
	At work	2.94	2.46	2.70
	Both	1.59	0.44	1.03
	Neither	4.92	11.80	8.29
Broad (SCHWRK3H)				
	At school	90.55	64.29	77.72
	At work	2.94	10.61	6.69
	Both	1.59	21.45	11.29
	Neither	4.92	3.65	4.30

Notes: Because the questions on domestic work were asked only for girls, boys' activity rates using the two labor force definitions are the same.
Source: Author's calculations using ELMS 98 data.

The interaction between child work and schooling has many implications for the future of these individuals. Children who are economically active are less likely to be enrolled in school. In Egypt, 96 percent of the 6 to 14 year-olds who were not economically active (using the broad definition) were enrolled in school, while only 70 percent of active children were in school.

Among children ages 6–14 "at school," the results obtained in comparing both labor force definitions are very striking. In fact, while the gender gap was only six percentage points with the standard definition, in adding domestic activities included in the broad definition, the gender gap became a highly significant 25 percentage points. As expected in both definitions, the results were much less favorable for girls, striking a low school enrollment rate of only 64 percent when using the inclusive definition in 1998.

In the other extreme situation—the "neither" category, comprised of children "deprived" of both employment and school—the rates decreased quite substantially, by half, when comparing both definitions. Girls were primarily "responsible" for this decline. While girls represented 70 percent of the "neither" category when using the standard definition, they became less important when using the inclusive definition, going down to 42 percent. Still, a sizeable proportion of half a million children were categorized as "neither" in the broad category in 1998. Were these children really doing nothing? For boys, the prevalence of "neither" is more likely to reflect unemployment and inactivity. Girls will continue to be ranked "neither" while they are hidden behind domestic chores and home work.

The decrease of children in the "at school" and "neither" categories seems to be the result of the rise of the two other categories, "at work" and "both." Of the children "at work," the standard definition shows activity rates were almost the same across gender, averaging 3 percent (the proportion of boys being slightly higher than girls). In adding home-based work, girls' activity rates increased quite significantly, reaching 11 percent. With a gender gap of 7 percentage points in their favor, girls counted for 77 percent of the "at work" category. Furthermore, a sizeable number of children—nearly 900,000—were categorized as "employed" in 1998, using the broad definition.

Many children who worked continued to attend school. Using the standard definition, the "both" category is the smallest one with no gender gap.[23] In contrast, by adding domestic work, girls' rates increased substantially, reaching a high of 22 percent—widening significantly the gender gap by 20 percentage points. Out of 1.5 million children in Egypt ages 6–14, 1.3 million were girls, and were the most likely to combine school with work. It is impressive that many children who worked in the labor force also attended school, given the long hours that some of them were working. It seems obvious that this category has benefited greatly from the decrease of both "at school" and "neither" categories.

The changing nature of labor markets and low returns to education have made education less attractive for many parents. This has especially been the case in rural areas, where formal education makes very little difference, given the limited formal sector opportunities, and most skills required are obtained by the "learning by doing" principle. Child labor is perceived as a process of socialization in many countries, and many believe that working, rather than education, enables a child to get acquainted with the skills for being employable (Grootaert and Kanbur, 1995).

8. Descriptive Analysis

Previous studies have shown that the demographic and socioeconomic characteristics of children provide greater insight about the supply of child work. The literature on child labor has identified several critical supply-and-demand factors (Grootaert and Patrinos, 1998). In the analysis below, we focus on supply factors at the household level, that is, the characteristics of children, their parents, and the households to which they belong. These can all influence the household decision to allocate children's time away from schooling and toward work.

In this section, we examine some of the factors that influence the probability of a child working, the relationship between work and school, and if these factors are the same for boys and girls. The descriptive analysis is based on simple cross-tabulations with selected demographic and socioeconomic variables available in ELMS 98. In Egypt, very little empirical research has been carried out to date with a view to uncovering the determinants of child work.

In order to better understand the factors that influence children's activities, three groups of explanatory variables are identified in the schooling-work choice. These are: 1) the child's characteristics, including the age, gender, and relationship to household head; (2) the parents' characteristics, including whether or not the father and/or mother is absent, the schooling of the parents, the father's employment status, etc.; (3) household composition characteristics, including family size, age and gender of the child's siblings; and 4) some socioeconomic background of the household, particularly family wealth, region of residence, availability of a farm enterprise in the family, and so on.

Of course, any conclusion from the descriptive analysis only raises possible hypotheses that need to be further tested in a multivariate framework. In what follows, only some relevant variables are examined.

Family wealth index[24]

The inevitable starting point in explaining child work is its relation to poverty. Most of the studies on child labor have documented the inverse relationship between family income and participation in the work force. Although there are exceptions, it may clearly be assumed that the lower the per-capita family income, the greater the proportion of children who work in order to contribute to the family budget. If family poverty could provide sufficient explanation for child work, one would ask why more children are not involved in such activities. In other words, poverty is a necessary factor underlying the existence of child work, but it is not sufficient to explain the persistence of the phenomenon. Further study of the labor-market structure is needed, including its trends and links to different stages of economic and social development, and to the conditions of supply and demand for children's labor. Economics alone can never explain social dynamics. Social, demographic, and cultural factors inevitably affect the incidence of child work.

Figure 6.4: School and Work: Mutually Exclusive Categories of Activities Among Urban Children by Wealth Quintile (%)

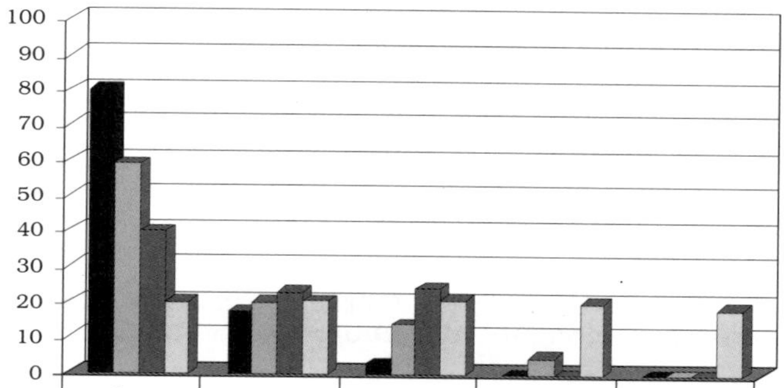

	1st Quintile	2nd Quintile	3rd Quintile	4th Quintile	5th Quintile
At Work	79.99	17.39	2.62	0.00	0.00
Neither	58.98	19.98	13.99	4.48	0.00
Both	39.71	22.94	24.00	0.00	0.00
At School	19.98	20.32	20.84	20.17	18.69

The ELMS 98 results on the link between children's activities and wealth are provided separately for urban and rural areas (although children working in the labor force are clearly more likely to be from poor families). In Egypt, wealth in urban areas clearly affects the children who are economically active. Nearly 80 percent of working children belong to families with the lowest wealth quintile Figure 6.4). In contrast, child work and wealth in the lowest quintile are not as intimately connected in rural areas, but there is still a strong connection (Figure 6.5). Can the decline of child labor in Egypt between 1988 and 1998 be partially explained by the decline of poverty, especially in rural areas, during the beginning of the 1990s? If a priori child labor seems clearly a phenomenon confined to the poor, what about employment opportunities (demand-side factors) being more responsible to child work? Econometric analysis suggest that "child work and school non-attendance are primarily a phenomenon among the poor households that arises more from the inability to finance education and to a lesser degree by a pressing need for paid and unpaid work" (Tzannatos, 1998).

Family size

In addition to poverty, family size is hypothesized to be a determining factor in the decision to enroll in school. That is, the larger the family, the lower the probability that a child is in school. As expected, results show that families of children ages 6–14 in rural areas (an average of 7.6 individuals) are larger than those in urban areas (an average of 6 individuals). Working children ages 6–14 seem to come from larger households. This is especially true for working girls. While urban girls from larger households are more likely to be "neither," girls from larger households in rural areas are more likely to be "at work." This is because it is easier to be counted at work with the standard definition in rural areas than in urban areas. However, in developing countries there is literature that suggests that larger families may facilitate schooling, at least for some children. Thus, it is important to examine the structure of the family and activities of the siblings.

Figure 6.5: School and Work: Mutually Exclusive Categories of Activities among Rural Children by Wealth Quintile (%)

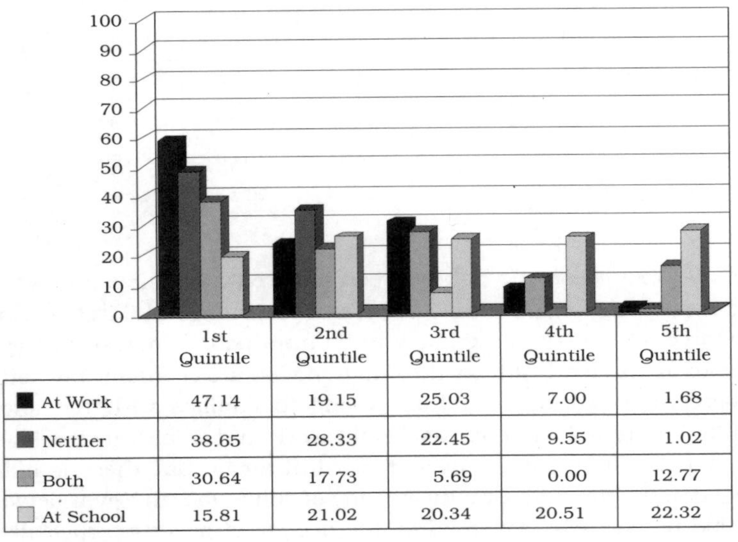

	1st Quintile	2nd Quintile	3rd Quintile	4th Quintile	5th Quintile
At Work	47.14	19.15	25.03	7.00	1.68
Neither	38.65	28.33	22.45	9.55	1.02
Both	30.64	17.73	5.69	0.00	12.77
At School	15.81	21.02	20.34	20.51	22.32

Household composition

The presence of other siblings, their ages, and their genders may influence the activities of a given child in a household. As shown earlier, boys are more likely to be engaged in market work, while girls are more likely to assist in farm work and domestic activities. For girls, the presence of younger children in the household increases quite substantially the likelihood to be at home—i.e., qualifying as "neither." This reflects that child-care activity is being done mostly by girls, a finding that is rather to be expected. Quite interestingly, the presence of young children (less than 2 years old) in the household strongly increases the likelihood of boys qualifying as "neither" as well. Is there a new phenomenon in Egypt—boys engaged in child care? Similar results are found when the children are slightly older (3–5 years old).

In a study of urban Brazil, Levison (1991) finds that child employment increases with the number of children in the family, especially when infants and preschool-age children are present. She argues that this may be due to children substituting for the mother in the labor force, or child care, or both.

Eldest child in the family. A variable indicating whether the child is the eldest son or daughter present in the household was made available. Data shows that being the eldest son reduces the likelihood of being put to work. However, being an eldest daughter seems to increase the likelihood of working.

Father present illiterate. Most studies identified the low level of education of parents as among the most important determinants of child labor. According to this survey, having a father that is illiterate increases strongly the likelihood for girls to be first "at work"—at even a much higher level than for boys—and second to be "neither," the two extreme situations. While for boys, having an illiterate father increases the chances in a similar way to belong in one of the three alternatives. In a sense, households with less-educated parents are less likely to keep their children in school and more likely to have child workers.

Father's employment status.[25] The most relevant results reveal very clearly that having a father who works in the public sector with all the social guarantees that this implies decreases the chance for both sexes to be "at work." In contrast, having a father who is an irregular wageworker[26] in the private sector increases the likelihood for children to be "at work"—quite surprisingly, more for girls than for boys. The intriguing result concerns the great likelihood to be "neither" as well, especially among girls.

Father absent. ELMS 98 includes unusual information on the characteristics of absent fathers. Children whose fathers are absent are much more likely to be working. Overall, this result applies primarily to boys, even though a similar but weaker relationship is obtained for girls.

Mother absent. In contrast to findings about absent fathers, in the case of absent mothers, the likelihood of being "neither" increases. An intriguing result concerns boys with absent mothers who are more likely to be "at work" as well, but also more likely than girls to be "neither." Girls with absent mothers are also more likely to be "at work" and much more likely to be "neither." It is known that, generally speaking, mothers' activities are much more compatible with home production activities than with full-time employment in the labor force. Because of the mother's traditional responsibilities, we expect that boys are more likely to substitute for her in labor force hours, and girls are more likely to do so in home production.

We find very interesting results when there is a presence in the household of other adult males, ages 18–59, who are nonwage workers[27] (excluding the father of the child). Living in a household that has adult nonwage workers highly increases the likelihood for boys to be "both," and also—but to a lesser extent—to be "at work." The same is observed for girls "at work."

The presence of other adult males who are irregular wageworkers[28] (excluding the father of the child) is another interesting variable. Quite intriguingly, girls seem to have a much higher likelihood of being "at work" than do boys.

Having a farm enterprise in the family increases substantially the likelihood for boys to be "both" and, quite noticeably, for both boys and girls to be "at work."

Conclusion

The inclusive definition of child work suggests that not only are girls as likely to undertake work activities as boys, but also that the phenomenon of child work is much more prevalent than suggested by estimates based on the traditional definitions of employment.

The results of this research underscore the important differences between the work activities of girls and those of boys, in both urban and rural areas. Traditional calculations of labor force participation tend to mask these differences and to understate the intensity of the work undertaken by girls. The differences in the occupational distribution of the work of males and females underscores the need to introduce more gender balance in the formulation of policies, programs, and legislation on behalf of working children. It is important to note that girls undertaking home-based domestic work are only protected via laws on the right to education.

The evidence collected in this paper suggests that schooling and work outcomes for children, labor supply outcomes for other members of the household, the household structure, and perhaps even the age and gender composition of the household are interconnected. There is still insufficient understanding of the true impact of work on a child's school attendance. However, no formal statistical tests are offered. Much work remains to be done before one can claim to have sorted out the complex set of endogeneity problems that characterize household resource allocation decisions.

Child labor is not independent of the decision to school. Hence, addressing school participation cannot be independent of demand side issues. The high cost of schooling pushes children into the labor market to enable them to afford school, or pulls them away from school as they cannot afford it. Hence, the official and unofficial fee charged for schooling is negatively correlated with school participation.

Notes

1 Examples include DeGraff, Bilsborrow, and Henin (1993) for the Phillippines; Jensen and Nielsen (1997) for Zambia; Canagarajah and Coulombe (1998) for Ghana, Knaul (1999, 1995) for Mexico and Colombia; Levison (1991) for Brazil; and Patrinos and Psacharopoulos (1997) for Peru.

2 Here the idea is to consider domestic work in the child's own home as an activity that is potentially competitive with educational attainment.

3 In Egypt, the census that first captured child labor dated back to 1917. In respect to official labor statistics, Egypt is one of the few countries considered among the Third World Countries that has a long statistical series on child labor in history (N. Zibani; EMA 94).

4 In comparison with the ELMS 98, it is worth noting that in the LFSS 88, the field workers were trained and more sensitive to the issue of child labor. This might have had an impact on the size of phenomenon measured.

5 Here, the standard employment definition refers to the International Labor Office definition of economic activity "all market production and certain types of non-market production, including production and processing of primary products for own consumption" (Hussmanns, Mehran, and Verma; 1990).

6 Both surveys include the summer school vacations in the last three months reference period.

7 Greater Cairo metropolitan region contains the entire governorate of Cairo, the urban parts of both Giza and Qaliubiya governorates.

8 This other metropolitan region includes the Alexandria, Suez and Port-Said governorates (mainly urban) and the city of Ismailia in the Ismailia governorate.

9 In Egypt, regulations on the employment of minors (term used in the labor laws to refer to children) date back to 1909 when a law prohibited the employment of minors below nine years of age in the cotton industry. The last child labor law dated back to 1996 No.12.

10 The MOE's One Classroom Schools initiative responded by calling for building three thousand one-room, multigrade primary schools without fees for girls 8–15. The schools were built in areas where no primary schools existed closer than 4–5 km.

11. UNICEF and MOE signed a cooperative agreement in 1992 to establish community schools in rural areas of Sohag, Assiut, and Qena in rural Upper Egypt where there were very low female literacy rates. The aim of the project was to develop an effective sustainable basic education program focusing on girls and serving small, rural communities where primary schools were either absent or some distance away. By 1995, 38 community schools were in operation, and by 1997 almost 200 schools.

12 "Greater appreciation for learning or more energy resulting from an improved diet (if wages are spent on nutritious food)", (Levison, 1991).

13 "Reduced ability to concentrate, less available time and/or energy for home work and study outside of school, and failure to pass into the next grade level" (Levison, 1991).

14 In her study, the author uses more encompassing questions regarding work activities among children aged 10 to 14 that includes household chores. In doing that she finds that an additional 36 percent of young females are working as compared to 25 percent of males.

15 The house chores were identified as doing laundry, cleaning, cooking, taking care of

siblings, shopping, fetching water, taking care of animals and chickens at home, and so on.

[16] Because the question on domestic work was asked only for girls, this percentage concerns only girls. Note that it is possible for a child who engages in market work to also participate in home work.

[17] Out of 37 girls working in market work, only 14 are combining market with domestic work (that is, there are very few observations).

[18] In the ELMS 98 questionnaire, the following questions on domestic work were asked only for female adults and young girls:
"In which of the following domestic activities (list of 8 choices) do you spend most of your time?"
"On average, how many hours a day do you spend on these household tasks?"
In the list of choices for domestic activities, husbandry—that is "taking care of animals and chickens in the home"—was mentioned. To avoid double counting of this particular activity with the question on the subsistence activity asked before, if the child is engaged in subsistence activities as well as doing husbandry as a domestic work, the answer "yes" on husbandry from the question on the domestic activities was removed.

[19] A test showed that there are no variations in the activity rates for both sexes and in both labor force definitions between 8 and 14 hours of work per week.

[20] In restricting the working children to those who worked at least 14 hours per week, the absolute number of working girls drops from nearly 515,000 to 180,000, which is reflected in the activity rates from nearly 7 percent to 3 percent, while for boys, the activity rates remain quite similar.

[21] Here the references are Jensen and Nielson (1997) for Zambia; Canagarajah and Coulombe (1998) for Ghana; Knaul (1999,1995) for Mexico and Colombia; Levison (1991) for Brazil; Patrinos and Psacharopoulos (1997) for Peru; and Psacharopoulos and Arriagada (1989) for Brazil.

[22] In the questionnaire, the responses "parents did not want to," and "traditions and culture" were distinct categories. I merged them into one category called "traditions and mentality" based on the idea that the father or the mother who does not send the child to school is more likely to do so because of similar factors, such as traditions, resistance, etc.

[23] It is worth mentioning that, based on the standard labor force definition, the number of observations are very small—only 10 observations for girls in the "both" category.

[24] In this study, the wealth index is not based on incomes or salaries (monetary being controversial), but rather on a variety of items. The wealth index constructed by Ragui Assaad is a composite variable based on the ownership by the household of a list of 23 durable goods, and on a series of housing characteristics such as type of floor and ceiling, connection to a sewage system, and access to piped water and electricity. Because wealth in urban and rural areas takes different forms, we opted to construct separate wealth scores for urban and rural households. Each group was then divided into quintiles based on its respective score. (Forthcoming paper)

[25] The employment status variable was a combination of three information sources.

[26] Irregular wageworkers in the private sector consist of intermittent and seasonal jobs.

[27] The category of nonwage workers is comprised of males who are working as self-employed, employer, or unpaid workers.

[28] Irregular wageworkers are those working temporary or occasionally.

Part IV. Labor Market Dynamic

7 Youth Labor Market Trajectories Over Time: A Comparison of the 1980s and 1990s

Mona Amer

Introduction

Youth unemployment has emerged as one of the most important problems plaguing the Egyptian labor market over the past two decades. The timing of the demographic transition in Egypt has led to severe demographic pressures on the labor market, which are expected to continue for at least another decade. This chapter aims to examine the labor market trajectories of youth in Egypt, with a focus on their transition from school to work. Nearly 90 percent of the unemployed in Egypt are looking for their first job, which suggests that the unemployment problem is primarily one of youth insertion into the labor market. Further, according to a number of studies on Egypt's labor market, a significantly high level of unemployment is found among women and graduates.

The first part of this study examines the major characteristics of the youth labor market. It provides a general overview of the manpower population, labor force population, participation rate, unemployed population, and unemployment rate—organized by gender, age group, educational level, and residence (urban vs. rural)—from 1988 to 1998. The second part focuses on youth labor-market trajectories. It presents the trends in transitions from school to the labor market over the 1980s and 1990s, and tracks labor market mobility.

1. Assessment of the Youth Labor Market

Youth population is defined here as individuals ages 15–34. To further distinguish this population, these have been divided into four age groups: 15–19; 20–24; 25–29 and 30–34. The youngest group (ages 15–34) represents approximately one-third of Egypt's 1998 population of 60.4 million people. The overall 15 to 34 year-old population has grown from 15.6 million in 1988 to 21.1 million in 1998, at an annual growth rate of 3 percent.

2 Labor Force Participation Trends

2.1. Trends by Gender, Urban/Rural Location, and Age Groups

From 1988 to 1998, the youth labor force grew from 8.6 million to 11.4 million, which is equivalent to an annual growth rate of 2.8 percent. Moreover, youth manpower has grown from 15.6 million to 20.9 million in the same period of time, which is at a rate of 3 percent per year. These similar growth trends lead to a stable participation rate of about 54–55 percent, slightly declining by about 0.1 percent per year. However, this result warrants a deeper analysis, as the apparent overall stability in labor force participation masks a number of different trends when distributions of labor force participation by gender, urban/rural location, and age composition are considered.

Distribution along gender lines highlights these different trends in labor force participation, as is shown in Table 7.1. Participation rates among males declined by 0.6 percent per year, as the male population has grown faster than the male labor force (2.4 percent vs. 3 percent). On the other hand, female participation rates increased by 0.5 percent annually, as the female labor force grew at a faster rate than the female population (3.4 percent vs. 2.9 percent).

Table 7.1: Growth of Manpower, Labor Force, and Labor Force Participation Rate Among Those Ages 15–34 (% per year)

		Urban	Rural	Egypt
Population	Male	1.2	4.6	3.0
	Female	1.1	4.3	2.9
	Total	1.2	4.5	3.0
Labor force	Male	0.7	3.8	2.4
	Female	1.0	4.7	3.4
	Total	0.8	4.2	2.8
Participation rate	Male	-0.5	-0.8	-0.6
	Female	-0.2	0.3	0.5
	Total	**-0.4**	**-0.3**	**-0.1**

Labor force participation according to urban/rural location shows nearly the same trend (See Table 7.1). The urban participation rate declined by about

0.4 percent per year, and the rural rate decreased by about 0.3 percent per year over the 10-year span of the studies. However, this similarity hides different patterns of labor force and manpower growth in urban and rural areas. The working-age population and the labor force have grown nearly four times faster in rural than in urban areas, for both males and females. But both urban and rural areas have experienced the same proportion of labor force growth that is lower than the population growth, leading to a small decrease in labor force participation rates. Distinction along gender lines also indicates different patterns. While male participation rates declined slightly in both urban and rural areas (by –0.5 percent and –0.8 percent per year, respectively), female participation rates decreased in urban areas but increased in rural locations (by –0.2 percent and 0.3 percent per year, respectively).

Table 7.2: Labor Force Participation Rates Among Youths Age 15–34 by Urban/Rural Location, Gender, and Age Group in 1988 and 1998 (%)

Age and Gender		**Urban**		**Rural**		**Egypt**	
		1988	**1998**	**1988**	**1998**	**1988**	**1998**
15–19	Male	40.6	27.3	56.1	40.7	48.4	35.5
	Female	17.8	15.3	41.5	39.7	30.5	30.5
	Total	**30.3**	**21.6**	**49.0**	**40.2**	**40.0**	**33.1**
20–24	Male	45.5	52.3	55.5	62.5	50.6	57.9
	Female	38.0	40.1	58.4	62.3	48.2	52.5
	Total	**41.9**	**46.6**	**56.9**	**62.4**	**49.5**	**55.4**
25–29	Male	90.7	90.6	91.6	92.3	91.1	91.6
	Female	45.4	39.4	58.0	62.2	51.9	52.5
	Total	**68.2**	**65.9**	**73.5**	**77.1**	**70.8**	**72.2**
30–34	Male	97.8	98.8	99.1	98.0	98.4	98.4
	Female	37.1	46.8	60.8	69.6	47.7	59.4
	Total	**64.8**	**71.6**	**79.8**	**83.2**	**71.8**	**78.0**
Total	Male	62.6	59.4	70.1	64.9	66.3	62.5
15–34	Female	33.7	33.1	53.1	54.8	43.5	45.8
	Total	**48.6**	**46.7**	**61.7**	**59.9**	**55.1**	**54.4**
Total	Male	73.5	75.6	77.3	80.3	75.3	78.2
20–34	Female	40.2	41.9	58.8	64.4	49.4	54.5
	Total	**56.8**	**59.2**	**68.1**	**72.5**	**62.4**	**66.6**

Notable differences appear in labor force participation trends among the various age groups (Table 7.2). Trends for the youngest age group, for example, were dissimilar to those of other age groups. The participation rate for those aged 15–19 declined from 49 to 40.2 percent, at an annual rate of 1.9 percent. The annual decline of participation for males was approximately

3 percent, while female participation remained stable from 1988 to 1998. In contrast, participation rates of individuals ages 20 and up increased annually by 0.7 percent (from 62.4 percent in 1988 to 66.6 percent in 1998).

It is interesting to note the distribution of labor force participation by gender. Participation among males ages 15–19 declined from 48.4 percent to 35.5 percent (an annual rate of 3.9 percent in urban areas and 3.2 percent in rural areas), and then increased by 1.4 percent per year among males ages 20–24. Participation rates of males ages 25 and up remains stable in both urban and rural areas. On the contrary, participation rates for females ages 15–29 remained stable or experienced a small increase over the 10-year period. The most interesting change concerns females ages 30–34. Their labor force participation rate increased substantially, from 47.7 percent in 1988 to 59.4 percent in 1998 (i.e., by 2.2 percent per year).

The important increase in female participation after age 30 leads to a new shape of female participation across all ages. Comparing results from LFSS 88 to ELMS 98, we can see that in 1988, the female partici-pation rate increased for those ages 15–29 and then declined for those ages 30–34. This tendency is no longer relevant in 1998, as the female participation rate increases continuously with age. Females tend to no longer quit the labor market after the age of 30.

Table 7.3: Labor Force Participation Rates by Gender and Urban/Rural Location According to Extended and Labor Market Definition of Economic Activity Among 15 to 34 Year-Olds in 1988 and 1998 (%)

Gender		Urban		Rural		Egypt	
		1988	1998	1988	1998	1988	1998
Male							
	Market labor force	N.A.	59.4	N.A.	64.7	N.A.	62.5
	Extended labor force	62.6	59.4	70.1	64.9	66.3	62.5
Female							
	Market labor force	N.A.	27.2	N.A.	22.6	N.A.	24.5
	Extended labor force	33.7	33.1	53.1	54.8	43.5	45.8
All							
	Market labor force	N.A.	43.8	N.A.	44.1	N.A.	44.0
	Extended labor force	48.6	46.7	61.7	59.9	55.1	54.4

Notes: N.A. = Not Available.

Finally, Table 7.3 provides participation rates according to the two definitions of economic activity as defined above. The comparison between the restrictive (labor-market production) and the extended (including agriculture subsistence) definition is only available for 1998. It shows that this distinction is only relevant for females—especially rural females. Indeed, participation rates among males are almost the same whatever the definition, the age group, and the urban/rural location. Therefore, young males participate exclusively in market-production economic activities. On the contrary, female participation increases substantially (from 24.5 percent to 45.8 percent for all of Egypt) if we use the extended definition rather than the market definition, as females are much more engaged in non-market production such as production and processing of primary products for own consumption (i.e., agriculture subsistence). Consequently, the female participation rate increases substantially in rural areas (from 22.6 percent to 54.8 percent).

Although the overall labor force participation rate among youth is stable from 1988 to 1998, further investigation shows that males and females experienced opposite trends. Male participation, particularly among men ages 15–19, decreased, while female participation increased, especially among those ages 30–34. The following section tries to provide some explanations to these results.

2.1 Determinants of Labor Force Participation Trends

Labor force participation rates are determined by demographic factors such as population age composition, demographic pressure, and behavioral changes, such as schooling enrollment and female withdrawal (Assaad, in this volume).

Male participation declined from 66.3 percent to 62.5 percent among 15 to 34 year-olds. However, men ages 15–19 experienced a remarkable fall in participation (from 48.4 percent to 35.5 percent over the study's 10-year period) while males older than 20 experienced increased participation. On the contrary, female participation increased from 43.5 percent to 45.8 percent, especially among women ages 20 and older (it increased from 49.4 percent to 54.5 percent from 1988 to 1998). The reduced male participation can be related to the rising school enrollment of males ages 15 to 19 (Table 1.2.4). This trend can also be related to an increase in schooling enrollment and educational attainment, as well as to the fact that women remain in the labor force longer (see Assaad, in this volume).

Table 7.4 shows that net enrollment rates among 15 to 24 year-olds have increased from 1988 to 1998 in both the 15–19 age group and the group of those ages 20–24. This is true for males and females, and in rural and urban areas. The overall growth rate was approximately 2.5 percent per year from 1988 to 1998. Nevertheless, this overall tendency masks different patterns along gender lines and between urban and rural residence. Female net enrollment rates have grown faster than that of males, narrowing the gap between male and female enrollment. Moreover, the enrollment gain from 1988 to 1998 is higher in rural than in urban areas. Rural females ages 15–24, then, represent the group that gained the most from improvement in school enrollment.

Table 7.4: Net Enrollment Rates Among 15 to 24 Year-Olds by Urban/Rural, Gender, and Age Group in 1988 and 1998
(in % per year)

Age and Gender		Urban		Rural		Egypt	
		1988	1998	1988	1998	1988	1998
15–19	Male	64.5	69.6	50.1	56.8	56.3	61.7
	Female	60.3	68.7	25.2	45.2	40.0	54.1
	Total	**62.5**	**69.2**	**37.8**	**51.1**	**48.3**	**58.1**
20–24	Male	21.9	28.0	11.7	17.1	16.2	21.9
	Female	17.9	26.0	4.2	7.3	10.6	15.5
	Total	**19.9**	**27.0**	**8.2**	**12.6**	**13.5**	**19.0**
Total	Male	44.4	50.1	32.5	40.3	37.7	44.3
15–24	Female	40.0	49.4	16.0	30.4	26.6	38.1
	Total	**42.3**	**49.8**	**24.6**	**35.6**	**32.3**	**41.4**

Figure A7.1 and Table 7.5 provide the evolution of educational attainment from 1988 to 1998 according to gender and urban/rural location among youth ages 15–34. These figures clearly show a noticeable decline of illiteracy and an improvement of educational attainment. However, distinguishable gaps prevail by gender and residence location.

Both young men and women acquired higher levels of education. However, women, who were much more disadvantaged in terms of education, experienced greater improvements than men. While half of women ages 15–34 were illiterate in 1988, they represented only 28.7 percent in 1998, which is equivalent to those with less-than-intermediate levels of education. Thus, women for the most part accomplished less-than-intermediate or intermediate levels of education in 1998. As for school enrollment, women were the ones who gained the most from educational improvement, inducing reduced gender differentials in educational attainment.

In urban areas, levels of education were very close for males and females, except that more young women suffer from illiteracy. In rural areas, gender differentials in favor of men persisted, notably for low levels of educational attainment (intermediate or less-than-intermediate levels) and among illiterates. For higher levels of education, gender differentials were reduced. Moreover, rural areas that were disadvantaged (more disadvantaged or most disadvantaged) in terms of education experienced the greater improvements at all levels of education, especially at low levels.

The overall improvement in educational attainment for both men and women can explain, in part, the fact that male participation decreased for those ages 15–19, and that female participation of those ages 15–34 increased. Moreover, a preliminary overview of labor-market trends from the 1980s to the 1990s by Ragui Assaad (in this collection) indicates that women tend to delay marriage and to continue working after marriage, leading to an increase in female participation across all ages.

Table 7.5: Educational Attainment Among 15 to 34 Year-Olds by Gender and Urban/Rural Location in 1988 and 1998 (in %)

Education Level[1]	Gender	Urban		Rural		Egypt	
		1988	1998	1988	1998	1988	1998
Illiterate	Male	17.0	7.7	36.3	17.8	26.6	13.5
	Female	29.5	14.0	71.5	39.2	50.7	28.7
	Total	**23.0**	**10.8**	**53.7**	**28.2**	**38.4**	**20.9**
Read and write	Male	10.7	4.1	11.4	7.5	11.0	6.1
	Female	7.8	4.0	4.3	5.1	6.1	4.6
	Total	**9.3**	**4.1**	**7.9**	**6.3**	**8.6**	**5.4**
Less than intermediate	Male	28.6	35.0	26.4	34.6	27.5	34.8
	Female	24.0	29.1	13.4	27.9	18.6	28.4
	Total	**26.3**	**32.2**	**19.9**	**31.3**	**23.1**	**31.7**
Intermediate	Male	27.4	35.8	20.3	31.5	23.9	33.3
	Female	25.9	36.9	8.4	21.5	17.1	28.0
	Total	**26.7**	**36.3**	**14.4**	**26.6**	**20.5**	**30.7**
Higher than intermediate	Male	5.2	5.4	1.6	3.1	3.4	4.1
	Female	3.1	6.1	1.1	3.5	2.1	4.6
	Total	**4.2**	**5.8**	**1.3**	**3.3**	**2.8**	**4.3**
University and higher	Male	11.1	11.4	4.1	4.9	7.6	7.7
	Female	9.7	9.6	1.2	2.5	5.4	5.5
	Total	**10.4**	**10.6**	**2.7**	**3.8**	**6.5**	**6.6**

Note: 1: Less than intermediate level refers to preparatory certificate; intermediate refers to general or technical secondary or azhari certificate; higher than intermediate designates two-year institute certificate or five-year technical secondary certificate; university and higher refers to bachelor, master higher diploma, or doctorate levels.

2.3 Unemployment

All figures concerning unemployment use a definition of unemployment that requires the search criterion, in both 1988 and 1998.

All studies on the Egyptian labor market underline the fact that unemployment is primarily experienced by young people. According to the extended definition of economic activity (including production and processing of primary products for own consumption), the number of unemployed among those ages 15–34 has grown from 0.7 million to 1.6 million over the 10-year period, i.e., an annual growth rate of 8.5 percent (see Table 7.6). Under the restrictive definition of economic activity (only available for 1998), the number of unemployed becomes much greater—growing from 1.6 million to 1.8 million in 1998—essentially because of the increased number of rural unemployed females.

Table 7.6: Unemployed Population Among 15 to 34 Year-Olds by Gender and Urban/Rural Residence in 1988 and 1998 ('000s)*

Gender		Urban 1988	Urban 1998	Rural 1988	Rural 1998	Egypt 1988	Egypt 1998
Male							
	Market labor force	N.A.	333	N.A.	492	N.A.	825
	Extended labor force	211	331	90	492	301	824
Female							
	Market labor force	N.A.	442	N.A.	576	N.A.	1018
	Extended labor force	281	400	113	351	394	751
All							
	Market labor force	N.A.	775	N.A.	1068	N.A.	1843
	Extended labor force	492	731	203	843	695	1575

* *Market and Extended Definition of Economic Activity.*

Table 7.7: Unemployment Rates Among 15 to 34 Year-Olds by Urban/Rural, Gender, and Age Group, in 1988 and 1998 (%)

Age and Gender		Urban 1988	Urban 1998	Rural 1988	Rural 1998	Egypt 1988	Egypt 1998
15–19	Male	10.9	20.3	3.5	15.5	6.6	16.9
	Female	40.7	25.8	6.9	8.2	16.0	11.5
	Total	**18.8**	**22.2**	**4.9**	**12.0**	**10.0**	**14.5**
20–24	Male	14.3	18.4	5.8	19.7	9.5	19.2
	Female	34.6	44.3	10.4	21.2	19.9	29.0
	Total	**23.0**	**28.7**	**8.0**	**20.4**	**14.3**	**23.5**
25–29	Male	8.4	11.2	2.4	10.0	5.5	10.5
	Female	13.9	28.1	2.6	8.8	7.4	15.0
	Total	**10.2**	**16.1**	**2.5**	**9.5**	**6.2**	**12.1**
30–34	Male	1.6	3.5	1.4	3.1	1.5	3.3
	Female	3.9	11.5	0.0	2.9	1.7	5.9
	Total	**2.3**	**6.3**	**0.9**	**3.0**	**1.5**	**4.3**
Total 15–34	Male	8.4	12.3	3.3	12.3	5.7	12.3
	Female	22.0	28.4	5.5	10.8	11.8	16.1
	Total	**13.0**	**17.8**	**4.2**	**11.6**	**8.1**	**13.8**

Table 7.7 gives unemployment rates by gender, urban/rural location, and age groups. According to the extended definition of economic activity, the overall unemployment rate among youth has grown from 8.1 percent in 1988 to 13.8 percent in 1998—a growth rate of 5.6 percent per year. The gender differential is still great, as women experienced very high unemployment

rates, but it has tended to reduce. The unemployment rate increased with age, reaching its peak for the 20 to 24 year-olds and then diminishing. The same pattern appeared in both 1988 and 1998.

Figure 7.1: Unemployment Rate Among 15–34 years old by Gender, and Urban/Rural Location in 1988 and 1998 (%)

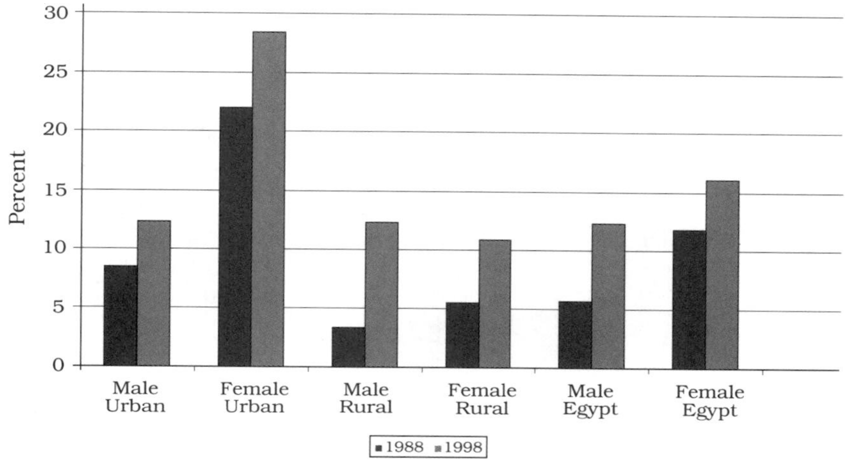

If we use a market definition of economic activity, this unemployment rate rises to 20 percent in 1998. As shown in Figure 7.1, regardless of the age group, the unemployment rate has increased faster in rural areas than in urban areas, especially among men (their unemployment rate has grown from 3.3 percent to 12.3 percent over the 10-year span). As the urban unemployment rate was higher in 1988, the gap between urban and rural areas tended to shrink.

Finally, Figure 7.2 shows the relation between educational attainment and unemployment rates. Unemployment rates increased with educational attainment, reaching a peak for individuals with intermediate levels of education. The uneducated individuals, and those who can just read and write, experienced very low levels of unemployment. However, different trends appeared for males and females. Unemployment rates increased for all levels of education among young men, but rose faster at high levels of education. On the other hand, female unemployment rates declined for low levels of education and increased for high levels of education.

In conclusion, young, educated people—particularly women—suffered the most from unemployment. Above all, the situation is deteriorating for people holding intermediate and higher levels of education.

Figure 7.2: Unemployment Rate and Educational Attainment in 1988 and 1998 (%)

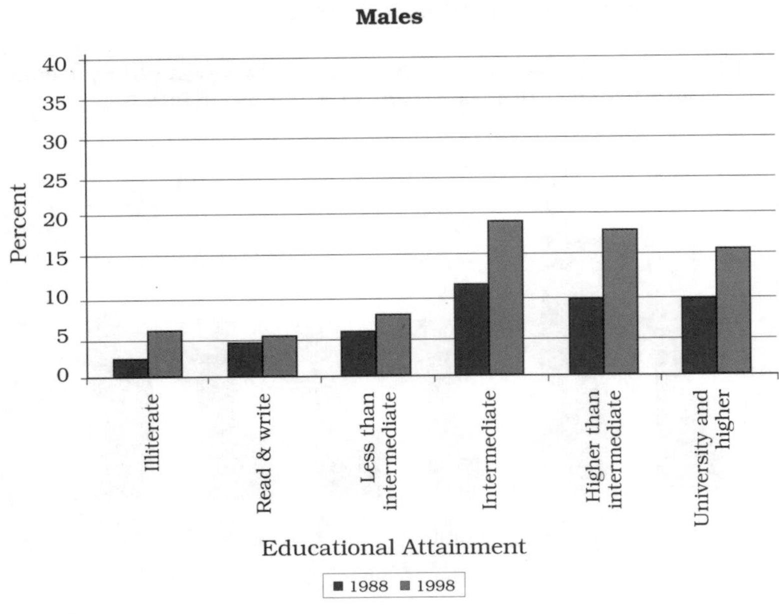

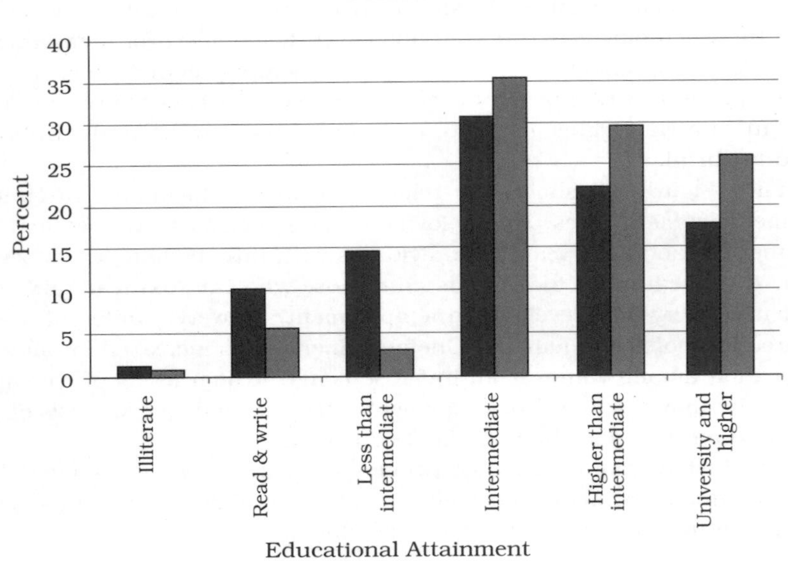

3. Mobility and Insertion Path Process

3.1 Transitions from School and Insertion into the Labor Market

This section explores the trend of transition from school to the Egyptian labor market, from the 1980s to the 1990s. The goal is to show how educated youth enter the labor market, and if there have been major changes over this decade. The comparison of periods is particularly critical and relevant since Egypt implemented a structural adjustment policy in 1991. It is important now to examine whether or not the government strategy of discouraging public employment—by allocating low wages and increasing queuing to government jobs—has led youth to adjust their expectations of employment. Private-sector employment, unlike that in the public sector, is characterized by little job security, low benefits, and higher levels of effort. The question is whether or not, as a result, Egyptian youth have reduced their expectations regarding employment security and social benefits. Particular focus is given here on female work strategies, since women are confronted by barriers when trying to enter the private sector (Assaad, 1997; El Khawaga, 1990).

This analysis is based on the mobility modules of LFSS 88 and ELMS 98 questionnaires. The LFSS 88 survey provides a history of employment at different dates—1973, 1981,[1] and 1988—and presents the employment status for all three. The ELMS 98 survey provides the same information, from 1990[2] to 1998. In order to compare the way youth have been inserted into the labor market in the 1980s and 1990s, the time intervals chosen here are 1981–88 and 1990–98. It is important to note that the time interval refers to eight years in the 1990s while referring to only seven years in the 1980s.

Moreover, modules on job history are restricted to a few categories. They take into account only individuals who have been employed for market purposes at any time during the "mobility period" (1981–88 and 1990–98). This implies that some people—mainly women—are excluded from the analysis, in particular those who never worked at all (e.g. discouraged unemployed or housewives), or those who never worked for market purposes (e.g. individuals who participated only in subsistence activities).

This part of the study focuses on youth ages 20–29 at the end of both periods (1988 and 1998) who were enrolled in school at the beginning of both periods (1981 and 1990). Restricting the study to this age group allows us to emphasize those with at least primary education[3] who are most likely to have finished school in 1988 or 1998. I then analyze their transitions by focusing on the beginning of their insertion into the labor market.

The purpose here is to establish trends of transitions from a predetermined status, which is school (the initial status in 1981 and 1990), to a final status in 1988 and 1998, which has to be determined. In order to define precisely the transitions, the final employment status is divided into the following categories:

- public job—includes employment in the public enterprises and in the government
- private regular wage-protected job—which refers to a permanent or temporary job with a written contract and/or social security
- private regular wage-unprotected job—which refers to a permanent or temporary job without a written contract or social security
- irregular wage job—which refers to a seasonal or casual job
- nonwage employment—which consists of employers, self-employed, and unpaid family workers
- unemployment—defined here with the search criterion
- out of the labor force—which includes those still in school, those who don't want to work, housewives, those permanently or temporarily disabled, workers on unpaid leave for a year or more, and others.

Figure 7.3 shows the evolution of the overall transition rates from school between two periods of time: 1981–88 and 1990–98.[4] There is no indication here whether these transitions are direct or not. The first and most striking result from the analysis of the transitions from 1981 to 1988 is that approximately 39 percent of those who where students in 1981 were not employed in 1988. They were either looking for a job (20 percent) or out of the labor force (19 percent). Second, there is no clear domination of the private sector against the public sector. Indeed, although the private sector is very heterogeneous (composed of protected and unprotected regular wage jobs, irregular wage jobs and nonwage employment), in 1988, it employed 33 percent of those who had been students in 1981. It is to be noted, however, that transition rates to irregular wage work were lowest within the private sector. The public sector was also a great employer, as 29 percent of former students were employed by public enterprises or by the government at the end of that period.

Transitions from 1990 to 1998 reveal that the primary, and first, employer is now clearly the private sector, as transition rates from school to private jobs reached 51 percent. The public sector is still an important employer, as 28 percent who were enrolled in school in 1990 were employed by public enterprises or by the government in 1998. Transitions to unemployment and inactivity are still at the high level of 22 percent (9 percent of unemployed and 13 percent of inactive).

Therefore, the main result from the analysis of trends in transitions among youth ages 20–29—from the 1980s to the 1990s—is that the rates of transition to employment have increased, whereas rates of transition from school to unemployment or inactivity have greatly decreased. However, while they may seem to reflect an improvement in the insertion of educated youth into the labor market in Egypt, these results are not complete without information on the type of employment that has resulted, and an analysis across gender and age groups.

Figure 7.3: Transitions Rates from School from the 1980s to the 1990s. Youth Aged 20–29 in 1988/1998

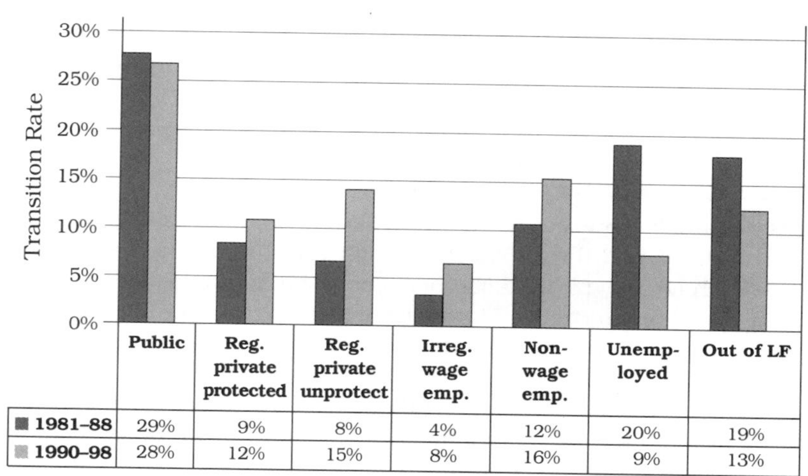

	Public	Reg. private protected	Reg. private unprotect	Irreg. wage emp.	Non-wage emp.	Unemp-loyed	Out of LF
1981–88	29%	9%	8%	4%	12%	20%	19%
1990–98	28%	12%	15%	8%	16%	9%	13%

Protected Versus Unprotected Jobs

Those who were students at the beginning of the period of analysis (1981 and 1990) were principally hired by the public sector seven years (in the case of 1981 to 1988) and eight years (in the case of 1990 to 1998) after graduation, even though transition rates from school to public jobs have declined slightly, from 29 percent in the 1980s to 28 percent in the 1990s.

The overall transitions from school to private employment have greatly increased, in particular those leading to irregular and unprotected jobs. While transition rates to regular private protected jobs have increased from 9 percent in the 1980s to 12 percent in the 1990s, transition rates to regular but unprotected jobs have grown faster (from 8 percent to 15 percent). Also, transition rates to irregular wage employment have doubled, from a low 4 percent in the 1980s to a substantial 8 percent in the 1990s. Figure 7.3 shows a similar trend regarding transitions from school to nonwage employment (12 percent in the period from 1981to 1988, compared to 16 percent from 1990 to 1998). As the nonwage employment category is heterogeneous, it is interesting to divide it into employer and self-employed on the one hand, and unpaid family workers on the other. When doing so, it appears that transitions to self-employment or employer (essentially in agriculture and trade) have increased from 5 percent to 7 percent, and that transitions to the situation of unpaid family worker have increased from 6 percent to 9 percent (essentially in agriculture).

Thus, Figure 7.3 clearly indicates that the two most desired types of jobs—i.e., jobs in the public sector (which we assume are protected by a written contract and offer social security) and regular wage-protected jobs—have experienced a decline or a very small increase. In contrast, the unsecured jobs (unprotected and/or irregular jobs) have experienced the biggest increase in transition rates. Although this expansion of undesired jobs seems to have compensated for the big fall in transition rates to unemployment and inactivity, the major trend is a deterioration of transitions to employment for educated youth.

20 to 24 Year-Olds Versus 25 to 29 Year-Olds

Figures 7.4 and 7.5 present age group differentials in transitions from school across the 1980s and the 1990s. Transition rates from school between 1981 and 1988 show the main differences between the two age groups. The youngest are characterized by lower transition rates to public jobs (18 percent compared to 45 percent among those ages 25–29) and higher transition rates to unemployment and inactivity (24 percent, compared to 13 percent and 11 percent, respectively, among those ages 25–29). Transitions to other employment statuses are quite similar across both age groups. Thus, while the 25 to 29 year-olds are well inserted into the labor market (62 percent have regular wage employment in 1988), the youngest group is still struggling with unemployment or inactivity (only 35 percent of those ages 20–24 had regular wage employment in 1988). The high level of unemployment seems to be related to the low level of public jobs among those ages 20–24, and probably reveals that those in this age group are unemployed because they are waiting for a government job.

Figure 7.4: Transitions Rates From School Among 20–24 Year-Olds

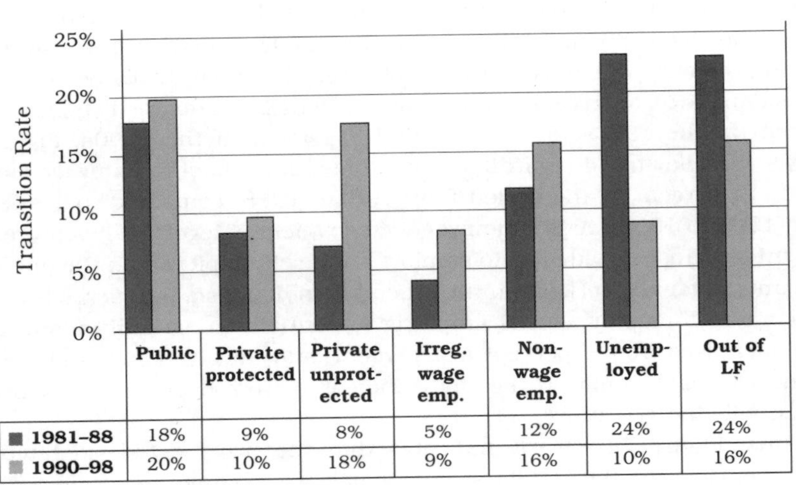

	Public	Private protected	Private unprot-ected	Irreg. wage emp.	Non-wage emp.	Unemp-loyed	Out of LF
■ 1981–88	18%	9%	8%	5%	12%	24%	24%
■ 1990–98	20%	10%	18%	9%	16%	10%	16%

Figure 7.5: Transitions Rates from School Among 25–29 Year-Olds

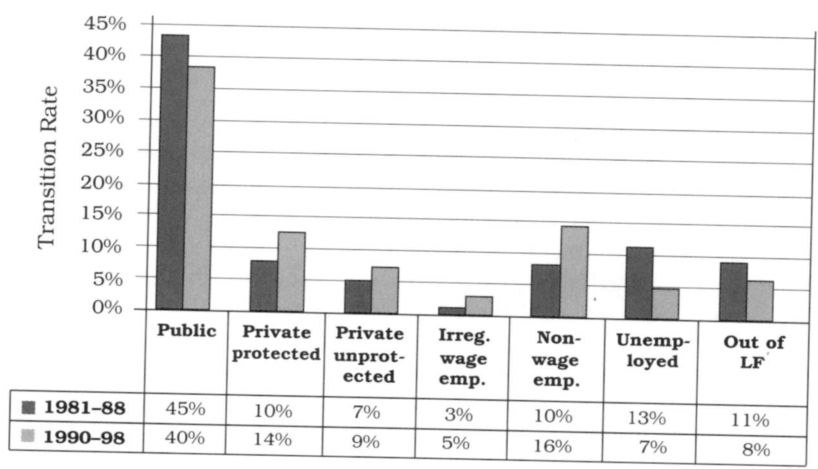

	Public	Private protected	Private unprotected	Irreg. wage emp.	Non-wage emp.	Unemployed	Out of LF
1981–88	45%	10%	7%	3%	10%	13%	11%
1990–98	40%	14%	9%	5%	16%	7%	8%

The transitions from 1990 to 1998, compared to those from 1981 to 1988, indicate that the overall transition rate from school to employment has grown among those ages 20–24. But transition rates to regular unprotected jobs and irregular wage jobs have increased more among this youngest group. While transition rates from school to regular protected and unprotected wage jobs were quite the same from 1981 to 1988 (9 percent and 8 percent respectively), transitions from school to regular protected jobs remained stable, while transitions to regular unprotected jobs more than doubled from 1990 to 1998. Also, transitions to irregular wage employment almost doubled (from 5 percent to 9 percent) from the 1980s to the 1990s, and transitions to non-wage employment increased from 12 percent to 16 percent. This result has to be linked with the high decrease in transitions to unemployment and inactivity. Thus, it seems that unemployment and inactivity have been replaced by irregular, unprotected, or nonwage employment among 20 to 24 year-olds.

The evolution of transition rates over the two decades among those ages 25–29 shows that even if the transition rate to the public sector has decreased (from 45 percent in the 1980s to 40 percent in the 1990s), the latter is still by far the main employer. In contrast to the youngest group, the 25 to 29 year-olds experienced a higher increase in transition rates to regular protected jobs than to regular unprotected jobs. Moreover, the main difference between the two age groups is the very slight increase (from 7 percent to 9 percent) in transitions to regular but unprotected jobs (compared to a substantial increase from 8 percent to 18 percent among the 20 to 24 year-olds). When comparing unpaid family work with self-employed and employer, it appears that both transitions have grown (from 5 percent to 9 percent, and from 5 percent to 7 percent, respectively).

In conclusion, the 20 to 24 year-olds experienced the greatest shifts from the 1980s to the 1990s compared to other age groups. The most noticeable result is the increase in transitions to unprotected jobs and the decrease of unemployment and inactivity.

Gender Differentials

Figures 7.6 and 7.7 give the evolution of transition rates of the students by gender, from the 1980s to the 1990s. The most noticeable fact is that both males and females experienced an important overall increase of transitions towards employment together with a large decline of transitions to unemployment. Nevertheless, while transitions to the public sector decreased slightly among males from the 1980s to the 1990s (from 25 percent to 22 percent), they substantially increased (from 34 percent to 43 percent) among females over the same period. The growth of the public sector shows that the main employer for females remains attractive compared to the private sector, even in the context of economic liberalization and structural adjustment.

Figure 7.6: Male Transitions From School from the 1980s to the 1990s. Youth Aged 20–29 in 1988/1998

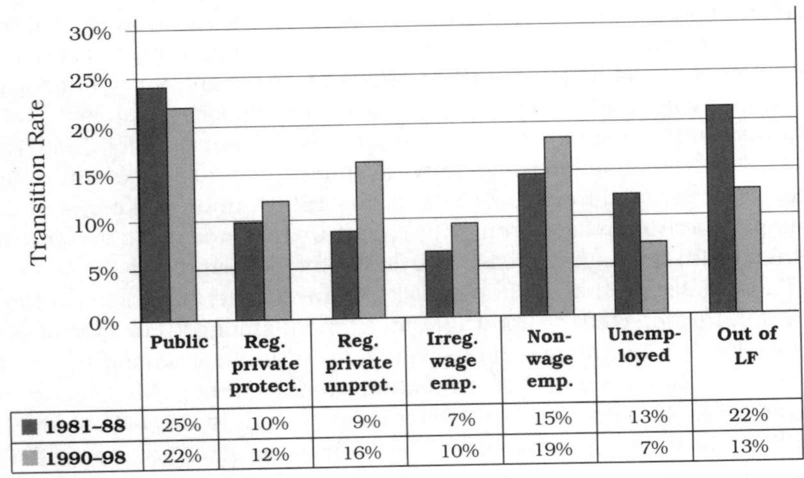

	Public	Reg. private protect.	Reg. private unprot.	Irreg. wage emp.	Non-wage emp.	Unemp-loyed	Out of LF
1981–88	25%	10%	9%	7%	15%	13%	22%
1990–98	22%	12%	16%	10%	19%	7%	13%

All transitions from school to private employment have grown, but what is most striking and particularly disturbing is that the transitions to unprotected employment have increased more. They almost doubled during the period of analysis for both men and women. Transitions to regular protected, irregular, and nonwage jobs have grown slowly. The big change is in the growth in transitions to regular unprotected jobs. This result has to be compared with the important fall in transitions from school to unemployment and to inactivity for both males and females. It seems, then, that unprotected jobs have replaced periods of unemployment. It is likely that a segment of the educated youth who were unemployed while queuing for government jobs have stopped waiting, and are working in unprotected jobs in the private sector. Thus, the most important shift is that unemployment has been replaced by unprotected or unpaid employment, for both men and women.

Figure 7.7: Female Transitions from School from the 1980s to the 1990s. Youth Aged 20–29 Years in 1988/1998

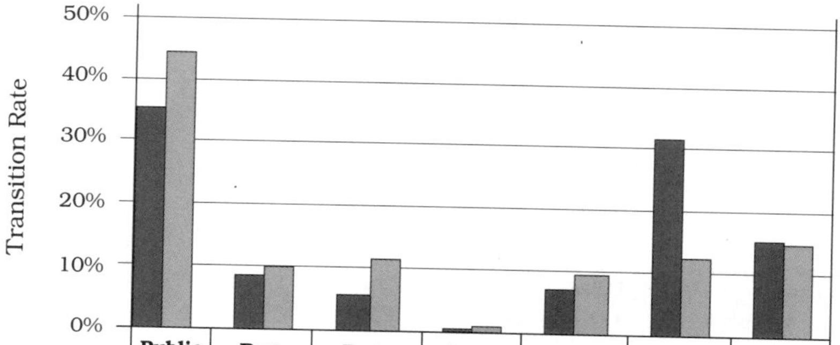

Transition Rate	Public	Reg. private protect.	Reg. private unprotect.	Irreg. wage emp.	Non-wage emp.	Unem-ployed	Out of LF
1981–88	34%	8%	5%	1%	7%	30%	15%
1990–98	43%	10%	11%	1%	9%	12%	14%

This result is confirmed by focusing on the evolution of the share of each employment category given in Table 7.8. The employment structure is characterized by an important contrast that persists over the period when comparing females and males. While the private sector is by far the major employer for males, it is the public sector that plays that role for females. Moreover, the private employment structure reveals gender differences. There is no clear domination of a certain type of job among males, even though nonwage employment represents almost one-fifth of total employment. This can be explained by the fact that nonwage employment comprises the self-employed, employers, and unpaid family workers. Female private employment is characterized by the fact that irregular jobs are very rare for females. However, regular and protected employment represents a similar share among men and women.

Although the structure of the private sector presents differences by gender, both females and males experienced the same trends of transitions from school to private and public jobs between the 1980s and the 1990s. The main changes concern the regular unprotected wage employment and public employment. Both men and women experienced a fall in the share of the public sector and an important increase in the share of unprotected wage employment. The share of other types of employment remains almost stable for both men and women.

Table 7.8: Employment Structure in 1988 and 1998 for Individuals Who Were Students in 1981 or 1990

Employment Status 1988/1998	Male 1981–88	Male 1990–98	Female 1990–98	Female 1981–88	Total 1981–88	Total 1990–98
Public sector	37.69	28.14	62.23	58.24	46.66	35.32
Regular private Protected	15.41	15.57	14.79	13.27	15.18	15.02
Regular private Unprotected	13.83	20.48	9.64	14.90	12.30	19.15
Irregular wage Employment	10.28	12.28	0.99	1.05	6.89	9.60
Nonwage Employment	22.78	23.54	12.35	12.54	18.97	20.91
Total	**100.00**	**100.00**	**100.00**	**100.00**	**100.00**	**100.00**
Sample size	***378***	***597***	***230***	***195***	***608***	***792***

This shift in the employment structure and, in particular, the fall of the public sector's share is expected in the context of an economic liberalization policy. It is clear that there is a disengagement from the state, but what is disturbing is that the protected private sector does not seem capable of replacing the state in its employment role.

3.2 Mobility in The Youth Labor Market at Different Period Length

This section aims to explore the main trajectories and mobility of youth in the Egyptian labor market through three periods of transitions: 1990–91; 1990–94; and 1990–98.

Comparing these three periods provides an insight into short, middle, and long-run transitions in the labor market. As the main objective of this section is still the analysis and understanding of youth mobility in the Egyptian labor market, the study is here restricted to individuals ages 15–29 in 1990 who were not in school in 1998.[5]

The results of this section have been obtained from data on the history of employment module of ELMS 98. As mentioned earlier, this module offers two kinds of information. First it presents the last three employment situations (current for late October, 1998, and the two previous to this). Second, it provides the employment status in August, 1990. Because only those who have ever entered the labor market answered this part of the questionnaire, some assumptions have been made in order to include all the youth ages 15–29 in

1990, whatever their employment situation. Employment status in 1990, 1991, 1994, and 1998 have been given the following assumptions:

- For those who were ever employed and thus answered the mobility section, their employment status in 1990 and 1998 are given. The dates of start of the current, previous, and pre-previous employment status allow us to easily determine their situation in 1991 and 1994.
- For those who never worked for market purposes, and therefore did not answer the mobility section, some assumptions had to be made. These individuals are divided into three categories:
  - Those currently unemployed (or "always unemployed"). The duration of their current unemployment spell and the year they finished school allow us to identify the beginning of their unemployment spell and then determine whether they were unemployed or students in 1990, 1991, and 1994.
  - Those currently out of the labor force (or "always out of the labor force"). It is assumed that they were also out of the labor force since the age of 6 if they were not students in 1990, 1991, and 1994.
  - Those currently unpaid family workers (or "always unpaid family workers"). It is assumed that if they were not students in 1990, 1991, or 1994, they were unpaid family workers.

Even with these assumptions, however, some transitions cannot be observed. This concerns all kind of mobility between unemployment, inactivity, and participation in subsistence activities for individuals who never worked for market purposes (e.g. discouraged unemployed). This implies that these individuals are considered here to be always in one of the three statuses, (i.e. are immobile). As females are more likely to belong to one of these three categories, this leads to an overestimation of female immobility.

The definition of unemployment used here depends on whether or not an individual is currently unemployed. If he or she is unemployed, the search criterion is applied; if not, there is no indication through the mobility section in the ELMS 98 questionnaire of whether or not he or she is looking for a job. Given the fact that the Egyptian labor market is highly segmented by gender, female and male trajectories of the youth are presented separately.

3.3 Female Labor-Market Trajectories: Toward Early Inactivity?

The analysis of female trajectories (those ages 15–29 in 1990) over the three time intervals is defined as transitions to and from different employment statuses, divided into the following categories: public employment; remunerated private employment; unemployment; student; and out of the labor force. The marital status has been included for each category except in the case of unpaid family workers, students, and those out of the labor force (only in 1990), as this information does not offer any further insight. These transitions are given in appendix tables (see Table A7.1, A7.2 and A7.3), with persistency rates in bold.

Table 7.9: Female Distribution of the Number of Changes by Periods of Transitions

Number of Changes	Period of Transition 1990–91	1990–94	1990–98
No change	94.81	82.07	72.31
1 Change	5.19	16.79	22.19
2 or More Changes	-	1.14	5.50
Total	**100.00**	**100.00**	**100.00**
Sample Size	***2437***	***2437***	***2437***

One of the main characteristics of youth female mobility in the Egyptian labor markets is well illustrated in Table 7.9. This table presents the distribution of the changes from one employment status to another according to the length of the transition period.

It is clearly shown that females are mainly immobile. Indeed, there is almost no mobility from one year to the next. Ninety-five percent of females ages 15–29 in 1990 have not changed their employment status. The very few who did change were students in 1990 who, by definition, were bound to move out of that state. The longer the interval, the more females are likely to change their employment status. Still, 82 percent remained in the same status from 1990 to 1994. Those who changed status did it just once (17 percent), and only 1 percent changed twice or more (which represents only 29 cases out of 2437 observations). The period of 1990–98 also finds a very high percentage (72 percent) of females remaining in one status. Only 22 percent changed once, and 5.5 percent changed twice or more over the eight-year period.

Since almost all females changed their employment status at least once, transitions from 1990–94 can be considered to be direct ones. Therefore, transitions from 1990–91 are included with those of 1990–94. It would be redundant to present transitions from 1990–91, so this section will present only female mobility (or immobility) for 1990–94 and 1990–98.

3.4 Mobility versus Immobility

In the transitions tables in the annex for 1990–94 and for 1990-98 (see Table A7.2 and A7.3), a clear distinction appears between the categories with mobility and the categories without mobility or high persistency rates. The first category includes students and unmarried women working in the private sector. The second category (with persistency rates above 90 percent) includes those employed by the public sector, unpaid family workers, and those out of the labor force. Those who are unemployed have intermediate transition rates relative to those in other states.

3.5 Employment Status with High Persistency

Transitions from 1990–94 and from 1990–98 reveal that, whatever their marital status, women out of the labor force or unpaid family workers experience very high persistency rates (95 percent and above). Once they are out of the labor force, there is almost no chance to enter or reenter the labor market.

The status of unpaid family workers, who are all participating in subsistence activities, is not affected by whether or not they get married. This can be explained by the fact that working as an unpaid family worker is compatible with domestic responsibilities. Once women belong to one of these two statuses, they remain there.

Transitions from employment in the public sector also show a very high persistency rate. Ninety-four percent of women ages 15–29 working in public enterprises or in the government in 1990 had kept their jobs by 1994. The characteristics of the public job (permanent job, social security, low productivity) seem appropriate to young working women.

As for unpaid family workers, being or not being married does not affect these transition rates. Indeed, 96 percent of the women already married and working in the public sector in 1990 remain working there in 1994. Moreover, those who were unmarried in 1990 also kept their jobs after marrying.

Persistency rates were still very high from 1990–98. Approximately 91 percent of females who were working in public enterprises or in the government in 1990 were still engaged in the same jobs eight years later. Only 6 percent had quit their jobs and were currently out of the labor force. As for transitions from 1990–94, marital status does not matter. The persistency rates among unmarried and married women are very close—89 percent and 92 percent, respectively. It appears, then, that working in the public sector is a very stable situation.

3.6 Employment Status with Low Persistency Rates

Most of those who were in school in 1990 had dropped out of school or had completed their education four years later. Indeed, only 30 percent were still in school in 1994. This result can be explained by the fact that they were in the 19–33 age group in 1994, and most of them finished secondary school, which is a determinant stage in the Egyptian education system. Those who left school entered the labor force (37 percent). They were searching for jobs (18 percent), were employed in the public sector (11 percent—probably benefiting from their direct nomination as teachers), or were working in the private sector (8 percent) in 1994. Nevertheless, a high percentage went directly from school to inactivity. Indeed, the most important transitions after school was being out of the labor force and married (19 percent). Even the 13 percent of women who left school and were unmarried and out of the labor force in 1994 were about to get married (about two-thirds married in 1995 or 1996). Thus, it seems that marriage strongly influences women to not get into the labor market. Transitions over the eight-year period reveal the same mobility structure compared to 1990–94, with lower persistency rates. Females experienced high levels of transition rates toward inactivity (44 percent) and, in particular, toward inactivity while married. The second possibility after finishing school is to be unemployed, and very few get the chance to be directly employed.

3.7 Unemployment

The most striking result concerning transitions from unemployment is that 77 percent of unemployed women in 1990 remained unemployed in 1994. Moreover, as they did not change their employment status between the two dates, we can say that they stayed continuously unemployed for at least four years. The very few (10 percent) who did not stay unemployed got jobs in the public sector in 1994 (mainly in the government). It is almost impossible, then, to find a job over a period of four years, and the only exit is to get a government nomination. Female unemployment is then a waiting period for the nomination to a government job.

Marital status does not effect transitions from unemployment. Indeed, while about half of the females unemployed in 1990 were married, persistency rates in unemployment over the 1990–94 period were about the same regardless of marital status.

Fifty-four percent of the women who were unemployed in 1990 were still looking for a job in 1998. The distribution of the number of changes reveals that almost none of them changed their situation between 1990 and 1998. Thus, they experienced unemployment without interruption, and their average duration of unemployment was 11 years. Only 10 percent got a private sector job, and 9 percent were out of the labor force (discouraged unemployed). If not still unemployed, these women, ages 23–37 in 1998, were primarily employed in the government (23 percent). Unemployment was then a necessary step before getting a job in the government. As for the period from 1990–94, marital status didn't seem to affect transitions from unemployment.

3.8 Private Sector

Female transitions from private employment between 1990–94 give interesting results in comparison with transitions from the public sector. While almost all women working in the public sector remained in it, only 67 percent of females working in the private sector in 1990 remained in their jobs in 1994. This result clearly contrasts with the very high persistency rate of public jobs from 1990–94. The high transition rate (18 percent) from private employment to inactivity reflects the difference between public and private jobs for women. Also, almost all women who quit their jobs for inactivity were married in 1994, while they were single in 1990. Moreover, this persistency rate in private employment masks differences by marital status. While the persistency rate in private jobs for women already married in 1990 was about 91 percent, it fell to 46 percent for unmarried women in 1990. So, it seems that there is a high correlation between marriage and withdrawal of women from their private jobs.

Only 55 percent of the women who worked in the private sector in 1990 had kept their jobs by 1998, compared to a persistency rate of 67 percent from 1990–94. A large number quit the labor force (27 percent). All of them were married women in 1998. The high rate of transition out of the labor force is especially true for unmarried women once they marry (39 percent).

In conclusion, these trajectories reveal that the female Egyptian labor market is highly segmented into public and private sectors. Women working in the private sector are very likely to quit the labor force, in contrast to those working in the public sector. Even though a very long period of unemployment is necessary to get a public job, it seems worth it to these women. Moreover, the results indicate that marriage is an important determinant of withdrawal from an economic activity, especially in the private sector. Being married and having a job in the private sector are not always compatible. Nevertheless, the timing between marriage and the beginning of the economic activity is determinant. Indeed, those who are already married when they get a job are more likely to keep it.

4. Male Trajectories or How To Get a Regular and Protected Job

This section presents male transitions over three periods: 1990–91, 1990–94; and 1990–98 (see Tables A7.4, A7.5 and A7.6).

The employment status is divided into the following categories: public employment; regular and protected private wage job, regular and unprotected private wage job, irregular employment in and out of agriculture, nonwage employment in or out of agriculture, unemployment, and out of the labor force.[6]

Contrary to females, males ages 15–29 in 1990 changed their employment status (See Table 7.10). Even if most of the males maintained the same employment status from one year to the next, a substantial percentage (13.5 percent) experienced a change in their situations. The longer the transition, the more males are mobile. Only 41 percent remained in the same status over the eight-year period (compared to 59 percent from 1990–94). In addition, the share of those who changed status twice or more has increased from 10 percent to 26 percent between the four- and eight-year periods.

4.1 Transitions from 1990–91

Male transitions from 1990–91 are characterized by high persistency rates. This result is confirmed by the fact that only 87 percent of males have moved from their initial status in 1990 to their status in 1991. Except for those out of the labor force, the initially unemployed or students experienced the lowest persistency rates—77 percent and 81 percent, respectively.

Even if persistency rates are high among all types of employment, it is interesting to note that those working in regular wage unprotected employment and regular protected jobs experienced the lowest persistency rates (89 percent and 91 percent, respectively). Thus, even over a very short period, regular jobs (protected or not) are the less stable.

Table 7.10: Male Distribution of the Number of Changes by Periods of Transitions

Number of Changes	**Period of Transition**		
	1990–91	**1990–94**	**1990–98**
No change	86.50	58.75	40.80
1 change	13.50	30.93	32.88
2 or more changes	-	10.31	26.32
Total	**100.00**	**100.00**	**100.00**
Sample Size	***2267***	***2313***	***2313***

4.2 Transitions from 1990–94 and from 1990-98

Only 10 percent of men ages 15–29 in 1990 changed twice or more over the four-year period. Thus, for 90 percent of males the observed states in 1990 and 1994 reflect at most a single transition. Indirect transitions primarily concern those who were students (50 percent), out of the labor force (10 percent), or engaged in regular unprotected jobs (10 percent) in 1990. This is not surprising, as being a student or being out of the labor force are, by definition, a temporary status for males. All other transitions can be considered more or less as direct transitions from 1990–94.

Unemployment

Most of the men unemployed in 1990 had found jobs in 1994. The first job found after being unemployed was either a public job (16 percent), a regular protected job (12 percent), or a regular unprotected job (16 percent). Almost all males who were unemployed in 1990 had found jobs by 1998. Only 17 percent remained continuously unemployed from 1990–98. This contrasts with the high persistency rates of unemployment among females. Again, as in the period of 1990–94, once men left the unemployed status, they found jobs in either the public sector (27 percent) or in the regular private sector (12 percent obtained a protected job and 21 percent an unprotected one). One explanation could be that these jobs are the most desired by males. The unemployment spell, then, represents the searching period for desired jobs such as these.

Students

Those who were students in 1990 were 19 to 33 year-olds in 1994, and had finished secondary school. As dropping out of school is frequent in Egypt after secondary school completion, the persistency rates in education are very low among this age group. Those who remained enrolled in 1994 (33 percent) were pursuing their educations at the university or in technical institutes.

No males remained students from 1990 to 1998 by construction of the sample. Moreover, the age group we are focusing on, which was 15–29 in 1990, was 23–37 in 1998. Tables in the annex show that almost all those who were students in 1990 were employed in 1998. This result confirms the fact that participation rates among males are very high. The three main transitions from school to job are to the public sector (24 percent), private protected workers (13 percent), and private unprotected workers (12 percent), which mainly employ educated workers. However, transition rates from school to unemployment are also important (16 percent), most likely because they concern educated youth, who are more demanding and need more time to find a job suitable to their qualifications.

Public Sector

Transition rates from the public sector show a very high persistency over four years. Almost 95 percent of the young men employed in public enterprises or in the government remained in it (in the corresponding sector). There were no significant transitions to other kinds of jobs for the very few who quit the public sector. Transition rates from public jobs are characterized by the highest persistency rate from 1990–98. Indeed, 89 percent of those who were already working in the public sector were still working in the sector in 1998. The distribution of the number of changes among this group confirms this, as 95 percent did not change their employment status. Thus, they stayed continuously employed in the public sector from 1990–98. Transitions from the public sector to other employment statuses are marginal (4 percent go to the private protected and 3 percent to the nonwage employment). As for females, these results confirm that the public sector is a very stable environment.

Private Protected

This category has similar characteristics to public employment. Indeed from 1990-94, persistency rates are high (82 percent), and there are no significant transitions from a regular private protected job, except to public employment, which could be interpreted as an improved situation. Persistency rates from 1990 to 1998 are high, as a majority (68 percent) of those who were already employed in a regular private wage job have kept these jobs. However, transitions to other statuses are not negligible, contrary to transitions from the public sector. Indeed, 10 percent have left regular protected jobs for public jobs, and 9 percent for nonwage nonagricultural jobs (in fact they were employers or self-employed). Other transitions from private protected jobs seem negligible.

Private Unprotected

If we exclude transitions to inactivity and consider only the mobility within the labor market, it appears that most people (70 percent) have kept their regular but unprotected jobs from 1990 to 1994. If not, they find regular but protected jobs, either in the public or the private sector. Thus, they change jobs to find a better situation for themselves. The transitions from 1990 to 1998 are characterized by the lowest persistency rates among all employment statuses. Only 57 percent of young men employed in this type of job in 1990 had kept it in 1998. Moreover, considering the number of changes among those who kept their jobs, only 80 percent kept them continuously from 1990–98. So this persistency rate of 57 percent is even overestimated.

Another interesting result is that those who changed their jobs had improved their situations. Indeed, main transitions from regular but unprotected wage employment from 1990 to 1998 have led to public jobs (16 percent) or to regular but protected wage jobs (10 percent). Other transitions can be considered as insignificant.

Moreover this is the only category that leads to a regular private protected job. It seems, then, very difficult to obtain a regular protected job.

Irregular Wage Employment in Agriculture

This category concerns essentially casual workers (86 percent) and people with low education levels (74 percent had less-than-primary educations). When excluding transitions to and from inactivity, the persistency rate in irregular agricultural jobs from 1990 to 1994 is about 91 percent. Moreover, this persistency rate reflects a real immobility, i.e., these workers remained in the same jobs from 1990–94. Also, if we look at this status by column, the table clearly shows that there is almost no transition from any kind of status to irregular job status in agriculture.

Transitions from 1990–98 indicate the same pattern as the pattern from 1990–94. Those who worked in this type of employment in 1990 experienced a very high persistency rate. Moreover, no transition to other statuses seemed to emerge.

Nonwage Nonagricultural Employment

Those belonging to this employment status are mainly self-employed or are employers, as only 20 percent are unpaid family workers. Their transition rates are similar to those of irregular agricultural work, as 83 percent remained in their status from 1990 to 1998, and there was no significant transition to any other employment status.

Irregular Wage Nonagricultural and Nonwage Agricultural Employment

Theses two categories concern primarily lower-educated males (50 percent have less-than-primary educations), and show very similar patterns in terms of transitions. Indeed, they both have very high persistency rates (65 percent and above), and the only significant exit is a public job.

5. Conclusion

In conclusion, male trajectories reveal a highly segmented labor market. The male labor market can be divided into two categories: regular protected jobs (public or private); and unprotected and/or irregular jobs. The first category employs the more-educated young males. Unemployment or regular unprotected jobs seem to be the only two paths to obtaining the most desired jobs. The second category is composed mainly of less-educated youth. Even though this category is less homogeneous, it is characterized by very high persistency rates and very few exits. All the people working in such jobs seem to stay there.

Notes

1 The dates 1973 and 1981 have been chosen because they refer to two memorable dates in the Egyptian modern history. 1973 refers to the Yom Kippur war, and 1981 to the assassination of former president Sadat.

2 The date of August 1990 is also a memorable date, as it refers to the invasion of Kuwait by Iraq.

3 They belong to two different age groups at the beginning of each period: the 13–22 year-olds in 1981 and the 12–21 year-olds in 1990.

4 There is no indication here whether these transitions are direct or not.

5 This restriction isn't very strong as the 15–29 year-olds in 1990 are aged 23–27 in 1998 and almost all of them have completed their education or have dropped out from school.

6 Transition rates from inactivity to other employment status states do not show a specific pattern. Male inactivity leads to all kinds of status. Also, except for public and private protected jobs, transitions to out of the labor force are substantial. These results might be explained by the fact that males aged 15–29 in 1990 are of age to do their military service (in Egypt, generally three years). Therefore this category is excluded from the analysis.

Appendix

Figure A7.1: Educational Attainment Among 15–34 Year Olds by Gender and Urban/Rural Location in 1988 and 1998 (in %)

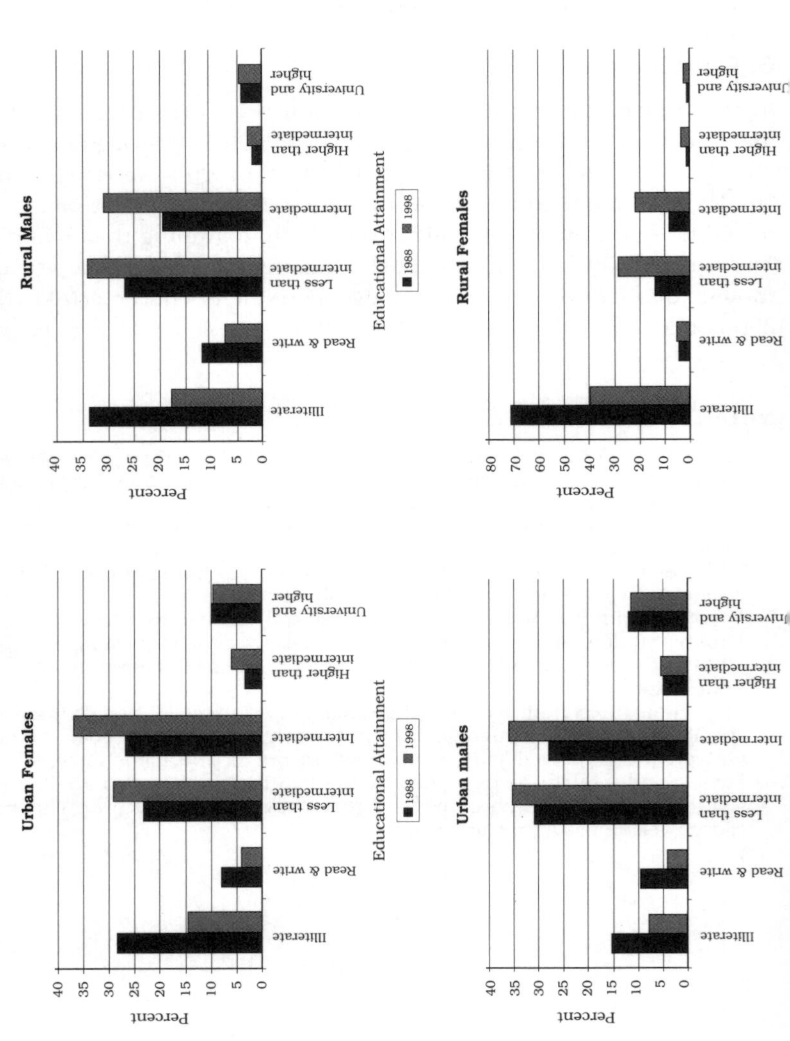

Table A7.1: Female Mobility from 1990 to 1991 in % (15 Year Olds in 1990)

Employment Status 1990		**Female Employment Status in 1991**										
		Public		**Private**		**Unpaid**	**Unemployment**		**Student**	**Out of the LF**		**Total**
		Not married	**Married**	**Not married**	**Married**		**Not married**	**Married**		**Not married**	**Married**	*(Sample size)*
Public	Not married	**79.97**	**18.15**	0.00	0.00	0.40	0.00	0.00	0.00	1.48	0.00	100.00 *(83)*
	Married	0.00	**98.46**	0.00	0.00	0.00	0.00	0.00	0.00	0.00	1.54	100.00 *(148)*
Private	Not married	3.77	0.00	**73.33**	**3.79**	3.17	1.60	0.00	0.00	6.24	8.10	100.00 *(54)*
	Married	0.00	1.24	0.00	**96.93**	0.00	0.00	0.00	0.00	0.00	1.84	100.00 *(44)*
Unpaid		0.00	0.00	0.00	0.00	**100.00**	0.00	0.00	0.00	0.00	0.00	100.00 *(537)*
Unemp.	Not married	4.15	1.27	0.00	1.55	0.00	**76.50**	**13.15**	0.00	3.38	0.00	100.00 *(55)*
	Married	0.00	3.32	0.00	0.00	6.28	0.00	**86.36**	0.00	0.00	4.04	100.00 *(57)*
Student		1.60	0.58	1.59	0.12	0.16	3.63	0.28	**81.99**	6.53	3.53	100.00 *(470)*
Out of LF		0.16	0.16	0.06	0.65	1.31	0.00	0.00	0.00	26.25	71.40	100.00 *(988)*
Total		**2.94**	**5.91**	**1.93**	**2.19**	**28.33**	**2.06**	**1.96**	**14.21**	**11.62**	**28.85**	**100.00**
Sample size		***89***	***164***	***48***	***52***	***554***	***60***	***60***	***388***	***282***	***739***	***2436***

Table A7.2: Female Mobility from 1990 to 1994 in % (15 Year Olds in 1990)

Employment Status 1990		Female Employment Status in 1994										
		Public		**Private**		**Unpaid**	**Unemployment**		**Student**	**Out of the LF**		**Total**
		Not married	**Married**	**Not married**	**Married**		**Not married**	**Married**		**Not married**	**Married**	*(Sample size)*
Public	Not married	**44.43**	**47.85**	0.92	0.92	0.40	0.92	0.00	0.00	2.11	2.46	100.00 *(84)*
	Married	0.00	**95.68**	0.00	0.00	0.00	0.00	0.00	0.00	0.00	4.32	100.00 *(148)*
Private	Not married	4.67	5.10	**33.96**	**12.03**	3.17	2.72	7.61	0.00	1.03	29.71	100.00 *(54)*
	Married	0.00	3.66	0.00	**91.07**	0.00	0.00	1.52	0.00	0.00	3.75	100.00 *(44)*
Unpaid		0.00	0.00	0.00	0.17	**99.46**	0.00	0.00	0.00	0.00	0.37	100.00 *(537)*
Unemp.	Not married	5.42	3.79	6.68	1.86	0.00	**41.58**	**37.26**	0.00	0.00	3.41	100.00 *(55)*
	Married	0.00	10.09	0.00	1.73	6.17	0.00	**75.72**	0.00	0.00	6.28	100.00 *(58)*
Student		6.91	4.55	7.38	0.56	0.38	12.50	5.65	**30.01**	13.34	18.73	100.00 *(470)*
Out of LF		0.25	0.76	0.48	1.28	2.19	0.07	0.08	0.09	**14.55**	**80.24**	100.00 *(988)*
Total		**2.87**	**7.94**	**2.37**	**2.70**	**28.54**	**3.04**	**3.38**	**5.23**	**8.07**	**35.86**	**100.00**
Sample size		***88***	***226***	***58***	***66***	***559***	***86***	***91***	***154***	***201***	***909***	***2438***

Table A7.3: Female Mobility from 1990 to 1998 in % (15 Year Olds in 1990)

Employment Status 1990		Female Employment Status in 1998									
		Public		Private		Unpaid	Unemployment		Out of the LF		Total
		Not married	Married	Not married	Married		Not married	Married	Not married	Married	*(Sample size)*
Public	Not married	**29.40**	**60.35**	0.00	0.92	0.40	0.92	1.78	1.47	4.77	100.0 *(84)*
	Married	0.00	**91.53**	0.00	1.52	0.00	0.00	0.55	0.00	6.41	100.0 *(148)*
Private	Not married	9.27	3.03	**21.30**	**10.63**	6.72	1.58	8.07	0.00	39.39	100.0 *(55)*
	Married	0.00	5.89	0.00	**80.94**	2.15	0.00	0.00	0.00	11.03	100.0 *(44)*
Unpaid		0.00	0.00	0.00	0.00	**99.46**	0.00	0.00	0.00	0.54	100.0 *(537)*
Unemp.	Not married	10.28	11.05	6.53	8.98	1.26	**16.09**	**40.62**	2.16	3.03	100.0 *(55)*
	Married	0.00	24.00	0.00	5.26	7.20	0.00	**50.83**	0.00	12.71	100.0 *(58)*
Student		12.91	7.96	8.99	2.21	0.92	13.73	9.75	8.99	34.53	100.0 *(468)*
Out of LF		0.59	2.20	0.38	4.56	2.55	0.52	0.70	**7.84**	**80.65**	100.0 *(983)*
Total		**3.77**	**9.68**	**2.30**	**4.28**	**28.99**	**2.94**	**3.97**	**4.69**	**39.38**	**100.0**
Sample size		***116***	***276***	***61***	***92***	***573***	***89***	***97***	***119***	***1009***	***2432***

Table A7.4: Male Mobility from 1990 to 1991 in % (15–29 Year Olds in 1990)

Employment Status 1990	Male Employment Status in 1991										
	Public	Private protected	Private unprotected	Irreg. Wg. agri.	Irreg. Wg. nonagri.	Nonwage agri.	Nonwage nonagri.	Unemp.	Student	Out of LF	Total *(Sample size)*
Public	**95.44**	0.82	0.00	0.00	0.00	0.00	0.00	0.00	0.30	3.43	100.00 *(301)*
Prv. protected	1.50	**91.08**	2.38	0.00	0.00	0.00	1.83	0.00	0.00	3.20	100.00 *(126)*
Prv. unprotected	2.07	1.67	**88.50**	0.66	0.65	0.00	0.00	0.33	0.00	6.12	100.00 *(317)*
Irreg. wage	0.00	0.00	0.00	**95.88**	0.00	0.00	0.00	0.00	0.00	4.12	100.00 *(88)*
Emp. agri. Irreg. wage	1.28	0.00	1.49	0.00	**93.76**	1.75	0.00	0.00	0.00	1.72	100.00 *(173)*
Emp. nonagri. Nonwage agri.	0.00	0.93	0.00	0.00	0.00	**95.81**	0.00	0.00	0.00	3.26	100.00 *(151)*
Nonwage	0.00	1.21	1.38	0.28	0.00	0.00	**92.74**	0.00	0.00	4.39	100.00 *(160)*
Nonagri. Unemployed	5.75	3.12	7.60	0.68	2.01	0.41	0.00	**76.76**	0.00	3.67	100.00 *(74)*
Student	1.17	0.51	1.55	0.00	1.13	3.85	0.78	2.76	**80.58**	7.68	100.00 *(619)*
Out of LF	3.08	1.82	8.11	3.14	5.79	3.63	3.97	0.28	1.33	**68.85**	100.00 *(258)*
Total	**12.81**	**5.36**	**13.92**	**5.45**	**8.27**	**11.22**	**6.48**	**3.26**	**21.31**	**11.92**	**100.00**
Sample size	***323***	***139***	***325***	***95***	***186***	***174***	***171***	***74***	***501***	***279***	***2267***

Table A7.5: Male Mobility from 1990 to 1994 in % (15–29 Year Olds in 1990)

Employment Status 1990	Male Employment Status in 1994										
	Public	Private protected	Private unprotected	Irreg. Wg. agri.	Irreg. Wg. nonagri.	Nonwage agri.	Nonwage nonagri.	Unemp.	Student	Out of LF	Total *(Sample size)*
Public	**94.60**	2.38	1.30	0.00	0.00	0.00	0.30	0.59	0.30	0.53	100.00 *(302)*
Prv. protected	6.95	**81.68**	2.17	0.43	2.03	0.61	2.51	0.61	0.00	3.02	100.00 *(128)*
Prv. unprotected	10.65	4.93	**69.73**	0.65	1.26	0.00	2.31	1.12	0.00	9.34	100.00 *(319)*
Irreg. wage Emp. agri.	2.95	0.58	0.00	**77.66**	0.00	0.93	4.71	0.00	0.00	13.17	100.00 *(89)*
Irreg. wage Emp. nonagri.	8.25	0.00	3.33	1.39	**78.33**	0.64	2.25	0.00	0.00	5.81	100.00 *(174)*
Nonwage agri.	7.60	0.48	1.47	0.00	0.00	**78.68**	2.46	0.00	0.00	9.31	100.00 *(154)*
Nonwage Nonagri.	1.03	2.40	2.40	0.00	1.31	0.00	**85.96**	0.00	0.00	6.89	100.00 *(160)*
Unemployed	15.50	12.31	16.47	0.67	2.93	2.77	1.52	**38.44**	0.00	9.37	100.00 *(75)*
Student	8.68	5.21	7.95	0.81	4.01	5.05	3.10	13.24	**33.45**	18.51	100.00 *(623)*
Out of LF	16.20	8.58	17.13	4.49	13.41	7.99	7.28	2.07	0.00	**22.84**	100.00 *(262)*
Total	**19.29**	**7.93**	**14.78**	**5.02**	**8.94**	**10.40**	**8.08**	**5.17**	**8.78**	**11.61**	**100.00**
Sample size	***468***	***202***	***365***	***89***	***200***	***164***	***212***	***117***	***220***	***249***	***2286***

Table A7.6: Male Mobility from 1990 to 1998 in % (15–29 Year Olds in 1990)

Employment Status 1990	Male Employment Status in 1998									
	Public	Private protected	Private unprotected	Irreg. Wg. agri.	Irreg. Wg. nonagri.	Nonwage agri.	Nonwage nonagri.	Unemp.	Out of LF	Total *(Sample size)*
Public	**89.12**	3.55	2.08	0.00	0.00	0.00	3.31	1.35	0.58	100.00 *(304)*
Prv. protected	10.30	**67.77**	5.21	0.20	3.21	0.00	8.57	2.56	2.17	100.00 *(129)*
Prv. unprotected	15.91	10.32	**56.53**	0.72	2.62	0.00	5.66	2.72	5.52	100.00 *(321)*
Irreg. wage Emp agri.	5.74	0.89	3.29	**73.79**	1.15	1.79	3.63	3.49	6.24	100.00 *(92)*
Irreg. wage Emp. nonagri.	12.70	0.00	6.99	2.20	**64.96**	0.00	4.55	5.22	3.39	100.00 *(176)*
Nonwage agri.	13.16	0.48	3.19	0.00	0.87	**75.45**	2.66	0.00	4.19	100.00 *(154)*
Nonwage Nonagri.	3.82	2.30	4.16	1.79	1.71	0.00	**83.23**	0.35	2.65	100.00 *(160)*
Unemployed	26.91	12.24	20.79	0.68	8.57	4.30	5.82	**17.16**	3.53	100.00 *(75)*
Student	24.41	13.46	12.09	1.21	4.81	7.18	8.58	16.29	11.95	100.00 *(624)*
Out of LF	23.81	10.21	16.41	3.69	13.87	7.56	8.04	5.42	**10.99**	100.00 *(245)*
Total	**26.02**	**10.45**	**15.06**	**5.15**	**8.80**	**10.56**	**10.81**	**6.67**	**6.49**	**100.00**
Sample size	***634***	***252***	***351***	***82***	***188***	***171***	***291***	***161***	***150***	***2280***

8 Labor Mobility in Egypt: Are the 1990s Any Different from the 1980s?

Jackline Wahba

Introduction

Economic reforms and structural adjustment programs affect labor markets and workers in several ways. These reforms involve economic liberalization of trade, privatization, changes in labor market policy, and an overall transition to a market economy. Structural adjustment requires a shift of resources from nontradable to tradable sectors, from noncompetitive sectors to more competitive ones, and from inefficient sectors to efficient ones. Hence, economic liberalization entails reallocation of workers between different sectors and labor markets. Labor mobility is seen as an important indicator of this reallocation (Horton et al., 1994). This chapter examines the extent of labor reallocation in Egypt by focusing on labor mobility during the period of economic reforms in the 1990s, and comparing it to the 1980s, using data from the 1988 Labor Force Sample Survey (LFSS 88) and the 1998 Egypt Labor Market Survey (ELMS 98). The Egyptian labor market has several features that are of significance to any economic reform measures. First, the public sector has played a major role in absorbing the increasing labor force during the past three decades. It accounted for more than 35 percent of nonagriculture employment in the 1980s. It has been the preferred sector of employment for many new entrants to the labor market, particularly women. Second, the guaranteed civil-service employment for graduates of secondary and higher educational institutions has led to the concentration of educated workers in the public sector. Third, by the early 1990s—prior to economic reforms—the public sector was overstaffed and inefficient, and its wage bills constituted a huge burden on government expenditure. Also, the growth of the private formal sector in job creation and absorption has been limited. Finally, the role of the agriculture sector has been declining.

Hence, economic reforms have been expected to have several direct and indirect impacts on the Egyptian labor market and its workers. First, reducing and downsizing the public sector would affect existing public sector workers and educated new entrants to the labor market who expect government jobs. It would be anticipated that educated female workers would feel the brunt of public sector downsizing, since approximately 90 percent of educated women are public sector employees (Assaad and Arntz, 2000). Second, an increase in the extent of informal employment has been expected to increase with the reduction of new hiring in the public sector (Wahba and Moktar, in this volume). Third, a shift in the pattern of production toward exportables and tradeables would involve a corresponding shift of labor to those sectors or markets.

The aim of this study is to identify the consequences of economic reforms on the reallocation of labor by focusing on the extent and pattern of labor mobility in the Egyptian labor market in the 1990s, the period of reforms, compared to that of the 1980s. This study will also attempt to answer the following questions: Which categories of workers have experienced the highest rates of mobility over the last decade? What has happened to the rate of mobility in wage employment in the 1990s? Has the rate of labor mobility from the public sector to the private sector accelerated during the period of economic changes? Has the rate of mobility from the formal sector to the informal sector increased or decreased as a result of the economic reform and structural adjustment?

The structure of this chapter is organized as follows: Section 1 presents mobility patterns for five employment characteristics: employment status, economic sectors, informality status, occupations, and economic activities, between 1981–88 and 1990–98. Section 2 provides overall rates of mobility over two seven-year periods in the 1980s and 1990s, and characteristics of those moving between employment statuses. Section 3 examines mobility rates to and from wage employment, public sector employment, and informal employment. Section 4 concludes by summarizing the main findings.

1. Mobility Patterns

This section examines mobility by comparing the period of 1981–88, covered in the LFSS 88 survey, to the period of 1990–98, captured in the ELMS 98 survey. The analysis is based on the work history and employment characteristics of respondents at those fixed dates. One of the problems in using two fixed dates is that it understates the number of movers, since it does not take into account individuals who have moved more than once or those who have moved but have returned back to their original status. Also, it should be noted that we are comparing mobility patterns between two slightly different time intervals, i.e. eight years in the 1990s and seven years in the 1980s.

This study examines mobility of those ages 15–64. An individual is included if he/she is at least 15 years old at the beginning of the period of analysis—in 1981 or in 1990—and less than 64 at the end of the period of analysis—1988 or 1998. To control for the effect of age on mobility, this paper also distinguishes between two age groups, the young and the old, by looking at those who were 35 years or younger and those who were more than 35 years old at the end of the two study periods.

1.1 Employment Status

The analysis in this subsection includes all individuals who have ever been in the labor market. Five states are defined: wageworkers, self-employed and employers, unpaid family workers, unemployed, and those of out the labor force (OLF). The last category includes all female subsistence-agriculture workers working less than 25 hours per week as well as students, housewives, and other economically inactive groups. Tables 8.1 to 8.6 present mobility patterns among employment statuses in 1981–88 and 1990–98.

Wageworkers

The first point that stands out from Tables 8.1 and 8.4 is that although the proportion of stayers among wageworkers is very stable across the two periods, the destination of movers is quite different. In the 1990s, wageworkers were less likely to move into self-employment or become employers than in the 1980s. Although with reforms, one would have expected the opposite—i.e. more movement into self-employment or becoming employers—it is interesting to note that wageworkers in the 1990s were moving out of the labor force at a higher rate, particularly older workers.

Self-employment and employers

Self-employed individuals and employers were the least mobile group of workers in both periods. Younger workers tended to be twice as likely as older workers to move from self-employment and being employers into wage employment in the 1980s and 1990s, indicating that many young workers became temporarily self-employed until they secured waged jobs.

Unpaid family workers

Among employed individuals, unpaid family workers were the most mobile, indicating that family work is a temporary strategy people engage in prior to getting independent employment. This is increasingly the case, since the proportion of stayers in this category has declined substantially from the 1981–88 period to the 1990–98 period. The bulk of unpaid family workers who move end up becoming employers or self-employed, indicating that they either take over the family business or start up a business on their own. Although a significant number of unpaid family male workers end up in wage work in both periods, in the 1990s, female unpaid workers seemed unlikely to move to wage employment and more likely to move out of the labor force or to subsistence agriculture, compared to the 1980s.

Table 8.1: Mobility of Individuals Between Employment Status: 1990–98

	Employment Status in 1998					
Employment Status in 1990	**Waged**	**Employer & self-employed**	**Unpaid**	**Unemployed**	**OLF**	**Total**
Waged	7238.00	400.00	24.00	0.2	793.00	8672.00
	83.46	4.62	0.27	2.50	9.14	100.00
Employer & self-employed	92.00	2082.00	0.00	28.00	88.00	2290.00
	4.04	90.92	0.00	1.21	3.38	100.00
Unpaid	131.00	151.00	413.00	6.00	78.00	779.00
	16.75	19.42	53.01	0.79	10.02	100.00
Unemployed	214.00	16.00	10.00	38.00	29.00	308.00
	69.58	5.15	3.41	12.32	9.55	100.00
OLF	1709.00	352.00	189.00	136.00	735.00	3121.00
	54.77	11.27	6.05	4.36	23.55	100.00
Total	**9384.00**	**3002.00**	**636.00**	**425.00**	**1723.00**	**15,170.00**
	61.86	**19.79**	**4.19**	**2.80**	**11.36**	**100.00**

Note: In each entry the top figure gives the absolute number in thousands; the second figure is the % of the row.

Table 8.2: Mobility of Individuals Between Employment Status by Age Group: 1990–98

	Employment Status in 1998					
Employment Status in 1990	**Waged**	**Employer & self-employed**	**Unpaid**	**Unemployed**	**OLF**	**Total**
Waged	(Y) 85.98	3.04	0.62	3.75	6.61	2587
	(O) 82.39	5.29	0.13	1.97	10.22	6085
Employer &	(Y) 7.53	91.87	0.00	0.29	0.32	406
self-employed	(O) 3.29	90.72	0.00	1.41	4.59	1884
Unpaid	(Y) 20.13	17.62	51.72	1.21	9.31	507
	(O) 10.47	22.78	55.42	0.00	11.34	272
Unemployed	(Y) 73.17	6.64	4.40	6.75	9.03	229
	(O) 57.20	0.00	0.00	31.48	11.32	69
OLF	(Y) 66.06	10.24	6.50	5.27	11.94	2466
	(O) 12.22	15.17	4.37	0.92	67.33	654
Total	**(Y) 67.06**	**13.04**	**7.23**	**4.04**	**8.63**	**6205**
	(O) 58.26	**24.46**	**2.09**	**1.95**	**13.25**	**8965**

Note: In each entry the top row (Y) is the % of the row for those who were 35 years old or less in 1998 and the second row (O) is the % of the row for those who were older than 35 in 1998. The total column is the absolute total number in thousands of that age group in that state in 1990.

Table 8.3: Mobility of Males and Females Between Employment Status: 1990–98

Employment Status in 1990		Employment Status in 1998				
	Waged	Employer & self-employed	Unpaid	Unemployed	OLF	Total
Waged	(M) 83.56	5.55	0.27	2.78	7.84	7101
	(F) 83.02	0.41	0.28	1.28	15.02	1571
Employer & self-employed	(M) 4.30	91.31	0.00	1.22	3.17	2100
	(F) 1.13	86.66	0.00	1.13	11.09	190
Unpaid	(M) 23.24	25.53	44.15	0.00	5.88	559
	(F) 0.00	3.52	75.57	2.80	18.01	220
Unemployed	(M) 76.91	5.35	4.55	10.01	3.06	181
	(F) 59.10	4.85	1.61	15.62	18.81	127
OLF	(M) 67.56	11.67	6.46	4.59	9.71	1829
	(F) 36.41	10.70	5.45	4.02	43.42	1282
Total	**(M) 63.97**	**22.74**	**3.34**	**2.76**	**7.18**	**11780**
	(F) 54.52	**9.51**	**7.15**	**2.94**	**25.87**	**3389**

Note: In each entry the top row (M) is the % of the row for males and the second row (F) is the % of the row for females. The total column is the absolute total number in thousands of that age group in that state in 1990.

Table 8.4: Mobility of Individuals Between Employment Status: 1981–88

Employment Status in 1981		Employment Status in 1988				
	Waged	Employer & self-employed	Unpaid	Unemployed	OLF	Total
Waged	4451.00	458.00	26.00	155.00	290.00	5380.00
	82.73	8.51	0.49	2.88	5.39	100.00
Employer & self-employed	95.00	2023.00	2.00	25.00	49.00	2194.00
	4.34	92.18	0.11	1.14	2.23	100.00
Unpaid	103.00	226.00	1135.00	7.00	150.00	1623.00
	6.33	13.95	69.97	0.48	9.27	100.00
Unemployed	201.00	16.00	3.00	19.00	17.00	256.00
	78.38	6.35	1.21	7.42	6.63	100.00
OLF	1282.00	277.00	206.00	357.00	2027.0	4149.00
	30.90	6.68	4.96	8.59	48.86	100.00
Total	**6132.00**	**3000.00**	**1373.00**	**563.00**	**2533.0**	**13,602.00**
	45.08	**22.06**	**10.10**	**4.14**	**18.62**	**100.00**

Note: In each entry the top figure gives the absolute number in thousands; the second figure is the % of the row.

Table 8.5: Mobility of Individuals Between Employment Status by Age Group: 1981–88

Employment Status in 1981	Employment Status in 1988					
	Waged	Employer & self-employed	Unpaid	Unemployed	OLF	Total
Waged	(Y) 82.79	8.02	0.81	3.50	4.88	2072
	(O) 82.70	8.83	0.29	2.48	5.70	3308
Employer& Self-employed	(Y) 7.76	86.45	0.27	2.17	3.36	444
	(O) 3.47	93.64	0.07	0.89	1.94	1750
Unpaid	(Y) 9.12	15.81	67.27	0.43	7.37	983
	(O) 2.04	11.10	74.12	0.55	12.18	640
Unemployed	(Y) 84.85	5.94	0.00	4.14	5.07	225
	(O) 31.71	9.31	9.97	31.10	17.90	31
OLF	(Y) 42.03	7.31	5.90	11.23	33.53	2937
	(O) 3.96	5.14	2.70	2.21	85.98	1212
Total	**(Y) 49.01**	**14.01**	**12.80**	**6.39**	**17.79**	**6661**
	(O) 41.31	**29.78**	**7.50**	**1.98**	**19.40**	**6941**

Note: In each entry the top row (Y) is the % of the row for those who were 35 years old or less in 1988 and the second row (O) is the % of the row for those who were older than 35 in 1988. The total column is the absolute total number in thousands of that age group in that state in 1981.

Unemployed

The unemployed were the most mobile group in both periods. The vast majority of the unemployed ended up in wage work, indicating that unemployment occurs primarily among those seeking wage work. However, that proportion has declined by almost 10 percentage points in the 1990s, implying that the probability of an unemployed finding wage employment dropped. Almost one-third of the older workers who were unemployed remained unemployed in the two periods under study, though the proportion of the younger workers who stayed unemployed increased in the 1990s. This may be due to the scarceness of new public sector jobs as a result of the decline in the growth of public sector employment in the 1990s. Also, the proportion of females who remained unemployed increased in the 1990s, compared to the 1980s, which again reflects the diminishing role of the public sector—the main employer of educated females—in absorbing new entrants.

Out of the labor force (OLF)

Since this group includes those who were students or in the military at the beginning of the period, it is not surprising that the bulk of that group ended up in wage work. Since OLF also includes female subsistence-agriculture workers who were over-sampled in the 1988 survey, the bulk of those out of the labor force stayed so in the 1980s, especially among females.

Table 8.6: Mobility of Individuals Between Employment Status by Gender: 1981–88

Employment Status in 1981		Employment Status in 1988					
		Waged	Employer & self-employed	Unpaid	Unemployed	OLF	Total
Waged	(M)	83.40	9.60	0.34	3.00	3.66	4516
	(F)	79.26	2.83	1.26	2.24	14.41	864
Employer & self-employed	(M)	4.84	92.93	0.06	1.30	0.87	1843
	(F)	1.69	88.27	0.34	0.34	9.37	351
Unpaid	(M)	14.04	24.42	56.94	0.42	4.18	578
	(F)	2.08	8.17	77.17	0.51	12.08	1045
Unemployed	(M)	73.94	12.76	2.44	5.43	5.43	127
	(F)	82.78	0.00	0.00	9.21	8.00	129
OLF	(M)	60.05	11.92	7.81	9.01	11.21	1375
	(F)	16.46	4.08	3.55	8.39	67.53	2774
Total	**(M)**	**57.54**	**29.24**	**5.40**	**3.47**	**4.34**	**8439**
	(F)	**24.71**	**10.31**	**17.76**	**5.24**	**41.97**	**5163**

Note: In each entry the top row (M) is the % of the row for males and the second row (F) is the % of the row for females. The total column is the absolute total number in thousands of that age group in that state in 1981.

1.2 Economic Sector of Ownership

For the study of economic sector of ownership, four states are defined: government; public enterprise; private, which includes private, joint venture, foreign, and other categories; and economic inactive, which includes unemployed female subsistence agriculture workers and those out of the labor force. Tables 8.7 to 8.12 show the sectoral mobility patterns for 1981–88 and 1990–91.

Government-sector employees

Government-sector employees are the least mobile group of workers. Civil servants value lifetime job security and the additional benefits they get as civil servants, so it is not surprising that they hold on to these government jobs (Assaad, 1996). These jobs are particularly valued by females, which is reflected in their higher stay rate in the 1990s, compared to the 1980s, and their higher stay rate than males in the 1990s. Female civil servants in the 1990s were less likely to move out of the labor force and lose their government jobs. It seems that structural adjustment has not negatively affected the existing female civil servants by pushing them out first. Another consequence of the adjustments is clear when we compare the proportion of older workers who left government employment and moved out of the labor market

(Table 8.8 and Table 8.11). Almost twice the proportion of older civil servants became inactive between 1990–98 than between 1981–88.

Table 8.7: Mobility of Individuals Between Economic Sectors: 1990–98

	Economic Sector in 1998				
Economic Sector in 1990	**Government**	**Public enterprise**	**Private**	**Economic inactive**	**Total**
Government	3385 87.18	5 0.14	166 4.27	327 8.41	3883 100
Public enterprise	41 3.71	791 72.52	82 7.49	178 16.28	1091 100
Private	422 6.26	64 0.96	5551 82.32	706 10.46	6743 100
Economic inactive	825 24.06	127 3.70	1538 44.87	938 27.37	3429 100
Total	**4673** **30.85**	**988** **6.52**	**7337** **48.44**	**2148** **14.18**	**15146** **100**

Note: In each entry the top figure gives the absolute number in thousands; the second figure is the % of the row.

Table 8.8: Mobility of Individuals Between Economic Sectors by Age Group: 1990–98

	Economic Sector in 1998				
Economic Sector in 1990	**Government**	**Public enterprise**	**Private**	**Economic inactive**	**Total**
Government	(Y) 88.55 (O) 86.88	0.42 0.08	5.56 4.01	5.36 9.03	655 3228
Public enterprise	(Y) 15.97 (O) 1.42	66.83 73.58	12.45 6.56	4.75 18.44	172 919
Private	(Y) 8.93 (O) 4.52	1.82 0.39	78.72 84.67	10.54 10.41	2664 4079
Economic inactive	(Y) 28.08 (O) 9.04	4.54 0.57	50.3 24.58	17.08 65.81	2705 724
Total	**(Y) 25.91** **(O) 34.27**	**4.66** **7.81**	**56.74** **42.70**	**12.69** **15.22**	**6196** **8950**

Note: In each entry the top row (Y) is the % of the row for those who were 35 years old or less in 1998 and the second row (O) is the % of the row for those who were older than 35 in 1998. The total column is the absolute total number in thousands of that age group in that state in 1990.

Table 8.9: Mobility of Individuals Between Economic Sectors by Gender: 1990–98

Economic Sector in 1990	Economic Sector in 1998				
	Government	Public enterprise	Private	Economic inactive	Total
Government	(M) 88.55	0.42	5.56	5.36	655
	(F) 86.88	0.08	4.01	9.03	3228
Public enterprise	(M) 15.97	66.83	12.45	4.75	172
	(F) 1.42	73.58	6.56	18.44	919
Private	(M) 8.93	1.82	78.72	10.54	2664
	(F) 4.52	0.39	84.67	10.41	4079
Economic inactive	(M) 28.08	4.54	50.3	17.08	2705
	(F) 9.04	0.57	24.58	65.81	724
Total	**(M) 25.91**	**4.66**	**56.74**	**12.69**	**6196**
	(F) 34.27	**7.81**	**42.70**	**15.22**	**8950**

Note: In each entry the top row (M) is the % of the row for males and the second row (F) is the % of the row for females. The total column is the absolute total number in thousands of that age group in that state in 1990.

Public enterprise workers

Public enterprise employees are the most mobile group of employed individuals. Twice the proportion (size, magnitude) of older public enterprise employees became economically inactive by 1998, compared to the period of 1981–88. This is a consequence of privatization of public enterprises, which started to gather momentum by the second half of the 1990s. Early retirement has been one of the means of reducing staffing in those enterprises. However, females in public enterprises were more likely in the 1990s to move out of the labor force than in the 1980s—an increase of 10 percent. Females were unlikely to move out of public enterprises to another sector of employment; they were more likely to move out of the labor market altogether. Public enterprise male employees were twice as likely to move to a private-sector job than to a government job. Thus, more adjustment has taken place among public enterprise employees than among government workers as a result of reforms in Egypt.

Private sector workers

Private sector workers have shown higher mobility rates in the 1990s than in the 1980s, particularly females. This is an indirect impact of reforms where females are crowded out of the private sector—pushed out of the labor force—and replaced by males. Therefore, it is important to note that, unlike what has been expected, it is the private female employees, not female government employees, who are actually bearing the brunt of the reforms.

Economically inactive

Those who were economically inactive in 1990—primarily the young, both students and new entrants to the labor market—were twice as likely to end up in the private sector than in the government sector. This again reflects the scarcity of new public sector jobs.

Table 8.10: Mobility of Individuals Between Economic Sectors: 1981–88

Economic Sector in 1981	Economic Sector in 1988				
	Government	Public enterprise	Private	Economic inactive	Total
Government	1740	15	140	111	200
	86.78	0.73	6.97	5.52	100
Public enterprise	39	842	90	95	1066
	3.62	79.04	8.43	8.91	100
Private	216	97	5343	469	6125
	3.52	1.59	87.22	7.66	100
Economic inactive	704	216	1064	2420	4404
	15.99	4.90	24.17	54.95	100
Total	**2699**	**1170**	**6637**	**3095**	**13600**
	19.84	**8.60**	**48.80**	**22.76**	**100**

Note: In each entry the top figure gives the absolute number in thousands; the second figure is the % of the row.

Table 8.11: Mobility of Individuals Between Economic Sectors by Age Group: 1981–88.

Economic Sector in 1981	Economic Sector in 1988				
	Government	Public enterprise	Private	Economic inactive	Total
Government	(Y) 86.05	1.30	7.06	5.59	573
	(O) 87.07	0.50	6.93	5.49	1432
Public enterprise	(Y) 9.54	72.62	9.76	8.08	293
	(O) 1.38	81.47	7.92	9.23	773
Private	(Y) 4.68	2.63	84.48	8.26	2634
	(O) 2.65	0.80	89.34	7.21	3491
Economic inactive	(Y) 21.66	6.57	29.52	42.25	3160
	(O) 1.58	0.65	10.56	87.22	1243
Total	**(Y) 19.95**	**7.46**	**48.43**	**24.15**	**6661**
	(O) 19.73	**9.70**	**49.15**	**21.42**	**6939**

Note: In each entry the top row (Y) is the % of the row for those who were 35 years old or less in 1988 and the second row (O) is the % of the row for those who were older than 35 in 1988. The total column is the absolute total number in thousands of that age group in that state in 1981.

Table 8.12: Mobility of Individuals Between Economic Sectors by Gender: 1981–88

Economic Sector in 1981	Economic Sector in 1988				
	Government	**Public enterprise**	**Private**	**Economic inactive**	**Total**
Government	87.76	0.77	7.93	3.55	1519
	83.74	0.61	3.97	11.68	486
Public enterprise	3.17	79.36	9.60	7.87	936
	6.88	76.73	0.00	16.39	130
Private	4.53	2.10	88.05	5.31	4481
	0.77	0.18	84.97	14.08	1645
Economic inactive	23.46	10.19	46.91	19.44	1501
	12.12	2.16	12.40	73.31	2902
Total	**22.73**	**11.87**	**57.60**	**7.79**	**8437**
	15.12	**3.26**	**34.41**	**47.21**	**5163**

Note: In each entry the top row (M) is the % of the row for males and the second row (F) is the % of the row for females. The total column is the absolute total number in thousands of that age group in that state in 1981.

1.3 Formality

The ELMS 1998 study collected information from employed persons on the basis of whether or not they had job contracts and social-security contributions. This information is used to draw a picture of informality in the Egyptian labor market. Unfortunately, similar information does not exist for the 1980s—it was not collected in the LFSS 88.

This study uses the existence of a job contract as its measure of formality, i.e. "formal employment" refers to workers who have job contracts. Since we also have information on social security, we differentiate between two types of informality: "semi-informal" refers to those who have no contract but do have social-security contributions; "informal" refers to workers who have neither job contracts nor social-security contributions.

For this analysis, we also identify six states of employment: public formal, nonagriculture private formal (have job contracts), nonagriculture private semiformal (have no job contracts but do have social security), nonagriculture private informal (have neither job contracts nor social security), agriculture, and economically inactive (those who are unemployed, female subsistence agriculture workers, and those out of the labor force). Tables 8.7 to 8.9 show the patterns of mobility among informality statuses between 1990–98.

Formal employment

Public formal employees were the least mobile group of workers. They tended to move mainly out of the labor force rather than to other sectors. There is no sign of labor moving out of public formal employment into private employment as a result of reforms (see Wahba and Moktar, 2000). Female public formal employees moved only out of the labor market, though the proportion that did so was the smallest among all employed females.

On the other hand, private formal nonagricultural workers seemed to be the most mobile group of workers. Younger workers and females were more mobile than older workers and males, respectively. Also, more private formal nonagricultural workers moved into public formal work than into informal employment. Yet the majority of private formal employees who did move ended up out of the labor force by 1998. Females, in particular, were more likely to leave the labor market from formal private employment—41 percent did so by 1998. In addition, females did not move into formal private jobs from other states, reflecting the existence of barriers to the hiring of females in the private sector.

Private nonformal employment

Private semi-formal nonagricultural workers—those who had no contracts but were contributing to social security—were the least mobile group of workers. Only younger workers and females tended to move out of that state and into public formal jobs.

Almost 30 percent of private informal nonagricultural workers moved between 1990 and 1998, indicating that for many, especially the young, informal employment is a waiting stage for the public formal job. Private informal female workers were the least likely among all employed females to move into public formal jobs.

Agriculture

The agriculture sector seemed to keep almost two-thirds of its workers. However, it was the least likely to attract workers from other sectors, which reflects the long-term decline in the growth of agricultural employment, compared to other sectors. Almost one-third of females engaged in agriculture tended to move into subsistence agriculture or out of the labor force altogether.

Economically inactive

An equal proportion of those who were economically inactive in 1990 ended up in public formal jobs and in private informal ones (26 percent). Only 8 percent managed to secure a formal private job by the end of the period under study. Younger individuals were more likely to move into formal private jobs than were older individuals. Males were more likely to end up with private informal jobs than with public formal work, while the opposite was true for women. Also, only 4 percent of economically inactive women moved to formal private employment by the end of the period.

1.4 Occupation

The analysis of occupation is confined to individuals who were employed at the beginning and end of the study periods. Female subsistence agriculture workers are excluded. Tables 8.13 and 8.14 present the mobility patterns among occupations between 1981–88 and 1990–98.

The first interesting change in the mobility pattern between the 1980s and the 1990s is that the stay rate in white-collar occupations (technical and scientific, management, and clerical) has increased, while the stay rate in blue-collar occupations (services, agriculture, and production) has decreased. In other words, it seems that blue-collar workers were more mobile in the 1990s than in the 1980s, while the white-collar workers were less mobile in the 1990s. In the 1980s, agricultural workers were the least mobile, while in the 1990s, technical and scientific workers were the least mobile. In addition, agriculture experienced net out-mobility, capturing the structural changes taking place in the economy as a result of reforms, which were having different impacts on agriculture.

Table 8.13: Mobility of Individuals Between Informality Status: 1990–98

	Formality Status in 1998						
Formality Status in 1990	**Public formal**	**Private formal**	**Private semi-formal**	**Private informal**	**Agriculture**	**Economic inactive**	**Total**
Public formal	4131 85.18	42 0.86	75 1.54	58 1.19	49 1.00	496 10.24	4850 100
Private formal	55 9.40	383 65.06	36 6.06	34 5.85	3 0.56	77 13.08	588 100
Private semiformal	16 1.92	3 0.41	759 91.45	10 1.26	0 0.00	41 4.96	830 100
Private informal	232 8.23	103 3.67	117 4.15	1981 70.40	48 1.71	333 11.84	2814 100
Agriculture	167 6.52	17 0.67	26 1.00	95 3.70	1996 78.07	257 10.04	2557 100
Economic inactive	890 26.33	282 8.35	144 4.25	886 26.20	241 7.13	938 27.75	3381 100
Total	**5491 36.56**	**830 5.53**	**1156 7.69**	**3064 20.4**	**2337 15.56**	**2143 14.27**	**15,020 100**

Note: In each entry the top figure gives the absolute number in thousands; the second figure is the % of the row.

Table 8.14: Mobility of Individuals Between Informality Status by Age: 1990–98

Formality Status in 1990	Formality Status in 1998						
	Public formal	Private formal	Private semi-formal	Private informal	Agriculture	Economic inactive	Total
Public formal	(Y) 89.08 (O) 84.43	2.01 0.64	1.50 1.54	2.07 1.02	0.00 1.20	5.35 11.17	777 4073
Private formal	(Y) 12.36 (O) 7.88	59.96 67.66	2.62 7.82	11.67 2.87	0.28 0.70	13.11 13.07	199 389
Private semiformal	(Y) 7.43 (O) 0.72	1.14 0.25	79.58 94.05	3.18 0.84	0.00 0.00	8.68 4.14	149 681
Private informal	(Y) 11.58 (O) 5.23	3.76 3.59	3.83 4.44	68.36 72.24	1.29 2.08	11.18 12.43	1332 1482
Agriculture	(Y) 8.54 (O) 5.24	1.06 0.42	0.28 1.46	5.59 2.50	75.17 79.91	9.36 10.46	990 1567
Economic inactive	(Y) 30.99 (O) 9.14	10.09 1.92	4.71 2.55	28.14 19.03	8.70 1.34	17.37 66.02	2659 721
Total	**(Y) 29.33** **(O) 41.51**	**7.62** **4.09**	**5.15** **9.43**	**28.79** **14.65**	**16.27** **15.08**	**12.84** **15.24**	**6108** **8913**

Note: In each entry the top row (Y) is the % of the row for those who were 35 years old or less in 1998 and the second row (O) is the % of the row for those who were older than 35 in 1998. The total column is the absolute total number in thousands of that age group in that state in 1990.

Table 8.15: Mobility of Individuals Between Informality Status by Gender: 1990–98

Formality Status in 1990	Formality Status in 1998						
	Public formal	Private formal	Private semi-formal	Private informal	Agriculture	Economic inactive	Total
Public formal	(M) 83.85 (F) 88.89	0.92 0.69	1.95 0.37	1.56 0.13	1.36 0.00	10.35 9.91	3573 1277
Private formal	(M) 8.55 (F) 14.58	68.80 41.97	7.04 0.00	6.39 2.50	0.65 0.00	8.56 40.95	506 82
Private semiformal	(M) 1.75 (F) 6.37	0.43 0.00	91.95 78.91	1.31 0.00	0.00 0.00	4.56 14.72	798 32
Private informal	(M) 9.06 (F) 2.10	4.08 0.64	4.63 0.61	70.32 70.96	1.94 0.00	9.97 25.68	2479 335
Agriculture	(M) 6.86 (F) 3.39	0.74 0.00	1.11 0.00	3.83 2.48	79.49 64.73	7.98 29.41	2311 246
Economic inactive	(M) 27.79 (F) 24.20	11.25 4.14	5.72 2.12	30.42 20.08	10.49 2.28	14.33 47.19	2000 1381
Total	**(M) 34.22** **(F) 44.70**	**6.24** **3.06**	**9.38** **1.83**	**21.76** **15.65**	**18.4** **5.69**	**10.01** **29.08**	**11668** **3353**

Note: In each entry the top row (M) is the % of the row for males and the second row (F) is the % of the row for females. The total column is the absolute total number in thousands of that age group in that state in 1990.

Table 8.16: Mobility of Employed Individuals Between Economic Activity: 1990–98

	Economic Activity in 1990							
Economic Activity	**Agri.**	**Mfg**	**Constr.**	**Trade**	**Trans.**	**Finc.**	**Services**	**Total**
Agriculture	2056	39	19	54	21	4	194	2387
	86.16	*1.63*	*0.79*	*2.24*	*0.89*	*0.16*	*8.12*	*100*
Manufacturing, mining & electricity	41	1619	32	39	29	4	96	1859
	2.20	*87.09*	*1.71*	*2.12*	*1.54*	*0.20*	*5.14*	*100*
Construction	19	32	536	27	30	5	73	722
	2.66	*4.41*	*74.25*	*3.80*	*4.09*	*0.65*	*10.14*	*100*
Trade	5	31	9	1169	21	2	71	1308
	0.39	*2.35*	*0.67*	*89.40*	*1.59*	*0.16*	*5.44*	*100*
Transport	23	10	0	14	548	1	13	610
	3.83	*1.61*	*0*	*2.33*	*89.82*	*0.21*	*2.20*	*100*
Finance	0	3	2	9	0	172	11	197
	0	*1.67*	*0.86*	*4.36*	*0*	*87.28*	*5.83*	*100*
Services	19	32	9	58	43	19	3243	3422
	0.55	*0.94*	*0.26*	*1.69*	*1.24*	*0.55*	*94.77*	*100*
Total	**2164**	**1766**	**606**	**1370**	**691**	**207**	**3702**	**10506**
	20.60	***16.81***	***5.77***	***13.04***	***6.58***	***1.97***	***35.24***	***100***

Note: In each entry the top figure gives the absolute number in thousands; the second figure (italics) is the % of the row.

Table 8.17: Mobility of Employed Individuals Between Economic Activity: 1981–88

	Economic Activity in 1988							
Economic Activity in 1981	**Agri.**	**Mfg.**	**Constr.**	**Trade**	**Trans.**	**Finc.**	**Services**	**Total**
Agriculture	3071	60	18	46	27	1	90	3313
	92.70	*1.80*	*0.55*	*1.39*	*0.82*	*0.03*	*2.70*	*100*
Manufacturing, mining & electricity	45	1251	16	45	33	11	51	1452
	3.11	*86.17*	*1.13*	*3.07*	*2.25*	*0.75*	*3.53*	*100*
Construction	44	28	347	43	6	4	37	508
	8.71	*5.45*	*68.26*	*8.39*	*1.15*	*0.69*	*7.36*	*100*
Trade	12	10	13	843	12	0.9	46	936
	1.24	*1.06*	*1.37*	*90.09*	*1.26*	*0.10*	*4.88*	*100*
Transport	4	9	0	8	392	0	2	414
	0.96	*2.07*	*0*	*1.85*	*94.62*	*0*	*0.51*	*100*
Finance	2	2	0	5	2	126	0.9	138
	1.47	*1.55*	*0*	*3.87*	*1.21*	*91.28*	*0.61*	*100*
Services	35	27	8	50	15	4	1650	1789
	1.95	*1.52*	*0.45*	*2.82*	*0.81*	*0.22*	*92.24*	*100*
Total	**3213**	**1387**	**402**	**1040**	**485**	**146**	**1877**	**8551**
	37.58	***16.22***	***4.70***	***12.17***	***5.67***	***1.71***	***21.95***	***100***

Note: In each entry the top figure gives the absolute number in thousands; the second figure (Italics) is the % of the row.

1.5 Economic Activity

The analysis of economic activity is confined to individuals who were employed at the beginning and end of the two study periods. Female subsistence agriculture workers are excluded. Tables 8.16 and 8.17 show the mobility patterns among economic activities.

Construction and services were the only two sectors where the stay rate of workers was higher in the 1990s than in the 1980s. However, construction workers were the most mobile workers in the 1990s, while services workers were the least mobile. Services seemed to be the sector attracting most of the mobile workers.

Agricultural workers had a lower stay rate in the 1990s than in the 1980s, and had higher out-mobility rates during the adjustment period. Prior to reforms, the agriculture sector had a large scale of controls and price-fixing rules, which made it subject to a number of reform measures. A priori, it is not clear whether structural adjustment that requires a resource shift toward tradeables would result in workers moving into or out of the agriculture sector. This is because a large part of the agriculture sector was competitive in the world economy, though a significant proportion of agricultural products was not traded, and was subject to the control of marketing boards and price fixing by the government.

Also, as a result of adjustment, labor is expected to move out of nontradeable sectors and into tradeables. Thus, it is not surprising that workers in transport and construction were more mobile in the 1990s than in the 1980s.

2. Overall Mobility Rates

This section compares the different mobility rates in the 1980s to those of the 1990s. To enable a better comparison between the two decades, we construct mobility rates for (two) seven-year periods: 1981–88 and 1991–98. Mobility here refers to a change of state (status, sector, location, etc.), regardless of the nature or the direction of that change. All female subsistence-agriculture workers are excluded from this analysis.

2.1 Employment Status

Table 8.18 shows that the rate of mobility among employment statuses between 1991–98 was less, by three percentage points, than it was between 1981–88. Females, young individuals, and urban dwellers all experienced lower mobility rates.

However, in the 1990s, as in the 1980s, females were more mobile than males, mainly because they were more likely to move out of the labor force. Younger workers were three times as mobile as older workers, because they were likely to have moved to several states before becoming employed (e.g., being students or unemployed). Also, urban dwellers were more mobile than rural dwellers, though the gap was closing down in the 1990s. And the educated were more mobile than the less educated, which is a common finding in studies.

Although young individuals showed lower mobility rates in the 1990s, compared to the 1980s, the mobility rates of older individuals did not change. However, if we look at those ages 50–59, we find that this group actually had higher mobility rates between 1991–98 than they did between 1981–88. This pinpoints them as the primary group pushed out of the labor market during the adjustment period.

2.2 Economic Sector

It is important to note at the outset that in this subsection, we are considering sectoral mobility, i.e. examining the mobility between different sectors of employment of those in the labor market at the beginning and end of the periods of study. Transition rates among economic sectors stayed the same between 1981–88 and 1991–98—7.5 percent in the 1980s, and 7 percent in the 1990s (Table 8.18). This is slightly surprising, as one would have expected greater sectoral mobility in the 1990s as a result of the downsizing of the public sector and privatization. Males experienced lower rates of transition in the 1990s (a drop of 1 percent), while females had higher mobility (a rise of 1 percent). The mobility rates by age were not so different in the two periods. There was no clear change in the pattern of mobility rates by educational level.

There is no evidence that reforms resulted in reallocation among sectors. This is primarily due to several factors: the downsizing of the public sector has resulted from limiting the creation of new jobs (i.e. a decline in the growth of the public sector); provisions were used for early retirement for existing civil servants rather than redundancies or firings and layoffs; privatization began to gain momentum in the second half of the 1990s; and public enterprise has been restructured through the formation of the Employee Shareholders Associations, which enable workers to buy stakes in their companies.

2.3 Occupation

In evaluating labor reallocation between occupations, we consider only those who were employed at the beginning and end of the period—we do not include movement into and out of the labor market. Overall, occupational mobility rates decreased by 1.5 percent from the 1980s to the 1990s. Males, older workers, and urban dwellers all experienced lower occupational mobility rates in the 1990s than in the 1980s. On the other hand, females, younger workers, and rural dwellers all had the same mobility rates in both periods. Again, education did not affect occupational mobility rates in any systematic manner.

Table 8.18: Mobility Rates (%) of Individuals 15–64 Years Old by Employment State: 1991–98 and 1981–88

State	Employment Status		Economic Sector		Occupation		Economic Activity		Informality
	1991–98	1981–88	1991–98	1981–88	1991–98	1981–88	1991–98	1981–88	1991–98
Gender									
Male	28.97	30.18	7.97	9.04	19.12	21.75	14.35	14.37	10.11
Female	35.96	41.01	3.39	2.40	12.35	12.77	7.27	5.03	2.65
Age									
≤ 35 years old	48.5	50.20	10.48	9.99	23.35	23.33	19.64	16.84	13.11
> 35 years old	17.05	17.24	5.93	6.24	15.57	17.42	10.44	9.63	7.08
Residence Location									
Urban	32.00	39.19	6.17	8.97	18.66	22.84	12.57	13.13	8.88
Rural	28.82	27.96	8.22	6.39	17.50	17.10	13.84	11.52	8.96
Educational level									
Illiterate	22.19	23.72	4.32	3.53	13.16	13.94	10.14	8.69	5.67
Read & write	22.57	26.13	4.44	9.89	12.90	20.90	9.75	15.60	6.86
Less than intermediate	25.70	32.98	9.34	10.94	21.37	21.92	16.79	16.18	12.42
Intermediate	36.77	48.62	10.25	13.77	20.00	30.61	16.06	17.37	11.42
Higher than intermediate	36.25	47.84	7.82	5.04	16.15	15.56	11.77	11.44	10.00
University	41.14	52.31	7.23	13.24	24.48	32.09	13.14	15.36	7.78
Post-graduate	26.69	26.19	14.35	12.90	33.99	25.80	19.14	8.75	10.71
Total	**30.43**	**33.38**	**7.25**	**7.48**	**18.05**	**19.53**	**13.24**	**12.20**	**8.92**

2.4 Economic Activity

The only employment characteristic to experience an increase in the overall rate of mobility in the 1990s is found among economic activities—but by just one percentage point. Males did not experience any change in their mobility rates between economic activities, while female workers showed a 2 percent rise between 1991–98, compared to 1981–88. It is interesting to note, however, that the mobility rate of the economic activities of male workers was twice that of female workers. Mobility rates of both younger and older workers increased, though the increase was greater among the younger group. Rural dwellers had higher mobility rates in the 1990s while urban dwellers did not, which can be attributed primarily to the rise in out-mobility from agriculture in rural areas.

2.5 Formality Status

A lack of data prevents a comparison of formality status between the 1980s and the 1990s; we have only transition rates for 1991–98. Overall, the mobility rate between formality statuses was almost 9 percent. In other words, 9 out of every 100 workers changed their formal/informal status between 1991 and 1998. There is a significant difference between the formality mobility rates when it comes to gender. Males had a 10.1 percent mobility rate, while females had just 2.7 percent—one-fifth the rate of males. Younger workers had almost twice as high a rate of mobility as older workers, which reflects how informal employment is still a transitory stage for many younger people until they secure public formal jobs.

2.6 Job Mobility

Table 8.19 summarizes the characteristics of job movers between 1981–88 and 1991–98, where a job move is a change in any of the following: employment status; economic sector of ownership, occupation; economic activity, or geographical job location (urban/rural, governorate, or district). Only those who were employed at the beginning and at the end of the period are included. Overall, job mobility rates were lower between 1991–98 compared to 1981–88, by nearly 6 percent. This is striking, since labor reallocation during reforms is expected as part of the adjustment process, and the extent and speed of that reallocation is crucial for the success of reforms.

It is also important to note that both new entrants to the labor market and existing workers experienced a drop in their job mobility rates between 1991–98, compared to the 1981–88 study period (Table 8.19). However, the fall in job mobility rates of new entrants was twice that of existing workers (a drop of 8 percent, compared to 4 percent).

Table 8.19: Job* Mobility Rates for 1991–98 and 1981–88

	1991–98	1981–88
Gender		
Male	23.69	29.48
Female	16.65	21.76
Age (At the end of the period)		
20–29	31.49	40.41
30–39	25.62	31.62
40–49	17.74	24.34
50–59	18.78	16.98
60–64	24.30	18.19
Residence Location		
Urban	25.14	34.23
Rural	20.17	22.62
Educational Level		
Illiterate	16.29	19.87
Read & Write	16.92	28.18
Less than intermediate	24.10	32.49
Intermediate	26.11	43.25
Higher than intermediate	23.07	21.25
University	30.84	43.66
Post-graduate	33.99	34.35
Total	**22.56**	**27.67**

*Notes: * Job characteristics are changes in either of the following: employment status, economic sector, occupation, economic activity, or geographical job location. Informality status is excluded because data are not available for 1981–88. If a public sector worker changed only geographical job location, that was not considered to be a change in job characteristics. Only those working at the beginning and end of the period are included.*

We can clearly identify the movers. Males had higher job mobility rates than females. It is not surprising that the most mobile age group included those ages of 20–29. However, it is important to note that between 1991–98, those older than 50 had higher job-mobility rates than they did in 1981–88. This may reflect the tendency of older workers in the 1990s to take early retirement. It is also notable that all educational levels experienced a drop in their mobility rates—except for those with higher-than-intermediate educations. However, university graduates stand out as having the biggest fall in their mobility rates among all groups—13 percent. Graduates had lower mobility rates throughout all vectors of employment in the 1980s and the 1990s, though they were still more mobile than the other less-educated groups between 1991–98.

Table 8.20: Job Location Mobility Rates (%) of Individuals 15–64 Years old: 1991–98 and 1981–88

	Urban/Rural		Governorate		District	
	1991–98	1981–88	1991–98	1981–88	1991–98	1981–88
Gender						
Male	6.28	3.92	6.16	4.97	10.29	10.52
Female	1.91	1.16	1.32	1.60	5.48	4.44
Age						
≤ 35 years old	8.79	4.75	9.09	5.30	14.66	10.68
> 35 years old	4.02	2.54	3.62	3.64	7.23	8.00
Residence location						
Urban	3.31	1.78	5.46	5.45	11.20	14.76
Rural	7.66	4.34	5.32	3.23	8.00	4.98
Educational level						
Illiterate	7.25	2.22	4.66	2.13	8.40	4.79
Read & write	4.36	4.15	4.38	4.58	6.39	8.93
Less than intermediate	7.21	5.42	6.40	6.83	10.56	14.55
Intermediate	4.92	4.72	5.13	5.62	9.11	13.92
Higher than intermediate	2.60	0.00	4.21	3.67	8.44	11.35
University	3.62	4.46	6.65	9.88	13.09	20.73
Post-graduate	4.75	4.62	9.4	12.41	21.50	21.43
Total	**5.58**	**3.26**	**5.39**	**4.16**	**9.52**	**9.05**

2.7 Geographical Job Location

Workers also responded to adjustments by changing their geographical job locations. In Table 8.20, job location mobility rates by urban/rural, governorate, and district movements are presented for 1981–88 and 1991–98. Overall, it seems that job location mobility rates were slightly higher in 1991–98, compared to 1981–88, suggesting that workers have responded to the labor market adjustment by being more geographically mobile. Males had higher urban/rural and intra-governorate mobility rates in the 1990s. Females had higher mobility rates only between districts, reflecting that distance is an important deterrent to female mobility. Cultural barriers prevent females from being geographically mobile. Younger workers, though, had twice the mobility rates as older individuals between 1991–98.

The mobility rates of illiterates were at least twice as much in the 1990s than in the 1980s. On the other hand, university graduates experienced a drop in all job location mobility rates. In the 1980s, university graduates were twice as mobile between urban and rural job locations as illiterates. However, that pattern was reversed in the 1990s.

In summary, and to respond to our first point of interest about which categories of workers have experienced the highest rates of mobility over the last decade, the above section shows that male, younger, and educated workers are the most mobile of all categories of workers.

Table 8.21: Mobility Rates of New and Existing Workers

	New Workers		Existing Workers	
	1991–98	**1981–88**	**1991–98**	**1981–88**
Job move*	58.78	66.13	21.46	25.87
Economic sector	7.46	19.33	7.26	7.20
Economic activity	19.69	29.57	13.05	11.77
Informality status	13.71	---	8.85	---
Job location				
Urban/Rural	3.99	3.47	5.53	3.20
Governorate	9.24	6.19	5.23	4.13
District	12.56	16.63	9.45	8.91

*Note: New workers are individuals who entered the labor market for the first time during the period of study, i.e., they were not in the labor market at the beginning of the period. Existing workers are those who entered the labor market for the first time before the start of the period of study; i.e., they were in the labor market at the start of the period. *Job moves are changes in either of the following: employment status, economic sector, occupation, economic activity, or geographical job location. Informality status is excluded because data are not available for 1981–88. If a public sector worker changed only geographical job location, that was not considered to be a change in job characteristics. Only those working at the beginning and end of the period are included.*

3. In-Mobility and Out-Mobility Rates

In this section, we address the rest of the points raised in the introduction. We examine in-mobility to and out-mobility rates from three areas: wage employment, public sector employment, and informal employment. Seven-year mobility rates are analyzed for the study periods of 1981–88 and 1991–98 (see Assaad and Arntz, 2000). Female subsistence agriculture workers are excluded from the analysis.

3.1 Wage Employment

Mobility is considered the movement into and out of wage employment. Here, we examine mobility into and out of wage employment from any other employment state, such as self-employment, employer, unpaid family worker, unemployment, or out of the labor force (students, housewives, etc.).

Overall, the mobility rate into wage employment increased between 1991–98, compared to 1981–88 (Figure 8.1). Rates of in-mobility to wage employment, for both males and females, were higher in the 1990s. Female in-mobility rates to wage employment in the 1990s caught up with that of males. Both genders experienced a fall in their out-mobility rates in the 1990s, though males experienced a smaller drop. Females witnessed a very high out-mobility rate in the 1980s. The difference in mobility patterns of female wage employees between the 1980s and 1990s can be attributed to the higher percentage (3.5 percent) of those who moved to self-employment and employers in the 1980s.

Figure 8.1: Mobility Rates by Gender (%): 1991–98 and 1981–88

Wage employment

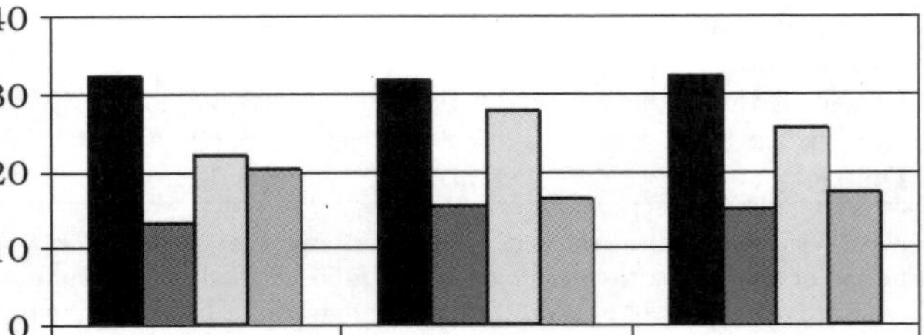

	Female	Male	All
In-mobility 1991–98	32.23	31.76	31.88
Out-mobility 1991–98	13.02	15.47	15.04
In-mobility 1981–88	22.04	27.49	25.29
Out-mobility 1981–88	20.03	16.33	16.95

Both younger and older workers experienced higher rates of mobility into wage employment in the 1990s compared to the 1980s, though the mobility rate of the younger group rose by 9 percent while that of the older group increased by just 3 percent. However, the younger workers also witnessed a bigger increase in their out-mobility rates in the 1990s compared to the 1980s.

Figure 8.2: Mobility Rates by Age (%): 1991–98 and 1981–88

Wage employment

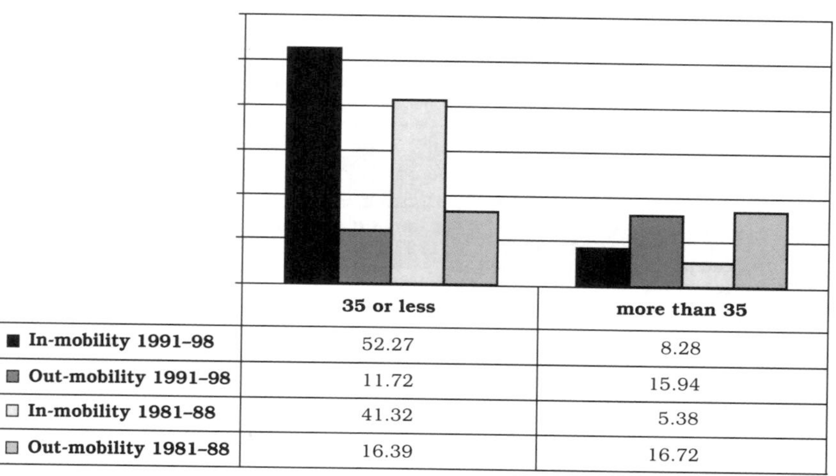

	35 or less	more than 35
■ In-mobility 1991–98	52.27	8.28
■ Out-mobility 1991–98	11.72	15.94
□ In-mobility 1981–88	41.32	5.38
□ Out-mobility 1981–88	16.39	16.72

Age applies to end of period

Examining the mobility rates according to educational level reveals a slightly different story. Only university graduates and post-graduate-educated individuals witnessed higher mobility rates into wage employment between 1991–98 than between 1981–88. This suggests that the increase in wage employment is the result of educated workers moving into wage work. Also, those with higher-than-intermediate educations had higher out-mobility rates from wage employment in the 1990s than in the 1980s, while their in-mobility rate stayed unchanged. In other words, workers with higher-than-intermediate educations and university-educated workers—who are expected to lose with any reduction in the public sector—are the two groups that did not experience lower in-mobility to wage employment, though they did have higher out-mobility rates from wage employment.

Figure 8.3: Mobility Rates by Education (%): 1991–98 and 1981–88

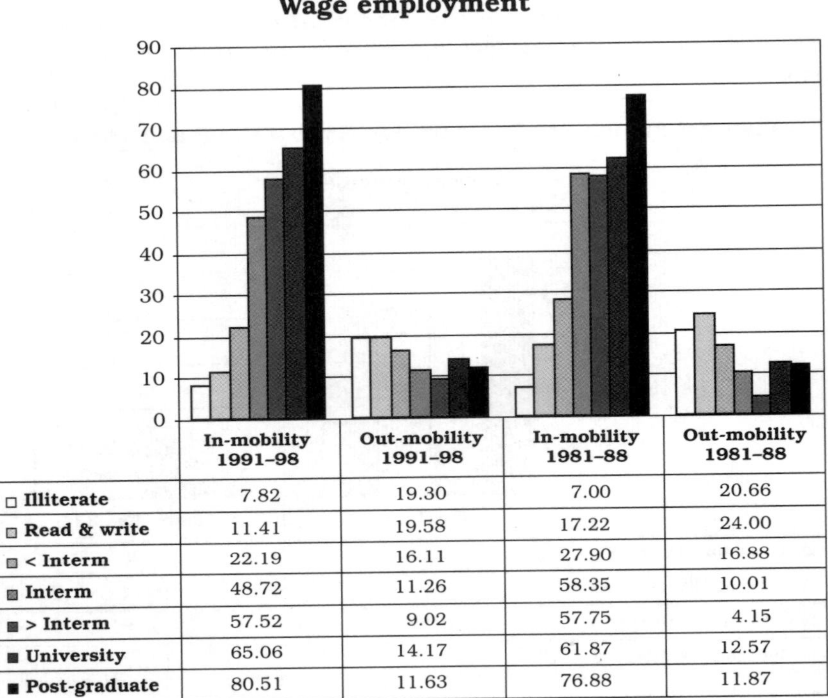

	In-mobility 1991–98	Out-mobility 1991–98	In-mobility 1981–88	Out-mobility 1981–88
Illiterate	7.82	19.30	7.00	20.66
Read & write	11.41	19.58	17.22	24.00
< Interm	22.19	16.11	27.90	16.88
Interm	48.72	11.26	58.35	10.01
> Interm	57.52	9.02	57.75	4.15
University	65.06	14.17	61.87	12.57
Post-graduate	80.51	11.63	76.88	11.87

3.2 Public Sector Employment

Public sector employment includes both government and public enterprise employment. Since we are interested in the rate of mobility into and out of the public sector during the process of adjustment, we will also consider movement to and from that sector by those who were economically inactive (unemployed, new entrants to the labor market, those retiring, etc.). Overall, in-mobility rates to public sector employment appear to have decreased slightly (approximately 1 percent) between 1991–98, compared to 1981–88 (Figure 8.4). Unlike the expectations of a process of reforms that involve downsizing and reducing the public sector, out-mobility rates from public employment did not change between 1991–98, compared to 1981–88.

However, if we examine the mobility rates into and out of public sector employment by gender (Figure 8.4), we find a different, gender-specific pattern. Females had higher in-mobility rates in the 1990s than in the 1980s. They also experienced lower out-mobility rates from the public sector. Males, on the other hand, had lower in-mobility rates between 1991–98 than in

1981–88. They also had higher out-mobility rates from public sector employment in the 1990s than they did in the 1980s. Thus, it seems that males were affected by the reforms more than females: males experienced a net out-mobility from the public sector in the 1990s; females did not, because female civil servants held on to their jobs longer than others (see Section 1.2).

Figure 8.4: Mobility Rates by Gender (%): 1991–98 and 1981–88

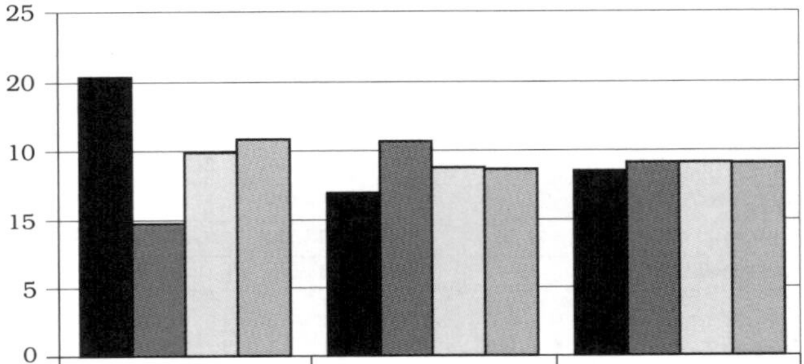

	Female	Male	All
■ In-mobility 1991–98	20.32	11.90	13.47
■ Out-mobility 1991–98	9.64	15.61	14.08
□ In-mobility 1981–88	14.85	13.73	14.09
■ Out-mobility 1981–88	15.82	13.59	14.04

Figure 8.5: Mobility Rates by Age (%): 1991–98 and 1981–88

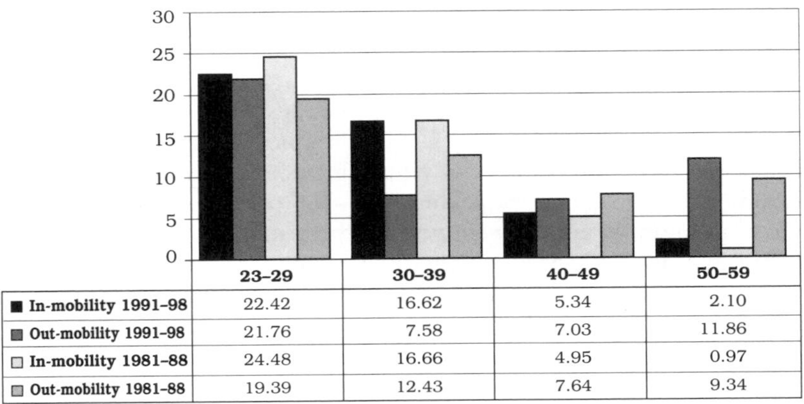

	23–29	30–39	40–49	50–59
■ In-mobility 1991–98	22.42	16.62	5.34	2.10
■ Out-mobility 1991–98	21.76	7.58	7.03	11.86
□ In-mobility 1981–88	24.48	16.66	4.95	0.97
■ Out-mobility 1981–88	19.39	12.43	7.64	9.34

Age applies to end of period

Figure 8.6: Mobility Rates by Education (%): 1991–98 and 1981–88

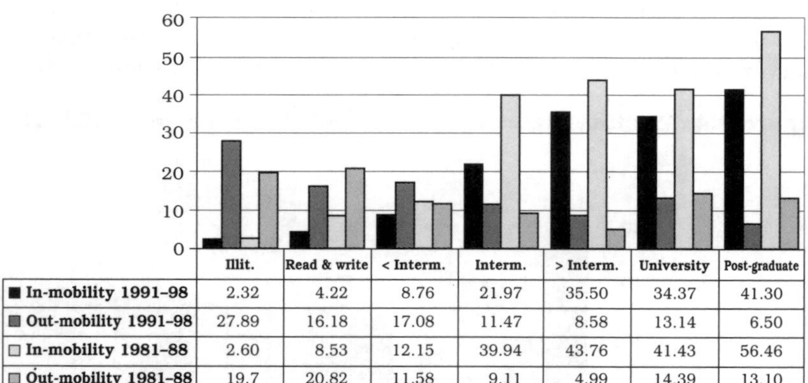

	Illit.	Read & write	< Interm.	Interm.	> Interm.	University	Post-graduate
■ In-mobility 1991–98	2.32	4.22	8.76	21.97	35.50	34.37	41.30
■ Out-mobility 1991–98	27.89	16.18	17.08	11.47	8.58	13.14	6.50
□ In-mobility 1981–88	2.60	8.53	12.15	39.94	43.76	41.43	56.46
■ Out-mobility 1981–88	19.7	20.82	11.58	9.11	4.99	14.39	13.10

Younger workers experienced a fall in their in-mobility rates to public sector employment in the 1990s, compared to the 1980s (Figure 8.5). Also, it is important to note that the older age group (50–59) experienced higher out-mobility rates from public sector employment between 1991–98 than between 1981–88. In short, public sector reforms seem to have affected new entrants to the labor market as well as workers over the age of 50.

Figure 8.6 presents the mobility rates into and out of public sector employment broken down by education levels. Regardless of educational levels, all workers experienced lower mobility rates into public sector employment between 1991–98, compared to 1981–88.

3.3 Informal Employment

For this analysis of in-mobility to and out-mobility from informal employment (private nonagricultural) between 1991–98, we include movement to economically inactive states from informal employment and vice versa. Overall, the in-mobility rate to informal employment was 9.5 percent, while the out-mobility rate from informal employment was 5.5 percent.

Figure 8.7 presents a summary of in-mobility to informal employment, and out-mobility from informal employment, broken down by gender. Females had higher in-mobility rates than males. On the other hand, they had lower out-mobility rates from informal employment than did males, which reasserts that females are less likely to move out of informal employment than are males.

Mobility rates by age group (Figure 8.8) show that between 1991–98, the mobility rate into informal employment for the 23–29 age group was 21 percent. It seems that the mobility rate into informal employment falls with age, while the mobility rate out of informal employment does not. Those with no education were twice as likely as university graduates to go into informal employment. However, those who could only just read and write had rates of in-mobility to informal employment similar to those with more-than-intermediate or university-level educations. Out-mobility rates increased with education—the more education, the higher the out-mobility rate.

Figure 8.7: Mobility Rates by Gender (%): 1991–98

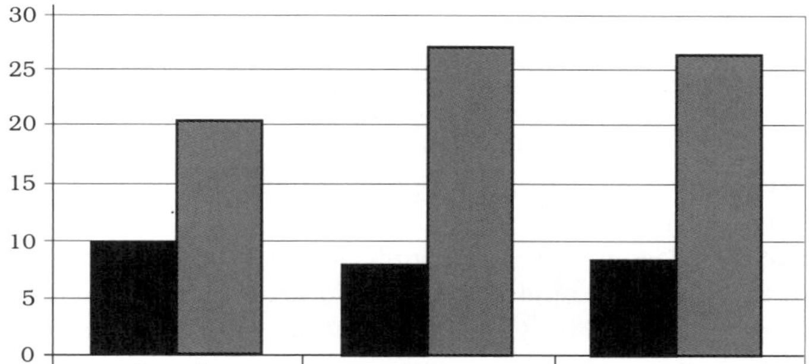

	Female	Male	All
■ In-mobility	9.63	7.59	8.07
■ Out-mobility	20.19	26.69	25.95

Figure 8.8: Mobility Rates by Age (%): 1991–98

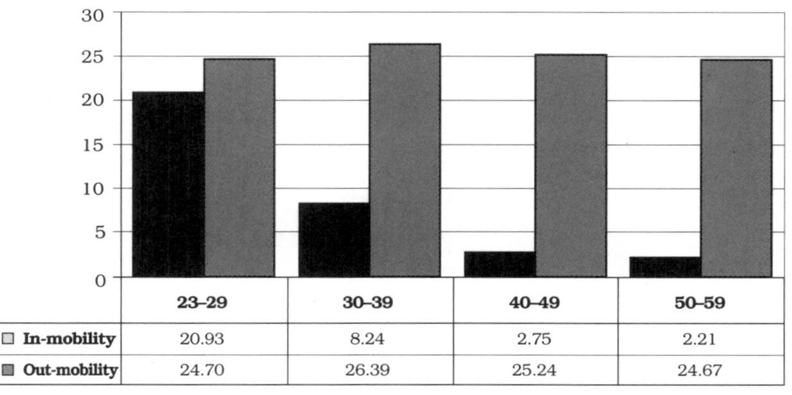

	23–29	30–39	40–49	50–59
□ In-mobility	20.93	8.24	2.75	2.21
■ Out-mobility	24.70	26.39	25.24	24.67

Age applies to the end of the period

Conclusion

Economic reforms entail reallocation of workers between different sectors and labor markets. The extent and the speed of that labor reallocation will affect the success of any reform measures. Labor mobility is essential for an efficient allocation of resources. Thus, the degree of labor mobility and labor market flexibility is crucial to the adjustment process. It is important to analyze the extent and pattern of labor mobility and labor reallocation if we are to assess the progress of economic reforms. For our analysis, we have explored the adjustment of the Egyptian labor market by examining the changes in mobility patterns and mobility rates during the period of reforms.

There are several main findings. Overall, job mobility rates were lower between 1991–98 than they were between 1981–88. When looking at mobility rates, employment status, economic sector by ownership, and occupations fell in the 1990s. Particularly striking is that during the era of adjustment, sectoral mobility was lower than the earlier period. Thus, there is no evidence that labor reallocation between economic sectors has taken place as a result of public sector downsizing or privatization.

However, the way the labor market and workers were adjusting to the reforms was affected by different processes. It was not brought about by existing workers changing sectors of employment. It occurred as the result of two different mechanisms: among existing workers, older workers (those between 50–59) were pushed out of the labor market altogether through early retirement. On the other hand, new entrants to the labor market were pushed more than ever before into the private sector and informal employment.

Bibliography

Al-Biblawy, Hayam (1990). *Labor Mobility. Final Report*. CAPMAS: Labor Information System Project. Cairo, Egypt.

Anker, Richard (1983). *Female Labour Force Participation in Developing Countries: A Critique of Current Definitions and Data Collection Methods*. Geneva, Switzerland: International Labour Office.

Anker, Richard (1990). "Methodological Considerations in Measuring Women's Labor Force Participation in Developing Countries: The Case of Egypt." *Research in Human Capital and Development*, 6: 26–58.

Arab Republic of Egypt, MOE (1994). *Growth in Girls Enrollments in the Public Primary Stage, 1981–82 to 1992–93*. Cairo: USAID, RTI, HIID, ARE, MOE, and EPID.

Assaad, Ragui (1996). "Structural Adjustment and Labor Market Reform in Egypt." In Hans Hopfinger, ed., *Economic Liberalization and Privatization in Socialist Arab Countries: Algeria, Egypt, Syria and Yemen as Examples*. Stuttgart: Justus Pertheses Verlag Gotha.

——— (1997a). "The Effects of Public Sector Hiring and Compensation Policies on the Egyptian Labor Market." *The World Bank Economic Review* 11: 85–118.

——— (1997b). "The Employment Crisis in Egypt: Current Trends and Future Prospects," *Research in Middle East Economics*, Volume 2. Greenwich, Conn.: JAI Press, pp. 39–66.

——— (1999). "The Transformation of the Egyptian Labor Market." Paper presented at Conference on Labor Market and Human Resource Development in Egypt, Cairo, November 29–30.

Assaad, Ragui and Fatma El-Hamidi. (Forthcoming). "Female Labor Supply in Egypt: Participation and Hours of Work." In I. Sirageldin, ed., *Population Challanges in the Middle East and North Africa: Towards the 21st Century*. London: I.B. Tauris.

Assaad, Ragui, Fatma El-Hamidi and Akhter Ahmed (2000). "The Determinants of Employment Status in Egypt." Discussion Paper 88, International Food Policy Research Institute. Washington D.C. (June).

——— (2001). "Is All Work the Same? A Comparison of the Determinants of Female Participation and Hours of Work in Various Employment States in Egypt." *The Economics of Women and Work in the Middle East and North Africa*. Mine Cinar (Ed.), *Research in Middle East Economics*, Vol. 4. Greenwich, Conn.: JAI Press pp. 117–150.

Assaad, Ragui and Ghada Barsoum (1999). "Egypt Labor Market Survey,

1998: Report on the Data Collection and Preparation." Report presented to Economic Research Forum, Cairo, Egypt.

Assaad, Ragui and M. Arntz (2000). "Does Structural Adjustment Contribute to a Growing Gender Gap in the Labor Market? Evidence from Egypt." Report for the Economic Research Forum, Cairo, Egypt.

Becker, Gary S. (1993). "Human Capital: A Theoretical and Empirical Analysis with Special Reference to Education," *Third Education*. Chicago: University of Chicago Press in conjunction with the NBER.

Beneria, Lourdes (1981). "Conceptualizing the Labor Force Underestimation of Women's Activities," *Journal of Development Studies*, Vol.17, No. 3, pp. 10–28.

Bequele Assefa and William Myers (1995). *First Things First in Child Labour: Eliminating Work Detrimental to Children*. Geneva, Switzerland: International Labour Office.

Blau, F.D. and Kahn, L.M. (1996). "International Differences in Male Wage Inequality: Institutions Versus Market Forces." *Journal of Political Economy*, Vol. 104, no. 4, pp. 791–837.

Burra, Neera (1989). "Out of Sight, Out of Mind: Working Girls in India," *International Labour Review*, Vol. 128, No. 5, pp. 651–660.

Canagarajah S. and H. Coulombe (1998). "Child Labor and Schooling in Ghana," World Bank Policy Research Working Paper No. 1844. Washington D.C.: The World Bank.

Cardiff, P.W. (1997). "The 1995–96 Household Income, Expenditure, and Consumption Survey. Final Analysis Report." In *Education*. Cardiff, ed. Cairo: USAID/Egypt.

Central Agency for Public Mobilization and Statistics (CAPMAS) (1988) *Labor Force Sample Survey*. Cairo, Egypt.

Cowell, F.A. (1995). *Measuring Inequality*. Second edition, Prentice-Hall/Harvester-Wheatsheath, Hemel Hempstead.

Cunningham, Hugh and Pier Paolo Viazzo, eds. (1996). *Child Labour in Historical Perspective – 1800–1850: Case Studies From Europe, Japan and Colombia*. Florence: Italy, UNICEF.

El Khawaga, Laila. (1990). "Le Chômage Apparent et la Structure du Marché du Travail en Egypte." *Revue Tiers Monde*, t. xxxi, n°. 121, January-March, 91–118.

Fergany, N. (1990). *Design, Implementation, and Appraisal of the October 1988 Round of the LFSS*. CAPMAS, Cairo, Egypt.

——— (1991a). "A Characterization of the Employment Problem in Egypt," *Employment and Structural Adjustment: Egypt in the 1990s*. H. Handoussa and G. Potter (eds.), Cairo: American University in Cairo Press.

——— (1991b). "Overview and General Features of Employment in the Domestic Economy," *Final Report, Labor Information System Project*. CAPMAS, Cairo, Egypt.

Fergany, N., A. Amina, D. Al-Islambouly, I. Farmaz, S. El-Sheneity, M. Mokhtar, and N. Ewais (1994). *Survey of Access to Primary Education and Acquisition of Basic Literacy Skills in Three Governorates of Egypt*. Cairo: UNICEF.

Goldschmidt-Clermont, Luisella (1982). *Unpaid Work in the Household*. Geneva, Switzerland: International Labour Office.

Grootaert, Christian and Harry Patrinos, (eds.), (1998). "The Policy Analysis of Child Labor: A Comparative Study," World Bank, New York: St. Martin's Press.

Grootaert, Christian and Kanbur Ravi (1995). "Child Labor: A Review," Background paper for the World Bank, *World Development Report 1995*, Mimeo. December.

Handoussa, Heba and Gillian Potter (1992). "Egypt's Informal Sector: Engine of Growth?" Paper presented at the MESA Conference, Portland, October 28–31, 1992.

——— (1991). *Employment and Structural Adjustment: Egypt in the 1990s*. Cairo: The American University in Cairo Press.

Hansen, Bent and Samir Radwan (1982). *Employment Opportunities and Equity in a Changing Economy: Egypt in the 1980s*. Geneva: ILO.

Hill and King (1993). Women's Education in Developing Countries. Baltimore, Maryland: The John Hopkins University Press.

Horton, S., R. Kanbur, and D. Mazumdar (1994). *Labor Markets in an Era of Adjustment*. Washington, D.C.: The World Bank.

Hua Haiyan (1996). "Which Students are Likely to Participate in Private Lessons or School Tutoring in Egypt?" Cambridge, MA: Ph.D. dissertation.

Hussmanns, Ralf, Fahrad Mehran, and Vijay Verma (1990). *Surveys of Economically Active Population, Employment, Unemployment and Underemployment: An ILO Manual on Concepts and Methods*. International Labour Office, Geneva.

Ibrahim, Barbara, Sunny Sallam, Sahar El Tawila, Omaima El Gibaly, and Fikrat El Sahn (2000). *Transitions to Adulthood: A National Survey of Egyptian Adolescents*. New York: The Population Council.

International Labour Office (1982). *Resolution Concerning Statistics of the Economically Active Population, Employment, Unemployment and Underemployment*. Adopted by the Thirteenth International Conference of Labour Statisticians.

——— (1996). *World Employment 1996/97: National Policies in a Global Context*. ILO, Geneva.

——— (1996b). *Economically Active Populations: Estimates and Projections, 1950-2010*. Geneva.

——— (1996c). *Child Labor: What is to be Done?* ILO: Geneva.

——— (1997). "Job Creation and Poverty Alleviation in Egypt: Strategy and Programmes," Geneva: Development Policies Department, ILO.

——— (1998). *Job Creation and Poverty Alleviation in Egypt: Strategy and Programmes*. Development Policies Department, ILO, Geneva.

Jenkins, S.P. (1995). "Accounting for Inequality Trends: Decomposition Analyses for the U.K., 1971–86," *Economica,* 62: 29–63.

Jensen, P. and H.S. Nielson (1997). "Child Labor or School Attendance? Evidence from Zambia." *Journal of Population Economics*, 10: 407–424.

Juhn, C., Murphy, K.M. and Pierce, B. (1993). "Wage Inequality and the Rise in Returns to Skill," *Journal of Political Economy*, vol. 101, No.3.

Knaul Felicia Marie (1995). "Young Workers, Street Life and Gender: The Effect of Education and Work Experience on Earnings in Columbia." Harvard University: Ph.D. dissertation.

——— (1998). "Incorporating Home-Based Domestic Work into Estimates of Child and Youth Labor: The Mexican Case." Paper written as part of the World Bank, LCSPR Project on "Human Capital Decisions, Labor Force Participation and Gender," under the direction of Olympia Icochea.

Knight, W.J. (1980). "The World's Exploited Children: Growing up Sadly." U.S. Department of Labor, Bureau of International Labor Affairs, Monograph No.4, Washington, D.C.

Levison, Deborah (1991). "Children's Labor Force Activity and Schooling in Brazil." The University of Michigan: Ph.D. dissertation.

Maloney, William (1998). "Are LDC Labor Markets Dualistic?" World Bank Research Policy Papers. Washington, D.C.: The World Bank.

Mills, Barbara and David Sahn, (1997). "Labor Market Segmentation and the Implications for Public Sector Retrenchment Programs." *Journal of Comparative Economics* 25: 385–402.

Moghadam, Valentine (1998). Women, Work, and Economic Reform in the Middle East and North Africa. Boulder: Lynne Rienner Publishers.

Patrinos, H. and Psacharopoulos, G. (1997). "Family Size, Schooling and Child Labor in Peru: An Empirical Analysis." *Journal of Population Economics*, 10: 387–404.

Psacharopoulos G. (1997). "Child Labor Versus Educational Attainment: Some Evidence from Latin America." *Journal of Population Economics* 10: 377–386.

Puhani, P.A. (1997). "All Quiet on the Wage Front?" ZEW Centre for European Economic Research Discussion Paper No. 97-03 E, SELAPO, University of Munich.

Ridker, Ronald G. (ed.) (1997). "Determinants of Educational Achievement and Attainment in Africa: Findings from Nine Case Studies." SD Publication Series, Technical Paper No. 62., Washington, D.C.: USAID, Office of Sustainable Development, Bureau for Africa.

Rizk, Soad K. (1991). "The Structure and Operation of the Informal Sector in Egypt," in Handoussa, H. and G. Potter (eds.), *Employment and Structural*

Adjustment: Egypt in the 1990s. Cairo: The American University in Cairo Press.

——— (1994). *Informal Economic Activity. Final Report*. Labor Information System Project. CAPMAS, Cairo, Egypt.

Rosenzweig, Mark R. (1978). "The Value of Children's Time, Family Size and Non-Household Child Activities in a Developing Country: Evidence from Household Data." *Research in Population Economics*, Vol.1, pp. 331–347.

Rugh, Andrea (2000). *Starting Now: Strategies for Helping Girls Complete Primary*. Strategies for Advancing Girls' Education (SAGE) Project. Academy for Educational Development. Washington, D.C.

Salazar, Maria Cristina and Walter Alarcon Glasinovich, (1996). "Better Schools: Less Child Work, Child Work and Education in Brazil, Columbia, Ecuador, Guatemala and Peru." *Innocenti* Essays No. 7, Florence: Italy, UNICEF International Child Development Center.

STATA Corporation (1999). "Analysis of Income Distributions." *STATA Technical Bulletin*, no. 48, March 1999.

Tunali, Insan (1996). "Labor Market Implications of the Demographic Window of Opportunity." *Forum:* Newletter of the Economic Research Forum for the Arab Countries, Iran, and Turkey. Vol. 3:4, pp.3-6.

Tzannatos, Zafiris (1998). "Child Labor and Schooling Enrollment in Thailand in the 1990s." Social Protection, (discussion paper no. 9818) The World Bank, December 1998.

UNICEF (1997). *The State of the World Children Report*. UNICEF: New York.

Weiner Myron (1991). *The Child and the State in India: Child Labor and Education Policy in Comparative Perspective*, Princeton University Press.

Williamson, Jeffery and Tarik Yousef (forthcoming). "Demographic Transitions and Economic Performance in the Middle East and North Africa." I. Sirageldin, ed., *Population Challenges in the Middle East and North Africa: Towards the 21st Century*. New York: I.B. Tauris.

Zibani, Nadia (1994). "Le Travail des Enfants en Egypte et ses Rapports avec la Scolarisation: Esquisse d'evolution." *l'Education en Egypte: les Processus*, Egypte, Monde Arabe No. 18–19- 2e et 3e Trimestres.

http://www.ilo.org/public/english/bureau/stat/res/ecacpop.html.

In this series:

Economic Trends in the Mena Region, 2002
Edited by The Economic Research Forum for the Arab Countries, Iran and Turkey

Employment Creation and Social Protection in the Middle East and North Africa: The Third Mediterranean Development Forum
Edited by Heba Handoussa and Zafiris Tzannatos

Human Capital: Population Economics in the Middle East
Edited by Ismail Serageldin

Institutional Reform and Economic Development in Egypt
Edited by Noha El-Mikawy and Heba Handoussa